MACRO PRACTICE

A Generalist Approach

Eighth Edition

MACRO PRACTICE

A Generalist Approach

Murali D. Nair
Cleveland State University

&

Ralph Brody
Cleveland State University

Gregory Publishing Company   **Wheaton, IL 60187**

Design and Production: Gregory Publishing Company
Typeface: New Century Schoolbook
Typesetting: Gregory Publishing Company
Cover Art: Sam Tolia

MACRO PRACTICE
A Generalist Approach

Eighth Edition 2007
Printed in the United States of America
Translation rights reserved by Publisher
ISBN 0-911541-79-9

ACKNOWLEDGMENTS

The following materials have been modified and are reprinted with permission from the publishers:

Effectively Managing Human Service Organizations by Ralph Brody, Sage Publications, 2005
        Organization's Culture
        Strategic Planning
        Developing Structures and Processes
        Handling Communications and Conflict
        Managing Time
        Humanizing the Organization
        Problem Solving

Problem Solving: Concepts and Methods for Community Organizations by Ralph Brody, Human Sciences Press, 1982
        Setting Doable Objectives
        Implementing Achievable Plans
        Solving Agency Problems
        Facilitating the Decision Making Process
        Generating Ideas Through Creative Thinking
        Collaborating and Negotiating with Other Organizations

"Preparing Effective Proposals" by Ralph Brody, in *Skills for Effective Human Service Management*, edited by R.L. Edwards and J.A. Yankey, NASW Press, 1991.

Organizing for Social Change: A Case Study Approach by Ralph Brody and Kay Cramer published by the Institute of Urban Studies, Cleveland State University, in cooperation with the Council for Economic Opportunities in Greater Cleveland, 1970 (excerpted and updated).

AUTHORS

Murali D. Nair is a Professor and Coordinator of the BSW Program at the School of Social Work, Cleveland State University. He has thirty years of experience in graduate and undergraduate social work education. He received his Doctorate in Social Welfare from Columbia University in New York. Dr. Nair is on the Editorial Board and is the Book Review Editor of the Journal of Baccalaureate Social Work. Cross-cultural and cross-national understanding of poverty is one of his research interests. For the past eight years he has been the Director for the Summer Study Abroad Program for social work professionals, faculty and students in India. He is also the Chairman of the Global Learning Advisory Committee and Co-Director of the Center for Healing Across Cultures. He conducts Social Work Licensure Examination Review Courses at universities across the country. His latest publications include *The Art of Community Service: Volunteering and Service Learning* with Dr. Brody, *Tsunami Victims: An Anthology of Writings of Children,* and *Genius in Public Housing* (ed).

Ralph Brody was an Associate Professor of Social Work at Cleveland State University (CSU). He held a Ph.D. in Social Policy from Case Western Reserve University and had over thirty years experience in health and human services. He had been the Executive Director of the Center for Community Solutions, an organization conducting research and planning on urban issues and had been a director of job training programs, multi-service centers, United Way Services allocations, and an associate director of a university urban institute. He provided consultation or training to more than thirty community agencies, including agencies in Kenya, Spain, India, the People's Republic of China, Nigeria, Ghana, Uganda, Ethiopia, and Egypt. Dr. Brody also wrote *Effectively Managing Human Service Organizations.*

Dedicated to

Ralph Brody

He tried to help those in need

and

He will always be remembered.

Table of Contents

INTRODUCTION

The profession of social work reflects two parallel trends: On the one hand, the profession has developed such highly specialized fields as child welfare, mental health, aging, substance abuse, and mental disabilities—to name a few of the many specializations. On the other hand, social work methods continue to emphasize a generalist approach, involving a basic understanding of how to work with individuals, families, small groups and organizations within a community context—regardless of a particular specialized field.

Most beginning social workers will likely work as generalists with individuals who have pressing needs. While it is, therefore, important for students to develop skills and understanding in working with individuals, it is also important to understand the community and organizational context within which social workers need to function. It is the premise of this book that by having an awareness and appreciation of the forces that impact our clients and our work, we can be more effective professionals.

This book is designed to prepare students to understand and work within and with "macro systems." In the terminology of social work methods, individuals, families, and small groups are viewed as "micro systems," meaning small and self-contained entities. In contrast, "macro systems" are large and complex units that can be identified at various levels: the general community, a system within the community (such as a mental health system), the interaction of agencies, and an individual agency that delivers specific services.

By understanding macro level issues better, social workers will be able to interpret information about the social and political communities in which they operate, and also gain a deeper understanding of how agencies function.[1] Through this increased understanding, social workers will be in a better position to help individuals and families.

Macro practice generally falls into three major categories: administration, community organization, and social planning. The following abbreviated definitions may be useful:[2]

Administration: A range of activities in a social welfare organization that transforms policies into concrete services. These activities involve planning, coordinating, and evaluating various aspects to achieve organizational goals.

Community organization: An intervention process that helps groups of people from the same geographic areas or with the same common interests deal with social problems and enhance social well-being through planned collective action.

Social Planning: A process designed to manage social change rationally. Usually this involves collecting facts, delineating alternative courses of action, and making recommendations to those empowered to implement them.

Social work generalist practitioners will likely relate to macro system issues involving administration, community organization, and social planning. The nature of social work compels interacting with others. Rarely do social workers function in isolation. They must work with others within their agency and with specialists in other settings.[3] Just as the medical generalist must draw upon a variety of skills, so the social work generalist must have the skills and the understanding of individual, group, organization, and community dynamics. This book focuses on those community forces and organizational aspects that impinge upon social work practice.

By having a wide-ranging repertoire upon which to draw, the social worker is in a better position to effectively work with clients. For example, social workers involved with parents who abuse their children need to understand the environmental context of the problem, the legal ramifications of their work, the budgetary constraints under which they operate, and the possible interventions that can be used by other agencies. Only by having this broad perspective can social workers determine how to leverage resources beyond their own individual efforts. The generalist practitioner also needs to understand how social services can best be developed and implemented. Moreover, the generalist practitioner must understand how community organizations can involve those impacted by human services so they can have a voice in the design and implementation of programs that are supposed to benefit them.

We have prepared this book to meet the requirements of two major organizations. The first entity is the Council on Social Work Education, which is the accrediting body for all social work educational programs in the United States and which establishes mandates for minimum requirements for the curricula of social work education.[4] Included in these mandates are the following:

the enhancement of social functioning of groups, organizations, and communities;

the planning and implementation of social policies to meet basic human needs;

the development of programs and resources that empower groups at risk and promote social and economic justice.

The other entity is the American Association of State Social Work Boards that prepares the State Social Work Licensure Examination for undergraduates and graduates. All states now require social workers to obtain state licensure after graduation from an accredited social work program. One major element of the exam deals with macro practice knowledge. This includes social work practice with communities, professional use of self, use of collaborative relationships in social work practice, techniques of communicating, use of professional relationships, professional values and ethics, supervision in social work (educational and administrative functions), and social work administration (staffing and personnel management, social work program management, social and institutional policies).[5]

In preparing this book, we have made several assumptions:

1) Students have already taken an introductory course and probably a micro practice course. They have a general familiarity with the basic concepts of the methods of social work.

2) Students have had a field placement or are presently in one so that they can draw upon some first-hand experiences of working in an agency.

3) To fulfill a particular assignment or to enrich their understanding further, students will draw upon the rich body of literature and research that has been accumulated. In addition to the references used in the preparation of this book, we provide a supplementary list of suggested readings.

4) To enhance student understanding of concepts, we provide numerous examples taken from actual experiences. In addition, wherever possible we provide practical tools and techniques that students will be able to use in their professional work. Brief summaries are provided at the end of each chapter.

5) To stimulate class discussion we provide a list of questions and possible assignments at the end of each chapter. We trust that these questions will stimulate students to explore more in depth some of the policies and practices of their field agency. Because some of these questions may require several weeks of preparation or exploration, students are advised to begin their assignments in advance of the week they will be discussed. If appropriate, students may wish to observe or interview staff or clients outside their field agency. Depending on the preference of the instructor, students may use the questions as a springboard for classroom discussion or as a basis for written assignments.

This book is divided into 23 chapters. Chapter 1 lays the groundwork by focusing on the environmental context within which all agencies must function. Chapter 2 reviews how agencies are part of a social system and how clients move through a service delivery system. Chapter 3, Client Advocacy, is added to this book to demonstrate the connection between working with individual clients and macro systems. Chapters 4-6 discuss general values and strategic planning that provide overall directions of an organization. Chapters 7-11 deal with such operational issues as setting objectives, implementing plans, solving day-to-day problems, improving communications, focusing on diversity and ethical issues, and developing effective structures and processes. Chapters 12-16 concentrate on specific skills needed to enhance agency and community organizational functioning and survival: running meetings, managing time and stress, managing and supervising, and writing proposals.

Although concepts and techniques in various chapters relate to both social agencies and community organizations (hence, the generalist perspective), chapters 17-22 give special attention to community wide issues and how neighborhood and community organizations can address them. Such issues include community problem analysis, community organization and development, advocacy and negotiation, and coalitions.

We have added a new chapter 20 on grassroots organizing, discussing how to help empower people to take charge of their lives.

Chapter 23, international social work practice, explains how students can consider opportunities abroad.

In the Appendix A we provide information on web sites that can be of interest to social work students. Appendix B provides twenty case examples, many drawn from actual situations, which can be used to stimulate class discussions.

Using *Macro Systems* as the basis for exploring ideas, students should gain an appreciation of the complex forces under which they will be operating, acquire specific tools to help them function better, and develop insights about the interactions between staff and agencies and the larger systems that affect the social work field.

At the heart of the social work process—whether at the individual organizational, or community level—is a commitment to improve the lives of people through the purposeful and professional use of oneself. Our strong belief is that those who enter the field want to be involved in more than a 9-5 job. They want to see their neighborhood and community improved. We hope that this book will stimulate inquiry, foster critical thinking, enhance understanding, and contribute to the problem-solving process in our agencies and our communities

Murali D. Nair
September 2006

Chapter Notes

[1]Meenaghan, T.M. (1987). "Macro Practice: Current Trends and Issues." In A., Minihan (Editor-in-chief), *Encyclopedia of Social Work*, (18th ed., Vol 1, pp. 82-89). Silver Spring, MD: National Association of Social Workers.

[2]Barker, R.L. (1999). *Dictionary of Social Work*, (4th ed., pp. 285, 90-91, 452). Silver Spring, MD: National Association of Social Workers.

[3]Johnson, L. (1995). *Social Work Practice: A Generalist Approach*, (4th ed., p. 24). Needham Heights, MA: Allyn and Bacon.

[4]*CCSWE Curriculum Policy Statement*. (Oct., 1997). Washington, D.C.: Council on Social Work Education, p. 7.

[5]*AASSWB Manual*. (1998). Alexandria, VA: American Association of State Social Work Board, p. 10.

CHAPTER 1

The Environmental Context
Affecting Human Services

The environmental context influences the way all social agencies function. Knowing the context and how outside forces can impinge on the way an agency functions can be useful in dealing with numerous issues confronting social workers.

We begin our discussion with the way human services are categorized, then discuss the various environmental factors that influence agency functioning, and finally review some of the major issues currently affecting agencies.

AGENCIES

Agencies can be categorized on the basis of the services they provide, their sources of funding (governmental or private), and on their emphasis of directly helping their members.

Single and Multi-Service Agencies

Almost all human service organizations do what their name conveys: provide direct services. Sometimes an agency is established to provide one service to a specific target population, for example, providing counseling to mothers who have recently delivered their babies and who suffer from depression. More often, agencies provide multiple services to a target population, for example, counseling and educational opportunities to recent school dropouts. Frequently, agencies provide multiple services to a variety of target populations, for example, a neighborhood center or a family counseling agency works with a wide variety of clients and offers several specialized services.

Agencies are greatly influenced to expand services as a result of both internal and external pressures. A single purpose agency, for example, may come across clients having many needs that do not seem to be met by other organizations and may therefore feel compelled to expand its services. An agency established to provide a service funded in part by its state legislature might add advocacy to its array of functions when public officials threaten to reduce funding.

On the other hand, multi-purpose organizations can be put under pressure to curtail their programs—especially when funding is reduced or when other agencies come on the scene to compete for their clients. Hence, in a dynamic environment agencies are constantly assessing whether to expand or contract their services.

Governmental Agencies

Public agencies include federal, state, regional, county, and city units. The Department of Health and Human Services is a prime example of a federal agency that provides funding, usually through state agencies, and then monitors the use of these funds. State agencies frequently match federal funding in grants to local communities as, for example, by providing funds for mental health services. Most public social services are administered at the county level, such as county departments of human services. At the city level, health services sometimes are augmented social services.

Public agencies are created by public law and are therefore subject to public mandates and public accountability. Services are prescribed and are limited by law—regardless of what clients' particular needs are. They must operate under clear boundaries and constraints.

Funds for services to older persons or those experiencing mental retardation or AIDS will typically flow from federal and state governmental bodies to the local community. Accompanying this funding will be regulations about who is to be served and what the nature of the services will be. Employees of governmental agencies are typically covered by civil service regulations.

Typically, client costs and fees are subsidized by the government entity (e.g., Medicaid) that establishes policies and rates for reimbursement. The difference between commercial transactions in the market place and one involving clients in most agencies is that in commercial firms the customers are those who purchase the goods and services and thus the organization is responsive directly to them. Generally public funding comes with strings attached and decisions on how to spend these funds may be imposed by the funding agency. Federal or state funding may greatly influence how funds are to be spent in a local community. As a consequence, clients do not have nearly the same influence as the commercial customer.

Funds received from governmental agencies can be in the form of grants paid in advance to the requesting agency providing service. Alternatively, funds can be distributed on a cost reimbursement basis, i.e., the organization must first provide a service over a period of time (e.g., three months) and then be reimbursed for services.

Private, Non-profit Agencies

Typically, a board of trustees governs nonprofit organizations and determines overall policies, provides oversight to the expenditure of funds, and evaluates the performance of the executive director. Non-profit agencies apply for a charter from their state government and are governed by Internal Revenue Service 501 (C)(3) regulations. Policy decisions of the director and trustees influence the selection of target populations and the services performed.

Voluntary agencies receive financial support from the private sector. Often, but not always, they are dependent on United Way funds and therefore must abide by the rules and constraints of this major funding organization. For example, agencies receiving funds are limited in their soliciting corporations that participate in the United Way drive. Other constraints could include the national charter of the organization (e.g., the local Red Cross must perform services mandated by the national office). Usually, voluntary organizations have great flexibility to perform services approved by their board of trustees.

Nonprofit agencies are not entirely autonomous in determining their services. Many are highly dependent on governmental funding, which can affect what they can or cannot do. Some even function as quasi-government entities, that is, even though they may have an independent board of trustees, they adhere closely to the legislation and regulations of a governmental agency.

A quasipublic organization is primarily a voluntary organization that uses public funding for its services. A child guidance center or a Lutheran counseling agency can receive public funding for a portion of its services and is accountable for how these funds are spent. A woman's drug referral service, for example, may receive almost all of its funding from the state alcohol and drug service board, but it may raise additional funds through a special event. The board of this organization must function within certain parameters set by the state body: it can hire and fire the director, establish personnel practices, and determine the location of the office. It cannot shift the service from a referral program to providing direct counseling or employment services—as much as these may be needed. The public body determines the function of the agency through its funding process.

Similarly, mental health agencies are created by public law and thus must function under legal constraints. They can, however, receive fees from clients, raise their own funds for services not mandated by law, and hire staff outside of the local and state civil service requirements. These quasipublic agencies are accountable to the public sector but have the autonomy to make service decisions beyond governmental requirements.[1]

NGO's or Nongovernmental Organizations are known in countries outside the U.S., especially in developing countries that rely on such outside funding sources as church organizations. Often they are established to provide very basic services, such as clothing and housing. Sometimes they are established to provide employment training designed to develop the craft skills for which the country or a particular community has a reputation. In Kenya, for example, YMCAs administer workshops for citizens who want to learn a craft skill, such as woodworking, which they can use to earn a living.

For-profit Agencies

Increasingly, the delivery of health and human services is being implemented through for-profit making organizations. These proprietary or for-profit organizations are readily apparent in the health-care arena as evidenced by corporations buying up private hospitals. Other examples include day-care facilities, home-based nursing, nursing homes, and correction facilities. Some corporations also provide counseling services through employee assistance programs. All of these examples have in common the desire of the owners or the stockholders to make a profit. This tendency toward privatization is likely to continue.

Voluntary and Self-Help Organizations

People who have special needs often turn to or form groups. Members who create these self-help associations pay dues and expect a service to meet their needs or achieve some change in the community that will benefit them. Credit unions, economic self-help groups, ethnic and minority fraternal associations, and neighborhood organizations provide support and advocate for changes in the community that benefit their members. Although not generally identified with providing direct social services, their members frequently turn to them for assistance with their problems.

Self-help groups address a variety of social problems, including the loss of loved ones, depression, abuse, and alcoholism. Often they work with minimal or no professional involvement. Alcoholics Anonymous is among the most well-known self-help organizations, but in every community there are dozens of groups formed to deal with the concerns of their members. Voluntary associations provide a structured group experience for people to advance their special interests. Community organizations, religious social improvement groups, and economic development corporations are examples. Members share a sense of community and strive to enhance the well being of their members.[2]

ENVIRONMENTAL FACTORS INFLUENCING SOCIAL AGENCIES

To paraphrase an old saying: no agency is an island onto itself. Outside factors are constantly influencing how an agency will select clients and deliver services. Below we list some of the most significant influences:

Resources

Previously we discussed how governmental funding could affect the work of nonprofit agencies. Governmental requirements are not the only influence. United Way budget panelists, major agency contributors, and local foundation decision makers can influence an agency's services. Third party payments and managed care impose new demands on agencies and their clients. These outside funding patterns can profoundly influence the kinds and lengths of service agencies provide to their clients. Wherever concentrated funding occurs, there always exists this twist on the "golden rule": whoever has the gold, rules. Agencies either respond to their expectations and evidence accountability to their funders or else risk the loss of a major source of support.

Sometimes the availability of resources plays an indirect influence on where and to whom an agency will deliver its services. Take, for example, a youth counseling center operating in the inner city. Initially funded through a foundation grant, this center was able to respond to inner city adolescents who experienced severe home problems. Because foundation funding was coming to an end, the agency decided to move to a wealthy suburb in order to expand its fund raising capacity. The organization continues to serve teenagers—mostly from the suburbs.

Public Opinion and the Media

The media play a powerful role in influencing public opinion, which in turn affects the attitudes, policies, and positions of public officials and financial supporters. Media reports can be quite damaging to the reputation of an agency. They can also generate public support and sympathy for a particular population—as, for example, homeless persons or abused women. Those not normally seen in a sympathetic light—for example, people on public assistance, drug addicts, or gang members—can receive the spotlight of attention from the media that can generate interest in providing them with special services.

Political Climate

Changes in political leadership at the federal, state, or local levels will often result in new priorities emerging. Where before, for example, only lip service was given to coordinating services, now, with a shifting political climate, state and local organizations are required to coordinate their services. Or new emphasis is given to providing social services in the schools. Political agendas will greatly influence agency programs.

Here is an example of how a change in the political agenda can affect a change in the way certain populations are served. Until the 1970s mentally ill persons were placed in large mental institutions. Then the emergence of psychotropic drugs, the growing commitment of many mental health professionals to move people out of institutions and into the community, and the motivation of state legislators to reduce costs of housing mentally ill persons resulted in the emptying of mental hospitals. Contrary to the rhetoric of the period, community mental health programs did not expand to keep pace with those who left institutions and those who might have been placed in them. As a consequence, new organizations have had to come into existence to deal with homeless persons, a portion of whom are mentally ill. Hence, political decisions made at one point of time can have an impact on how programs are fashioned at another point in time.

Concerns of the Community

How people in the community feel about particular programs and the people they are designed to serve can have a tremendous impact on an agency. Fears of residents living near a children's institution may make that agency wary of letting the children out in the community. A newly proposed teen center can be squelched if neighborhood block clubs fear that this will detrimentally affect the tranquillity of the neighborhood. This common fear of residents resisting change—sometimes referred to as "NIMBY" (Not In MY Back Yard)—must often be dealt with by agencies that want to develop community based programs.

Professional Associations and Unions

These wield tremendous power in the internal aspects of agencies. For example, agencies that violate the NASW code of ethics are subject to sanctions. Periodically, agencies have to undergo accreditation from their national organizations and alter their practices to conform to standards. Unions influence how their members will be deployed and what standards will be applied to caseload size.

Educational and Theoretical Perspectives

The training they receive obviously influences the staff, both before they enter the field and subsequent training they receive as part of their continuing education. They learn about treatment modalities and about desirable agency practices. Sometimes these ideas are not congruent with the realities operating within the agency itself, setting up the possibility of conflict and change. Staff, for example, may attend an outside workshop on improving communications in the workplace and expect to implement new procedures. Ideas from outside the organization may initially be resisted (sometimes for appropriate reasons), but the tension that is created sets up the possibility of change now or in the future.

Religious and Moral Values

The values of the community can greatly affect how an agency responds to its clients. A local department of human services, for example, may take as a community mandate that families must be helped to stay together. It may therefore determine to take extraordinary measures to work with acting out adolescents so they can be kept in their own homes rather than be sent to institutions. Religious values about homosexuality and abortion can effect responses to client concerns. Attitudes (sometimes subtle) about sex, age, and race influence practice. For example, should children needing foster homes be placed only with families of the same ethnic or racial background? The answer in part may rest with the philosophical values of the organization and the community.

Special Circumstances

Suddenly a natural disaster hits a community—a hurricane or a flood—and the total population becomes mobilized to deal with the problem. Counseling agencies, for example, may be called upon to deal with helping families cope with the loss of possessions. Communities are often able to mobilize many resources in times of crisis.

Sometimes a circumstance is long festering, a chronic condition that suddenly is made manifest. Teenage alienation brought about by the lack of job opportunities and feelings about their bleak future can explode into gang warfare. Agencies that previously may not have experienced community support for their work with angry teenagers now, perhaps because of media publicity, will become the focus of positive attention.

Technological Advances

New technologies can alter how an agency deals with clients. Examples: One organization, wanting to reach reticent adolescents, provides for conference calls in the evenings during which time teenagers can discuss their problems anonymously. Another organization provides a computer service in which persons with sexual concerns can have them addressed by a pool of psychiatrists, psychologists, and social workers who are experts on various aspects of sexual dysfunction. Information systems are now being developed so that inventories of services can be developed to meet particular client needs.

Response of Other Agencies

The approaches of other organizations in the community can significantly affect how an agency works with its clients. If collateral organizations are cooperative, then appropriate referrals can be made. If, on the other hand, others are competitive in their response to clients and resources, then internal strategies and procedures will be developed in response to this reality. If other agencies are not able to meet special needs of clients, new service offerings may need to be developed.

Cooperative arrangements among agencies can take a variety of forms. Staff from one agency can be placed in another, e.g., a mental health professional placed in a YMCA. Agencies can agree to informal compacts to work together on family situations of common concern, e.g., a tutorial program of a neighborhood center and a substance abuse prevention agency.

Agencies can also enter into formal contracts to guarantee services in exchange for funds, e.g., a health services clinic that contracts with an organization that serves the homeless. In all these instances working in collaboration with other agencies affects service delivery.

The Environment of the Host Organization

Sometimes the staff of a social work unit must operate within a host organization and it is possible under these circumstances that work styles, values, and perspectives differ. The unit must then deal with not only the environment outside but also inside the organization. The staff of a social work department within a large hospital, for example, may have to advocate for services to battered women. School social workers may have to sensitize principals and teachers on ways to work with children from different cultures and ethnic groups.

Effects of the Environment on Clients

Clients bring with them the effects of their environment, which in turn affect how agencies need to respond. For example, cultural differences may require various modes of interaction. In certain Hispanic cultures, family supports, the use of folk healers, and home remedies have traditionally played a role in determining how Latinos deal with health and illness. Hence, it is important to understand the customs and traditions that affect how people feel and behave.

A TWO WAY STREET: INFLUENCING THE ENVIRONMENT

We have emphasized the importance of environmental factors on agencies, but we should also stress that agencies can influence their environment. For example, agencies can document unmet needs, thereby influencing funders and legislators. They can work with others to influence legislation. They can influence community values by working with the media to communicate issues that have emotional impact. They can encourage other agencies to be more responsive to the special needs of their clients. In these and many other ways agencies can exert influence to change the environmental climate.

One illustration of this is a mental health agency that takes on the responsibility of educating employers to hire those with mental disabilities. Agency staff aggressively seek employment opportunities and advocate that their clients can function productively on the job. Employers who participate in the program are touted at an annual luncheon, and they in turn are encouraged to recruit other employers.

Client life experiences must also be understood and addressed. Clients may have difficulty with transportation, with child-care arrangements, and with fear of traveling at certain hours because of safety concerns. Knowing that these life experiences can deter clients from seeking services can be an important first step in stimulating an agency to determine whether services can be provided in different ways. For example, the staff of an agency wanting to reach out to clients may consider altering the hours of service, providing child care on the premises, or meeting with clients in localities closer to their homes.

RATIONING SOCIAL SERVICES

Human service agencies are increasingly faced with having less resources than they need to meet the needs of their clients. As funding is reduced from the public sector at the federal, state, and local levels and as fundraising through local United Ways and other private sources of funding remain at a plateau or are in some instances diminished, agencies find that they must curtail their services. Though repugnant to the fundamental values of social work, more and more agencies have come to resort to some form of rationing.[3]

Rationing is a means of allocating scarce resources. Agencies can resort to rationing either through explicit decisions and actions or, more commonly, they implicitly let certain practices evolve over time. Among the more frequently used rationing methods are the following:

Queuing is a rationing mechanism that permits people to be served on a first come, first served basis. A family counseling agency, for example, that establishes a waiting list requires people to "stand in line." This form of rationing is commonly used because the agency does not have to be in a position to select whom it serves and is therefore not likely to experience criticism. Those who get tired of waiting for a service drop out themselves. For some this process could present a tremendous hardship, as for example, a homeless mother being told that she cannot have access to a housing shelter because it is already filled up.

Service inaccessibility is often unintended but nevertheless becomes a convenient way to prevent agencies from being deluged. If people don't know that they are eligible for certain benefits and the organizations responsible don't go out of their way to inform them, demand will be contained. If people are unable to get to a downtown office because of limited bus transportation and if a purposeful decision is made not to establish neighborhood offices based on the rational of being unable to handle all those who want our services, then this form of rationing accomplishes its purpose.

Triage is a form of rationing in which agencies select who they will and won't serve. Originally the term, "triage," (meaning, "sorting," in French) came from the experience in World War I when surgeons had to make decisions about dealing with the flood of wounded soldiers brought in from the battle field. They had to make difficult, heart wrenching choices about where to devote their limited time and resources. The soldiers they could not help were left to die; others had superficial wounds and would likely recover with minimal effort. This left them time and energy to concentrate on those soldiers who could benefit from their surgery.

In the same way, agencies determine those who are not appropriate for their services either because they are functioning too well to meet their criteria or because they are not likely to respond to the services provided. A mental health agency that restricts its clients only to those who are a danger to themselves and others reflects triage. So does an agency that refuses to accept for counseling persons whose urine tests reflect drug use.

Creaming involves selecting only those clients who have the greatest chance of success. This mechanism of rationing occurs in job-training agencies where the pressure is on to produce high results in job placement. The term, "creaming," probably comes from the old fashioned way milk was bottled, with the cream rising to the top—this was supposed to be the best tasting part of the milk. A job-training agency that accepts only those welfare recipients that have a high school education practices creaming.

Equal parceling is a way of distributing limited resources to everyone who is eligible. A food distribution center, for example, gives everyone who seeks food the same amount, regardless of particular needs. By giving each person an equal share the agency avoids the appearance of unfairness, even though some are much more needy than others are.

Protecting society is a way of rationing that focuses on those persons who could potentially harm others. In a neighborhood center focused attention is given to gang members over other needy, but less potentially disruptive, individuals. Similarly, a juvenile court caseload may be portioned out so that those with the highest potential for recidivism will be under closer scrutiny.

Preferred recipients are given preferential treatment because of their role in the community or because they have very appealing characteristics. Often considerations are based not on the inherent characteristics but on political factors. One obvious group that receives special treatment are veterans. A decision might be made that because a service is offered on the north side of the city, those who live on the south side should be equally served. If one ethnic group is scheduled for a service, then other ethnic groups must also be served.

Market rationing is based on the ability to pay for services. With the advent of managed care more and more agencies find themselves restricting services based on the decisions of third party payers (insurance companies) to determine the kind and duration of services. Sometimes market rationing is more subtle, as when an agency decides to open an office in an outlying suburb which results in having fewer services available through its central city office.

Serving the neediest is often based on mandates created by a public agency or by law. Local human service departments only serve those children who meet the criteria of neglected and abused. Some voluntary agencies are established to care for children of drug addicted mothers, others to care for dying AIDS patients. Because of the care required, only a few of the total needy can be served by voluntary agencies.

Setting boundaries affects how agencies may put limits on whom they will serve. They may, for example, determine to only make programs available to people who live in a designated geographic area. Or they may confine service—or reach out—to people who meet pre-determined demographic characteristics based on gender ("battered women") ethnicity (Hispanics) or age (Senior Citizens). Agencies may profess to be open to everyone, but the reality of how they reach out to their clientele and the way they discourage those that do not meet preset criteria clearly indicate de facto rationing.

In an era of reduced funding for health and human services, rationing is becoming a way of life. Choices have to be made, priorities determined. With limited resources should a few be served intensely or more be served less intensely? Should the survival needs of the agency supersede those most in need of services? Should serving youth take precedence over older persons? Clearly, political, service, and ethical questions will be debated as we examine the pros and cons of various rationing methods. And certainly macro practitioners will need to become more purposeful and conscious of the rationing methods they consider.

USING RESOURCES IN THE ENVIRONMENT

Faced with dwindling resources and expanding needs social agencies increasingly find it difficult to add or sustain programs. At a time when funding for agencies is being curtailed, staff are being asked to do more with less. Under these circumstances agencies are seeking other ways to provide needed services. Two approaches are becoming more prevalent: the use of volunteers and the use of information and referral services.

Involving Volunteers

Volunteerism involves the mobilizing of unpaid individuals or groups to provide services.[4] People are motivated to volunteer for a variety of reasons. Some seek a voluntary experience because of a desire to help others; some want to network, some seek business contacts, and many, of course, want the joy of having an impact on other people's lives. Religious institutions, corporations, and schools encourage their constituents to participate in the fabric of community life through volunteer activities.

At the federal level volunteerism is being encouraged by some political officials in the hopes that this will take pressure off of the need for government funding for human services. Other public officials see genuine benefit in providing funding to support voluntary efforts so as to foster a partnership between the public and private sectors. The Federal Government has created the Corporation for National and Community Services which in turn has stimulated each state to provide its own vehicle to encourage volunteerism. Also, the National Self Help Resource Center and the National Center for Voluntary Action promote volunteerism throughout the nation.

At the local level United Way organizations either provide a source of volunteers for agencies or can identify the specific organization in each community that has this responsibility. Another source is the yellow pages of the telephone directory, which lists such service organizations as the Rotary Club, Lions Club, Kiwanis, and the Junior League.

Colleges and universities, through their community affairs, student affairs, or student government office, are other sources of volunteers. University internship programs in nursing, social work, and urban affairs provide appropriate supervision. Some universities and high schools require students to volunteer in order to graduate.

If you participate in an agency that wants to develop a role for volunteers, consider the following: 1) Provide an application form to collect basic information. 2) Check references the same as you would for a person seeking a job. 3) Provide adequate supervision and appropriate training. A major complaint the volunteers have is that they are left too much on their own. Hence, while volunteers may save staff time, they also demand time.

4) Provide adequate insurance through an umbrella insurance policy—especially make sure that automobile insurance is adequate.

Information and Referral Service

Since typically it is not possible for agencies to provide all the services their clients need, a good understanding of the availability of community resources is essential. Many communities provide an information and referral service. These can be affiliated with the local United Way, the county administration, or be a free standing agency. If the community is large enough there may be several specialized information and referral agencies devoted to such areas as women's issues, mental health, or older person's issues. In some communities the local community planning counsel may provide a directory or even a computerized service.

Within an agency one or more staff persons may be designated as a specialist in a given category, for example, housing services or employment services. If the need to make referrals is important enough, agencies appoint a case manager who has the responsibility for referring clients to services within the agency or to outside organizations. Case managers assess a client's needs, develop a service plan, and, after making a referral, monitors the results.[5]

To insure that clients will be served, some agencies develop contracts involving payment. In exchange for funding clients of agency A will be given priority consideration by agency B. Usually, however, agencies do not pay each other, but they may have compacts that encourage Agency A to give priority to Agency B's clients without funding. For example, an agency that works with chemically dependent persons will make referrals to a crisis child-care facility. The organization that receives the referrals has the assurance and confidence that the referring agency makes appropriate referrals.

DEALING WITH ENVIRONMENTAL ISSUES

Because their environment can be in a constant state of flux, all agencies must grapple with ongoing service delivery questions. Among these questions are the following:

1) *To what extent should we make our services accessible?*

Agencies must continuously balance the demand for services with the resources to meet them. Here are two examples: (a) A family counseling agency provides services both in the inner city and the suburbs. Faced with a reduction in funding, it determines to close its inner city office and concentrate its services on fee-paying clients in the suburbs. (b) A public agency has until now provided educational and prevention services to young mothers so they can better meet the developmental needs of their children. But new state regulations of agencies that provide intervention services to families with abused and neglected children now require those agencies to concentrate on the legal mandates and drop successful prevention services.

Agencies today must determine where they must concentrate their intervention efforts. Given limited resources, to whom should they make their services accessible? This is a perennial question that all agencies must come to terms with through setting priorities for their services. Further curtailment of funding is likely to force agencies to make hard priority decisions about whom they will serve—and whom they will not.

2) *How can we balance conflicting demands from our environment?*

Because many agencies receive funding from multiple sources, they must meet different and sometimes incompatible demands. The local drug board, for example, may want one kind of information and the mental health board another. The county commissioners may want to move clients off welfare, but employment opportunities are limited for low skilled people. A family planning agency is prepared to offer its services to teenagers, but the religious community is opposed to any efforts that appear to promote sexual activity. An accrediting body determines that an agency is not in compliance with certain professional standards, but to meet these requirements would mean that the board of trustees would have to make difficult policy changes. Each agency is acutely aware of these kinds of incompatible demands and must determine its course of action accordingly.

3) *How can we prepare for the continuous changes that are bound to occur in our environment?*

Agencies must be continuously tuned into their environment and determine what events may have a direct or an indirect impact on their services. For example, a downturn in the United Way campaign may not have an immediate consequence for the delivery of an agency's services. Several months may go by before the loss of funds is actually felt. Staff can be alerted that shortfalls in funding community campaigns will eventually have consequences and begin early on to anticipate these consequences. Similarly, the opening of a new agency serving the same client base, a shift in funding priorities of local foundations, the emergence of new political leadership, and other changes could create serious repercussions that must be anticipated.

SUMMARY

The environmental context within which all agencies must operate will greatly influence the formation and functioning of human services. A variety of forces impinge upon organizations that can affect directly or indirectly how staff respond. At the same time agencies can take steps to influence environmental forces.

QUESTIONS FOR DISCUSSION

1) What are some of the most important environmental factors affecting your agency?

2) With which organization does your agency relate?

3) What kinds of rationing does your agency use?

4) What are some ways your agency influences its environment?

5) Your neighborhood center has a major program designed to work with students so they can graduate from high school and become employed by the ten companies with whom you have an agreement. Your efforts consist of counseling students and arranging for tutoring. In the past you have worked with high-risk students, as well as students who have excellent prospects for going on to college. You have just received word that because of funding cuts, you will have to reduce the number of students in the program. You are now faced with the difficult decision of choosing which students you will serve—and which you will not—in order to be responsive to the companies that are committed to hiring your students.

    a. What criteria should be established regarding which students you would include?

    b. What should you do about those high-risk students who are in danger of dropping out because of their taking drugs, even though they are intelligent enough to graduate?

    c. What should you do about those students who probably will go to college even without the support of your program?

Chapter Notes

[1]Meenaghan, T.M., Washington, R.O., Ryan, R.M. (1982) *Macro Practice in the Human Services*. New York: The Free Press, p. 41.

[2] Netting, F., Kettner, P., & McCurtry, S. (1996). *Social Work Macro Practice* (2nd ed.). USA: Addison Wesley Longman, Inc.

[3]Coultan, C.J., Rosenberg, M. & Yankey, J.A. (1982, Summer). "Scarcity and the Rationing Services." *Public Welfare*, pp. 15-21.

[4]Brilliant, E. (1995). "Volunteerism." *Encyclopedia of Social Work*, (19th ed.). Washington, D.C.: NASW Press.

[5]Rosenberg M. and Brody, R. (1974). *Systems Serving People*. Cleveland, OH: Case Western Reserve University.

REFERENCES FOR CHAPTER 1

Brody, Ralph (2005). *Effectively Managing Human Service Organizations*. (3rd edition) Thousand Oaks, CA: Sage Publications.

DeMontigny, Gerald (2005). "Constructing Clienthood in Social Work and Human Services: Interaction, Identities and Practices." *Qualitative Social Work* Vol. 4, Issue: 2, June 2005. pp. 229-236.

Dominelli, Lena (2005). "Constructing Clienthood in Social Work and Human Services: Interaction, Identities and Practices." *Journal of Social Work*. Vol. 5, Issue 3. December 2005. pp. 363-364.

Kahn, William (2005). *Holding Fast: The Struggle to Create Resilient Caregiving Organizations*. Hove, East Sussex, New York: Brunner-Routledge

Seldon, Arthur (2005). *The Welfare State:Pensions, Health, and Education*. Indianapolis: Liberty Fund

CHAPTER 2

The Service Delivery System

SOCIAL SYSTEMS ANALYSIS

Before discussing various service delivery systems, including case management, it is useful to provide some understanding of Social System Analysis. Derived from General Systems Theory, Social Systems Analysis aims at discovering how a system functions with its various interdependent parts. It provides a useful framework for examining how agencies function within a health and human service delivery system and how agencies' clients move through this system.

The essence of a social system analytic model is understanding "the complex of components in mutual interaction...any whole consisting of interacting parts."[1] Each system has distinctive properties and a unity of its own, so that it is more than just the sum of its parts. The parts can be understood only in relation to the larger whole that they constitute. In every community, agencies are part of a social service delivery system network.

Several social system terms are useful to understand more fully the service delivery system through which clients must flow:[2]

1) The Suprasystem
2) Collateral systems
3) Subsystems
4) Inputs
5) Conversion
6) Outputs

7) Feedback
8) System boundaries

The **suprasystem** represents the unit to which the organization must be responsible. Human service organizations must respond to directions and be accountable to some higher unit. For example, local organizations have to be responsive to mandates from their state or national organization (e.g., mental health or alcohol and drug boards) or they may be funded and be accountable to their United Way or other outside funders. They may also be accountable for meeting external regulations or legislation.

Collateral systems involve all those agencies that are involved in reciprocal relationships with the organization. Almost all agencies have relationships with other entities in the community. They either refer clients to them or receive clients from them. They may participate with them on common community efforts, such as a general fund raising drive. Exchanges between agencies are common.

Subsystem(s) are units that are part of, and contribute to, the overall system. They can operate with considerable autonomy on the one hand and, on the other, have to be responsive to the needs and demands of the system of which they are a part. A social work department in a hospital is an example of a subsystem. Within an agency, units that specialize in particular services (e.g., day care, job search, and training) function as subsystems within the larger organization.

Inputs into an agency can be of various kinds. Resource inputs in the form of staff, funding, and programs energize an agency and make it ready to function. These may be termed active inputs in the sense that they will be used by the agency to act upon consumers. In contrast, object inputs are service clients or consumers towards whom the active inputs are directed.

The **conversion** process, sometimes known as "throughput or transformation," involves several elements: 1) assessing clients, 2) conducting transactions between staff and clients, 3) negotiating with internal and external service providers, 4) providing services, and 5) altering the client or his/her environment in some significant way.

Social Systems Analysis recognizes that in the process of conducting its transforming activities an organization may tend to run down. This is analogous to entropy, the tendency of physical matter to run its course. The tendency decreases when there is a higher input and exchange of energy and information from the environment. The system survives and maintains its characteristic internal order only so long as it imports from its environment more energy and matter (active inputs) than it expends. In the social service system this would mean a balanced supply of consumers and resources must be maintained in order to resist entropy, or winding down. To continue to provide services, all agencies must strive for this balance or equilibrium between inputs and outputs.

Outputs refer to those products that the organization discharges. The survival of most organizations requires that they deliver products that are acceptable to their environment and especially to their suprasystem. Sometimes a distinction is made between outputs and outcomes. Outputs are quantitative activity service units provided to those clients who have become engaged in the organization. Outcomes refer to the impact these services have on the processed clients as they relate to previously specified objectives. Outcomes reflect a change in the problem or needs status of a client, such as improved personal functioning, improved housing, or change in employment status.

Feedback is defined as an information input about how the organization is functioning in relation to its goals and its environment. Agencies develop information systems to indicate whether they are on course in meeting goals and to control for deviations that might make them veer off from their intended accomplishments. Feedback is obtained through follow up with clients and with collateral agencies.

System boundaries may be characterized as either rigid and impermeable or open and permeable. Agency boundaries function to regulate the kind and rate of the flow of inputs and outputs. Through the process of setting boundaries, agencies control which clients they will process and also to what extent they will connect their clients with other agencies. The boundaries connecting agency A with agency B are called the interfaces and the extent to which these two agencies provide an exchange will indicate the permeability of their respective boundaries. Some agencies are more rigid while others are more open regarding how they deal with prospective clients and with collateral organizations.

Service Delivery Within One Agency

Some agencies strive to meet the total needs of their clients by forming their own internal array of services. The agency itself constitutes the totality of the service delivery system. For example, an agency is established to find welfare recipients jobs, and it determines that it must provide a wide range of services to achieve its primary objective. In addition to providing training programs and employer recruitment, it decides to offer the following services: a day nursery program, a health services program, a camping program so parents can drop their kids off in the summer, and a legal program so that those involved with disputes with their landlords or those who seek to erase juvenile records that interfere with potential employment can obtain legal assistance.

The advantage of this build up of a variety of services within the same organization is the ease with which clients can be referred from one unit to another. If, for example, a newly trained person is unable to continue on the job because of the lack of day care or because she/he needs a safe and stimulating program for a preschool child, the employment agency has a facility on its premises for taking care of the children.

Agencies are tempted to provide the full range of services themselves, rather than rely on outside organizations—until they realize the problems that come from being self-contained. One problem is cost. The resources required to provide "one stop shopping" are a tremendous burden for all but the largest agencies—and even they have to struggle to find financial support. Few agencies can afford the extra expenses, as desirable as they might be, to meet the varied needs of their clients.

A second disadvantage is that in attempting to meet the disparate needs of its clients, an agency may so dilute its resources that it becomes less able to do the essential work for which it was originally established. In the example of the employment agency, staff might become so diverted from their original focus of job development and job finding, that these become less effective programs. All agencies have to be mindful of their primary focus even as they become aware of the many different needs of their clients.

Hence, service delivery entails a combination of both internally and externally provided services. Depending on their resources and the configuration of services in a particular community, agencies evolve their own style of meeting their clients' needs. Agencies must then assist clients with the various pathways they can take to resolve their concerns.

CLIENT PATHWAYS THROUGH THE SOCIAL SERVICE SYSTEM

Clients move through social service delivery systems in various ways depending on the permeability of the boundaries they encounter, on the success of the transformation process, and the degree to which the collateral agencies with whom they come in contact can make adjustments and obtain the input resources to meet their needs.

The term "pathways" is used to describe a sequence of structured contacts with clients as they move through the service delivery system. Pathways can be a single route or multiple routes. A client's movement through the system is not random but represents clearly delineated directions he/she can take. A client flowchart can illustrate a finite set of options available to clients.

Constructing a Client Flowchart

To understand how clients might move through a service delivery system, review the Generic Client Flowchart. (See figure 2.2) Different agencies might, of course, have different routes for their clients. Moreover, different clients going through the same agency might take different routes. The value of a Client Flowchart is to identify the various points along the process where crucial decisions have to be made, where activities need to be monitored for feedback, and where different alternatives might need to be considered. Sometimes this process of identifying clients' pathways through the community into a service agency is called channeling. This involves providing the client with proper information about services, generating motivation, and making sure that the services are available and accessible.[3]

Symbols Used in Creating a Client Flowchart

The purpose of a flowchart is to describe various pathways clients may take into, through, and out of an agency. Symbols used for describing the client pathways are shown in Figure 2.1.

Figure 2.1
Client Pathway Symbols

*An arrow connects another process, question, or ending symbol.
*Dotted arrows reflect returning to a previous step.
*Three methods for closing a case are:
    (1) The agency could make a referral to another agency
    (2) The client could voluntarily discontinue
    (3) The agency could terminate

REVIEW OF A GENERIC FLOWCHART MODEL

Figure 2.2, a Generic Client Flowchart, reflects a "typical" client through an agency that provides mental health counseling but is also mindful that clients could require such external services as housing, employment, or day care. Note that the client can be referred to the agency from several sources, such as self-referral, another family member, or the local school. During the intake process staff determines whether the client is eligible for the service and meets appropriate requirements, such as motivation and need. If not, the agency ends the contact with the client and, if appropriate, makes a referral elsewhere.

If the client continues, an intervention plan involving specific objectives to be achieved is mutually agreed upon. Subsequently the agency provides the agreed upon service(s). If the objectives are achieved then the agency terminates the client. If not, the agency works to resolve the barriers either within the client or in the environment. For example, a client may be poorly motivated to work on his substance abuse problem, or he may be in a social environment that stimulates his drinking. Before treatment can proceed, the barriers that prevent him from working on his problems will need to be resolved.

In this generic flow chart, we indicate several instances of clients being at yes/no decision points that may involve their leaving the agency, returning to a previous process, or being referred to an outside agency. Client pathways should make these decision points clear because they focus attention on those instances where clients' needs may require new or different ways of delivering services. In developing client pathways be especially mindful of the possible drop out points.

If the agency determines that the client would benefit from another agency's services, then a referral would be made and the agency would monitor the delivery of services and the achievement of objectives. Again, if barriers were encountered in agency B, agency A would take steps to influence the removal of those barriers or to find suitable alternatives.

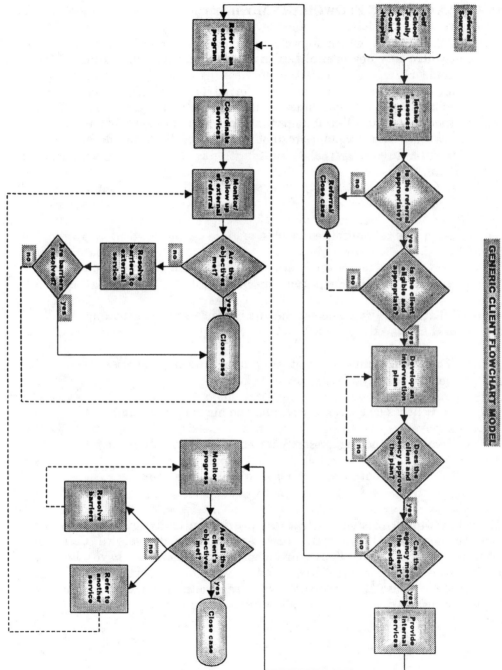

Figure 2.2

GENERIC CLIENT FLOWCHART MODEL

In examining client pathways through a particular service system or agency consider the following questions:

Is there only one or are there multiple pathways through the system?

After going through intake if the client is referred to a specialist, must the client return to a central point before going on to a second specialist or can the first specialist make a direct referral?

Can a client go directly to a specialist, thus bypassing a central intake?

Can there be multiple entry points?

How permeable are the agency's boundaries in letting people in (e.g., eligibility requirements, waiting lists, "red tape")?

What pathways are open to clients if their conditions change or their objectives are not met?

If certain objectives are met, but others are not, what does the agency do?

Can clients be recycled back into the agency's program?

Does the agency aggressively pursue clients who drop out?

Are clients routinely channeled to outside agencies?

The value of these questions is that they provide an analytic perspective for viewing how clients are being processed through the service delivery system.   To facilitate client movement, some agencies have devised mechanisms for tracking clients.   We will focus next on two such mechanisms: Case Management, and Wraparound Services. In Chapter 22, we discuss various other forms of agency coordination.

CASE MANAGEMENT

Need for Case Management

Case management has emerged as one of the more common mechanisms through which services can be coordinated in such areas as the following: mental health, child welfare, frail elderly, health care, welfare reform, children with special needs, and such specialty target populations as those affected by AIDS, substance abuse, homelessness, and developmental disabilities. Case management cuts across public and private sectors and all fields of practice. Settings include hospitals, schools, and health and mental health clinics. Increasingly policy makers, agency administrators, and direct service practitioners are turning to case management as the method of choice for delivery of services to clients and their families with complex, multiple problems or disabilities. Case management has become a permanent part of the service delivery system.[4]

Not all agencies use the term case management to describe a professional generalist. Some use the title "generalist social worker," others "service manager," and others "client advocates." With the advent of social welfare reform, the term "self sufficiency coaches" has come into vogue. Because "case manager" is the most recognizable term, we will use it in this book.

Features of Case Management

Either a designated person or team coordinates, organizes, or develops a network of formal and informal efforts designed to improve the way clients who have multiple needs function. A client, for example, suffering from both mental illness and kidney disease has no family members to turn to and may need monitoring. Help may be needed in taking prescribed medication and in working out a variety of housing, mental health, and employment services. All of these need to be coordinated through a case manager.[5]

The following features are typical of case management: 1) Services are individualized, meaning they are specifically designed to meet specific client needs. 2) Services are comprehensive, meaning they can be related to all facets of a client's life, such as housing, recreation, and finances. 3) Duplication of services is discouraged, resulting in better use of community resources. 4) Clients are generally encouraged to make their own decisions and to be empowered to take action. 5) Follow up with clients ensures better use of services and determines what further help may be needed beyond the initial request. 6) Formal support systems of agencies and services are integrated with that of the informal support system involving family and friends.[6]

Case management is defined in relation to outcomes it is expected to achieve: the client will receive services in a supportive, effective, and efficient manner through a process of interaction with a service network. The outcomes can include improving access to services, fixing responsibility for coordinating and monitoring care, ensuring optimal outcomes, and providing for cost controls.[7]

Functions of the Case Manager

The following core functions are typical of case management programs regardless of the specific area:

Outreach
Screening and intake
Assessment and diagnosis
Service planning
Service arrangement
Making referrals
Advocacy
Monitoring

Outreach activities are intended to identify and enroll appropriate clients. For example, a program designed for homeless persons may make special efforts to seek out persons living under bridges or in cars. Another example would be reaching out to people with AIDS. Because of the fears of disclosure, abandonment, and helplessness, many are reluctant to seek help and often delay getting treatment and support. Case managers may become part of a staff team to reach out to the persons with AIDS.[8]

Screening is a preliminary assessment to determine client eligibility. Almost every agency will impose criteria for determining whether people will be eligible for their services. Often these eligibility requirements are established by federal or state regulations. For example, mentally ill patients may have to meet a specific mental health diagnosis to qualify for services.

Assessment and diagnosis involves learning about the current and future needs of the client. This entails collecting information about the person's social situation and physical, mental, and psychological functioning. Moreover, attention is given to the client's strengths and capabilities. Among the questions that would be explored in the assessment process are the following:[9]

- Can the client's needs be met with minimal outside support through family and friends?

- Does the client have the capacity to seek services with minimal outside assistance?

- Is the request for help the result of a particular life episode or a chronic condition?

- Will the client need ongoing assistance?

- Are there resources in the community to meet the client's needs?

- Is the client willing to accept the service(s) being offered?

- Is the resource accessible, either within the agency or elsewhere in the community?

During the assessment the case manager determines the extent to which the client can function independently and appropriately through the use of agency or community resources. Because of the skills involved in the assessment process, highly trained case managers with good diagnostic skills and awareness of community resources are essential.[10]

Service planning is based on information gathered during the assessment process, and the case manager works out a plan with the client. The case manager must determine whether to provide services directly to the client or coordinate the work of other service providers or specialists. The primary job of the case manager is to work with clients to identify the type of help needed and then to identify and overcome barriers that prevent the use of this help.[11]

The essence of the planning process is the mutual determination by both the client and the case manager of the objectives that need to be achieved. It is assumed that generally clients can articulate their needs, and it is the responsibility of the case manager to assist in clarifying and prioritizing these needs to achieve client objectives. Case managers must determine how extensively and intensively to probe the client's problems. Is it best to accept the problem as stated or delve into others areas? In the planning process, the client acts as an informed, authorizing agent by knowing the reason for the referral, what can be expected, and the purpose of the plan in relation to objectives. The client thus becomes an active participant, a co-producer of his or her own use of resources.[12]

Ideally, service planning should entail a written statement of specific, achievable objectives. For example, suppose a battered woman requires temporary housing in the short run and more permanent housing eventually. The service plan might specify that the case manager will first contact battered woman shelters for temporary housing followed by explorations with public housing authorities and low cost rental properties. The client might agree to search for employment while in the shelter and also look for low cost rentals. This client-centered focus allows the client to have a very direct involvement in the planning process.[13]

Service arranging involves contacting service providers to arrange for services developed in the service plan. Often this entails a searching out of scarce resources, determining whether they are available, and negotiating the extent to which they can be provided. Sometimes case managers are put in the futile position of attempting to coordinate resources that do not exist.[14] For example, many communities have very limited or no residential facilities for substance abusing women. Similarly, communities frequently lack facilities for dual diagnosed individuals (e.g., severe depression **and substance** abuse). On the other hand, where services are available the case manager provides an essential brokering role of connecting clients to agencies.

In some agencies case managers develop an expertise and become specialists about specific services. For example, in an agency where there are four or five case managers, one might be a specialist in housing, another in employment, and another in day-care services.[15] Typically where an agency provides both counseling and case management, the roles are very distinctive, with the case manager being responsible for connecting the client to both internal and external services, while the counselor is responsible for ongoing treatment. Ideally, the case manager ought to have available a directory of resources that clients will typically use. Sometimes a community resource directory is tailored to specific clients. Or the case manager may have to develop a specific directory of services likely to be used.

Whether case managers should provide direct service is open to question. In some agencies case managers are prohibited from providing direct service on the basis that this can be time consuming and would result in a breakdown of the case management system. In many other agencies service managers are given flexibility to offer direct service, such as providing temporary housing, transportation, or even limited counseling in crisis situations. Because there is a natural tendency for case managers to want to have more then a time-limited relationship with their clients, this is an issue requiring continuous attention.

Making referrals requires more than simply giving the client the name and address of a potential service provider. The case manager can prepare the client by discussing the role of the agency, what services can be expected, and how they can best make use of external services. Clients should have a contact person, know what procedures will be followed, and what follow up assistance will be forthcoming. Some case managers may even coach their clients about how to go through intake. Through role playing and anticipating the first visit, the client is prepared to deal with potential difficulties. Occasionally, the case manager may have to accompany the client to help in the adjustment process. In many instances, though, the case managers may determine that the clients are capable of taking initiative in the referral process and will encourage their doing so. When clients can do things for themselves, they should be encouraged to take independent action.[16]

Advocacy is one of the major functions of the case manager who strives to elicit improved policies and procedures for referred clients. In dealing with major systemic trends involving homelessness, lack of access to health care, inadequate housing, and family burdens, case managers must confront long waiting lists, overburdened bureaucracies, and administrative "red tape." Agencies may establish constraining eligibility requirements or agency personnel may be resistant to change. They may establish such rationing methods as "creaming," i.e., accepting only those individuals who have the best success in their program. For example, an employment agency may prefer a welfare recipient with a work history to one who has not had a work experience.[17] Although case managers by themselves cannot produce systemic change, they can provide the information and the impetus for their agency to become engaged in trying to make substantial changes in organizational relationships and even in legislation.[18] Case managers should anticipate that they and their clients will frequently encounter barriers to services. The case manager's commitment and ingenuity can lead to positive changes. (Note: Chapter 3 will discuss client advocacy in depth.)

Monitoring and follow up occur by obtaining feedback of the internal or external service. Ideally the case manager should receive a disposition report from the service provider. Depending on the agency and nature of service needed, some case managers will terminate their services at the end of a finite period (e.g., 90 days). Others can go on for a long time period—in some instances, indefinitely. A mental health agency, for example, may provide brief sessions year after year for chronically mentally ill persons.

Follow up of clients is what distinguishes case management from an information and referral program. The case manager wants to know whether the objectives established with the client are achieved. If objectives are not achieved, the case manager will need to reassess with the client what needs to be done and to determine how to make service providers more responsive, or whether to explore other services.[19] Unfortunately, because of huge demands on the case manager's time and the need to continually deal with new clients, case managers tend to limit the amount of monitoring that they can provide to their clients. Some agencies deal with this problem by limiting case management follow up to three or four times a year.

ISSUES AFFECTING CASE MANAGEMENT

Several issues affect the delivery of case management services. First, as was previously noted, caseloads can become unmanageably large, resulting in case managers being limited to responding only to crises. Sometimes, an agency will create a backlog by only providing a limited number of staff in relation to the number of people needing to be served. Sometimes, case managers themselves contribute to the build up by retaining clients longer than the system is designed for. Case managers may understandably want to hold on to their clients because they have developed a relationship and because their clients express a wish to continue. Note that we have not included counseling as one of the case manager's roles. Although some agencies with small caseloads may be able to include limited counseling, usually agencies will use other internal staff or those from outside the agency designated for this purpose, and case managers have to accept that their role is delimited.

Second, the case manager must watch that confidentiality is not compromised when dealing with external agencies. A case manager will need to balance the need to advocate on behalf of clients to gain access to needed services with the concern of divulging too much information about the client. This is particularly true of those involved in substance abuse, mental health, or homelessness.[20]

Third, we have described the functions of the case manager as if the process were linear, meaning that first case managers would conduct outreach, then determine eligibility, then make an assessment, etc. In reality the case management process does not necessarily follow a rational, linear course. Objectives may change, unanticipated issues may emerge, or previously undetected strengths may allow the case manager to work with the client in reframing directions. Hence, case management should be seen as a dynamic process, one requiring continuous, skillful judgement.[21]

Fourth, also as discussed previously is the harsh reality of the accessibility of services. Access relates to whether resources are made available in ways that clients can use them. Are language specialists available to assist those whose primary language is different from the provider? Are the agencies' hours conducive to seeing clients whose work hours limit their ability to come during the daytime? Are day-care providers located in low-income neighborhoods so that people can take advantage of training programs?[22] The case manager must assess these issues of accessibility.

Finally, since so much a part of the case manager's job is to serve as an advocate, case managers may face inherent conflicts when they deal in an environment and an atmosphere of increasing restrictions and limitations. Operating within a public policy environment based on a "meaner and leaner" philosophy, case managers are increasingly being required to restrict service choices and instead to seek out the informal support network involving family and friends. This is an atmosphere, regrettably, that requires clients to do more with less. Managed care in the health and mental health arena is reflective of this ideology.[23]

WRAPAROUND SERVICES

Wraparound reflects an overall approach that mandates services be customized to the specific needs of children and families, even when these services are part of different categorical funding arrangements, such as child welfare, juvenile justice, and mental health. The term, "wraparound process," refers to a specific set of policies and practices used to provide individualized services and supports for children and families.[24] It is possible that some agencies use some, but not all, elements of a wraparound program. The following elements constitute the basis for wraparound services:

1) **Anchored in the community**: A community team is composed of key stakeholders, including members from various agencies involved with a particular child and family members. Family members are an integral part of the team because they will be involved in carrying out plans, and they can sensitize other members of the team to the family's culture.

2) **Planning is highly individualized**: Many communities initially target children and families where the children are either currently placed in restrictive care or are at risk of being placed outside of the home. After the child is determined to be eligible for the wraparound process, their records are typically sent to a "broker" agency that is responsible for hiring a resource coordinator. The coordinator brings together members of the team and assists the team in identifying the strengths of

the family and child and determining what issues need to be focused on. Among the questions that would be explored are the following:

- Are current living arrangements appropriate?
- What are the strengths and limitations of family functioning?
- What are the social relationships outside of the family?
- Are there emotional issues that affect family interactions?
- What is involved in ensuring a viable education for the child?
- Is the child, as well as other family members, safe?
- Are the health needs being taken care of?
- If they desire spiritual guidance, is this available?
- Are financial needs being addressed through employment or public support?

An example of the kinds of services provided by a wraparound program for adjudicated adolescents would include the following:

- individualized youth assessment
- intensive meetings involving youth and family members
- recreational youth groups
- chemical dependency services
- educational assistance (tutoring)
- vocational training
- linkages to community support groups
- intensive in-home family treatment

The aims of these services are to strengthen family skills, mobilize community resources, prevent delinquency recidivism, and avoid future placement or incarceration of the adolescent.

The ideal plan would focus both on informal supports and formal services, inasmuch as services will eventually end while informal family supports will likely continue. In addition, the plan would anticipate potential crises based on previous episodes and responsibility for action steps would be assigned to the specific team members. The plan would include the following elements: strengths, needs, outcomes, strategies to produce outcomes, who is responsible for what, funding requirements, and methods of assessing outcomes.[25]

3) **Flexible, non-categorized funding**: In some communities arrangements are made to pool funds or at least to reserve funding for children who have multiple needs. For example, a child who is both mentally ill and physically disabled would have access to both emotional counseling services and handicapped services. Similarly, youth recently released from incarceration and needing to return to school could draw upon tutoring resources and substance abuse counseling. In this example the resources of the school system, juvenile justice system, and substance abuse agency would provide a combination of resources for the multi-need youngster.

4) **Follow up and measuring results**: Following the creation of the plan, periodic follow up occurs to determine whether the plan needs to be revised. Outcomes will reflect such behavioral data as reduction and drug and alcohol abuse, reduction in aggression, or improvement in school attendance. Sometimes consumer surveys are used to measure family reaction and service responsiveness.

MAKING THE WRAPAROUND PROCESS WORK

Wraparound process is not a "model" that rests on one formula. Rather, it is a process that reflects the particular needs of an individual situation. There are, however, certain features that contribute to its potential success. First, the wraparound process requires interagency collaboration. Agencies must share power and funding and be willing to come together in a collaborative effort. Second, the wraparound process must recognize that each child and family is unique and therefore must be individualized. What works for one family may not necessarily work for another. Third, flexibility of funding is absolutely essential to pay for services that cannot be provided in other ways. Often these flexible funds are spent on short-term supports, such as respite services for families. Because flexible funding is usually limited, these funds should avoid being used to purchase items that can be obtained in other ways. Fourth, the wraparound process requires top administrative commitments in the state or community and local agency level support. One without the other will doom the process. Fifth, parental advocacy and parent-professional partnerships are crucial. The wraparound process requires a different relationship with parents in engaging them in advocacy efforts and involving them in planning for children.[26] Finally, the services offered must have sufficient strength and integrity. If the intensity of services is insufficient, if staff commitment is lacking, and if flexible funding is too small, the program may not be strong enough to have an impact on the children and families served.[27]

SUMMARY

Social systems analysis helps explain how organizations that provide services operate within a social service delivery system. Clients may be able to get their needs met through one organization or, more frequently, they need to be referred to other agencies. Client flowcharts are used to describe how clients move through a service delivery system. Case management is one of the most prevalent forms of assisting clients through the service delivery system. A wraparound program is a way of customizing a broad spectrum of interdisciplinary services to meet the special needs of children and families.

QUESTIONS FOR DISCUSSION

1) Using Figure 2.2 as a guide, prepare a flow chart of a typical client moving through your agency. Discuss points where a client might discontinue. Should the agency consider ways to deal with dropouts?

2) A meeting has been called of representatives of the local mental health board, the mental retardation board, the United Way, the county human services department, local health department, and public schools. Your purpose is to determine whether you could devise a case management system at the neighborhood level so that families needing multiple services could have their needs coordinated. What are the pros and cons of setting up a centralized office to deal with multi-need families?

3) You are in a mental health agency that works with mildly mentally ill persons. They are able to function in the community, but they need jobs. What are the pros and cons of a) offering job counseling and job finding through the agency and b) partnering with another organization that is in the business of job development?

    If you decide to work with another organization, what would you need to consider to make the program work for the benefit of your clients?

Chapter Notes

[1]Bertalanffy, L. (1966). "General Systems Theory and Psychiatry." *American Handbook of Psychiatry,* 3, Ed. S. Arieti (New York: Basic Books).

[2]Rosenberg, M. & Brody, R. (1974). *Systems Serving People: A Breakthrough in Service Delivery.* Cleveland, OH: Case Western Reserve University.

[3]Rothman, J. & Sager, J. (1998). *Case Management: Integrating Individual and Community Practice.* (2nd Ed.). Needham Heights, MA: Allyn & Bacon.

[4]Rosenberg & Brody op.cit.; Biegel, D., Tracy, E., & Corvo, K. (Aug. 1994). "Strengthening Social Networks: Intervention Strategies for Mental Health Case Managers." *Health & Social Work,* 19, pp. 206-216; Austin, C., & McClelland, R. (1996). *Perspectives on Case Management Practice.* Milwaukee, WI: Families International, Inc. pp.1-16; Vourlekis, B., & Greene, R. (1992). *Social Work Case Management.* New York: Walter de Gruyter, pp. 1-25.

[5]Kirst-Ashman, K., & Hull, G., Jr. (1997). *Generalist Practice with Organizations and Communities.* Chicago, IL: Nelson-Hall, pp. 327-353.

[6]Kirst-Ashman, K., & Hull, G., Jr. (1993). *Understanding Generalist Practice.* IN: Nelson-Hall, pp. 493-520.

[7]Vourlekis, B., & Greene, R. (1992). *Social Work Case Management.* New York: Walter de Gruyter, pp. 1-25.

[8]Greene, R. (1992). "Case Management: Arena for Social Work Practice." In Vourlekis, B. & Greene, R, *Social Work Case Management.* New York: Walter de Gruyter, pp. 11-25.

[9]Kirsh-Ashman & Hull, *Understanding Generalist Practice* op.cit. 509-511; Rosenberg & Brody op.cit. 31-36; Austin & McClelland op.cit. 6-8.

[10]Greene, R., op.cit. 10.

[11]Ballew, J., & Mink, G. (1996). *Case Management in Social Work (2nd Ed.).* Springfield, IL: Charles C. Thomas, p. 11; Rosenberg & Brody op.cit. 34.

[12]Rose, S. (1992). *Case Management & Social Work Practice.* White Plains, NY: Longman, pp. 271-297; Greene op.cit. 19, 20.

[13]Rosenberg & Brody op.cit. 34, 35.

[14]Moore, S. (Sept. 1992). "Case Management and the Integration of Services: How Service Delivery Systems Shape Case Management." *Social Work,* 37, pp. 418-423.

[15]Ballew op.cit. 8.

[16]Kirsh-Ashman & Hull, *Understanding Generalist Practice* op.cit. 504; Rotherman & Sager op.cit. 121.

[17]Rothman op.cit. 118.

[18]Austin & McClelland op.cit. 24-28.

[20]Berger, C. (1996). "Case Management in Health Care." In Austin, Carol D. & McClelland, Robert W. (Eds.), *Perspectives on Case Management Practice*. Milwaukee, WI: Families International, Inc., pp.175-174.

[21]Rose op.cit. 282.

[22]Rose op.cit. 287,288; Rosenberg & Brody op.cit. 68.

[23]Austin & McClelland op.cit. 260.

[24]Clark, H. & Clarke, R. (Mar. 1996). "Research on the Wraparound Process and Individualized Services for Children with Multi-System Needs." *Journal of Child and Family Studies*, 5, pp.1-5; VanDenBerg, J., & Grealish, E. (Mar. 1996). "Individualized Services and Supports Through the Wraparound Process: Philosophy and Procedures." *Journal of Child and Family Studies*, 5, pp. 7-21.

[25]VanDenBerg op.cit. 7-21.

[26]VanDenBerg op.cit. 7-21.

[27]Rosenblatt, A. (Mar. 1996). "Bows and Ribbons, Tape and Twine: Wrapping the Wraparound Process for Children with Multi-System Needs." *Journal of Child and Family Studies*, 5, pp. 101-116.

REFERENCES FOR CHAPTER 2

Chan, Fong (2005). *Case Management for Rehabilitaion Health Professionals*. Osage Beach, MO: Aspen Professional Services

Dennis, Carl (2006). *Everything is Normal Until Proven Otherwise: A Book About Wraparound Services*. Washington Child Welfare League

Neada, Rhoda (2006). *Case Management: A Palliative Perspective*. Mustang, OK: Tate Publications

Saleh, Shadi (2005). "Cost-Effectiveness of Case Management in Substance Abuse Treatment." *Research on Social Work Practice*. Vol. 16, Issue 1. pp. 38-47.

Woodside, Marianne (2005*). Generalist Case Management: A Method of Human Service Delivery*. (3rd edition) Belmont, CA: Thomson Brooks/Cole

CHAPTER 3

Client Advocacy at
the Macro Level

Readers of this text probably are, or will be, direct practitioners working with individuals, families, or small groups. Even so, you are likely to be engaged at the macro level with social agencies, school systems, courts, and other community institutions. During the course of your working on behalf of clients you will undoubtedly try to influence outside organizations to be more responsive to client needs. As a client advocate, you will be committed to helping your clients obtain the most appropriate resources and actions.

By *client advocacy* we mean the power to influence a change or behavior in others so as to accomplish client goals. Sometimes clients need only a slight boost to accomplish their goals; they can manage the advocacy process mostly on their own. At other times, through mutual decision with your clients, you will need to take full and complete responsibility because you are able to intervene more effectively, because you have cultivated significant external relationships, because of client limitations in taking action, or because of constraints inherent in their situation.[1] A degree of professional judgment is necessary to determine when to foster clients' independence and self-sufficiency and when to act more proactively on their behalf.

Advocating on behalf of clients is not a simple process; rather, it often involves the challenge of careful planning and delicately timed actions.

The decision to become an advocate is dictated by 1) the nature of the problem, 2) an assessment of the client, 3) the actual or potential availability of resources, 4) the receptivity of the practitioner to use advocacy methods, and 5) the anticipated response of those who can act on your client's needs. Being an advocate can be daunting because, though your clients have strengths, they likely have also experienced many adverse situations that heighten their vulnerability in dealing with the vicissitudes of their lives. For many of them, one more adverse situation, on top of the many that they already have experienced, can make them wary of advocating for themselves, and they may become highly dependent on your advocacy assistance.

In addition to responding to the overwhelming situations your clients face, you may also have to deal with limits of time and resources. Advocates typically have demanding schedules and constraints of large caseloads. Moreover, agency and community resources may be limited and even unavailable. Progress is often, therefore, "two steps forward, one step backward." Fortunately, there are enough experiences with success—even limited success—that the challenges inherent in advocacy are worthwhile.

In fulfilling their role as advocate, direct practitioners carry out the following commonly practiced professional activities:

- Identify issues of concern to the client.
- Obtain facts and information that can help determine a course of action.
- Plan long-term strategies and short-term tactics that can help influence a change in the client's situation.
- Encourage the client to deal with the situation or, if this is not possible, take leadership to get desired results.
- Determine where there are appropriate resources and marshal these for the client's benefit.
- Assess the results to determine whether corrective action will be necessary.
- Where possible engage the client in every step along the way to ensure a better chance of success.

Because of the temptation to control the advocacy process, the advocate must constantly revisit the question: "Are my clients in a position to take a more active role?" An unintended consequence of taking over for clients is that you reinforce their inadequacy about handling situations on their own. As a professional, you must be willing to examine your own need to experience gratification that you have accomplished results for your clients—while inadvertently quashing their own sense of mastery over their lives.[2]

With these general caveats in mind we present ten principles of advocacy involving macro systems. The crystallizing of these principles emerged after discussion with scores of social workers, case managers, and human service advocates. Reflecting success, partial success, and even failure, the case examples have been edited and disguised to protect confidentiality and illustrate these ten principles.

I. DOCUMENT FACTS AND OBTAIN RELEVANT INFORMATION

In reviewing the situation with your clients, you may easily obtain some facts; you may have to dig out others, much as a reporter or a detective does in searching for relevant information. You may need to learn more about your clients and their situation directly from them or from third parties. You may have to search out what resources are available through numerous phone calls, e-mail inquires or personal visits. In advocating for your client, information is power. Nothing speaks louder than facts in making a strong case.

Case #1: Liang Ku

> Recently I received a case involving a Chinese minor who needed to be enrolled in our local high school. The family had just moved to Greatsville, and the teenager was eager to attend school. His main problem: he spoke no English.
>
> I contacted the Board of Education to determine the school's responsibility. I learned that English as a Second Language (ESL) was available for Spanish-speaking students only. In checking with the high school, I learned that school officials were reluctant to hire a private tutor to teach English because of the costs involved for only one student. I then checked with an immigration attorney who informed me that it was the school's responsibility to enroll foreign students and provide them with ESL courses.
>
> In a meeting with the school's principal, the student, and his family, it became clear to me that the school administration was reluctant to provide for tutoring. The principal would not accept proof of residency and requested more information. She refused to enroll the student, saying that no one from the school board had contacted her. I stated that having talked with an immigration attorney, I was aware that once proof of residency was obtained, the school was obligated to provide tutoring to a foreign student.

I encouraged the family to obtain proof of residency, which they did, and subsequently he was enrolled. He now has a tutor paid by the school to help him with his work.

QUESTIONS FOR DISCUSSION

1) What facts were essential to make this situation work out successfully?

2) Can you provide examples from your caseload where obtaining the facts or information was essential to getting results?

3) What special methods have you used to obtain needed facts?

II. EMPOWER CLIENTS TO ACT ON THEIR OWN BEHALF

An important element of good advocacy is to get clients to act for themselves. Their own self-esteem not only increases, but also they become emboldened to take on future courses of action without relying on outside assistance. They become masters of their own fate. But the empowerment process does not occur by happenstance. Acting as a facilitator, rather than the prime mover, the client advocate carefully prepares the client to act on his or her own behalf. Sometimes this can happen through a simple suggestion, or it may be accomplished through more involved methods. For example, through role playing, the client and social worker could plan the actual dialogue the client might use in a given situation. Regardless of the particular method, empowering clients helps them develop the courage and the competency to proceed on their own behalf.[3]

Case # 2: Mr. Brown

As a social worker for the Senior Activity Center, I had responsibility of working with Mr. B., a 73-year-old man who lives in an efficiency apartment. His water bill has been $9 monthly for several years. This month, however, his bill totaled $43. Thinking that he should pay whatever he was billed, Mr. B. was in the midst of writing a check when I called to remind him of our appointment the next day. He told me he didn't understand why it had jumped so much, but he did not want to appear negative. I asked him to hold off payment until we had a chance to talk together.

Though I could have easily called the water department myself, I thought it was important to empower Mr. B. by having him make the call. I showed him where the number was written on the back of the bill and offered him the use of my phone, since he was hesitant about making the call completely on his own. After about a two-minute conversation, the water company representative apparently realized that the company had made a mistake and agreed to send him a revised statement. My client was delighted he did not have to pay and felt very proud that he had corrected the situation by himself.

QUESTIONS FOR DISCUSSION

1) What if Mr. B. didn't want to call the water company?   What should the social advocate do?

2) Have you or your colleagues worked with clients to prepare them for a confrontation with a person they wanted to influence?

III.   ASSIST IN OBTAINING BASIC RESOURCES NECESSARY FOR A DECENT STANDARD OF LIVING

Some clients come with so little esteem and are so fragile that they require help with the basic skills of surviving. True, they may have some external and internal strengths. Externally, they may have friends or family who will help sustain them. Their internal strengths may include the ability to live off the streets, negotiate with others for food and shelter in exchange for simple housekeeping, or find a job that pays at or slightly above the minimum wage. Still, even slight reversals may throw them off. These highly vulnerable persons need an advocate who can work with various community institutions to clear the way for urgent resources to sustain a decent quality of life.

Case#3: Ms. Thomas

Diagnosed as mildly mentally retarded, Ms. T. is a person who uses poor judgment, and, as a result, her child has been taken from her. I was assigned to work with her because of an episode in which her girlfriend, in a fit of anger, threw scalding hot water at her two-year-old son. The friend was jailed, and Ms. T. was charged with neglect because this episode reflected a pattern of her not providing a safe environment for her child.

My objectives are to assist her in 1) improving her decision making capacity, 2) finding and holding a job, 3) keeping stable housing, 4) developing better budgeting, and 5) improving her parenting skills.   Although I wish that she would be able to function more independently, she is constantly calling and asking me how to handle situations. I hope that eventually she will be able to work things out on her own.

Ms. T. was living in the apartment with the friend who threw the hot water, so I was determined to get Ms. T. into another rental property, but her SSI monthly check of $551 barely covered her rental costs. So I called Public Housing Authority and pushed their moving her up the priority list, explaining this would help her become reunited with her son. Now she pays only a nominal amount of rent.

In addition, I went to the local antipoverty program and succeeded in getting them to help reduce some of the utility costs. Then I requested Children and Family Services to place special furniture in her new housing. I also started her keeping a notebook of decisions she made so she can see if there are any patterns that are not constructive for her. For example, after her third purchase of a junk car that broke down like the others, she realized that this was not a good idea, and she has begun taking a bus. I encouraged her to turn in her checkbook because she was continuously overdrawing.

Last week she called me to say that she just found out that she was nine weeks pregnant. When I asked her how it happened, she said she didn't know why she had slept with the man for whom she has no special feelings. I have been meeting with her to help her weigh her options. Though I am personally pro choice, I am careful to encourage her to make her own decision. She is very upset that her family is rejecting her at this time when she needs considerable support. Probably putting up the child for adoption is the best course, but I want her to make the decision.

QUESTIONS FOR DISCUSSION

1) What other community resources could the case advocate call upon? Are these available in your community?

2) Is the case advocate doing enough? Too much?

3) How have you had to deal with resource limitations?

IV.   DEVELOP A STRONG SERVICE NETWORK THROUGH FORMAL AND INFORMAL CONTACTS

Because resources typically may not be located within one organization but may be available throughout the community, it is vitally important that the client advocate have access to a broad and vibrant network of resource possibilities. Through printed directories and the use of the Internet it is possible in most communities to be aware of resources that can benefit your client. But competent client advocates do more than have access to printed or electronic information; they actively cultivate contacts to connect with the appropriate resources. Moreover, they develop a rapport with staff from other agencies so that when it comes time to make a referral, a degree of trust and respect already exists. Some agencies encourage various advocates to become specialists (e.g., housing, employment, or day care specialists) who actively cultivate relationships in their area of expertise and assist other client advocates in making the proper networking connections.

Case #4:   Ms. Williams

Ms. W. is a 25-year-old mother who came to our Domestic Violence Center because she has been physically, emotionally and sexually abused by many men, the latest of whom was her partner for five stormy years. On the day that she came to us, she had awakened with the urge to kill her perpetrator for beating her the night before. She first called the mental health center that then referred her to us on the hot line.

The first thing I did after meeting her and her children was to enroll them in the neighborhood school system. I have a relationship with the principal, who has agreed to keep the children's names anonymous so that their father could not find them. Next, I referred Ms. W. into counseling at the local hospital by calling the social worker with whom I have dealt in the past. I then called the Human Services Department to arrange for her to enter the volunteer program so she could obtain experience in office duties: filing, word processing and limited record keeping.

Her son, Lamier, age 8, is verbally and physically aggressive, so I referred him to the Child Guidance Center. Though this agency has a waiting list, they were responsive to my request because I have a long-standing relationship with the agency and they know that I make appropriate referrals.   He and his mother are now going for family sessions, and he is learning to deal with his anger. This past week I referred Ms. W. to a job specialist in our agency to help her with her résumé and to locate possible jobs through his contacts. I appreciate that my agency has hired a job specialist because he has the time and the relationships to find suitable jobs for our clients. Ms. W. now works part time as an intake person in the detoxification ward at a nearby hospital. Through our contacts at Section 8 we have helped her to obtain housing. Yesterday I went to court as her advocate to prevent the father from getting custody of their children. I spoke on her behalf to the judge; based on my testimony, she received full custody.

I am pleased that the many contacts that my co-workers and I have in the community came through for her.

QUESTIONS FOR DISCUSSION

1) In this case illustration, Ms. W. was referred to an internal job specialist who apparently worked with a number of the agency's clients to find them jobs. What are the advantages and disadvantages of having an internal job specialist rather than referring clients to organizations specifically set up for this purpose (e.g., job finding agencies)? What are the pros and cons of having various service specialists within the agency rather than using outside agencies?

2) Do you think that it is proper for advocates to purposefully cultivate relationships with other professionals and then call upon these relationships to aid their clients?

3) In your agency can you relate instances where having relationships with service providers have benefited your clients?

V.   WORK DILIGENTLY ON BEHALF OF YOUR CLIENT, BUT BE MINDFUL THAT YOU ALSO HAVE A RESPONSIBILITY TO THE COMMUNITY

This principle stipulates that your clients are your primary focus. Your allegiance is to them. As their client advocate, you develop a high commitment and a constant vigilance to ensure that community institutions are being responsive to your client's needs. At the same time you have to assume that your clients will make the proper efforts to play their part in resolving issues that stand in the way of working out their problems. In some instances you may have to work against their interests for the sake of other family members or for the good of the community.

Case #5: Sasha Witbla

Ms. W., age 26, has five children, each from a different father. The county's Children and Family Services (CFS) has temporary custody of all of them because of child neglect and her inability to complete drug treatment.

As an outside contracting neighborhood agency, we provide counseling and advocacy services to clients like Ms. W. so that they can have their children returned to them. My plan is to get her into treatment, develop stable housing, maintain financial stability, and ultimately get her children back to her. My initial attempt to have her stay in a residential drug treatment facility resulted in failure. She became hostile, flipped over a table, and threw a chair across the room. She then called a male friend to pick her up. Later she told me "I can't go for more than a day without having sex."

Some background on Ms. W.: She herself has been in and out of foster homes since the age of nine. Originally she was placed because of being molested by her mother's boyfriend. She has been involved in several domestic violence situations—she being the molester. Almost everyone at CFS knows her or knows about her because of her fits of violence. Her children love to see her fight. One of them recently told me, "My mom will jack you up if you mess with the kids." I speculate that they feel her aggressiveness serves to protect them.

After she left the treatment facility, she said to me that I should trust that she could manage on an outpatient basis. Although I had my doubts, I decided to risk that she could turn herself around, so I referred her to a drug outpatient treatment program. At first she did well. She attended regularly and the counselor said that she was involved in discussions. She tested negatively on urine tests—no signs of using PCPs. She was regularly attending AA meetings.

This progress went on for three months, and I was prepared to advocate strongly for her during her court hearing to determine if her youngest child would be returned to her. Just before her court hearing, however, I picked up her urine test, and it was positive. When I told her the news, she cried. She pleaded with me not to tell the court because she knew what would happen. It was heart wrenching for me, but I knew I had to tell the court the truth, even though, as I feared, the court decided to award permanent custody to CFS.

I consider Ms. W. a good mother who deeply cares about her children, and she has shown some progress. I knew that I could not lie to the court about the urine results, because this could eventually result in harm to the children, especially if Ms W. were to have a relapse. She was my primary client, but I also had to be concerned about the children.

There is a long- range possibility that she may still get her children back. I was able to get her a job packing fruits for truck delivery. But she no longer is making an effort to go for urine tests—not a good sign. I'm trying not to lose hope, and I care for her. I'm her only lifeline. I hope I don't become so swamped with the rest of my caseload that I lose touch with her.

QUESTIONS FOR DISCUSSION

1) If the client advocate's first duty is to her client, was there anything she might have done that could have prevented the court from awarding permanent custody to CFS?

2) What if you felt that you could do more to assist this client? What would your position be with your agency that wants you to move on to other cases?

3) You work hard to develop resources for your client (as in this case). You get her into a drug rehab program, find suitable housing, and encourage an employer to take a chance to hire her. In short, you do all you can to help the client and then she relapses. How do you manage your own feelings that you have been betrayed? How do you approach the next client that resembles Ms. W.?

VI.   UNDERSTAND THAT RESISTANCE TO CHANGE IS A NATURAL PART OF THE ADVOCACY PROCESS AND BE PREPARED TO DEAL WITH IT

Resistance to change comes with the territory. Expect that the parties that need to change have reasons to maintain their positions. At times the client advocate has to engage in "shuttle diplomacy," working first with clients to make changes and then showing the other parties that they too need to modify their positions in light of the clients' willingness to modify behavior and attitudes. Sometimes by working to alter client behavior and conditions, the client advocate helps the other party to become more receptive to making changes. The client advocate is thus constantly figuring out ways to overcome roadblocks. An old expression states, "Many roads lead to Rome." Faced with a roadblock, a good client advocate will figure out another path that will work to achieve client objectives. Finding alternative approaches entails creative thinking, coming at the problem from a different perspective, and arriving at a solution that can be acceptable and workable both for the client and for the other party.

Case #6a: Kimberly and Tanya Laniel

I work in a middle school system (grades 6-8) as a school social worker. Usually the teachers refer students to me who encounter such problems as school truancy, challenging authority, acting out behavior, inattention, and under achievement.

Working with the Laniel family presented a special challenge. The middle school teacher referred two sisters to me: Kimberly, age 11, and Tanya, age 12. As is my usual procedure, I mailed a parental release to the home, but after two weeks still did not receive a reply. Until I received permission, I couldn't work with the youth. Meanwhile, they were about to be suspended for not attending an in-school detention. I was feeling extremely frustrated at the mother's irresponsible behavior. How was I to be able to help the kids if the parents wouldn't give me permission?

I decided that I needed to "butt heads" with the mother, so I went to her home in the early evening. She said that she just had been so busy that she hadn't gotten around to sending back the release. Although I wanted to convey how annoyed I was that she was being irresponsible, I held my anger in check, sensing that she was feeling overwhelmed by working full-time and having to raise alone two daughters who were both bright and feisty.

Things have gotten worse since the teacher first referred the girls to me three weeks ago. Although they were seen as bright students and had until this year a good academic record, their situation had deteriorated. They had accumulated 10 days of absences and had not shown up for in-school suspensions. The principal was now threatening to suspend them (out of school) for 10 days, almost certainly guaranteeing that they would not pass on to the next grade.

Feeling that the situation required my active intervention, I immediately contacted the principal and the truant officer and requested that they give me a week to work with the family to determine if we could get at the issues that were contributing to the deteriorating school situation. I set up a meeting with the mother and the two girls and learned that they were upset because their friends were teasing them for wearing ill-fitting clothing. Apparently, the mother had bought clothing from a second hand clothing store for the girls but hadn't bothered to sew the clothing for better fitting. At my urging the mother agreed to do the necessary sewing.

Having worked out the problem that was making Kimberly and Tanya upset, I then returned to talk with the teacher who complained to me that she was already spread too thin to give the girls the special attention they would need to catch up with the rest of the class. So then I arranged for the girls to have special tutoring to make up for their absences. And I told them that the school would immediately contact the mother if the girls skipped school. I then returned to the principal, telling her that the family was going to work together and asked her to modify her original plan of out-of-school suspension, which would have resulted in the girls missing more classes; instead, they would have a one-week after-school detention. The girls complied with this punishment and are on their way to being productive students.

QUESTIONS FOR DISCUSSION

1) In this situation should the advocate have been more demanding of the girls to straighten up—or else face consequences?

2) Did the advocate take the right approach with the school personnel? Could he/she have considered other options?

3) Should the school social worker have encouraged the mother to work directly with the school, rather than be the go-between? If so, how should the client advocate have gone about doing this?

Case 6b: Mrs. Pierce

Mrs. P. is a 62-year-old woman who lives in a low-income senior citizen apartment. Evicted from her last residence because of foul odors, she is again facing eviction because of smells emanating from her new apartment. Her neighbors and management would be appeased if the odor were eliminated. I thought that perhaps a home health-care provider could clean the apartment, thereby eliminating the odors, but she did not like the idea.

During our meeting, Mrs. P. communicated to me that she had a medical condition known as ulcer sores. After seeing the sores, I asked if I could have a registered nurse visit her at home. She agreed and the nurse subsequently determined that the foul odor was from fluid that had drained from the sores and saturated the furniture coverings. Mrs. Price's sores were now past the point of weeping and almost healed. All the bedding and furniture coverings of Mrs. Price's were washed and the stench subsided.

With Mrs. P.'s permission, I spoke to the management of the apartment and explained what had caused the foul odors. The manager's annoyance turned to sympathy and understanding now that he knew that the odor wasn't from trash and that Mrs. P. had been ailing. He promised to call if any other problems arose.

QUESTIONS FOR DISCUSSION

1) Have you encountered situations like this where the action that needed to be taken "was right under your nose"? In retrospect what would you look for the next time you encountered such a situation?

2) Have you been in situations where getting your client to make a change resulted in your stimulating the other party to make an adjustment?

Case #6c: Ms. Jones

My job with the Disabled Services Office requires that I travel to different public housing sites in rural county public housing units. Recently I was assigned to work with Ms. J., a 55-year-old woman who suffers from severe asthma and whose diabetes has limited her mobility. She has had no telephone service during the two months of moving into a low-income apartment. It is critical that Ms. J. have a telephone because she must remain in contact with her family members and her health-care providers.

I told Ms. J. that she needed to contact the local phone company and request telephone services for her residence. I gave her the number and showed her to a vacant office near mine where she could use the phone. After awhile Ms. J. returned to my office with no success. She explained that she had trouble understanding the representative. Ms. Jones told me she would have her son call, but I was concerned about this course of action because she had previously communicated to me how her children were unreliable due to their drug use and alcoholism.

 I decided to make the call to the phone company myself. While Ms. J. waited I spoke with the phone representative who explained that Ms. J. had an outstanding bill of $100, which had not been paid for two years. The representative explained that the bill would have to be paid before services could be rendered. I explained Ms. J.'s need for a telephone and her low-income situation to the representative. Then after conferring with her I asked if Ms. J. could be put on a payment plan while receiving services. Fortunately, we were able to arrive at a solution acceptable to both my client and the phone company. The representative set up a payment plan of $5.00 a month and agreed to allow Ms. J. to receive a telephone line. Ms. J. gladly agreed to the arrangement.

QUESTIONS FOR DISCUSSION

1) Should the client advocate have had her client call from her office and provided more guidance?

2) Can you recall situations where it was necessary for you to act on behalf of your clients, rather than encourage them to act on their own behalf? In retrospect do you think that this was the appropriate course of action?

VII. IDENTIFY PRESSURE POINTS THAT WILL ENCOURAGE THE TARGET OF CHANGE TO BE MORE RESPONSIVE

Being a client advocate involves knowing the best source of pressure. Each person has certain people to whom they are more likely to be responsive. In many instances your target of change will be more responsive if they must deal with a higher-level of authority. Most people are more likely to respond to authority figures than to people on their same or lower organizational level. Your focus of attention, therefore, is to convince a person of authority who can become your spokesperson for change. Seek allies to ensure a better chance that your advocacy efforts will be successful.

Case #7: The Smith Family

I work for a Catholic Services agency in a rural community, and we are under contract with the local juvenile court's Court Diversion Program. Recently I was assigned the Smith family. The court had earlier decided to award temporary custody to the Department of Human Services (DHS) because of family deterioration, and I was given the ongoing responsibility to come up with a viable plan that would permit custody to be given back to the family.

Background: The family came to the court's attention when ten-year old Jeremy ran away from home. When the police returned him to the home, they discovered that the family had experienced domestic violence and drug abuse. The DHS then filed for custody, and Jeremy was placed in a foster home. As a case manager in Catholic Family Counseling, I was responsible for arranging services for the family. Although both parents were responding to our services, I began to realize that the social worker at DHS kept "raising the bar." As soon as the parents responded to one program, she would insist on their having to complete another. For example, we arranged for the father to undergo an anger management group; when he completed this, the social worker insisted that he be enrolled in a parent-training program. Mrs. S. was successfully involved in drug counseling and her urine tested negative for three months, but the social worker insisted that she go to a Drug Anonymous group.

At the end of the three months, I felt that the family was ready to be reunited, but the social worker insisted that more time was needed to be sure. I then learned that this particular worker had had a previous case that had disastrous results when a youngster was prematurely reunited with the family and subsequently experienced severe burns from an abusive father. I felt that she was overacting to this situation based on her previous experience.

Having tried unsuccessfully to convince her that the family was ready to have the boy returned, I then told my supervisor, who agreed with me, and who then contacted the DHS supervisor. In a joint conference with both supervisors, we agreed together that the boy was ready to be returned, and DHS supported our recommendation to the court.

Fortunately, my supervisor interceded on my behalf and was able to convince the other social worker's supervisor. I doubt if I would have been able to convince the social worker on my own.

QUESTIONS FOR DISCUSSION

1) What odds would you give that without the supervisor's intercession the social worker would have been able to persuade the DHS staff to allow the family to be reunited?

2) Should the client advocate have considered going over the DHS person's head and directly appeal to her supervisor? What are the advantages and disadvantages of doing so?

3) Have you encountered situations where you have had to convince an authority person to intercede with someone in another department or agency on behalf of your client?

4) Do you know of situations where pressure has been applied to a person who was in a decision making position?

VIII. USE PROFESSIONAL DISCRETION IN DETERMINING THE APPROPRIATE LEVEL OF GUIDANCE TO EMPOWER CLIENTS

The use of advocacy requires professional judgment about when to be active—even directive—in assisting clients and when to take a step back and let the client act as his/her own advocate. No hard and fast rule or formula is available; professional judgment is necessary. Being nondirective when your clients clearly need suggestions can leave them in the lurch. In contrast, being overly influential and dictating a script can be stifling and not conducive to growth. The best suggestion is to be mindful that you have to make judgment calls about how far (or how limited) you need to go—depending on the client and the situation.

Case #8: Lucretia Sella

I work as an advocate for a Domestic Violence Organization (DVO), which assists battered women to take control of their lives. In many ways Ms. S. represents our typical client, for she came to us after having been severely beaten by her perpetrator. Before coming to us she had been seen by a case manager at a mental health center for depression and drug and alcohol abuse. Because she lived in a deteriorated, cockroach-infested house, Children's Services Agency (CSA) was considering taking her two children from her. I believe that part of her motivation for coming to DVO was to avoid this from happening.

Our normal policy is to limit the time that a family can be with us to 90 days. In general, I go along with this rule, knowing that if clients overstay we would not be able to deal with the continuous flow of clients to our agency. Usually we are able to find housing and develop an employment plan in less than the 90-day limit. But in Ms. S.'s case I advocated a longer time period so she and I could focus on several courses of action.

The first thing I did was arrange to have her transferred to another mental health facility because I felt that the counselor was too rigid in her approach of focusing only on her drug dependency and not on her feelings of depression. In my opinion, she needed dual diagnostic treatment.

Meanwhile, I communicated with the case manager at CSA whose assessment was that Ms. S.'s mental instability warranted the children's removal. I then requested an emergency meeting with her and her supervisor at which time we communicated that Ms. S. was doing much better with the new mental health counselor and that the children were being well cared for. Ms. S. was attending mandatory group counseling sessions that we conduct, and she was regularly attending Alcoholics Anonymous three times a week.

I then helped Ms. S. prepare for her own hearing at CSA. She had a tendency to wear very short shorts (daisy dukes) and tops that revealed her stomach, and I told to wear more conservative clothing. We role played what she would communicate to CSA. Later she described that she was able to communicate to CSA that she intended to obtain a job in the near future so she could support her children and that she was on the waiting list for Section 8 public housing. As a result, the CSA backed off of the idea that she would need to go into inpatient treatment and would not pursue taking her children from her.

She was very proud of herself, saying, "I stood up for myself and my children." She is now completing her GED and participating in the Homemaker Program at the community college. When Section 8 housing comes through next month, she will move out of our facility and enter a nurse's aid training program. I'm glad that I was able to convince both my agency and CSA that with the right support Ms. S. had the ability to turn herself around.

QUESTIONS FOR DISCUSSION

1) Did the advocate act properly in giving specific guidance to Ms. S. in how to handle the interview with CSA?

2) Have you had clients who required specific directions and who then were able to manage on their own?

IX. CHALLENGE THE STATUS QUO BY FIGHTING FOR WHAT YOU BELIEVE IS THE RIGHT THING TO DO

At the heart of being a client advocate is the willingness to question the usual way of doing things. At times this will involve actively campaigning for your cause, usually in relation to other organizations. You will want to appeal to the hearts and minds of those you seek to influence. Oftentimes the rightness of your cause may not be sufficient, and you will need to develop strategies and tactics that bring to bear pressures your target cannot resist.

Case #9: Lobbying the Governor and the State Legislature

As a case manager who works for a treatment program for the mentally disabled in a rural area in the largest county of the state, I am constantly aware that my clients live fragile lives and are in a constant struggle to survive. Several are able to work part time, barely managing to pay their rent, utilities and food. They are, however, proud that they can live independently—thanks in part to the small subsidies they receive from the state. So when I heard that the governor, faced with a tight budget for the upcoming year, was proposing a cut in the human services that would affect my clients, I became very angry. In my state there has been a long history of cutting services rather than considering tax increases. This proposed cut would mean that my clients would just not be able to survive. I had to do something to challenge the usual way of handling state financial crises.

With the backing of my agency, I first organized a letter writing campaign, inviting clients and their families to come to the agency in the evenings over a one-week period. We were able to send over 100 letters to our governor, the budget office and our state representatives. Unfortunately, this didn't work. The governor remained adamant that severe cuts would have to be made, maintaining that the state constitution requires that he submit a balance budget. Nor did the conservative legislature respond to our letters. We had to find another, more powerful way of dealing with our state government.

We decided to organize a bus tour from our city to the state capitol. Although we were the largest city in the state, we realized that if we were to go it alone, this would not generate as much interest as organizing other cities around the state so that legislators from various localities could see that they had constituents that were committed to the mentally disabled. We therefore contacted agencies like ours throughout the state and asked them to organize a "Day for the Disabled" in our state capitol. All together we had 32 buses with over a thousand people marching on the capitol. Five different newspapers made it front page news to show that they cared. Editorials were written supporting our cause.

I'm pleased to report that the governor capitulated and restored the cuts. He and his advisors came up with the idea of finding new money by taxing car leases and legal services. Now my clients can feel confident that they can weather life's ups and downs.

QUESTIONS FOR DISCUSSION

1) Can you identify situations that require advocacy efforts to persuade public officials (mayor, city council, county commissioners, state representatives, and governor) to support a policy that would benefit your clients?

2) What strategies do you think would be most effective in convincing them to make changes? (Note: Chapter 21 discusses negotiation and advocacy in more depth.)

3) If the bus tour had not been effective in this case, what other tactics might have been considered?

4) Can you think of situations in which a human service professional has taken on the role of advocate to push for legislative or policy change?

X.   TAKE A PUBLIC STAND TO EMPOWER YOUR CLIENTS TO COME FORTH WITH THEIR OWN ADVOCACY EFFORTS

Sometimes it is essential that you take a public stand and battle with opponents to win the hearts and minds of the community.[4] In turn a public position serves to reinforce the sentiments of those who might stay on the sidelines and who can now lend their support to a mutually felt cause. Having initially stimulated latent concerns, you can recede into the background as citizens express their own commitment. Someone has to start the ball rolling and then it takes on a momentum of its own.

Case #10: Kohoga County vs. Foster Parents

I am one of 10 foster care workers in a county that is a bedroom community for a large metropolitan area. Six months ago we learned from the media that two of our foster care kids, ages 12 and 14, shot and killed a popular gas station owner. We were devastated by the news because while we knew that these particular kids had serious emotional problems, we were hopeful that we could help them become productive citizens. They were convicted and sent to the reformatory until their 21st birthday, as required by law.

We soon realized that the consequences of this horrific crime went beyond the particular individuals involved and could potentially jeopardize our entire foster care program, affecting some 200 families. In a sense, the entire community was placing the foster care program on trial. Public meetings were held and people began clamoring that the foster care program be discontinued. The suburban newspaper reported that at PTA meetings parents expressed their fears that foster children were corrupting the other children in the schools.

As an agency we decided that we had to take action to respond to the growing crisis for the sake of the kids and the foster families. We asked our foster parents to join us for several nights during a two-week period to write letters on their own stationary to the local newspapers, and several of these were published. Emboldened, a delegation of foster parents and staff (myself included) met with the editorial board of the newspaper and provided them with information packets plus testimonials of how well the foster care program was working. We were also able to arrange for several couples from the foster care program to speak at four community forums. Their calm, but positive, demeanor served to allay the fears of the community and ultimately helped cool the passions that had been directed against the agency's program. During the forums, several other foster parents expressed their positive experiences. I am glad to report that we have had an increase in foster home applications since we began our advocacy efforts.

QUESTIONS FOR DISCUSSION

1) In addition to the approaches taken in this case, could other efforts have been undertaken to empower foster parents who were feeling under attack to come forward?

2) Can you think of instances where your agency has taken (or should have taken) a stand on an issue that was vital to your clients?

In summary, these ten principles form the foundation of the advocacy process. We trust that you will be inspired by these examples and advocate on behalf of your clients at the macro level.

Chapter Notes

[1]Frankel, A. J. & Gelman, S. R. (1998). *Case Management*. Chicago, IL: Lyceum Books Inc., pp. 38-9.

[2]Schneider, R. L. & Lester, L. (2001), *Social Work Advocacy*. Belmont, CA: Wadsworth/Thompson Learning. pp. 152-193.

[3]Rose, S. (1991). "Strategies of Mental Health Programming: A Client Driven Model of Case Management." In C. Hudson & Cox, (Eds.), *Dimensions of Mental Health Policy*. New York: Praeger pp. 138-154.

[4]Gutierrez, L. M., Parsons, R. J., Cox, E. O. (1998). *Empowerment in Social Work Practice*. Pacific Grove, CA: Brooks/Cole, pp. 176-177.

REFERENCES FOR CHAPTER 3

Anders, Thomas (2005). "Who's Advocating What?" *Public Management*. Vol. 88, No.2. pp.16-20, 22.

Eisenstadt, Donna (2005). "Dissonance and Importance: Attitude Change Effects of Personal Relevance and Race of the Beneficiary of a Counter Attitudinal Advocacy." *The Journal of Social Psychology*. Vol. 145. No.4 August pp. 447-67.

Freeman, Iris (2005). "Advocacy in Aging: Notes for the Next Generation." *Families in Society*. Vol. 86, No.3 July/September pp. 419-23.

Fuentes, Claudio (2005). *Contesting the Iron Fist: Advocacy Networks and Police Violence in Democratic Argentina and Chile / Claudio A. Fuentes*. New York: Routledge, p. 221.

Hoefer, Richard (2006). *Advocacy Practice for Social Justice*. Chicago, IL: Lyceum Books, p. 203.

CHAPTER 4

The Organization's Culture

THE IMPORTANCE OF VALUES

Because all practitioners function within an organization and their work and their attitudes are affected by the dynamics of their setting, they should strive to develop an understanding of these unique forces. One of the most significant of these factors is the culture or predominant value system that permeates an organization.

By culture we mean the style, traditions, rituals, and beliefs—the fundamental values of the organization—that influence the way staff think and behave.[1] It is the system of values that a given group has invented, discovered, or developed in learning to cope with its problems of external adaptation and internal integration.[2]

Culture is "the right way to do things around here."[3] Usually cultural values develop over a long time, serve to stabilize the group, and are highly resistant to change. Frequently these values are taken for granted and may not even be part of the staff's conscious thought process.

Shared values give the organization a sense of direction so that individual staff see how to fulfill their professional goals in relation to the organization's goals. Above all, organizational values provide a profound sense of meaning to staff work. When influenced by a strong organizational culture, staff truly care about their work; they significantly invest themselves in what the organization represents.

In some organizations where values are weak or unenforced, those staff who do not subscribe to them (often known as "rebels" or "uncommitted drones") can contaminate the organization's culture. Where a strong culture exists, people either buy into organizational norms or they are encouraged to leave. Those who remain identify deeply with the organization's value system. They adopt the organization's values as their own, and their professional lives have greater significance because of this affiliation.

Changes in Organizational Culture

Sometimes the culture of an organization dramatically changes. This can occur in a number of ways. For example, a newly hired director may convey a new set of values that depart significantly from the previous administration. Example: A long time director has fostered a family atmosphere: staff were encouraged to relate to each other as peers rather than on the basis of their role in the organization. The new director wants the organization to be more efficient. He insists that staff meet less informally and be more mindful about how they are spending their time. Staff wonder what has happened to "the way we operate here."

Sometimes a new project or program with new staff can seriously affect the tone of an organization. Suppose a children's institution were to add a family preservation unit whose main purpose is to keep abused and neglected children in their homes. Two different philosophies—preserving family unity and working for the best interests of the children—now have to be reconciled.

Then, too, outside demands of funders can play a significant role in changing the agency's culture by imposing constraints on the kind and time limits of services. Staff who at one time spent time to develop a relationship of trust with clients find now that they must limit their involvement.

Thus, although usually the important values of human service organizations will be fairly constant, circumstances operating either from within or from without the organization can cause fundamental values to change.

Experiencing "Cultural Shock"

The term, "cultural shock," is normally applied to persons who experience going from one country or community to another. For example, someone who is used to the diversity of urban life in the U.S. might find that the values and life style of a South Dakota farm will require a substantial adjustment. So, too, it is quite possible that those who move from one agency to another will experience culture shock. For example, moving from a neighborhood agency that encourages considerable latitude in programming to working in a probation department that must operate under legislative and judicial rules and decisions will require significant changes in attitudes and behavior. Knowing that organizations will differ in their cultures can be a factor in your own decision making about where to work as a professional and can also prepare you for the adjustment that will be required.

Values, then, constitute the sum total of an organization's culture. Staff attitudes and behavior are greatly influenced by the organizational values and, in turn, affect how they respond to the clients they serve. In social agencies two major values likely to endure are 1) job ownership and 2) the primacy of the client.

JOB OWNERSHIP AS A CENTRAL VALUE

One of the highest values an organization can engender in its staff is that of job ownership. Employees must care so much about their work and be so invested in it that they do whatever it takes to get the job done. When they are this committed and dedicated, they work as if they were in business for themselves. This could mean working extra hours, responding in special ways to the needs of the people they serve, or advocating changes in organizational procedures for the benefit of their clientele. How does this profound commitment in the job come about? The organizational culture can promote a climate that furthers job performance by instilling in staff a sense of higher purpose, emotional bonding, trust, stakeholder involvement, and pride in their work. The result is that staff feel good about their work and want to invest themselves more fully in it.[4]

A Sense of Higher Purpose

Fortunately, most staff who work in the human services field prefer an organizational culture that emphasizes making a contribution, serving others, and feeling that they are a part of something larger than themselves. They typify the third worker in this story: A traveler meets three men at work. Each is asked what he is doing. The first says, "I am laying bricks."

The second says, "I am making a wall." The third replies, "I am building a cathedral." If staff feel the work of the organization can make a difference in the lives of the people it serves, they will be inspired to invest themselves more fully.

A Sense of Emotional Bonding

An organization in which people deeply care about each other fosters strong allegiances and a powerful sense of togetherness. This sense of bonding produces feelings of comfort and security. Feeling wanted and cared about, they like to come to work because they find their relationships emotionally and intellectually fulfilling.

This feeling of camaraderie is particularly important in organizations where clients make high demands and work pressures are tremendous. Staff are required to be so giving and so responsive to others' needs that care and support fostered by positive work relationships is especially important. Well-administered agencies, therefore, encourage a congenial work atmosphere and positive interpersonal relationships among staff. Of course, it must preserve balance, as too much of a good thing can be problematic. Weekly parties to celebrate birthdays that result in prolonged lunch hours can reduce productivity. Staff greeting each other with daily hugs can push an affectionate atmosphere beyond the realm of professional conduct. Hence, emotional bonding, while desirable, may need to have boundaries.

A Sense of Trust

This value is not easily defined, but employees know it when they have it, and they also sense when it does not exist. Perhaps when trust exists, we tend to take it for granted, but its absence can cause tremendous problems for an organization. If the organization's leadership conveys the expectation that everyone should work hard but managers are seen taking long lunch breaks and not investing time in their own work, they will be mistrusted. In contrast, a sense of fairness is conveyed throughout the organization if, for example, when an agency experiences a severe reduction in funding, everyone is required to take a salary cut.

Honest interpersonal relationships build trust. It is based on the assumption that staff are all trying to work for the common good. Certainly, they may evidence self-interest at times, but they must also be willing to put aside their individual agendas for a greater benefit. This value encourages and promotes mutual commitment.

A Sense of Stakeholder Involvement

An organization that espouses this value fosters stakeholders at every level. All staff feel they must invest themselves for the common goals to be achieved. Throughout the organization, there is a sense of empowerment to make decisions, to be invested, and to care about what is happening. At the same time, they understand and appreciate that various parts of the organization—management, supervisors, service staff, clients, support staff, and board members—participate in the overall purpose of the organization. They all feel that they are partners in a common venture.

A Sense of Pride in One's Work

Effective managers instill the idea that staff should be the very best they can be. Because of a collective sense of pride, each organizational member gains a reputation for providing a superior quality of service. In business, slogans such as "Quality is our most important product" or "Quality is Job #1" are created to promote this value. These could just as easily be the maxims of human service organizations. Periodically, staff are asked, "What makes you most proud of the organization? What gives you the most satisfaction?"

THE PRIMACY OF THE CONSUMER

Human service organizations must emphasize the primacy of the client. This sign was hung in the administrative offices of a public housing authority:

> We believe that our clients are not an interruption of our work; they are the very purpose of it. We are not doing them a favor by serving them; they are doing us a favor by giving us an opportunity to do so.

Even when human service organizations espouse the belief that their clients are their reason for being, a number of factors can prohibit this from being their core purpose. If program funding is received from a third party, consumers may not have a direct way to express their concerns because they are not paying for the service. If consumers are considered replaceable, that is, if there are so many people waiting to be served that dissatisfied ones can easily be exchanged for others, then there may be little or no impetus to deal with discontent. If too great an emphasis is placed on administrative or staff convenience, then meeting the needs of consumers becomes secondary.

Suppose, for example, that working parents can only attend marital counseling before or after work. If an agency serving these working couples places more importance on staff desires not to work early or late hours, then the needs of clients become secondary.

The antidote for these inhibitive factors is a value commitment to—even an obsession with—meeting consumer needs. Organizations must develop a good feedback system and a method for reminding staff of the primacy of consumers. One major way of obtaining feedback is through periodic formal surveys. Just as hotels, restaurants, and car repair shops ask their customers regularly for suggestions on how to improve their services, so human service organizations could undoubtedly benefit from such formal surveys of their constituents. It is important, of course, that surveys be conducted with the intent that issues identified will be carefully reviewed and corrective actions considered.

Some organizations use a feedback device entitled "Give us a Grade" in which the service consumer is asked to answer a variety of questions regarding expectations, description of care provided, and a rating of services. Encouraging comment cards and letters—both positive and negative—will help staff understand how their services are perceived.

Other organizations even assign management staff to pretend they are consumers. They may call or visit an office where they are unrecognized to see first-hand how their concerns are handled.[5] This is a common practice in retail stores that arrange for management, staff, or outside "professional shoppers" to experience what it is like to be treated as a customer. The purpose is not to evaluate specific individuals as much as it is to determine how responsive the system is to consumer needs. Experiencing the organization as a consumer can reveal discrepancies between how things should work and what actually takes place.

In addition to feedback, organizational management can provide orientation and training to improve staff proficiency and performance and to help them better tune-in to consumer needs. Applauding staff who have gone out of their way to be responsive to consumer needs and to obtain results furthers this fundamental organizational value. Role-playing exercises and problem solving simulations provide concrete, clearly understandable examples of how the organization can work to add value to the lives of consumers they serve.

A number of obvious clues indicate whether an organization is "consumer-friendly." Telephone calls are answered promptly. The reception room is inviting, and the receptionist conveys a warm welcome to visitors. Staff genuinely convey positive acceptance and go the extra distance to be helpful to clients. Appointments are promptly kept; apologies are given if clients have to wait. Clients are treated as genuine partners by engaging them in activities that assist the agency. They may, for example, be asked to serve on advisory committees to improve agency services.[6]

These are small efforts, perhaps, but they project the organization's fundamental emphasis on the dignity and importance of the client/customer. They convey the message that those served by the agency are very important. These efforts do not occur by happenstance. The culture of caring permeates the entire organization as it continually reinforces this primary value in staff meetings, annual reports, training programs, and documents describing particular programs. Through special training and supervision, staff learn how to treat clients with respect and dignity even when having to cope with hostility and complaints. By frequently stressing its commitment to caring and proving that commitment time and again, the organization develops a reputation for being responsive to the needs of the people it serves.[7]

Articulating the Organization's Culture

The organization's culture is expressed in a variety of ways: New staff are oriented about the ways the organization wants to treat its clients.   The way staff meetings are conducted and staff are treated give evidence of important values. The use of newsletters, the honoring staff for their outstanding work, even the way the agency disciplines or lets go of staff will reflect the agencies fundamental values. More often than not, values are not written out; they can only be assumed by the way staff behave toward each other and toward clients. Frequently, then, agency values can only be surmised by spoken (and unspoken) informal communications.

Occasionally agencies may even put in writing a "values statement." Figure 4.1 presents one such statement from an agency that spent considerable time and thought on this endeavor. While some of these values may be adaptable to other agencies, some are unique to this particular organization.

We should caution that very few agencies will have their values written out. Unless the administrators or the staff have the will to expend time and energy in this endeavor—in addition to their already demanding schedules— it simply will not get done. Moreover, making values explicit invites exposure to the possibility that there may be discrepancies between what the agency should be striving for and what actually occurs. Making values explicit also raises the possibility that while certain values may be desirable, the cost for attaining them may be too high. Or certain values may be in conflict with each other. Thus it may be necessary to couch some values in language that recognizes constraints.   Example: "When resources become available we will strive to provide the highest quality training for our staff."

A values statement encourages the agency—staff, clients, administration, trustees (if a voluntary agency), public officials (if a public agency)—to examine their practices in light of their espoused values and to determine if changes need to be considered to develop a congruency between what they say is valued and what they are actually doing.   Sometimes this examination will show that while some practices and behavior are in keeping with the organization's values, improvements can still be made. Figure 4.2 illustrates a way of analyzing how an organization can improve the connection between its practices and its values.

Figure 4.1
Values of a Children's Services Center

1. We are committed to work on **THE CUTTING EDGE** with the most difficult cases, the children and families other programs reject.

2. We believe effective **TEAMING** is essential to good therapeutic services.

3. We want to offer the finest **TRAINING** for our staff.

4. We want to **IDENTIFY** and **SOLVE** our problems, not **LIVE** with them.

5. We believe that **EXCELLENCE** is achieved through vigorous **GOAL SETTING/GOAL ATTAINMENT** processes and we want to be very self-conscious about our results.

6. We are a service-driven organization, committed to being **RESPONSIVE** to those who come to us for help.

7. We are committed to treating one another and all we seek to serve with **RESPECT** and **DIGNITY**.

8. We believe we need to establish the **POWER OF FAMILIES** whenever possible.

9. We are a mental health **MASH** unit and should always be responsive to the needs of those **WAITING** to access our services.

10. We are committed to **PROGRAM INNOVATION** and will continue to introduce new concepts, new approaches, and new technologies to meet emerging needs.

11. We believe that children should be served in the **LEAST RESTRICTIVE** and **MOST APPROPRIATE** service alternative.

12. We believe in the importance of **AFTER CARE**.

13. We believe in the principles of **EQUAL OPPORTUNITY** for clients and staff.

14. We believe that services to children and families should be offered with the highest level of **CULTURAL SENSITIVITY.**

15. We want to **PARTNER** with others in the development and delivery of services.

16. We believe the **QUALITY OF OUR SERVICES** can always be improved.

SOURCE: Adapted from Parmadale Children's Village *Value Statement* (1991).

Figure 4.2
Values in Practice

CURRENT VALUES	CURRENT MANIFESTATIONS	POTENTIAL IMPROVEMENT PRACTICES
Clients should understand their rights	Provide a "Bill of Rights" to all patients. Provide in service training to staff	Check patient hospital records to determine if all patients have been given the "Bill of Rights."
We want staff to communicate their concerns	Discuss in orientation of all new staff	Provide a staff suggestion box. Director would periodically announce this value at staff meetings and set aside time to meet with staff.
Foster a supportive atmosphere	Communicate in staff meetings that they can discuss their concerns without fear of reprisal.	Assign a buddy to new staff

SUMMARY

The organization's culture has a strong influence on staff behavior and performance. Cultural values are entrenched as traditional ways of thinking and doing and are developed over a long time period. Administrative staff can influence the shape and strength of staff values by stressing job ownership and by emphasizing the importance of meeting the needs of service consumers. Every organization would benefit from a periodic examination of its values to determine which ones need clarifying or modifying.

QUESTIONS FOR DISCUSSION

1) What are some of the values explicitly stated in your organization?

2) How are values expressed formally or informally in your organization?

3) Are there discrepancies between agency expressed values and actual practices? How are these resolved?

Chapter Notes

[1]Schein, E.H. (1986). *Organizational Culture and Leadership*. San Francisco: Jossey-Bass, p.6. Deal, T.E. & Kennedy, A.A. (1982). *Corporate Cultures*. Readings, MA: Addison-Wesley, p. 78.

[2]Townsend, R. (1970). *Up the Organization*. New York: Fawcett, p. 13.

[3]Commitment Plus (1985). *What is Culture*, p. 1.

[4]Beer, M., Eisenstat, R.A., & Spector, B. (1990). "Why Change Programs Don't Produce Change." *Harvard Business Review*, 6 pp. 158-66; Boyett, J.H. & Conn, H.P. (1988). *Maximum Performance Measurement*. Macomb, IL: Glenbridge; Herman, R.E. (1990). *Keeping Good People: Strategies for Solving the Dilemma of the Decade*. Cleveland, OH: Oakhill Press.

[5]Townsend, p. 13.

[6]Carl, J. & Stokes, G. (1991). *Seven Keys to an Excellent Organization: Fostering Innovation and Respect*. Nonprofit World, 5, pp. 18-22.

[7]Garner, L.H., Jr. (1989). *Leadership in Human Services: How to Articulate a Vision to Achieve Results*. San Francisco: Jossey-Bass, pp. 152-4.

CHAPTER 5

Strategic Planning

DEALING WITH CHANGE

Human service organizations operate in a continually changing and even turbulent environment. The needs of clients change over time, funding patterns shift, staff come and go, and the attention of community leaders and the media move to different social issues. Today's focus on homelessness, substance abuse, and child welfare may be ephemeral. Social issues that momentarily capture the community's attention can be replaced by another "social fad." Because of the inevitable and constant nature of change, both internal and external, staff must not only be prepared to cope with it but also to initiate and embrace it.

Not all change is necessarily good, nor is all resistance to change necessarily inappropriate. Too much change, the wrong kind of change, or change from one activity to another without clear purpose can create special problems, be disorienting, and even threaten the organization's survival. Maintaining the status quo can be stabilizing and can keep an organization from being in constant flux.

Strategic planning is the most common term used to describe the process of addressing change. It is the development of a set of future goals, accompanied by a set of actions to help achieve these goals.[1] Typically, strategic planning charts a course for a multi-year period. It helps the organization focus on fundamental issues that require ongoing, concentrated attention.

Two circumstances invite a strategic review. The first involves a threat to the organization. Funding cutbacks, legislation that is detrimental to the organization, competition from another human service organization that could lure clients away—these are the kinds of crises that compel a response. Business cannot go on as usual when the organization faces major difficulties; it must react to the crisis or face serious consequences.

The second circumstance is more subtle and, on the surface, might not seem to prompt strategic planning. When everything is going right—when the organization is strong, when funding is ample, when clients are being well served, when staff and volunteers are feeling positive about the organization—introspection might seem unwarranted. It is at just such a time, however, that the organization must discern whether there are dark clouds on the horizon in the form of staff and volunteer leader complacency, potential competition for funds, or possible change in community interest.

If the normal pattern of the organization is to continue providing services without questioning whether they can be improved, then there will be little stimulus for making modifications. An interesting aphorism states, "If you always think what you've always thought, then you'll always get what you've always gotten." By proactively searching for new ways to improve programs or processes that develop staff, you invite the organization to reach higher levels of productivity. You want to be able to slough off yesterday's less productive and less relevant programs and procedures to make staff and other resources available to meet emerging needs and to better fulfill the organization's mission.[2]

For example, suppose your organization has been providing a teenage counseling service for many years, but you now find that attendance is waning, though not enough to discontinue the counseling program altogether. The situation is not yet at a crisis but could be in a year or two. Your analysis shows that teenagers do want the opportunity to talk with someone, though in a more informal setting than is now provided by the agency. Your approach is to change your point of contact from in-office interviews to a more informal crafts and sports facility. Your willingness to improve propels you to seek other ways to reach your adolescent population.

It is useful to distinguish strategic planning from operational planning, which deals with immediate situations or current crises. The establishment of the annual work plan or the setting of this year's objectives are examples of operational planning. The value of strategic planning is that it disciplines the organization to move beyond the natural tendency to plan for the present and instead focuses on the future—to look beyond the next mountain.

Hence, by forecasting its future, setting goals, and considering new opportunities and threats, an organization can concentrate on its most critical problems and choices. Through strategic planning, it can engage key organizational members on every level in communicating and forming a consensus on significant decisions about their future.

CONDUCTING STRATEGIC PLANNING

A good strategic planning process requires widespread participation, thinking through your mission statement, asking fundamental questions, and examining external and internal processes.

Involving All Parts of the Organization

All segments of an organization, not just the management staff and trustees and public officials, should play a part in strategic planning. Input from staff and even clients is important. In a large organization representatives of some or all of the units may be involved with a strategic planning committee, or different constituencies could complete a questionnaire or submit their thoughts in writing. Through involvement, people do not feel left out and will be more inclined to carry forward the ideas that eventually will have to be implemented at all levels of the organization. This process of involvement may be as important—or even more important—as the final written product.

Developing a Mission Statement

Agencies should either already have a good mission statement or use the strategic planning process to prepare one. The statement should be lofty and inspiring, concise, capable of being easily understood and remembered, a reflection of the organization's fundamental purpose, and an indication of what it wants to accomplish in relation to the beneficiaries of its work. A major emphasis is on defining what impact the organization wants to effect.[3] Keep the mission broad enough to allow for flexible expansion but narrow enough to make clear its central purpose. Avoid on the one hand being "all things to all people" and, on the other, so restrictive that you cannot respond to changing needs and opportunities. Develop a statement that conveys your unique niche that makes you stand out above other similar organizations. Here are some examples of mission statements:

The mission of the neighborhood centers is to support the strengthening of Acorn City neighborhoods through programs and activities that are designed to:

- provide social services to families
- increase community education
- facilitate the support of social, economic, and political participation of neighborhood people
- advocate institutional change

As an integral member of the community, our mission is to assist individuals with mental retardation and developmental disabilities in choosing and achieving a life of increasing capability such that they can live, learn, work, and play in the community and to assist and support their families in achieving this objective.

Our mission is to ensure that appropriate, timely, accessible, and effective mental health and substance abuse services are available to people of all ages. Highest priority is to be given to adults and children with severe mental health disabilities who live or work in our geographic area.

Most organizations take considerable time and many rewrites before they can arrive at a simple statement. To make their mission statements readily apparent to both staff and outsiders, many organizations place them on their stationery, calling cards, and signs at their building entrance. Most importantly, the mission statement should be used to guide fundamental organizational decisions, such as whether to seek certain kinds of funding, whether to alter population mix, or whether to add or diminish functions or services.

When new projects are under consideration, determine whether they are in keeping with the mission. Sometimes it may be necessary to turn down a potential project, because it diverts from your main purpose. On rare occasions consider altering your mission because you want to serve a new client group, or be in a different target area. Example: Suppose that you have limited your clients to the county in which you are located. Because you want to raise badly needed funds, your staff could become trainers or consultants to organizations outside your community. Do you reject the idea or do you alter the mission statement to include services outside your county? This is the kind of issue that must be aired in the strategic planning process.

Certainly, modifying a mission statement can have tremendous impact on the way an agency responds to its clients. An agency sponsored by a religious body may proclaim in its mission that it will serve all people (not just those of its own religious faith), with the potential result that a large percentage of those served might be of different faiths. Another agency may determine through its strategic planning process that it will now provide a continuum of care for children under its care, thus broadening its service delivery commitment. Hence, a mission statement sends out a message to both internal stakeholders and to the world at large whom the agency will serve and how it will serve them.

Asking Fundamental Questions

Although each organization is unlike any other and will differ in relation to its mission, funding, and style of operating, all must grapple with four fundamental questions as part of the strategic planning process.

What business are we in? Most organizations perform several services and serve multiple populations. How the organization defines these services determines which services and clients it will emphasize. A child welfare agency, for example, could define its basic purpose as assuring the well being of children under its care, or it could define its focus as keeping families intact. The former might involve long term foster care; the latter, intensive family counseling.

What business should we be in now? As part of this analysis, you will also want to review why you exist now. The organization may have been formed ten or thirty years ago with a mission to serve a particular target population but now serves different populations with different needs. Some organizational members may be operating under a myth that the organization continues to provide services for those it is no longer able to serve. One of the values of strategic planning is that it forces organization members to ask, "If we did not currently exist, would we be created to meet the needs we are now trying to meet?"

What business do we want to be in a few years down the road? As a strategic planning exercise, it may be useful to imagine what the organization might be emphasizing three to five years hence. Are there new clients to be served or can the organization prepare itself to serve current clients better in the future? Is there new legislation in the offing that could provide needed funding? To give shape to this "crystal ball" thinking, the organization may want to capture its ideas about the future in a "vision statement." The group would go through an exercise of thinking how clients, services, staff, funding, and other aspects of the organization might be the same or different.

In considering the vision, the agency could improve on what the organization is doing now, and/or it could change its directions entirely. For example, an organization providing activities for the mentally and physically disabled could shift from seeing itself as a good caretaker (offering recreational activities and limited workshop experiences) to providing programs and advocating for legislation that helps disabled persons function more adequately in the mainstream of society. The vision statement might then describe how the organization would add job developers and group home staff so disabled persons might function more independently. Thus, the vision statement encourages strategic planning participants to think about what they would like their organization to be in the future.

What will happen if we stay in the same business? Continuing in the same direction could have negative consequences in a changing world. For example, you find in your day-care program that, because of a change in the law, teen mothers are now returning to school. You may decide to keep your current location, or you may conclude that you should relocate centers in the schools.

The strategic planning process, therefore, requires you to intensely examine not only your current relevance but also whether you need to make changes that will better position the organization to deal with its future.[4]

Examining External and Internal Processes

Included in the analysis phase should be an assessment of internal (organizational) and external (environmental) factors. The acronym, SWOT, is intended to convey that for the internal analysis, you would want to review Strengths and Weaknesses and, for the external analysis, Opportunities and Threats.

In looking at your organization's internal strengths, you would obviously want to continue doing the things you do well. You would ask, "What are our staff and volunteers best able to do, and how can we build on these assets?"

Examining weaknesses requires candid discussions about where things are falling short or, in the case of programs, what needs are beginning to wind down. Are staff not as prepared as they should be for doing their jobs? Is your organization encountering severe financial constraints? Are you losing clients because the program is no longer relevant or for other reasons? Focusing on weaknesses or constraints will provide imperatives for directing new energies or redirecting efforts to make needed changes. Identified weaknesses can give clues about what issues you need to address.

External realities can cause internal weaknesses. For example, in a public agency the lack of statutory authority and funding to carry out needed programs may limit the ability to serve some clients, even though they need the agency's services. Conversely, the legal requirement to process every client who walks into a public agency may limit the desired quality of service. These constraints suggest that focusing only on internal improvements may not be sufficient to improve services. By being aware of these external constraints, the strategic planning group can begin to consider ways to mitigate them. Instead of concentrating only on improving staff performance, for example, attention would be given to changing regulations or the law itself.

The term, "scanning the environment," is used to describe a process of looking at both opportunities and threats. Scanning involves selectively examining relevant economic, social, and political trends that now or in the future could affect your organization. A change in local public administration, reduced federal funding, expansion of women in the work force, and many other factors can have a powerful impact on the directions of the organization.

Some organizations prefer to conduct the scanning process prior to preparing the mission statement because the scan may influence the organization's essential emphasis. As an alternative, the strategic planning group can develop a tentative mission position and be prepared to modify it if the scanning process reveals new insights.

Scanning the environment is no easy task. Thousands of dollars can be spent on surveys with little to show except a momentary snapshot of community perceptions. Most organizations have limited resources and so may have to rely on published census data and studies sponsored by local universities, United Way, or a local planning council. In addition, the strategic planning group could compile its own list of major assumptions or "key realities" that could have an impact on the organization. An agency serving adolescents, for example, might identify such key realities as:

1. Teen pregnancy, already at a high rate, will continue.
2. AIDS among heterosexual adolescents will reach epidemic proportions.
3. Teen unemployment is likely to decline for those who graduate from high school but increase for those who do not.

4. The school dropout rate will continue to increase unless steps can be taken at the elementary school level to keep students from failing.

These and other key realities would be based in part on data and in part on the general knowledge of professionals or community experts. They should be considered to help determine the future focus of the organization.

Opportunities can be manifested in various ways. A possible new funding source, such as United Way announcing a special grants program for children, may open up opportunities not previously considered. A recently recognized community problem, such as a drastic reduction in welfare grants, severe overcrowding in detention home facilities, or an increase in the high school dropout rate, may offer opportunities for new services and special funding. Unfortunately, in the human service field, community crises sometimes provide opportunities.

External threats or constraints can be obvious or subtle. A reduction in funding can obviously affect the effectiveness of programs and even whether the organization will continue to exist. Subtle threats are often difficult to discern. For example, another organization beefs up its staff to replicate what you are doing, or a formerly successful camping program begins to lose some participants because of the growing availability of other recreation options. Loss of funds, competition from other organizations, or change in community interest are ever-present threats that may—or may not—require special attention, depending on how events unfold. These threats could either be bogeymen or genuine.

A particular change could be both an opportunity and a threat. Example: Changes in legislation that reduce welfare for single adults and childless couples certainly present hardships for certain clients but at the same time opens up the possibility of expanding services and seeking grant funds to meet the needs of this target population. Similarly, the loss of funding from a particular source could galvanize an organization to seek funding from other sources and to strive to beef-up its own fund raising capacity.

In the strategic planning process, members of the organization may find it desirable to specify anticipated opportunities and threats and then assess whether they have the capability to deal with them. Further, the staff must determine whether they have the requisite resources—time, funding, expertise, experience—to address the future. If not, are they prepared to do what is required to strengthen their capability? A candid assessment of capabilities will affect planning for the future.

Conducting a Retreat

Many organizations use the vehicle of a retreat (sometimes referred to as an "advance") to develop or revise their strategies. Two major factors need to be considered before embarking on this format. First, to get the most out of the session(s) (it could involve the equivalent of a day to as many as five days over an extended period of time), plan to do a considerable amount of homework. At a minimum, prepare basic facts about the organization—who, when and how clients are served. Also prepare relevant information about the community. This way everyone has the same facts to refer to. Then, too, consider preparing options regarding fundamental issues. When people have limited time to give to a retreat, it is advisable to provide materials in advance for their reaction and revision.

The second consideration relates to what happens after the retreat. Sometimes, members of an organization crank up their energies for the retreat and then go about their business with little regard to implementing what they intend to do. To avoid this, develop a timetable with specific assignments before the retreat concludes. Then arrange for an oversight committee that is responsible for monitoring the implementation process.

Because most social agencies have already gone through a strategic planning process, they undoubtedly have developed a clear idea of the clients they intend to serve and how they will serve them. Periodically, all organizations need to revisit their mission statement, identify significant developments, review where they have been, and explore possible new directions.

FOCUSING ON CRITICAL ISSUES

To keep the strategic planning process from becoming a perfunctory ritual in which participants go through the motions of involving themselves superficially, you must focus on critical issues. You need to ponder what significant problems, what burning issues, cry out for resolution. If you are primarily concerned with how to attract clients to the organization, for example, you may need to focus your strategic planning on various ways to reach them. If your burning issue is poor staff morale, then you would concentrate on how to improve it. If future funding is a concern, this would become your focus of attention. Thus, a critical issue is an unsolved problem requiring resolution because of its potential impact on the organization. Critical issues are "strategic" when they delineate where the organization should be going.[5]

Suppose the critical issue at hand is how well the agency's services are designed to meet client needs. The following are examples of the kinds of questions the strategic planning group would consider in planning organizational programs:

> Should our program be improved by (1) penetrating our market to serve more clients with current services, (2) expanding our product offerings (e.g., group counseling and job finding) to our existing clients, (3) marketing our current services to different clients (e.g., different geographic areas), or (4) diversifying both our services and clients (e.g., offering a new service—vocational training—to new general assistance clients).

> Should we phase out certain services or programs that are declining or are incompatible with other services?

> Should our basic funding pattern be modified, diversified, or more focused?

> Should we make major modifications in the organization by (1) replacing some staff with others having different skills or (2) retraining staff to perform their functions differently?
> Should we abandon programs or services, or contract with others?

These are illustrative of the kinds of critical issues and questions that could be raised, depending on the organization's focus of interest. An essential part of the strategic planning process is for each organization to identify its unique critical issues. Identifying critical issues concentrates attention on areas that are either currently or potentially of greatest concern.

Because every organization has finite resources, it is not likely that more than a few critical issues can be addressed at any one time. Priority decisions must not only be based on the organization's ability to have an impact but also on the cost of not addressing a particular issue.[6] Once you have selected a few critical issues, formulate actions appropriate for each. Then pinpoint who specifically within the organization will be responsible for follow-up and the timetable by when the task is to be accomplished.

DYNAMIC PLANNING

To counter what can end up as an inflexible strategic plan, a counterpoint approach is sometimes proposed. This approach may be referred to as "dynamic planning" or "logical incrementalism," meaning that strategies evolve over time and are based on modest attempts to deal with changing circumstances. This spontaneous decision-making process is continuously responsive to change resulting from opportunities or setbacks.

When changes occur (e.g., new technologies, legislation, funding alterations), planners may find it beneficial to review mission statements, reformulate goals and objectives, and redraft action plans—in an ongoing process that has no beginning point and no end point. In contrast to a comprehensive plan that may attempt to accomplish too much in too little time, dynamic planning continually tests out ideas, obtains feedback, and reshapes plans.[7]

For example, an opportunity may arise which allows the organization to implement services to a previously unserved population. In turn, this may require revising the mission statement to encompass new directions emerging from changing programs and target populations. Thus, dynamic planning helps the organization deal with political, social, and economic realities and also helps ensure that risks involved in embarking on new directions can be dealt with realistically.

Fundamental to dynamic strategic planning is thinking opportunistically. Ask, "What new opportunities can we take advantage of?" This is part of a never-ending search for new possibilities. Risk-taking is built into a trial and error process in which failure is always a realistic possibility.

Through a dynamic strategic planning process, "little visions" frequently emerge. These are small-scale ideas, which, if worthwhile, develop into ambitious undertakings. Not all of these emerging ideas necessarily emanate from managerial staff. Consider this example:

> A counselor expressed concern that she could not concentrate on the psychological needs of her clients because they were so deeply concerned about keeping their children fed. Moved by the plight of her clients, the counselor asked her director to allocate space for agency volunteers to bring in bags of food. From this small beginning emerged a greatly expanded food bank, which now provides supplementary food for public assistant recipients seen by the agency.

Dynamic strategic planning fosters an ability to seize the moment of opportunity, take corrective action, and reformulate plans. It prevents premature commitment to a rigid solution that may not allow the organization to be responsive to unpredictable events. The key elements, then, of dynamic planning are flexibility and experimentation.

A meaningful strategic plan, therefore, combines a comprehensive strategic plan and a dynamic planning process that sensitize the organization to changing circumstances. Strategic planning provides a general course, a direction with specific action steps focused on critical issues identified by participants at a particular point in time. But as new events precipitate unforeseen changes—new competition, shifts in funding, and new client requests—adjustments are made, including, if necessary, the very mission of the organization.

Incorporating dynamic planning into the strategic planning process can periodically affirm your current directions and activities or persuade you to embark on new directions based upon contingencies. Thus, if an organization has taken two or three months to formulate a three-to-five-year strategic plan, it may wish to conduct an annual "dynamic" review to determine whether modifications are necessary.

During strategic planning, the organization takes stock to determine how best to position itself to deal with its future. The process disciplines the organization to make tough decisions about priorities, since not everything it wants to do will be possible with the resources available. Strategic planning clarifies what must be pruned in order to take advantage of new growth opportunities.[8] It helps establish boundaries of what the organization will do—and what it will not. Through strategic planning, the organization also determines what special needs must be addressed to develop a plan that is both comprehensive and capable of being modified in the ever-changing human service environment.

SUMMARY

Determine why you want to develop a plan for your organization's future. What benefits do you see from embarking on an intensive process? Do these clearly outweigh possible disadvantages?

After ensuring that the organization's leadership is committed to the process, form a strategic planning group. An analysis of the organization would then be conducted which would include strengths, weaknesses, opportunities, and threats. Then develop a vision of what the organization would be like in three to five years. Prepare (or revise) a tentative mission statement, which may be altered later in the strategic planning process. Identify the most critical issues facing the organization. Prepare action plans containing three-to-five-year goals, implementation activities for the first year, and names of those accountable for follow-through. Draft a plan that is reviewed by a planning group, staff, board, and selected persons outside the organization. Implement the plan with the intent of making changes as circumstances change. Update the plan annually and, at least every five years, conduct another in-depth analysis.

QUESTIONS FOR DISCUSSION

1) What are the key elements contained in your agency's mission statement?

2) What steps has your agency taken to update its strategic plan?

3) What opportunities or threats has your agency had to deal with?

4) You are an organization established to provide recreation and socializing for older persons who live in public housing. Recently the public housing authority has offered you a considerable amount of funding to include younger single, disabled adults who reside in public housing and who need your services. Your mission statement clearly focuses on senior citizens. What should you consider doing?

Chapter Notes

[1]Espy, S.N. (1988). "Planning for Success: Strategic Planning in Nonprofits." *Nonprofit World*, 5, pp. 23-4.

[2]Drucker, P. (1985). *The Effective Executive.* New York: Harper & Row.

[3]Drucker, P. (1989). "What Business Can Learn From Nonprofits." *Harvard Business Review,* 4, pp. 89-93.

[4]Espy, S.N. (1988). "Where are You, and Where Do You Think You're Going?" *Nonprofit World*, 6, pp. 19-20.

[5]Weber, W., Laws, B., & Weber, S. (1987). "Real World Planning: Fresh Approaches To Old Problems." *Nonprofit World*, 2, pp. 25-27;

Barry, B.W. (1986). *Strategic Planning Workbook for Nonprofit Organizations.* St. Paul, MN: Amherst H. Wilder Foundation, p. 40.

[6]Eadie, D.C. (1991). "Planning and Managing Strategically." In R.L. Edwards & J.A. Yankey (Eds.), *Skills for Effective Human Services Management* (p. 294). Silver Spring, MD: NASW Press.

[7]Wolf, T. (1984). *The Nonprofit Organization: An Operating Manual.* Englewood Cliffs, NJ: Prentice-Hall;

Quinn, J.B. (1978, Fall). "Strategic Change: Logical Incrementalism." *Sloan Management Review*, pp. 3-16.

[8]Caplow, T. (1976). *How to Run Any Organization.* Hinsdale, IL: Dryden, p. 205;

Drucker, P. (1990). *Managing the Nonprofit Organization.* New York: Harper Collins Publishers, pp. 46-8, 55, 102, 142.

CHAPTER 6

Setting Doable Objectives

Good strategic planning can easily go nowhere unless an organization is astute about how to carry out its plans. The best-laid decisions can go astray unless an agency develops a well-thought out plan of action.

To properly carry out plans, staff must establish objectives. In some organizations, the terms "goals" and "objectives" are used interchangeably, but it is usually useful to distinguish between the two.[1] Typically, goals represent long-term endeavors, sometimes as long as three to five years, and may even be timeless. Examples of these goal statements would be "improving access to health care services for low-income persons" or "improving communications between board members and staff." A goal statement containing a time horizon might be "increasing the financial resources of the organization by 30 percent within four years."

Objectives represent relevant, attainable, measurable, and time-limited ends to be achieved. They are relevant because they fit within the general mission and goals of the organization and because they relate to problems identified by the organization.[2] They are attainable because they can be realized. They are measurable because achievement is based upon tangible, concrete, and usually quantifiable results. They are time-limited (usually a year) to help the organization demonstrate concrete results within a specified time limit.

KINDS OF OBJECTIVES

Impact Objectives specify outcomes to be achieved as a result of program activities. They detail the return expected on the organization's investment of time, personnel, and resources. The following are examples:

- To place 20 children in adoptive homes in one year
- To secure jobs for 35 juvenile delinquents in five months
- To increase the number of foster children reunited with their natural parents from 40 to 50 by June 30

In writing impact objective statements, consider the following criteria:

1. Use an action verb that describes an observable change in a condition—"to reduce," "to improve," "to strengthen," "to enhance."

2. State only one specific result per objective. An objective that states two results may require two different implementations and could cause confusion about which of the two objectives was achieved. For instance, "to reduce the recidivism rate by 10 percent and obtain employment for twenty former delinquents" is an objective with two very distinct aims.

3. Make objective statements realistic. Do not decide to decrease recidivism rates by 50 percent if staff and financial resources would at most allow you to reduce recidivism by 25 percent. On the other hand, do not set such unreasonably low objectives that the organization's credibility is called into question.

Service Objectives are the organization's tally of services rendered. Examples might be:

- To serve 300 clients in the program year
- To conduct 680 interviews
- To provide 17 neighborhood assemblies
- To interview 20 children needing foster homes

Operational Objectives convey the intent to improve the general operation of the organization. Examples include the following:

- To sponsor four in-service training workshops for 40 staff
- To obtain a pilot project grant of $10,000 within six months
- To increase the number of volunteers by 150
- To reduce staff turnover from 20 percent to 10 percent annually

Operational Objectives are essential to enhance the way an organization functions. They are a means to the end for which the organization was established. By providing in-service training, for example, an organization improves the way it serves its target populations.

Product Objectives are designed to provide a tangible outcome presumed to benefit a target population. They are used to achieve impact or service objectives. Sometimes these objectives are referred to as "deliverables." Some examples of product objectives might be:

- To obtain passage of House Bill 41 by the end of this legislative year
- To develop a neighborhood family support system in six months
- To review and critique a specific piece of legislation by April 20th
- To open four schools in the evening for recreation in time for the spring semester
- To provide a media effort on teen pregnancy prevention during the months of July and August
- To develop positions on three legislative initiatives in one month
- To prepare and distribute 2000 brochures on substance abuse prevention in time for Red Ribbon Week
- To sponsor a conference or a forum on Managed Care in two months
- To get 5000 residents to sign legislative petitions within three months
- To develop a mental health media campaign one month prior to the Mental Health Levy Campaign

The more specifically you can state your product objectives, the better. For example, indicate the time frame that you will use to complete your movie or put on your workshop.

FORMATTING GOALS AND OBJECTIVES

Which of these four types of objectives should an organization emphasize? The answer depends on the goals of the organization and its primary work efforts. Within the organization, different units may need to emphasize different type of objectives. For example, the unit dealing with clients will likely use process and impact objectives; an administrative unit would likely develop product or operational objectives. Some might argue that impact objectives are the most important. It is not enough for an organization to proclaim how well its processes are working and ignore whether it is having an impact on those it was established to serve. Because impact objectives emphasize measured outcomes, they should be the focal point for most service organizations. Agencies are in business to achieve results, which means they must demonstrate the impact they are having on clients. The focus, therefore, should be on attaining the impact objectives through the other kinds of objectives previously described. The following illustrates the relationship between an impact objective and other objectives that contribute to it:

Goal: To improve foster care services

Impact Objective: To decrease the number of children waiting each month for a foster home from an average of 150 to 170 to an average of 100 to 120

Service Objective: To conduct a recruitment campaign that will increase the pool of prospective foster parents from 10 to 60

Operational Objective: To conduct three in-house training programs on foster care within a three-month period

Product Objective: To produce a documentary film on the need for foster care

The advantage of this format is that it makes quite clear that the achievement of an interim service or operating objective is not an end in itself but a means to an end. In the above example, the organization can only consider itself successful if it reduces the number of children waiting for a foster home. The interim objectives of conducting a recruitment campaign and persuading commissioners to hire additional staff, even if successful, are means to accomplishing the primary or impact objective of reducing the number of children waiting for foster homes.[3]

In establishing objectives for serving clients, the organization should clarify *risk*, *target*, and *impact* populations. The *risk* population is the total group in need of help. To illustrate, in a certain community there may be two hundred ex-offenders who need to be employed. The *target* population is the group toward which the program is focused. For example, only 70 out of 200 are eligible for a 12-month high skill-training program and therefore qualify for services. The *impact* population is the group that actually benefits from the program. For example, of the 70 served, only 45 may actually find jobs.

CAUTIONS ABOUT OBJECTIVES

It is important that objectives be developed with certain caveats in mind. As powerful a tool as it is, objective setting does have its limitations. Keep the following cautions[4] in mind.

1) Not all objectives lend themselves to quantifiable measurement. For example, counseling programs are more difficult to quantify than, say, employment or housing programs where results are measurable. Be careful not to limit the selection to only those objectives that are quantifiable. Perhaps the most important things your organization does cannot be quantified.

Impact objectives are especially difficult to measure in relation to counseling activities because the achievement of objectives is so highly subjective and idiosyncratic.   Suppose, for example, that the agency provides family counseling. Each situation is different; each requires its own individually determined set of objectives. And each will require its own individually determined progress. So while each case record will reflect degrees of progress, these cannot easily be aggregated in some uniform way for the entire organization.

Of course, some will be more easily measured than others: recidivism of juveniles, repeat pregnancies, remaining sober—these are impact indicators that can be standardized and aggregated. Hence, the state of the art in human services dictates that some organizations will be able to document the results of their impacts more easily than others.

2) Objectives may conflict with each other. For example, the objective statement "to improve the recording of staff accomplishments" may actually reduce the effectiveness of the agency's services as staff devote more time to documenting services than to carrying them out. Achieving the objective "to reduce organizational costs" may result in serving fewer people, since part of the cost reduction may limit public information about the organization. Be mindful of possible undesirable ramifications and of objectives not being compatible with each other.

3) Be wary that organizational units may tend to set objectives for their own benefit rather than for the benefit the organization as a whole. Because

objectives may be in conflict with each other, and because over-emphasis on one objective may have a detrimental effect on the achievement of others, agencies must continually seek a proper balance and a way of integrating the organization's various objectives. There is always the danger that each unit in an organization may independently go about setting and achieving its own objectives, unmindful of its impact on objectives of other units. For example, in striving to achieve the objective of making the organization better known in the community, the public information unit may be making such extensive demands on staff to handle speaking engagements that less time is available to achieve the objective of increasing client services.

4)   The setting of objectives requires everyone in the organization, including the board of trustees, management, and front-line staff, to be responsible for their work. Constituents of all parts of the organization should understand how they are contributing to the objectives and hence to achieving the organization's mission. This is risky because when objectives are not achieved, there is a tendency to blame those who let the organization down. But insight that leads to further improvement in service delivery, not blame, must be the outgrowth of heightened account-ability.

On the positive side, setting objectives influences an agency to take certain actions. It has committed itself to achieve results, and if the agency has early warning signals that it will fall short then it may be propelled to take more drastic and urgent action. This is not dissimilar to a business that learns that its first three months earnings are falling short of its projections and therefore special actions are required.   Suppose, for example, that an agency has received funds to provide health services to the homeless and it projects that it would reach out to three hundred in the course of the year. By April it becomes aware that this is not an achievable number. As a result, the agency rents a mobile van to travel to hunger centers and assigns staff to search under the bridges of the city where homeless persons are likely to exist.   This agency is clearly committed to achieving its objectives.

5)   Be mindful of engaging in an objective setting process that has integrity and realism.   If funding is cut back, for example, then you need to set less ambitious objectives than you had earlier contemplated.   Watch out for a tendency to play games by purposefully setting objectives too low and then exceeding them in order to show how well you are succeeding. How an organization writes objective statements will greatly determine "success." For example, an employment related agency could write, "To secure jobs for 100 people within one year."   Or it could write, "To secure jobs for 100 people within one year, of whom 80 will continue to be employed six months

after placement." If the focus is on job finding and not retention, then success is more limited—and easier to attain. On the other hand, including retention expands the agency's commitment.

6) Be aware that some organizations use goals and objectives as if they were interchangeable; they are not—the former is general and ideal, the latter, specific and concrete. Having made this distinction, it is possible that in some organizations the word "goal" is used to convey specific accomplishments and "objective" is the word applied to the ideal to be general. This is perhaps a semantic issue that will be resolved over time with usage.

(7) Finally, objectives should be designed to stretch, but not break, staff. The value of objectives is that they stimulate staff to extend themselves to reach a predetermined target. If the target is set too high and is virtually unachievable, the result will be a highly frustrated and even disgruntled staff. If set too low, objectives lose their potency to foster staff investment and productivity.

SUMMARY

All organizations must establish objectives so that they can demonstrate to themselves and to their funders that they are achieving results as a result of the community's investment. By setting objectives in advance of the expenditure of staff and financial resources, an agency has a yardstick against which it can later measure outcomes. While it is important to keep in mind certain inherent cautions and limitations involved in the setting of objectives, still, this is a tool that all organizations must apply.

QUESTIONS FOR DISCUSSION

1) In your agency what are the examples of the following?
   risk population
   target population
   impact population

2) What examples can you give in each of the following categories?
   goal statement
   impact objectives
   service objectives
   product objectives
   operational objectives

Chapter Notes

[1]Schaffer, R.H. (1991). "Demand Better Results And Get Them." *Harvard Business Review*, pp. 2, 142-9.

[2]Patti, R. J. (1983). *Social Welfare Administration*. Englewood Cliffs, NJ: Prentice-Hall, Inc., pp. 78-80.

[3]Kettner, P.M., Moroney, R.M., & Martin, L.L. (1999). *Designing and Managing Programs*. Thousand Oaks, CA: Sage Publications, pp. 105-10.

[4]Brody, R., (2000). *Effectively Managing Human Service Organizations*. Thousand Oaks, CA: Sage Publications, pp. 66-7.

CHAPTER 7

Implementing Achievable Plans

ANTICIPATING UNINTENDED CONSEQUENCES

Human service organizations inadvertently experience unintended consequences, either because members do not sufficiently do their homework or because situations arise that nobody could have predicted. Obviously you can do little about unforeseen events, but with a little extra effort and disciplined thinking, you can identify potential trouble spots.

Preparation is essential before taking action. Painters do not just start painting; they devote as much as 80 percent of their total time preparing a job before ever making their first brush stroke. Similarly, it is important to think through in detail ahead of time what will happen as a result of a decision before you embark on it. Regrettably, many efforts fail because not enough time is spent making sure that those who will implement a decision are prepared to do so.[1]

Consider this example. In a juvenile court, a decision is made to provide intensive probation for delinquents who evidence high-risk behavior, such as repeated felonious offenses. To carry out intensive probation, 10 percent of the probation officers are given a small caseload—no larger than ten clients—who are seen frequently.

The decision appears to be a good one because their clients begin to manifest a low rate of recidivism. But a by-product is that the remaining probation officers have to take on an even larger caseload, with unintended results being lower staff morale and less time available to work with clients, who then evidence an overall increase in recidivism. Had the focus of attention not been entirely upon the new program, perhaps the potential negative consequence of the decision could have been prevented.

In the medical field, the word "iatrogenic" is defined as an inadvertent, medically-induced illness. No such word exists in the human service field, but there are certainly many instances where a particular decision, while beneficial in many ways, can produce negative side effects. Just as penicillin, prescribed to cure pneumonia, may cause patients who are allergic to it to go into shock, so specially-created social programs can also have negative side effects.

Subjecting unemployed persons to a job training program with no possibility of employment, placing clients in jobs without providing adequate day care for their children, releasing mentally disabled patients in the absence of proper community supports, or incarcerating juveniles with no provision for rehabilitation—these are among many examples of plans that can produce negative results because the agency did not adequately anticipate the negative consequences of the intervention.

Thus, certain plans may possibly lead to a detrimental condition that is as bad as, or even worse than, the original problem. Carefully weigh whether implementation of the plan may be worse than the problem it is intended to solve.

INITIATING PILOT PROJECTS

Agencies often must maintain current programs and services and, at the same time, consider making significant changes. Social agencies must determine how to generate projects without creating such great resistance and conflict that they are doomed before being tested. One way to deal with this is to create ad hoc, temporary staff teams to work on pilot projects. These teams can try out new ideas and work out any project glitches before they are diffused through the rest of the organization. Through pilot projects, staff develop flexibility to experiment with new ventures. If the pilots fail, they can be aborted without serious consequence to the rest of the organization; if they succeed, they can be expanded.[2]

When staff embark on a small-scale, manageable undertaking, when they are committed to the task, and when they operate within a climate that favors innovation, pilot projects are more likely to succeed.[3] The pilot project must be conceived with a reasonable chance for success. By having a clear beginning and end, by having focus, and by achieving modest and measurable improvements, the pilot project team is spurred on to continue its efforts and later to spread the word about its success. A project that focuses on achievable, short-term, and urgently needed results has the best chance of success. A task group can be quickly assembled to focus on problems requiring immediate and urgent resolution. Staff are assigned based on their expertise, experience, or other strengths to contribute. Their focus of attention should be on developing a breakthrough that can have great implications for the rest of the organization. They must strive for success in a few weeks (not months), be eager to tackle the challenge, and concentrate on achieving results with available resources.[4]

Pilot projects can involve a variety of efforts: reformulating the information flow of the organization, experimenting with new services, or developing new procedures. Whatever the project, its small-scale nature allows staff to try out ideas, be creative, and determine under what conditions the project works. By approaching the project on an incremental, trial-and-error basis, the organization avoids the possibility of a large-scale failure. If something does not work, the team can make corrections before implementing them on a larger scale.[5]

Unfortunately, even successful pilot projects may not spread throughout the organization. A project can fizzle because of insufficient efforts to institutionalize it or because current policies and practices are not in harmony with it.[6] For example, a specially-designed support program for school dropouts could be conducted outside the schools. But it may not be absorbed into the system because of such incompatible values and practices as the inability to give special attention to at-risk students or resistance to modifying the curriculum. In addition, some pilot projects tend to attract extra resources and highly motivated staff that are not available on an ongoing basis.

It is one thing to initiate change by engaging a small number of staff in a pilot project and dealing with their initial resistances; it is quite another to spread the change throughout the organization, to make it stick so that it becomes a permanent part of the way the organization operates. If the groundwork has been laid well, staff will be receptive to the change. If they have been involved in diagnosing what needs to be improved so they do not feel that the change has been foisted upon them, staff are much more likely to accept the change. The key, then, is not to over-manage the change process, not to convey from on high, but to engage staff from all levels of the organization in thinking through and implementing the change.[7]

CONTINGENCY PLANNING

Events can get in the way of implementing plans as originally conceived. Contingency planning imagines the unlikely; by thinking of the range of possibilities in advance, you may be able to gain mastery over them should they occur. The unexpected is expected.

Suppose, for example, your agency is experiencing a great increase in the number of clients needing service. Staff are already overextended. To meet your obligations, you have applied for additional funding and a decision is pending. Among your contingency plans could be the following:

Plan A: If you receive less funds than hoped for, you could consider hiring para-professionals working under close supervision.

Plan B: If the funding request is rejected, you could determine the reasons and be prepared to reapply.

Plan C: If expanded funding continues to be unavailable from this one source, you could consider an aggressive fund raising campaign.

Plan D: If, after reapplying, you are again rejected, you could consider either cutting staff or reducing salaries.

Plan E: If no funding is available, you could restrict the number of clients and redirect unserved persons to other agencies.

Plan F: If new funding is not possible, you could consider an innovative way of working with clients that achieves results at lower costs, such as group counseling sessions or telephone conferences.

As can be seen from this illustration, contingency planning helps the agency develop the discipline of walking through a situation to prepare for possible events that could have an impact on the organization. In fact, a special form of contingency planning is called "failsafe" analysis, in which you purposefully give attention to those possibilities that could cause your plan to fail.

Before embarking on a program, search for potential mine fields: "What political leader or board member or staff could torpedo the idea?" "What staff or resource constraints could keep the program from getting off the ground?" "Which organizations must cooperate if the program is to succeed?" Sometimes a colleague outside the organization can be asked to give an objective critique or even serve as the "devil's advocate" to ferret out potentially explosive situations.

Decisions that do not allow for the possibility of glitches are dangerous ones because they give the agency the false sense of security that nothing can go wrong. The reality is that plans have a low probability of succeeding unless major problems are anticipated and addressed. Failsafe contingency planning focuses attention on possible problem areas and gets you to think about solving them before they explode.

Contingency planning is like a game of chess. You have to anticipate your opponent's moves and consider protecting your flank, even as you take the offensive. You cannot be so concentrated in moving ahead with your plans that you lose sight of where you might be vulnerable. As in chess, contingency planning requires your constant assessment of the potential consequences of every move. Unlike a game of chess, the forces that can unravel a plan may not reside in an "opponent" but in more amorphous forces, such as the lack of adequate staff training. The point of the chess metaphor is to encourage your being on guard for unexpected possibilities even as you are moving forward.

"What if. . . ." scenarios or questions can stimulate contingency planning. In a foster home recruitment drive, for example, you would ask, "What if recruitment materials don't come on time . . . if it rains on the day of the promotional event . . . if staff are unable to answer inquiries?" Of course, these things may not happen, but if they do, you will have thought about them in advance and taken the proper precautions.[8]

Thus, contingency planning helps to anticipate and thus prevent problems before they arise. Planning is proactive, in contrast to reacting only to things as they happen. Of course, not all events can be anticipated, and, under some circumstances, you want to have the flexibility to respond to unexpected opportunities. The advantage of proactive planning is that you can minimize or neutralize the possibility of downside risks by anticipating how you will deal with them.

APPLYING CRITICAL CRITERIA TO ALTERNATIVES

As an organization begins to identify a potential plan of action, it is important to ask a series of critical questions that will aid in determining the feasibility of the final selection process.

As Figure 7.1 indicates, a children's treatment institution is considering options regarding the expansion of housing for adolescent mentally challenged offenders. Although its analysis would undoubtedly be quite extensive, for purposes of this discussion, the alternatives under consideration would be as follows:

Alternative A: Request that the county commissioners seek voter approval for a $2 million facility for mentally challenged offenders.

Alternative B: Request an existing children's institution to reserve thirty juvenile mentally challenged offender spaces.

Alternative C: Create three group homes that would house mentally challenged offenders. Provide necessary support services.

The following questions would need to be explored:

1) Based on a review of experience elsewhere, how successful is this alternative likely to be? How is this particular problem being tackled by other communities? What conditions operate in these communities to suggest success (or failure)? By examining what others are doing or have done, the organization can capitalize on success and avoid pitfalls.

2) What resources are available? Among the resources to be considered are the following: personnel, money, time, equipment facilities knowledge and skill, political influence, energy and commitment. Each alternative should be considered in light of the question, "Does it require more resources than are available, given certain priorities?" If so, "Is there a good chance of developing needed resources to carry out a particular action plan?"

3) Is the action plan in keeping with the purpose and style of the organization? If the organization relies on good will to effect coordination of various elements, is a strategy of confrontation appropriate?

Figure 7.1
Critical Criteria Applied to Options

	Alternative A New Facility	Alternative B Use Existing Homes	Alternative C Create Group Homes
	High/Med/Low	High/Med/Low	High/Med/Low
How successful based on experience elsewhere?	X	X	X
How feasible based on availability of resources?	X	X	X
How appropriate in relation to the basic style of the organization?	X	X	X
Extent alternative deals with scope of the problem?	X	X	X
How efficient is alternative in relation to potential accomplish-ments?	X	X	X
Negative side effects or new demands?	X	X	X

4) Does the action plan deal adequately with the scope of the problem? If three hundred people need a special kind of service, but the action plan will only provide enough service units to meet the needs of 60 people, will the organization be satisfied with limited scope?

5) How efficient is the action plan? How do the costs of this action plan compare with the costs of other plans, and how do the costs relate to the potential benefits?

6) What negative side effects or new demands could occur from the action plan?

Figure 7.1 shows, in abbreviated form, how the organization might go through its review and selection process. Note that the organization staff rate each of the options in relation to its predetermined criteria.

This review reveals that of the three alternatives, using existing facilities has the greatest promise of meeting most of the critical criteria. Note that criteria established for this situation may be different from criteria applied to other situations.

OBTAINING ACCEPTANCE OF AN ACTION PLAN

From the perspective of a group wanting to produce change, resistance must be taken into account. If not, the best analytic problem definition, the most coherent set of objectives, and the most creative planning ideas will go nowhere.

Although it is difficult to formulate universal guidelines that can apply to all situations where a group has settled on an action plan and must convince others to accept it, some general guidelines follow:

Involve those who will be implementing the action plan in its creation. This guideline is based on the assumption that people who have an investment in a plan they helped to shape will be more willing to carry it out. They feel a sense of ownership and commitment to seeing it through. This is why a committee established to study a problem should include those who will be involved in implementing recommendations. If, because of time constraints or other reasons, the implementors or approvers of the action plan cannot be involved, the next best thing is to keep them apprised on a continuous basis. There should be no surprises.

When an action plan calls for changes involving considerable risk and dealing with unanticipated, future events, build in go/no-go points. This approach will permit investing resources in incremental steps. The group could review progress before it makes a longer range commitment. Action plan advocates can gain acceptance by assuring group members and the organization's leadership (who may tend to be more cautious and conservative) that if the action plan does not work out as planned, the organization can abort the project and consider other ventures.

By determining at various stages whether or not to continue to proceed, the group avoids risking resources to a long-term project that may not prove feasible. For example, a community organization may decide it wants to establish a special program for school dropouts. Before embarking on the project, it might establish a 3 month study process to determine whether 1) the local school system is interested in cooperating in the venture, 2) local or state funding could be made available, and 3) a sample of youngsters not in school could be interested in the program. If these three basic conditions could not be met at the end of the time period, a no-go decision would be made. If, after the initial 3 month period, tentative funding is provided for a building, but not for operating costs, then a decision not to proceed can again be made. In this way a long-term commitment and investment in high-risk ventures can be based on the extent to which fundamental conditions can be met.

Because nothing succeeds like success, action plan advocates should consider proposals that have a high chance of achieving results. Building upon achievements which foster a sense of confidence, action plan advocates can become emboldened to propose more radical actions. In addition, action plan advocates should be wary of proposing a plan that, if it fails, may make it much more difficult to try again. This is why frequently an organization may undertake a pilot project: it will try out an idea to determine pitfalls before embarking on a large-scale program.

Advocates of an action plan must think of themselves as salespeople. Advocates are selling an idea. They cannot complacently assume that because they are enthusiastic about the plan, other key persons will be easily convinced. Resistances of others will have to be understood and dealt with. Just as in the business world, where good salespeople develop a point of sale, so, too, a convincing case must be developed in selling human service and community programs. The advantages of the program must be clearly spelled out—who will benefit and how.

At the same time, disadvantages and potential concerns must be anticipated: Whose vested interest, status, or power is threatened by the proposed change? A good strategy includes analyzing how objections might be prevented or neutralized. Hence, by understanding fully the nature of the resistances, advocates can prepare convincing proposals.

Anticipate controversial situations. When proposals or programs are controversial and the organization is composed of a broad cross section of the community, then those proposing the plan must anticipate likely reactions and how they will respond to them. It is never too early to begin asking how the organization will deal with controversial questions both internally and with other organizations.

Because resistance to change is sometimes based on lack of complete understanding of the proposal and how it can be carried out, the advocates of the action plan should do the following:

1) Work out details of the plan with special attention as to how it can be implemented. If, for example, the proposal is going to cost money, proponents should determine how much and from what sources it can be derived.

2) Prepare visual aids—charts, graphs, and other materials—to present to people needing to be convinced.

3) Spell out the action steps that will be required to implement the plan.

These guidelines may not be all inclusive because, as noted earlier, every situation is unique and will require its own special kind of preparation. Regardless of the situation, however, it is important to conduct a mental trial run of how the group expects significant others not directly involved in the initial development of the action plan to react. Doing this kind of homework will eventually increase the likelihood of acceptance.

IMPLEMENTING A PLAN

Attention to detail is a prerequisite for implementing a successful project. By anticipating specific outcomes as much as possible, you increase the likelihood that plans will be carried out properly. Even so, planning involves some degree of speculation; therefore, be prepared to revise even the most well thought-out work plans.[9]

To systematically structure the implementation phase, it is useful to think of major activities and specific tasks. Major activities can be completed within a specified time period and include the following elements:

- They are essential for achieving an objective.
- They should result in one identifiable product, such as a report, a meeting, or completion of a major assignment.

- They can occur either in sequence or simultaneously with other activities.

Tasks are specific jobs required to accomplish a major activity. Feeding into a major activity, tasks are usually achievable over a few days or weeks by specified individuals or units of the organization. Although explaining tasks can sometimes be time-consuming and tedious, the process more readily ensures completing major activities and implementing proper actions. Moreover, preparing the work plan can help determine whether adequate resources are available to properly complete the job or whether resources should be redeployed from low to high priority endeavors. If later there appears to be a lack of progress in achieving a major activity, staff can more readily pinpoint the specific unfinished tasks that led to the breakdown.

Carrying Out Task Assignments

Two approaches can be considered in specifying tasks: (1) reverse-order and (2) forward-sequence planning.[10]

In reverse-order planning, the organization begins with the final result to be achieved and identifies the tasks that feed into activities by reviewing, "What must we do just before reaching our final result, and then what needs to be done before that, and before that?" and so forth, until it arrives at the beginning point. For example, in organizing a staff speakers' bureau, the process of reverse order might include the following tasks:

Promote speaking engagements (last task)
Train speakers (fourth task)
Prepare speakers' kits (third task)
Recruit volunteer speakers (second task)
Plan training sessions (first task)

In forward-sequence planning the organization begins with what it considers to be the appropriate first set of tasks and then asks, "What should we do next, and what after that, and so forth?" until reaching the end result.

Whether the organization uses the reverse-order or forward-sequence planning approach, it is important to consider what preparation will be necessary to complete each task.

In actual decision-making situations, organizations usually combine reverse-order with forward-sequence planning. That is, staff typically consider by what date they want to achieve a particular result and then review all the tasks they need to complete prior to that deadline. If the predominant approach is reverse-order planning, staff will find it useful to employ forward-sequence planning (and vice versa) to double check that no task has been omitted.

Time line chart

The implementation process requires that controls and reporting procedures be developed to determine the rate of progress compared to the original implementation schedule. The process pinpoints responsibility and identifies reporting dates. By establishing accountability for who does what by when, you have a warning system that will tell you when you are in trouble.

A time line chart (sometimes referred to as a Gantt Chart) is useful for implementing decisions and projects because it provides a visual overview of what needs to be done, who needs to do it, and within what specific time frame it should be accomplished.[11] A time line illustrates how various tasks should be subsumed under major activities in a comprehensible, easy-to-construct format. The chart clarifies the beginning and ending points projected for each task and shows at a glance what efforts must be made within a specific time period. (See figure A and B.)

Suppose, for example, an organization responsible for foster children wants to conduct a campaign to recruit 100 foster parents in a nine-month period, beginning in April. To carry out this project it prepares a time line chart (shown in Figure 7.2 A & B) that lists major activities and tasks.

By displaying the timeline on a chart, one can determine at a glance where resources and staff time may need to be concentrated. For example, note in 7.2 A that the months of July and August appear to make heavy demands on staff time. This visual review allows management and staff to examine whether the timeline is realistic, given that many staff members like to take vacations in July and August. Either staff may be asked to take their vacations during another part of the year or the timeline needs to be modified to accommodate to the staff's personal plans.

As the project progresses, it will likely be necessary to modify the schedule because of unforeseen circumstances or because new information becomes available. The staff should continuously review the timeline and make necessary modifications either in the concentration of resources or in developing a more realistic schedule.

Figure 7.2 A: Time Line

Objective: To recruit an additional 100 foster parents by the end of the year

	Apr	May	Jun	Jul	Aug	Sept	Oct	Nov	Dec
Develop a plan and structure									
Appoint Task Force	—								
Interview foster care agencies parents, and H.S. Dept. staff	⊢——⊣								
Formulate foster care plan		⊢							
Prepare Public Relations Materials									
Identify profile of unserved children			⊢						
Identify profile of potential foster parents			⊢						
Prepare PR campaign strategy			⊢——⊣						
Prepare bus poster				⊢——⊣					
Prepare radio tapes				⊢——⊣					
Prepare TV ads				⊢——⊣					
Prepare written materials for speakers' kits				⊢————⊣					
Contact public media					⊢				
Submit materials to media							⊢		
Organize Speakers' Bureau									
Plan speakers' bureau					⊢				
Recruit volunteers and staff					⊢————⊣				
Prepare speakers' kits							⊢		
Train speakers								⊢	
Distribute PR materials								⊢	
Promote speaking engagements									⊢

**Figure 7.2 B
Time Line**

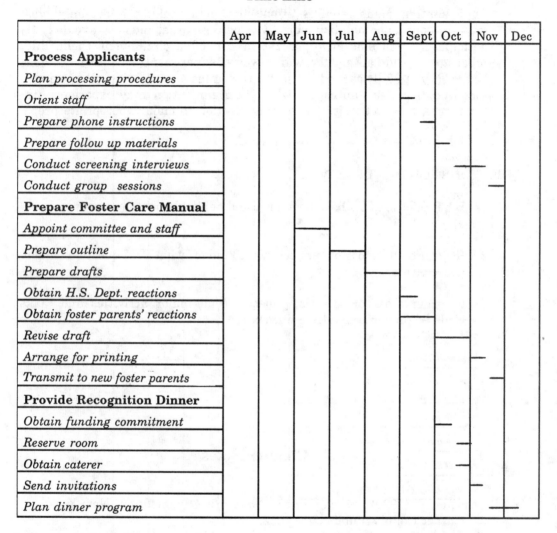

	Apr	May	Jun	Jul	Aug	Sept	Oct	Nov	Dec
Process Applicants									
Plan processing procedures					▬				
Orient staff						▬			
Prepare phone instructions						▬			
Prepare follow up materials							▬		
Conduct screening interviews							▬		
Conduct group sessions								▬	
Prepare Foster Care Manual									
Appoint committee and staff			▬						
Prepare outline				▬					
Prepare drafts					▬				
Obtain H.S. Dept. reactions						▬			
Obtain foster parents' reactions						▬			
Revise draft							▬		
Arrange for printing								▬	
Transmit to new foster parents								▬	
Provide Recognition Dinner									
Obtain funding commitment						▬			
Reserve room							▬		
Obtain caterer							▬		
Send invitations								▬	
Plan dinner program								▬	

The use of the time line chart tells the organization whether it is on schedule in achieving all it must do to carry out successfully its objectives.

SUMMARY

Implementing plans requires attention to detail related to not only what must be done to accomplish objectives but also what must be avoided. By anticipating problems an organization can often circumvent them. Pilot programs provide an agency with a way of experimenting with new ideas before they are fully carried out in the rest of the organization. Preparing a time line chart helps anticipate when the organization may experience unusual pressures so that it is in a better position to make appropriate preparations.

QUESTIONS FOR DISCUSSION

1) What pilot projects have been (or could be) implemented in your agency?

2) In regards to a possible project, what kind of "what if..." questions might you consider?

3) Consider a past or potential project. What major activities and tasks could be prepared in a time line chart?

Chapter Notes

[1]Drucker, P. (1990). *Managing the Nonprofit Organization*. New York: Harper Collins Publishers, p. 32.

[2]Schaefer, M. (1987). *Implementing Change in Service Programs*. Newbury Park, CA: Sage Publications, pp. 72-4.

[3]Work in America Institute, (1982). *Productivity Through Work Innovations*. New York: Pergamon Press, pp. 110-11.

[4]Schaffer, R.H. (1981). "Productivity Improvement Strategy: Make Success The Building Block." *Management Review*, August, pp. 46-52; Schaffer, R.H. (1989). *The Breakthrough Strategy*. Cambridge, MA: Ballanger Publishing Co, (c).p. 5.

[5]Schaffer, R.H. & Michaelson, K.E. (1989). "The Incremental Strategy For Consulting Success," *Journal of Management Consulting*, 2 (a).

[6]Lawler, E.E. (1986). *High Involvement Management*, San Francisco, CA: Jossey Bass.

[7]Beer, M., Eisenstat, R.A., & Spector, B. (1990). "Why Change Programs Don't Produce Change." *Harvard Business Review*, 6, pp. 158-166; Work in America Institute, p. 135.

[8]Von Oech, R., (1983). *A Whack On The Side Of The Head*. New York: Warner Books, p. 62.

[9]Espy, S.N. (1989). "Putting Your Plan into Action." *Nonprofit World*, 1, p. 28.

[10]Brody, R., (1982). *Problem Solving: Concepts and Methods for Community Organization*. New York: Human Sciences Press, Inc., p.149-151.

[11]Schaefer, *Implementing Change in Service Programs*, p. 88-9.

REFERENCES FOR CHAPTER 7

Harrison, Barbara (2006). *Collaborative Programs in Indigenous Communities from Field Work to Practice*. Walnut Creek, CA: Altamira Press

Lankes, David R. (2006). *Implementing Digital Reference Services: Setting Standards & Making it Real*. New York: Neal-Schuman Publishers

CHAPTER 8

Solving Operational Problems

Once an organization has determined its strategic plan, which includes its mission and goals, it is able to concentrate on its daily efforts. Many of these day-to-day tactics are focused on solving problems and making decisions. Often problems are complex, ambiguous, cumulative, and multi-faceted. Sometimes their causes cannot be fully known and their resolutions may require the involvement of many different participants. Hence, the problem-solving process requires an effective manager's keen judgment, intuition, and understanding of the dynamics of a situation.

Although there are no cookbook solutions, no simple formulas, it is useful to consider several dimensions to solving problems on a day-to-day basis. These dimensions include analyzing the problem, considering alternative solutions, making decisions and monitoring results, and making necessary corrections.

ANALYZING PROBLEMS

The term "analysis" denotes separating a whole into its component parts. Problem analysis thus entails breaking generalized concerns into delineated segments. Good problem solving requires moving beyond such generalized statements as "staff morale is low," or "absenteeism is too high," or "there is poor communication between departments" to achieve greater clarity about the nature of the problem. It involves examining discrepancies between goals and actual results, specifying the problem as clearly as possible, determining the boundaries of the problem, clarifying different perspectives, and identifying insidious problems.

Identifying Discrepancies

A problem can be defined as a felt need or a discrepancy between an existing condition and one that is desired.[1]

Establishing measurable objectives and then determining later whether they have been achieved alerts the agency as to whether a problem exists. For example, in an adult training workshop for the disabled, if your objective of having 80 percent function independently within one year is not met, you know a problem exists that must be addressed. Similarly, a problem becomes obvious, for example, when a unit of the organization does not meet its predetermined objective of contacting 125 clients in a given month. The fact that the unit is reaching only 85 clients should signal concern because of the gap between the predetermined benchmark and actual performance.

Specifying the Problem

Even if concrete objectives have not been established, staff or management may feel a vague sense of uneasiness: something is wrong, but, at least initially, there is a lack of clarity about what the problem is. Someone might ask, for example, "Why aren't we serving more clients?" A general consensus might be that more clients could be served, but ambiguity exists about whether "the problem" pertains to clients in general or clients from a particular geographic area or income level. Does "the problem" reside in the clients—something operating within them or their situation? Do they have difficulty in coming to the agency because of changes in public transportation, or have their perceptions changed about their safety in coming to the agency? By taking the time to obtain facts in any problem situation, you can avoid premature and impulsive solutions, or what is captured in the phrase, "Ready, shoot, aim."

To analyze a generalized problem more specifically, be clear about exactly when the problem occurs, who is affected by it, and where it takes place. Furthermore, strive to understand the causes and underlying conditions of the problem. If, for example, you note that absenteeism among staff has increased, determine whether the problem is pervasive and therefore indicative of a morale issue, or limited to a few staff, requiring disciplinary considerations.

Trying to identify the cause of a problem can be exceedingly difficult. In reality, a cause-effect chain of relationships can exist for any problem. We could analyze, for example, that low morale is causing absenteeism, which is caused by feelings of being ignored, which in turn is caused by an organization that is built on an authoritarian structure in which little communication occurs. To isolate one simple cause contributing to one single effect can be an oversimplification. You may not know until after you have diagnosed a problem, formulated a response to it, and obtained feedback that your "solution" is not working. You then may need to concentrate on another possible solution.

In analyzing problems, an inductive approach of identifying concrete examples or critical incidents can be useful, especially if the nature of the problem is vague. By pinpointing under what specific situations the problem occurs, you begin to get a handle on it. You move from specific incidents to determining the nature of the problem.

Determining the Boundaries of the Problem

By defining a problem, you set boundaries around it; you determine what it is—and what it is not. A good procedure to ensure accuracy of focus on a problem is to prepare a written problem statement. By putting your thoughts in writing, you develop more precision, and you discipline your thinking. In addition, you have a statement that you can refer back to and revise if necessary. The danger of not putting your problem in writing is that your thoughts may remain vague and amorphous and hinder the problem-solving process.

Typically, problems tend to be narrowed too quickly, thereby cloaking the real problem. In conducting a problem analysis, determine whether a particular manifest problem is exceptional or whether it reflects a larger issue. Does a particular problem reflect an idiosyncratic situation or a more general pattern? If it is unique, then pragmatic, expedient approaches may be used. If it is a general problem, then more fundamental change may be required. To treat a general situation as if it were a series of unique events can be a major miscalculation.[2]

Clarifying Problem Perspectives

In any discussion, participants invariably come to the table with their own perspectives. There is an old fable of six blind men touching different parts of an elephant. Each one describes the elephant in a particular way based on the part he touches. So too with problem analysis—people will sense a problem based on their individual experience with it.[3] Imagine this kind of group discussion on why the agency is not achieving its objective of reaching its predetermined quota of clients per month:

Employee A: "The problem is that I schedule appointments but my clients continually cancel, and so I find that I have time on my hands."

Employee B: "The problem is that clients do not find it easy to get to our agency from where they live. Public transportation has deteriorated, and, unless clients have a car, they are not able to keep their appointments."

Supervisor: "The problem is that clients cannot schedule appointments when we're open. When I have followed up with people who have missed appointments, they tell me that if we were open evenings and weekends, they would find it easier to leave their children with someone."

Administrator: "The problem is that too many staff seem to be absent on Mondays or Fridays and this is affecting our client count. It would be higher if staff were more available on those days."

Each one has a different perspective of "the problem," and therefore each will have an approach about how "it" should be analyzed and eventually addressed. If, for example, staff member B's perspective is to be pursued, then one solution may be to design ways to deliver services to clients outside the agency building. If, however, the focus turns to the administrator's perspective, then emphasis would be placed on reducing staff absences. Because perspective is so influential in determining both problems and their solutions, it is crucial that the various perspectives be articulated as explicitly as possible. The way to do this is to ask participants to convey their different perspectives. As a particular perspective on the problem develops, those with different views will have to decide whether or not to "buy in" to the problem as it is eventually defined.[4]

In all organizations, various individuals and groups are likely to have vested interests, i.e., issues they consider vital to their own functioning. These vested interests will certainly influence their perspectives. The management of the organization, for example, is likely to focus on efficiency problems, whereas these may be of little concern to employees. Fringe benefits are likely to be of special concern to employees, whereas meeting legal requirements will be of paramount concern to management. Because of these different perspectives, it is always desirable in formulating the problem to ask, "Who owns which part of the problem?" The ownership of the problem will greatly influence who wants to do something about it, i.e., who owns the solution.

Identifying Insidious Problems

Sometimes problems lurk beneath the surface, accumulating or growing over time until finally they explode. We can use several analogies to describe this phenomenon: small waves forming in the distance culminating in a tidal wave that capsizes a boat; or a small leak in the roof going undetected for many years, finally resulting in its collapse; or a symptomless cancer doing its damage to the body; or a smoldering fire needing only a slight breeze to cause it to burst into flames. The common aspect of these insidious problems is that they seem too small to require attention, but unless detected early, they can cause great damage.

In a similar fashion, incipient problems exist in organizations. They can take the form of small annoyances that, if not addressed, can become significant and explosive problems. Just as clients can resort to denying the existence of problems, so, too, organizations can develop the attitude, "If we don't look for trouble, we won't find it." But then the proverbial straw breaks the camel's back, that is, something that appears small and insignificant but inexplicably causes an outburst of negative feeling. Only on review might one be able to trace the series of earlier episodes that contributed to what appears to be an inappropriate reaction. Had the problem been identified while it was minor, the later, more damaging, crisis might have been avoided. Clearly, "small" problems should be handled before they become too immense to deal with effectively.

CONSIDERING ALTERNATIVE SOLUTIONS

In any attempt to address a problem, it is important to develop and then evaluate alternative solutions. This approach rests on the assumption that for every decision to be considered, there can be a range of alternatives. It is essential to realize that any action we take, any decision we make, is only one possibility out of a multitude of options.[5]

The reason we must consider alternatives is that there are usually a number of paths we can take to resolve a problem. This concept is especially useful for those managers who are prone to think their way is the only way. In the event that one of the paths leads us astray, we have others to fall back on. Considering alternatives also sharpens our thinking for the approach we finally select. Sometimes, it is the second or third or tenth idea that can help solve the problem, not the first.

In examining how to solve a problem, several precepts should be considered to guide the process:

Developing Criteria

Problem-solving criteria should be established as benchmarks against which to compare alternatives. They should encompass the organization's limits and expectations and should vary according to the problem under consideration.

Suppose the agency needs to alter office space. As you consider different plans, you might establish these criteria: a) cost under $7,000, b) reduced background noise levels, c) increased intraoffice communication, and d) reduced movement between work areas. As you evaluate each plan, you would compare it to the pre-established criteria, realizing that some alternatives will better meet the criteria than others.[6]

Making Ideas Concrete

As you consider various possibilities, think in concrete, future-oriented terms by asking, "Suppose we were to select a particular approach, what would we expect one year from now?" By anticipating the future, you discipline your thinking to walk through one or more of the proposed ideas to see how they would play out in reality.

Making abstract ideas or plans concrete is especially important in considering ways of serving clients. By visualizing how clients would be served, you determine how they would be routed through your system and how the information flow should occur.

One of the best antidotes to thinking too abstractly in the decision process is to go on the firing line for a period of time. Walk in the same door that your clients do and follow their path through your system. Sit where they sit for a while to get a feel for what it is like to wait in the waiting room. Hear their conversations and observe the professionals who serve them. Call the office as if you are a client to sense how the organization responds. Get out in the field and actually see how the operations are working. Through this type of direct experience you may be in a better position to judge the value of your current and proposed decisions.

Considering Tradeoffs

Every plan, however good, probably has inherent limitations. In your zeal to convince others of the efficacy of one approach over another, you may tend to overlook limitations or negative consequences. To combat these blind spots, build into your thinking the concept of tradeoffs to acknowledge that there are disadvantages as well as advantages inherent in any course of action.

For example, your plan to reach out to clients by sending staff to their homes will greatly improve contacts with those who formerly did not come for interviews but at a cost of reducing the total number of clients served in a given period. The concept of tradeoffs means accepting that every benefit has a cost. Considering any one alternative idea over others is a matter of weighing whether the advantages or disadvantages of one are greater than those of other options. This probing injects a greater degree of reality into the problem-solving process and forces you to look at the downside of even a good idea before you make your final determination.

Sometimes the word "satisficing" is used to express the thought that there may be no one best solution to a given problem. The word was coined to convey the idea of finding solutions that both satisfy and suffice. Further, it suggests that the search for an ideal but perhaps unattainable solution should be discontinued if a reasonable one—perhaps having some inherent limitations—can be found.[7]

We can thus accept the reality that even good decisions have their inherent limitations and therefore not be immobilized into thinking we have to make decisions that will have to satisfy everyone. For example, a decision to shift staffing to serve a selected group of clients means that others will be receiving less. Moreover, if we know our decisions will be "satisficing," we can experiment with courses of action that, if they do not work out, can be abandoned and replaced by another alternative under consideration.[8] Agonizing over alternatives can result in indecision, which can be worse than making a less than perfect decision.[9] In short, "satisficing" decisions help us to overcome paralysis by analysis.

MAKING DECISIONS

If problem solving encompasses formulating a problem statement and examining potential alternatives, then decision making is the process of choosing from among alternatives and implementing an approach to deal with the problem.

Making Risk-Taking Decisions Prudently

Most decisions involve some degree of risk because their impact cannot fully be appreciated until they are implemented and because no one can predict the future with complete accuracy. Since uncertainty is inherent in risk-taking decisions, the possibility of failure always exists. One way of dealing with risk is to embark on an experimental project. For example, the organization makes a decision to provide services away from the main office, but you are not certain which locations clients are most likely to use even after you have conducted surveys. For a period of time you might try using libraries, shopping malls, or religious facilities. After trying out different places, staff will learn which are best—or whether none of them is suitable. The experimental approach allows staff to be open-minded before making a final decision.

To reduce unnecessary risks, consider whether the potential negative consequences of a decision are so great that such a decision should not be made. Suppose productivity is being affected by interpersonal rivalry between two units in the organization. Should there be a major reorganization of moving staff and activities because supervisors are feuding with each other? A painful reorganization to accommodate a rivalry between two units may or may not result in a reduction in tension. Once the reorganization has taken place, even if the results are much less than desired, the decision cannot easily be undone. In sum, you must weigh the benefits of a particular decision against its costs. Indeed, the costs may outweigh advantages and may therefore serve as a deterrent to making what seems like a more appropriate decision.

Risk taking can have both minor and major consequences. Some decisions can be reversed; that is, if something goes wrong, you can shift to another course of action without the organization or the clients suffering. These are risks that you can afford to take. On the other hand, some risks have momentous significance, financially or otherwise, and may not be reversible; the consequences could be felt for years to come. These are the decisions you must weigh most heavily. In your analysis, therefore, the agency must determine whether the downside risks are such that the organization could withstand them if things go wrong.

EVALUATING RESULTS

The decision-making process is not complete until managers and staff review the results of their efforts. In the course of carrying out activities and tasks, you will find that some actions will result in partial or even complete failures. Staff will make mistakes, errors in judgment will occur, and things will inevitably go wrong. Evaluating results is the best way to assess whether current reality compares with plans made earlier.

Evaluating results should be based on objectives that have been written in advance. Objectives should be quantifiable or measurable in some clear way so that their success or failure can be seen during the review process. This helps the organization conduct an assessment by allowing it to compare intended results with actual outcomes.

To ensure accountability for results, organizations must determine standards for monitoring and controlling activities. For every objective there should be a performance indicator that will clearly demonstrate the extent to which the objective is being achieved.

This is no easy matter for many human service organizations because the outcomes of services are quite variable and do not easily lend themselves to quantifiable and objective data analysis. It is difficult enough to determine in some quantifiable way the extent to which, for instance, a couple has improved their marital relationship through counseling; trying to aggregate in some reasonable format the progress made by the 220 couples seen in the course of a year is indeed formidable. Demands for increased accountability, however, make evaluation of results one of the major challenges human service organizations must address.

Because agencies face a tremendous challenge in assessing results, they continually seek to develop measurement indicators that can reflect the impact of their services. A youth serving agency, for example, might develop the following indicators in relation to youth who are referred by their schools as having behavioral and emotional difficulties:

- Improvement in reading level by one grade
- Overall improvement in school grade average
- Reduction in juvenile arrests
- Improved youth/parent communication episodes
- Improvement in school attendance
- Reduction in fighting episodes

An employment agency would identify the number of persons who remained employed for six months. A substance abuse agency would track the rate of recidivism among convicted drug addicts. A senior nutrition agency would evaluate the number of elderly persons who maintain their independent living status.

COMMONLY USED EVALUATION DESIGNS

Agencies may consider a variety of evaluation designs to convey the results of their interventions:

One-Group Post test Only Design involves a single group in which progress is measures only at the end of the intervention, for example, asking adolescents who complete a drug reduction program if they had reduced or ended their drug-taking behavior. The problem with a post test design is that we can never be certain whether other variables operate that resulted in the discontinuance of a particular behavior.

Post test Only Design with Nonequivalent Groups employs a comparison group that may or may not be similar to the group being worked with. Suppose, for example, an intervention is attempted with a group of adolescents involved in illegal behavior. At the conclusion of the intervention effort a comparison might be made between this group and another group of adolescents with similar characteristics.

One Group Pretest/Post test Design measures the change over time using the same test or a variation of the same test at two points. For example, a measurement could be taken of the change in knowledge or attitudes regarding taking drugs.

Quasi-Experimental Design use two groups, both of which are given pretests and post tests. The groups are similar on important variables (such as gender and age), but there is no random assignment. This method allows us to rule out some alternative explanations for outcomes because we have tried to control for such possibilities as creaming and maturation.

Another quasi-experimental design would use a series before and after an intervention between a comparison group and the group being intervened with. The fact that the two groups have not been randomly selected limits the ability to make generalizations about the intervention.

Ideally an experimental design would give a more valid indication of the results of the intervention. This design would incorporate such features as appropriate sampling techniques, assignment of subject to control and experimental groups, and control over exposure to treatment variables. The use of experimental control presumably would allow evaluators to eliminate competing explanations for observed results and to generalize findings. But its disadvantages of very high costs, randomizing which individuals receive treatment, and restrictive delays make the experimental design unfeasible for most agencies.[10]

By not using experimental design, agencies may be subject to criticism if the results are not completely valid. A child's attendance might be improved, but is this a valid measure of success if the child is spending most days in the principal's office? A program designed to work with delinquent youth may demonstrate the reduction in recidivism, but we may not be completely certain that this result happens because of the program or because of other factors in the environment. In spite of these concerns agencies are working to provide an outcome framework that measures in some degree the quality and quantity of their services. [11]

Agencies may consider two other monitoring designs. One is client satisfaction surveys that attempt to measure satisfaction with the service or with the achievement of specific objectives. The results of this information can be useful in determining how clients perceive staff behavior. Client perception of the accessibility of services may provide an explanation for why they drop out of the program.[12] A second measurement relates to the improvement in service efficiency. Examples could include the following measurements: 1) average length of time on a waiting list, 2) average time between arrival in an agency and being seen, 3) length of time in foster care, 4) cost of providing units of service. These efficiency measures alert the agency to making possible changes and procedures.

Effective evaluation requires good input of information and proper packaging for decision makers. With the prevalence of the computer, reports can now be generated to reveal deviations from targets. In this way, client information audits can reveal discrepancies between predetermined objectives and actual performance in much the same way that budget analyses are conducted to reveal variances in financial projections.

For information to be useful in the monitoring process, it must be timely and relevant. The information must be significant both for reporting to external funders and policy makers and for internal decision making. It must be user-friendly and not so complicated that it overwhelms the staff. Such information should not only be useful for analyzing the impact of services, as discussed above, but also in conducting analyses of the activities and work of the organization's units. A good information system should be able to answer questions like these:

- Are the activities of the unit contributing to the accomplishment of objectives?
- Are costs for conducting the work excessive in relation to meeting objectives?
- Are services provided in a timely manner?
- Is the level of service improving or declining?
- Are staffing levels appropriate for accomplishing objectives?

CORRECTIVE ACTION

The purpose of monitoring is to identify performance deviations so that corrective action can be taken.[13] The value of identifying deviations from predetermined standards is to stimulate staff to think about how they could get back on course—or to revise the objectives so that they are more realistic. Self-correction is possible only if, as a result of the self-assessment process, the organization is prepared to ask hard questions. If the organization does achieve its objectives, these questions could be asked:

- Given the nature of the problem and the resources that were available, were the objectives set too low?
- Was the cost worth the accomplishment?
- Even though you achieved the objectives, does the basic problem remain essentially unchanged?
- Does solving this particular problem create other problems to deal with?
- Has reaching these particular goals interfered with the achievement of other objectives; if so, do the balances have to be redressed?

If the organization does not achieve its objectives, these questions could be asked:

- Were adequate resources (staff and funding) available to do the job?
- Were objectives set unreasonably high?
- Was the timetable appropriate?
- Given the time and financial constraints and other demands, should the organization redirect its energies to other broad problem areas?

The review of success, partial success, or failure of objectives provides a springboard for future decision making. Because organizations generally operate under less than ideal conditions, they may achieve some objectives partially and others not at all. Through the monitoring process, staff may become keenly aware that a discrepancy exists between their aspirations and the actual outcomes. They may not have been able to select the optimum solution for a given problem because of inadequate resources, political constraints, time pressures, or finances. Not being able to provide the optimum solution, they may have to settle on a second or third-best approach. Confronted with this reality, staff can either despair or do nothing, or they can use the opportunity to determine what changes need to be made in the problem-solving, self-correcting process.

This dynamic quality of decision making occurs, paradoxically, even if you succeed. Solving one problem sometimes creates or uncovers another. Suppose, for example, in order to encourage staff to develop more initiative and independence, you send them to special training programs. As a result, they are more prone to challenge supervisors and the organization's authority. This newly-created problem may require supervisors to be trained in dealing with staff who raise provocative issues that challenge traditional ways of doing things. Thus, the resolving of one problem may create other problems that then must be dealt with, suggesting that the decision-making process is never-ending. Obviously, this does not apply in all instances, but it may help to explain why one can never fully relax in the affairs of an organization.

The problem-solving process is dynamic and subject to continuous revision. It involves analyzing problems, establishing objectives, developing alternatives through both rational and creative approaches, and designing and implementing action plans. Monitoring and assessing results promotes a review of whether to make changes at any point along the process. Perhaps problems need to be redefined because their objectives are set too low and are unchallenging, or because they are set too high and are too difficult to achieve, or because achieving the objectives did not solve the problem and new objectives need to be developed that are more on target. Perhaps you need to consider a different strategy that reflects changing circumstances. Finally, the activities and tasks you choose may require alteration if it becomes obvious that they are insufficient and will not achieve your desired objectives. It is through this continuous review and revision that an organization can take necessary corrective actions.

SUMMARY

The willingness to base decisions on a critical review of changing circumstances is at the core of the problem-solving process. This attitude reflects a planning style that is open to constantly changing conditions, flexible in adapting to new needs, and willing to make modifications based on new situations.[14] By accompanying a built-in review with flexibility, an organization can avoid adhering to an approach that goes nowhere. It embraces the complex and kaleidoscopic nature of the real world in which everything is in constant flux. The problem-solving process is never-ending and ever-challenging.

QUESTIONS FOR DISCUSSION

1. Define a particular problem in your organization. How might you redefine it more broadly or narrowly?

2. How might various people in your agency have different perspectives of a problem?

3. In regard to a particular program your agency sponsors, what are its advantages and disadvantages?

4. How does your organization monitor its programs?

Chapter Notes

[1]Kepner, C.H. & Tregoe, B.B. (1974). *The Rational Manager*. New York: McGraw-Hill, pp. 20, 44-47;
Murdock, R.G. & Ross, J.E. (1975). *Information Systems for Modern Management*. Englewood Cliffs, NJ: Prentice Hall, p. 471.

[2]Drucker, P. (1985). *The Effective Executive*. New York: Harper & Row, p. 125.

[3]Kettner, P.M., Moroney, R.M., & Martin, L.L. (1990). *Designing and Managing Programs*. Newbury Park, CA: Sage Publications, pp. 39-40.

[4]Brody, R. (1982). *Problem Solving: Concepts and Methods for Community Organization*. New York: Human Sciences Press, Inc., p. 27.

[5]Dishy, V. (1989). *Inner Fitness*. New York: Doubleday, p. 75.

[6]Doyle, M. & Straus, D. (1976). *How to Make Meetings Work*. New York: Berkley Publishing Group, p. 84.

[7]Murdock & Ross, p. 485.

[8]Peters, T.J., & Waterman, R.H. (1982). *In Search of Excellence: Lessons from America's Best Run Companies*. New York: Harper & Row, pp. 134-5.

[9]Bliss, E. (1976). *Getting Things Done*. New York: Bantam, p. 71.

[10]Brody & Krailo (Nov. 1978). "An Approach to Reviewing the Effectiveness of Programs." *Australian Social Welfare* Vol. 23. No. 3.

[11] Consortium of the American Human Association (1998). *Assessing Outcomes in Child Welfare Services: Principles, Concepts, and Framework of Core Outcome Indicators*. The Casey Outcomes & Decision Making Project.

[12] Kirst-Ashman, K. & Hull, G., Jr. (1997). *Generalist Practice with Organizations and Communities*. Chicago, IL.: Nelson-Hall, pp. 336-346.

[13]Crow, R.T. & Odewahn, C.A. (1987). *Management for the Human Services*. Englewood Cliffs, NJ: Prentice-Hall, p. 97.

[14]Brody, R. (1982). *Problem Solving: Concepts and Methods for Community Organization*. New York: Human Sciences Press, Inc., p. 198.

REFERENCE FOR CHAPTER 8

Thomas Stephe J. (2005). *Improving Maintenance Through Cultural Change*. New York: Industrial Press.

CHAPTER 9

Handling Communications and Conflict

THE IMPORTANCE OF GOOD COMMUNICATIONS

When employees are adequately informed about their organization and have opportunities to convey their ideas, they are likely to be more involved and more invested in their work. This section discusses ways an agency can improve communication to heighten staff's commitment to the organization.

Good communications occur when staff feel their concerns will be listened to and dealt with promptly, when mistakes can be quickly identified and corrected, when staff understand what is taking place, and when they are clear how their work is contributing to the organization. In short, communication involves both upward and downward movement of ideas, suggestions, and values. It is a process of continuously sharing and transmitting important information throughout the organization. A positive flow of information is the result of an attitude that respects people for their ideas and that sees information, not as a source of power, but as a tool for accomplishing the organization's important work. As discussed in Chapter 3, good communications can make the organization's culture more meaningful.

While communication is generally desirable, under certain circumstances it is essential. When an organization is considering changes in strategy or structure, communication takes on special significance. The greater the change, the greater the need for communication.[1] Even when the basic structure of the organization is not changing, the tendency for organizations to delegate responsibilities to the lowest practical level means that every staff member will be involved in making choices. To make good decisions, staff must share in the basic understanding and purpose of the organization.

At a time of crisis, communication is especially essential. For example, when an organization goes through a period of severe retrenchment, discussions must be held openly with staff to encourage their input regarding the situation. To do otherwise runs the risk of creating discontent in employees who remain with the organization but who feel that management cannot be trusted.[2]

Communication is also vitally important when staff are expected to implement important projects. The more they understand the significance of the project to the organization and to the community, the more willing they will be to dedicate themselves to it.

Finally, communication is essential in enhancing staff loyalty to the organization. Staff may appreciate the work of their own unit but may not be aware of how it must mesh with other parts of the organization to accomplish the overall mission. By understanding their part in the whole picture, they come to feel pride in their organization. Proud people are committed people.

Misperceptions

The possibility always exists that staff will misinterpret what has been communicated to them. Suppose, for example, that administrative staff are seen separately from those that provide direct service to review a new directive from the state. Some service staff may become resentful that they are being treated differently and as "second-class citizens." Or a consultant is hired on a temporary basis, resulting in staff misinterpreting this as dissatisfaction with their own performance. Or staff are asked to write a report detailing their current activities that makes them wonder why you are singling them out. In all these instances, staff perception is quite different from what may have been intended.

Because the communication process can be so easily taken for granted, there is the ever-present danger of spoiling a positive organizational climate. Staff feel ignored or misunderstood, morale suffers, and complaints increase. And then tremendous energy has to go into undoing the unintended harm. Continuous communication involving ongoing feedback is essential.

HANDLING CONFLICTS

In every organization, staff interactions produce inevitable conflict; there is no conceivable way of avoiding it. Most of the conflicts do not threaten productivity and are not very painful to the people involved. In fact, constructive conflict can bring about genuine growth as participants gain new insights and perspectives different from their own. Positive conflict can be used to explore opposing ideas so that outmoded ideas can be challenged, and the group can discover new ways of working.[3] In many instances, disagreements should be encouraged if they provide alternatives that ought to be examined before decisions are made.[4]

But if conflicts get out of hand, they can be devastating and tie up huge amounts of the organization's energy. The normal pattern of cooperation is disrupted, the organization may even undergo a great loss of resources, and its own survival may be at stake. Those who are forced to concede in a conflicting situation are not inclined to stay on or, if they do, are not committed to the organization as before. Morale is likely to deteriorate throughout the organization. For these reasons, it is much better to address conflicts before they escalate to the point of being destructive.

Personal feuds between key members of an organization usually occur when they have mutual grievances, and they can lead to suspicion and hostility. Each party wants others in the organization to take sides. Under some circumstances involving low-level conflicts, it may be desirable for the manager to take one side or the other in order to quickly resolve an issue so that staff can get back to work.[5] Because arbitrarily taking sides can produce long-term animosities, an even better approach is to meet with the participants, individually and together, to sort out their grievances and reach a mutually acceptable resolution.[6]

Struggles between two units of an organization occur when one feels the other is encroaching upon its sphere of responsibility. Commonly this is known as a "turf battle." Unit A refuses to cooperate with Unit B as a way of protesting or even stopping the intrusion into its territory or functions. When such a rivalry occurs, the best approach is to clarify roles and assignments. If this does not succeed, it may be necessary to reorganize the functions of each unit so that their boundaries are made quite clear. This is not a time for indecisiveness or ambiguity.

Units within an organization can conflict with each other in different ways: they fight because the staff perceive different objectives to be achieved, they compete for scarce resources, or they believe other units are being treated more favorably.[7] In general, these conflicts are best handled when the feuding units or parties work out their own solutions. If this is not possible, effective managers must play a more vigorous role in helping the units come to resolution, particularly if the conflict becomes highly disruptive.

WAYS TO IMPROVE COMMUNICATIONS

Good communication throughout the organization is obviously needed when conflict exists. It is also essential for the ongoing functioning of the organization. When people know what is going on, they are less inclined to resort to rumors and gossip. They become more committed to the organization because timely information is a major way people build their sense of loyalty and commitment to their work and their organization.

No single method of communication is useful for all situations. If staff number in the hundreds, formal written communications may be necessary, but would likely be inappropriate in communicating to a staff of ten. Most of the time the chief executive will communicate through a network of key staff people, who in turn communicate with their staff, and so on throughout the organization. To further clarify ways to enhance communication, consider these suggestions:

Top-Down Communications

A common complaint among staff is that they lack information about developments in their organization. This can be quite demoralizing to staff who want to feel they are a part of and contribute to the organization. Thus, communication must be given high priority. Communication should not be limited to "professionals," but should include every staff member. By communicating with all staff you indicate that everyone is important and plays a significant role in accomplishing the organization's mission.

In large organizations, communication flows down from the top of the structure. Usually the agency is organized so that top management is responsible for formulating positions or carrying out policies of outside funders or policy makers. Typically, the span of control involves four to seven managers who then meet with division heads under them. This hierarchy can be quite extensive, depending on the size of the organization. The more complex the structure, the more each manager is a key link in the communications network. Breakdowns in communications can easily occur when messages are lost or poorly conveyed, especially when middle managers feel free to add their subjective interpretations, which can engender problematic reactions. The results can be disastrous for the organization.

Clear explanations about the reasons for changes in assignments or procedures should always accompany communiqués to staff. Staff should understand the rationale behind the procedure; otherwise they may resent what appear to be arbitrary and capricious decisions, ultimately preventing them from carrying out the request. They need to have clear, candid explanations about how the change will benefit them, their clients, or the organization.

Suppose, for example, that management decides that staff who work with foster children must see them at least once weekly. Managers should communicate to staff that the children will benefit from the increased continuity that results from these visits. To ensure that staff understand and accept the top-down communication, a monitoring system should be established so that supervisors can determine whether the children are actually being seen once weekly.

In addition to this hierarchical network, there are other ways of communicating from the top of the organization. Organizational newsletters, public announcements, phone mail, bulletin boards, e-mail, large staff meetings, and staff all-day retreats are among the ways that staff can learn about the latest developments.

Bottom-Up Communications

Staff should have ample opportunity to communicate ideas and give reactions to their immediate supervisors as well as top management. This upward communication network can help managers determine whether staff understand and accept requests, or whether they have concerns or problems. Furthermore, a bottom-up approach can solicit valuable suggestions and provide information from those directly on the firing line. Most importantly, when staff are encouraged to send information to top management, they feel better about their own role in the organization.

Unfortunately, some organizations give the illusion of being an information network while treating staff ideas in a cavalier fashion or ignoring them altogether. If staff sense an insincere gesture, expect an even more demoralizing atmosphere than if no effort was made in the first place.[8] If you cannot carry forward their ideas, make certain that you give them an explanation. Nothing is more frustrating to staff than when management claims their ideas will be taken seriously but then does not follow through.

Employee Surveys

One way to encourage good communication is to have an opinion survey when a new policy is under consideration or a program needs to be implemented. Staff can be of particular help in identifying the problems they are encountering with a new program idea. They may not have the answers, but their ability to articulate problems can be invaluable to management.

Surveys are often used because they are inexpensive, they collect information from everyone in the organization, and they permit management to see trends. Management could ask staff such questions as, "What in this organization would you retain? What would you want to see discontinued? What do you think the organization expects of you? What do you expect of the organization?" Answers to these questions can provide insight about what is uppermost on the minds of the staff and permit management to consider new directions. Surveys, however, have the disadvantage of inviting bias in the way they are worded and of causing staff to become disenchanted if they see little response to their feedback.[9] Certainly, if staff feel that their suggestions are not taken seriously, they will be less likely to be responsive to future surveys. It is essential that some form of follow-up occur to convey respect for their ideas—even if they could not all be implemented.

Client Surveys

Some agencies regularly survey their clients because they genuinely want to know how they can best serve their clients. Of course, client surveys may be motivated by the demands of a funding body or some other higher authority and so they are conducted in a perfunctory, ritualistic manner. Asking such questions as the following can provide the basis for good decision making.

> Were the services provided in a timely manner?
> Were staff courteous?
> Were staff responsive to client requests?

Suggestion Systems

To identify concerns from the entire staff, try the old-fashioned suggestion box. This permits people to communicate their concerns anonymously and could reveal festering problems. The suggestion box allows staff to present their complaints and concerns without feeling intimidated. Perhaps staff are talking too loudly in the corridors. Perhaps clients in the waiting room are not being treated courteously. Perhaps there is concern about the consistency of how all staff should dress for work. Normally, without a suggestion box, these concerns might go undetected and therefore unaddressed. Through the anonymity of the suggestion box, everyone—telephone operator, mail clerk, computer programmer, and manager—can express concerns or make suggestions.

Still another way to encourage communication is to have an open-door policy in which top management is available on either a continuous basis or for scheduled appointments. Some managers, for example, formally schedule "open houses" on a certain weekday afternoon. Staff welcome the opportunity to talk with top managers on matters that bother them. This approach may create problems for supervisors who feel that their subordinates "go over their heads," and it may tempt top management to try to resolve matters that are better left within the units. Still, safeguards can be built in so that staff do not inappropriately bypass supervisors. For instance, a manager could suggest that employees follow-up the issue with their supervisors, or that supervisors form ad-hoc task groups to address staff concerns. Furthermore, discussion could be limited to systemic rather than interpersonal or individual issues.

Active one-on-one consultation with subordinates is another way to foster good communications. On the negative side, individual consultation with several staff can result in delays between the formulation and execution of a top-management idea, elicit irrelevant suggestions, and even invite criticism. But actively soliciting advice and information, you can determine if there are mistakes in your plan as well as whether and how a decision might work.[10] If you are particularly interested in staff productivity, then supervisors can individually determine what makes staff feel productive by asking them such questions as the following:

> When do you work at your peak?
> What do you like most about your job?
> What bothers you about your work?
> What resources do you need to be more productive?
> What policies and procedures should be modified so you can be more
>   productive?

From the responses, you can determine what is highly individualized and idiosyncratic and what concerns are held in common.

A variation of one-on-one consultation is for management to meet with small groups of employees. These face-to-face meetings, sometimes composed of staff from several different sections, can provide helpful responses to policies under consideration. These meetings can be time-consuming but worthwhile, not only for obtaining valuable input but also for squelching rumors.[11]

Informal Communications

One of the best ways to keep in touch with staff is through informal contacts. In the hallways, on the elevator, in the lunchroom, you can always to take a few moments to ask how a project is going, how the copy machine is working, or how a spouse is recuperating. Sometimes these spontaneous communications take place right after a formal meeting and, interestingly enough, can be even more important than the meeting itself. By asking people about their jobs as you walk through the building, you pick up ideas and suggestions that you would never obtain by sitting at your desk. The tag name for this is MBWA—Management by Walking Around.[12] Some managers make a point of regularly scheduling time to walk through their unit so they can obtain feedback from their staff. Be careful, however, that a daily walk may be perceived as the prison guard making rounds. An alternative is to engage in impromptu discussions to and from your office.

Good Feedback

At the heart of any communication is feedback, a process that requires a reaction to actions or situations in the organization. High reliance must be placed on good feedback because it is the basis for taking necessary corrective actions. To encourage good feedback, the ability and the commitment to listen are essential.

Unfortunately, meaningful listening, though subscribed to, is often breached. We all have a tendency to concentrate on our own agendas and concerns so that we resort at times to "pretend" or selective listening. Meaningful listening requires tremendous effort and total concentration.[13] It is quite human for all of us to want to hear only what we are doing right and to avoid hearing negative responses. Some supervisors, for example, avoid listening to employees complain because it spoils their own good moods. Yet, by taking the time to listen, a minor complaint can be handled with minimal energy or a hidden problem can surface. Nothing is worse than for a staff member to express a concern, only to feel later that no one cared enough to respond to it. If nothing can be done, for whatever reason, staff should be given an explanation and a sense of appreciation for having raised the concern. This paves the way for improved communication in the future. Only when staff know that they will be taken seriously will they feel right about communicating their concerns.

Just as a supervisor has a responsibility to listen to a staff's concern, so staff has a responsibility to communicate good feedback. The reality is that agency managers rely on staff to let them know when policies are not working well and when decisions may need to be modified based on client responses. One example: hospital social work staff are reassigned because of administrative convenience even though the wards are far apart, thus resulting in an inefficient use of time. Only by alerting supervisors of this inefficiency could changes in deployment be considered. Another example: new forms are developed without consultation with staff, resulting in duplication of efforts. Staff feedback leads to further modifications and considerable savings in staff time.

To be sure, there is the possibility that a "whistle blower" could experience some degree of insecurity. In the real world, people seen as "trouble makers" or as messengers of bad tidings can be downgraded, shut out, or even have their jobs placed in jeopardy. On the other hand, it is also possible that staff may feel intimidated more from their own inner fears than is warranted by the situation. Some supervisors and managers may be tremendously pleased that staff care enough about the organization that they are willing to come forward with concerns and suggestions. In those situations where staff feel uneasy about conveying criticism, they should encourage the use of an anonymity mechanism such as a suggestion box or staff survey. A particularly useful arrangement is to have the organization conduct a survey of staff concerns and suggestions, followed up with a general meeting with the managers to discuss the findings and to build in an opportunity for response.

CLIENT FOCUSED COMMUNICATIONS

Some organizations become quite intent staying in touch with their clients. They may even purposefully refer to them as "customers" to convey that even though their clients may not be paying directly for their services, they are to be treated as if they were paying customers whose good will and concerns are paramount. These organizations may create a Customer Relations Team whose job is to answer questions, resolve problems, and ensure that all clients receive prompt service with courtesy and professionalism. Moreover, they provide information on all services available at the agency and relevant services provided elsewhere. They also provide a conciliation procedure that invites clients to talk first with the staff, then a supervisor, and then to a Customer Relations Specialist who can meet with staff and clients to resolve issues in a conciliation process before they have to be carried to a county state hearing level.

Some agencies, especially health-care facilities, will distribute a brochure to their clients, encouraging them to express their concerns. In a nursing facility, for example, a publication might suggest that clients first bring any concerns to the staff, encourage their active participation in care planning, and invite them to ask questions. They are informed that a Resident's Council can hear grievances. They can also communicate directly to administrative staff without fear of recrimination. They can either put their concerns in writing or use a "Customer Satisfaction Hotline," which allows for a confidential voice mail system and can trigger an investigation. Hence, the organization informs clients of various ways they can communicate their concerns, and they are aware that mechanisms exist for investigating and resolving their issues.

The reason for developing communication procedures is becoming more and more obvious: ensuring proper and professional response to client concerns and working to resolve issues before they become unmanageable.

SUMMARY

All organizations must ensure good communications to convey the organization's values, promote staff commitment, and handle conflict. Communicating is a two-way process that involves transmitting ideas and tuning into staff's thinking and feelings. Good communicators are good listeners.

QUESTIONS FOR DISCUSSION

1) What are examples of top-down or bottom-up communications in your organization?

2) What are some ways that would help improve communications in your organization?

3) How is information communicated informally in your agency?

4) Your supervisor seeks your advice, saying that the suggestion box is not being used by staff or staff have been using it to place nonsense ideas. You know from past discussions with staff that they have not taken the suggestion box seriously. What would you suggest to your supervisor that would invite more serious use of the suggestion box?

Chapter Notes

[1]Gaylin, D.H. (1990, Summer). "Break Down Barriers by Communicating Your Company's Strategy." *The Human Resources Professional*, pp. 20-21.

[2]Barton, G.M. (1990). "Manage Words Effectively." *Personnel Journal*, 1, pp. 32-33.

[3]Tjosvold, D. (1991). *The Conflict-Positive Organization.* Reading, MA: Addison-Wesley, p.11.

[4]Drucker, P. (1985). *The Effective Executive.* New York: Harper & Row, pp.150-53;

Lauffer, A. (1985). *Careers, Colleagues, and Conflicts: Understanding Gender, Race, and Ethnicity in the Workplace.* Beverly Hills, CA: Sage Publication, pp.145-46.

[5]Caplow, T. (1976). *How to Run Any Organization.* Hinsdale, IL: Dryden, p. 170.

[6]Bisno, H. (1988). *Managing Conflict.* Newbury Park, CA: Sage Publications, p.66.

[7]Crow, R.T. & Odewahn, C.A. (1987). *Management for the Human Services.* Englewood Cliffs, NJ: Prentice-Hall, pp. 145-6.

[8]Zaremba, 1989, p. 36.

[9]Boyett, J.H. & Conn, H.P. (1987). *Maximum Performance Measurement.* Macomb, IL: Glenbridge, pp. 255-6.

[10]Caplow, p. 170.

[11]Barton, p. 3.

[12]Herman, R.E. (1990). *Keeping Good People: Strategies for Solving the Dilemma of the Decade.* Cleveland, OH: Oakhill Press, p.140.

[13]Peck, M.S. (1978). *The Road Less Traveled.* New York: Touchstone, Simon & Schuster, p. 125.

REFERENCE FOR CHAPTER 9

Gramsbergen-Hoogland (2005). *Communication in Organizations: Basic Skills & Conversation Models.* NY: Psychology Press

CHAPTER 10

Perspectives on Diversity and
Ethical Behavior

Social workers functioning in both social agencies and community organizations must address fundamental challenges of diversity and ethical professional behavior.

MANAGING DIVERSITY IN SOCIAL AGENCIES

Some organizations consider that by complying with affirmative action requirements they have achieved their ultimate responsibility. Agencies hire qualified minority and female applicants and then place the burden on these new staff members to make the necessary adjustments. Simply placing people of diverse backgrounds together does not necessarily create a positive, culturally rich work atmosphere. Employees may tend to cluster with people like themselves and with whom they feel comfortable, which can produce cultural misunderstandings and feelings of prejudice in other staff members.

Moreover, as a result of the changing work force, agencies will find themselves dealing not just with diversity, but with unassimilated diversity. People with different cultural backgrounds are increasingly reluctant to accept assimilation.[1] So affirmative action is a necessary, but not sufficient, means of addressing diversity.

To move beyond affirmative action, organizations need to manage diversity in a way that achieves the same level of productivity and quality from a heterogeneous work force that was obtained from the formerly homogenous work force.[2] This should not require compromising standards or denying upward mobility to those who have merit, including white males. Rather, competence must count more than ever as each member of the organization is encouraged to perform at his or her fullest potential. The emphasis must be on creating an organizational climate in which all members of the staff will be stimulated to do their best work.

Managing diversity is not a single program for addressing discrimination. Rather, it is a process for developing an environment that works for all employees.[3] It involves a holistic approach of creating a cooperative environment in which all kinds of people can reach their full potential in pursuit of organizational objectives. It is not a program just for addressing discrimination.[4]

To take advantage of a heterogeneous work force, agencies can take such proactive measures as those listed below.[5]

- Establish guidelines and goals so that managers are responsible for promoting competent minorities and women (e.g., "Increase women in upper level positions from 5 percent to 20 percent within the next three years"). Evaluate individual managers on the basis of their assigning high potential minorities and women to pivotal jobs that could lead to upward mobility.

- Develop policies that reflect the gender diversity of the work force. Some organizations provide alternatives for maternity, disability, and dependent care benefits. They also provide part-time work, flexible work hours, job sharing, work-at-home arrangements, and paternity and maternity leaves.

- Establish quality improvement teams or committees headed by senior staff to encourage progress for talented minorities and women. They could, for example, initiate mandatory gender and racial awareness training designed to identify practices, procedures, and individual behaviors that work against minorities and women.

- Sponsor frequent celebrations of racial, gender, ethnic and religious differences. Print articles about the diverse work force in the organization's newsletter with emphasis on successful employee experiences. Assure equal celebration of holidays special to different religious and ethnic groups.

- Develop or expand summer intern programs with emphasis on minorities and women. Establish recruiting contacts with minority and women's organizations.

- Conduct regular attitude surveys of the entire organization to determine how and in what ways women and minorities experience prejudicial attitudes. Include in exit interviews questions that determine whether biases played a factor in decisions to leave.

- Establish "core groups" of eight to ten people led, if possible, by a skilled facilitator to stimulate informal discussion and self-development and to allow staff to candidly express experiences with prejudice in the organization. Those who have concerns about their supervisors' prejudicial attitudes may be more likely to communicate directly with them based on support and feedback from the group. The result is that both staff and managers will become more aware of their own biases.

- Concentrate staff and managerial training on issues affecting everyone in the organization on the basis that interpersonal relationships and people-managing skills are not limited to dealing with issues of prejudice.

- Assign a coach, personal advocate, or sponsor to promising minorities and women so that they have the same opportunity as other employees to move up the organizational ladder. Coaches should encourage those with whom they are working to ask for help, especially if roadblocks are encountered.

These are some of the ways organizations are implementing their commitment to diversity. The approaches do not intend to give special advantages to minorities and women but to ensure that those with talent have an opportunity to get ahead. They are based on the fundamental assumption that diversity is now a reality in the workplace requiring awareness, vigilance, and proactive efforts so that all staff can achieve their potential and contribute fully to the organization.

DEVELOPING A CULTURALLY SENSITIVE PERSPECTIVE

In attempting to broaden their cultural sensitivity to diverse populations, staff in human service organization are increasingly having to address the issue of separate vs. integrated delivery of services.

Suppose, for example, that a drug counseling agency concludes that it must expand the number of Latino staff because of its growing number of Latino clients. Suppose, further, that there are few specially trained Latino staff available. Should the agency consider hiring less formally trained Latino staff? To resolve this dilemma, some agencies seek Latinos and arrange to have them undergo intensive and accelerated training; others require trained staff to participate in culturally sensitive training and language instruction. Still others hire Latinos to be interpreters.

In addition, there is growing interest in developing specialized services geared to respond sensitively to group specific populations: services for African-American men, lesbian women, and Hispanic persons. Suppose that a man who happens to be homosexual has a substance abuse problem that leads him to seek counseling. Should he have available to him only a therapist who is also homosexual? The answer will depend in part on the preference of the client. To some clients seeing a counselor who does not have the same dominant characteristic (e.g., sexual preference, color of skin, ethnic heritage) may not matter—as long as the counselor is competent to perform the work and is sensitive to the issues of concern to the client. To other clients, having a social worker who is similar may be extremely important.[6]

Frequently social workers find themselves dealing with people who are different from themselves in significant ways. A young worker has to deal with an older person; a single man has to work with an unmarried woman with three children; a healthy woman has to help a male with AIDS. In these instances it is essential that staff come to terms with their own possible prejudices and biases about people who are different from themselves. They must develop the capacity for empathy and go out of their way to understand the background and the concerns of their clients.

If, for example, a staff member must work with a large number of Latino clients, it is imperative that the worker takes courses in Spanish and makes an effort to understand their life experiences and cultural practices. Similarly, if one is assigned to work with African-American youth who are at risk of failing in elementary school, it is essential to understand their family patterns, the role of the adult males in their lives, the kind of street environment that surrounds them, and the effects of their school performance.

Through heightened sensitivity social workers convey their respect for the dignity of the people with whom they work. One of the best approaches, when in doubt, is to ask people. Would they prefer to be called Latinos or Hispanics; African Americans or blacks; Mrs. Jones or Sally? Some may not care, but others will have tremendously strong feelings that must be taken into account.

To be sure, cultural sensitivity can be complicated. There is no guarantee, for example, that an African-American middle class, suburban-raised male can automatically be sensitive to an African-American inner city youth. Their outer appearance may be the same, but they live in two different worlds and biases and antagonisms can occur.

Thus, at the heart of much of social work practice is the ability to tune in to fundamental concerns of our clients, to understand—emotionally as well as intellectually—what they are going through, and to communicate that sense of understanding.

CHALLENGES OF DIVERSITY IN COMMUNITY ORGANIZATIONS

Community organization staff work frequently entails working with groups whose life styles and values are different from yours. It can also involve bringing together groups who are antagonistic toward each other. We offer the following suggestions for dealing with some of the formidable challenges related to dealing with diversity:

Discern and Accept Differences Among People

All of us have a tendency to generalize based upon our experiences with certain people. For most people this ability to generalize is a way of ordering a complex world. It is no wonder, then, that bias and prejudice creep into our thinking. Even social workers who pride themselves on being open minded are subject to subtle forms of stereotypical thinking.

Suppose, for example, you are asked to work with the Latino community to help develop a cultural center. What you will soon discover is that there is not one but many Latino communities. They may have the same language in common, but their ethnicity and consequently their values and styles of operating may be different. Some, for example, may come from a culture that results in their being highly critical and demanding of themselves and others. Others may stress the close knit family and not want to take on leadership roles that would divert their energies from their families. These differences must be understood and respected.

Even within the same ethnic or racial group, differences can occur that must be taken into account. Is their background from a small rural town where everyone knew each other or from a large urban city? Was education stressed or played down? Did they live an isolated experience or were they exposed to a variety of experiences outside their community? Was religion a significant part of their upbringing? In their communities did most of the parents work? All of these cultural variables and more will greatly influence how people perceive and respond to the world around them. By understanding these variations in people, community organization staff can avoid automatically trying to transplant a program or an approach that works with one group to another that could result in failure.

You Need to Earn Their Trust

In community organization work people would generally prefer to have the organizer reflect their basic characteristic. African-American communities prefer an African American; Puerto Ricans the same; battered women the same. There is a certain comfort level in having the organizer be closely identified with the group. For them the organizer can offer the appealing message: "I've experienced what you're going through."

It is our experience that community organizers can also work with groups different from themselves. Community people have powerful antennae; they can quickly spot those who are not sincere in their desire to genuinely help them strengthen themselves. They can be demanding that the community organizer demonstrate clearly that they can bring added value to the community.

Community people can, however, also respond to genuine efforts to reach out to them and to a commitment to help them improve their lives. Trust is established over time. Many one-on-one contacts will be necessary, and some testing out of sincerity may occur. Community organizers need to convey that not only do they understand what people are going through but that they can assist them in finding concrete ways of dealing with their problems.

Suppose you are a white male working in a Latino community. One of the first requisites is to be able to speak Spanish. In the same vein, if you were working with a Soviet Jewish community you would need to learn Russian or Yiddish. If you were from outside the African-American community, you would be expected to know black history, including the impact of slavery. The special challenge of being the outsider is that you will be continually asked to prove your sincere commitment.

Prejudice Can Breed Prejudice

It should come as no surprise that prejudice can be a two-way street. Polish Americans concentrated in a certain geographic area of a city suddenly begin to abandon their area when the first African Americans move in. Over time the community becomes African American but ownership of the small neighborhood stores becomes largely Korean. Soon friction develops between the African-American community and the Korean store owners, exacerbated by the shooting of an African-American male.

Community organizers are sometimes called upon to enter situations involving tension between groups. They must understand the dynamics of the situation, the immediate cause of the conflicts, and the long standing frictions that may have existed. Further, they will have to bring the parties to the table to air concerns, to express common frustrations, and to work out common solutions. The most useful approach is a nonjudgmental attitude that encourages the parties in the dispute to find common ground so that both sides feel they can gain by settling their differences.

DEALING WITH ETHICAL ISSUES

As a profession, social work relies on the integrity and comportment of its practitioners. Because social work professionals often work closely with those who are most vulnerable in our society, they must have an inner clarity of their own values, of what is proper and appropriate behavior. Most of the time these values are obvious and readily accepted; sometimes ethical dilemmas occur that must be addressed.

Most of the social work values are articulated in the National Association of Social Work (NASW) Code of Ethics. The Code emphasizes the profession's primary responsibility to clients (or client organizations) and asks social workers to make every effort to foster maximum self-determination among the people they serve. It further calls on social workers to act in accordance with the highest standards of professional integrity, and it proscribes exploiting professional relationships for personal gain. Under no circumstances, for example, would a referring social worker accept a payback from a therapist to whom he had referred a client. The Code further states that social workers should never engage in sexual activities with clients. Nor should social workers exploit a dispute between a colleague and employers to obtain a position or otherwise advance the social worker's interest.[7]

Even so, the ethics of the profession—and the NASW Code of Ethics itself—are not without ambiguity. Sometimes inherent conflicts will occur between the needs of the individual client, the agency, and the community. Some examples:

1) You work for a community center and in the course of your contacts with a youth group, you learn that several are selling cocaine. The Code of Ethics states that social workers should hold in confidence all information obtained in the course of professional service.

2) You work for a community agency that is located near a local factory, which contributes a sizable annual donation. In your community organization work you meet with neighbors who are greatly perturbed by the pollution emitted by the factory. Because the agency is concerned with its economic survival, you are receiving subtle suggestions to focus on other worthwhile community issues. You are torn because you know that the Code of Ethics states that social workers should be alert to and resist the influences and pressures that interfere with the exercise of professional discretion and impartial judgment required for the performance of professional functions.

3) You work with a citizen's organization that wants to improve the appearance of its surroundings. Members are becoming stronger in asserting the need for better police protection, improved lighting, and painting and fixing up houses in the neighborhood. One of the neighbors, though, seems to relish collecting junk. You believe strongly in the principle of self-determination, but now find that this is in conflict with the interests of the neighborhood.

The list of examples goes on: the homeless person who refuses to accept medical treatment, the mother who neglects her child while she studies for a GED, the battered woman who decides to return to her husband who himself refuses counseling services. These and many other examples are part of the daily experience of those on the firing line.

There are no easy answers to these ethical dilemmas. The best way to approach them is to honestly examine the implications for the client, the agency, and the community. You may want to confer with supervisors and colleagues whom you trust and whose values you consider to be solid. Certainly, you will want to understand various perspectives, clarify ethical values of a particular situation, consider which ones are most important, examine consequences for various courses of actions, and then make a decision based on your inner conviction and your own sense of integrity. In those instances where you think that the agency is in serious violation of the Code of Ethics, you can report it to local or national NASW offices. If the matter is serious enough, sanctions can be imposed.

DEALING WITH SEXUAL HARASSMENT

In any organization, sexual harassment can be grounds for dismissal. Accusations by clients that staff have made overt sexual advances or have pressured them into sexual acts are a violation of professional ethics and compel termination hearings. Supervisors who use their position to make overt demands for sex from subordinates abuse their power and should also be subject to termination.

There is, to be sure, a "gray area" involving sexual harassment. Co-workers can mutually agree to engage in intimate relationships without harassment being a factor. When mutuality is absent and when men and women have different perspectives about their relationships, personal and organizational turmoil will most likely follow. For example, while men may think that sexual references or jokes are harmless amusement, women often feel these comments are offensive. When a man puts his arm around a woman's shoulder, is it a sign of friendly affection or a sexual overture? Is telling a woman that she looks attractive a genuine compliment or a subtle come-on? Is a request to go out for a drink after work a sign of camaraderie or a prelude to a sexual advance?

These interactions between staff in the work place can be fraught with ambiguities. They can be reflections of friendships or they can border on unwelcome advances. The courts have defined sexual harassment on the job as, "any unwelcome sexually oriented behavior, demand, comment, or physical contact, initiated by an individual at the workplace, that is a term or condition of employment, a basis for employment decisions, or that interferes with the employee's work or creates a hostile or offensive working environment."[8] Heterosexual overtures of men to women are the dominant pattern of harassment. Female supervisors can harass men, and both men and women may experience homosexual advances.[9]

A fundamental prerequisite for preventing sexual harassment in the workplace is for the chief executive and official policies to convey that it will not be tolerated. The climate and the organizational culture must be such that women will feel comfortable refusing overtures. They need to be able to say, "This joke, this behavior, this comment, offends me—please stop." Just as racial jokes have become taboo in the workplace, so too must behavior suggestive of a sexual overture be considered out of bounds.

If offensive behavior or comments persist, women (or men) need to know they can talk with supervisors who will not trivialize their concerns. If the banter or sexual jokes or flirtations move beyond an acceptable range, however staff define it, they must feel they have recourse. In those instances where the supervisor is unresponsive or where a male supervisor is himself the cause of the problem, the female employee must feel free to communicate to someone else in the organization who can deal effectively with her concerns. Women must feel that they work in a non-threatening environment that protects their sense of self-respect and personal dignity.

To resolve problems of sexual harassment, managers should consider taking the following steps:[10]

- Make it easy for an employee to register a complaint by establishing clear written procedures describing how to file a complaint, with whom, and in what form.

- Appoint an investigator from outside the department. This is especially important when a supervisor is accused of harassment. Inform staff that complaints may be registered with the supervisor's boss or with top management.

- Make sure the accuser and the accused understand that false statements can be grounds for discharge.

- If a supervisor is accused of harassment, make sure he or she understands that any form of retaliation will not be tolerated.

- Give the accused fair and objective consideration when obtaining his or her side of the story.

- Have witnesses sign statements.

Employees should be made aware that if they wish to pursue a legal remedy, they can contact their state discrimination agency or the federal Equal Employment Opportunity Commission. They need not have an attorney to file a claim, but they may wish to speak with one who specializes in employment discrimination. Under the Civil Rights Act of 1991, victims of sexual harassment are entitled to damages for pain and suffering as well as any lost pay.[11]

Because sexual harassment can be highly subjective, it is important that protocols be observed so as not to recklessly impugn the reputation of staff. They may not have ulterior motives and may not be aware their remarks or behavior are offensive. Each situation must be assessed on its own merits, with both parties having an opportunity to resolve their concerns. Dialogues should take place throughout the organization on possible misuses of power, misperceptions, and insensitivities. The goal should be an atmosphere in which men and women operate on a cordial, professional basis.

Some observed behaviors in the workplace, though not technically sexual harassment, are clearly unprofessional. For example, a staff member in your department may be dating a supervisor in another department. They are seen hugging each other and making gestures that make you and other staff uncomfortable. This may not be cause for a lawsuit but can be sufficient reason to complain to your supervisor regarding the inappropriate behavior.

PROVIDING MEANINGFUL PERSONNEL PRACTICES

Agencies convey their expectations of staff behavior and provide safeguards for a professional atmosphere through carefully prepared personnel policies that have been approved by their governing body. While each agency must formulate a set of policies that deals with their unique situation, almost every agency observes—or should observe—the following minimum standards:[12]

Affirmative Action and Nondiscrimination

To achieve a work force free of discrimination and prejudice, agencies must develop strong policies that reflect a clear commitment to implement affirmative action. Written policies should reflect how the agency will actively search for qualified minorities. The responsibility and authority for administering the program should be assigned to a top agency executive. The policies should contain explicit language that there will be no discrimination based on personal characteristics (race, religion, physical handicap, sexual orientation, age, national origin, or political belief) that do not relate to the performance of duties.

Personnel Selection

Personnel should be selected on the basis of professional competence and the best qualifications to implement effectively the agency's functions. Prospective employees should be aware of the specific requirements, salary, and qualifications required of the position. Current staff should have the first opportunity to fill vacancies. The training (probationary) period should be specified.

Problem Solving or Grievance Procedures

Provisions should be made for a fair and impartial hearing if an employee believes that he/she has been unjustly affected by a personnel action or policy of the agency. The personnel policies should explain procedures for due process, the right of appeal, the provision for a written statement, the establishment of a review committee, and a delineation of the person(s) having final decision making authority.

Classification Plan and Benefits

All positions should be classified based on their relative complexity and responsibility. Job descriptions should include the quality and quantity of work expected, minimum qualifications, and designation of the supervisor.

Salaries should be based on levels that are comparable to similar positions in the community. Within constraints of the budget, normally staff may expect annual increments and merit increases for exceptional performance. Sick leave, vacation time, and health and retirement benefits should be articulated.

Special Policies

Recent federal legislation, court rulings and the changing ethical climate make it imperative that agency personnel policies be updated to reflect provisions on family and medical leave, nondiscrimination of staff with AIDS and other disabilities, and procedures for handling substance abuse.

Agencies must have a written policy on sexual harassment which would cover the following points: a statement that it is not acceptable and will not be tolerated, encouragement for victims to report incidents, provision of names of at least two persons to whom reports can be made, (one of whom is not the victim's immediate supervisor), and assurance that all charges will be fully investigated.

Security of Employment

Some employees of nonprofit and public agencies function under the protection of labor unions, and state labor laws guarantee collective bargaining rights for those who wish to be so covered. Where unions exist, labor and management use a variety of methods to resolve differences, including continuing negotiations, mediation, arbitration, fact finding panels, and strikes.

Under some circumstances staff serve under a specific time contract to perform a special function. In keeping with current law, many personnel practices now include provisions that employment may be terminated at the will of either the employee or the organization at any time, for any reason.

SUMMARY

The work of an organization can be affected by the way it handles such issues as the diversity of its work force, cultural sensitivity, sexual harassment, and its personnel practices. Being proactive in dealing with diversity issues can result in improved staff attitudes toward the organization and their work. Sexual harassment cannot be tolerated, and all agencies would do well to have definitive policies and procedures in place to address this problem. Personnel practices and procedures should be written so as to cover a wide range of personnel topics. Among the types that should be available are the following:

- A written human resource plan
- A job description for each position
- A plan for recruitment and selection
- A plan for enhancing agency diversity
- A plan for staff development and training
- A performance evaluation system in place
- Written procedures for employee termination

QUESTIONS FOR DISCUSSION

1) What is your agency's policy with respect to the following: a) affirmative action b) sexual harassment c) AIDS   d) substance abuse?

2) Select one of the following groups of potential clients: a) Gay/Lesbian people b) Latinos c) substance abusers. Assume you are not from the group that you select. How you would address the challenges of working with a client that is different from yourself?

3) What are the ways your agency communicates a code of ethical behavior?

4) You are working in a neighborhood recreation center and a thirteen-year-old girl has confided in you that she is in her second month of pregnancy as a result of her relationship with a nineteen-year-old man who also is living with a friend of her mother's. She tells you in confidence that she is planning to wear clothes that will not reveal her pregnancy until much later. Other than her girlfriend, no one else knows, and she feels that she cannot tell her mother. In order to avoid getting her mother's friend upset she plans to have sex with another teenager in the neighborhood and blame him for her pregnancy. You know that she trusts you and that she is not ready to voluntarily connect with a counselor in another agency.

Among your many concerns is the likely possibility of inadequate prenatal care.

> Should the staff person reveal this situation to the girl's mother?
> How might the staff person help the girl to do so?
> How should the staff person handle the issue of confidentiality, especially in the event that she does attempt to have sex with another teen?
> What should the staff person do in regards to the legal liability of the 19-year-old?

5) You are working in an aftercare mental rehabilitation program with clients who are trying to improve their social relationships through group experiences and discussions. In the course of your work you become aware that one of the female participants is making overtures that make you uncomfortable. Her friendliness begins to take on a quality of flirtation. She has attempted to put her hand on your knee.

> What steps can you take to discourage her overtures—while being sensitive to her past experiences of rejection?
> If she persists, what steps do you need to consider?

6) You are working in an agency that provides support for persons with AIDS. Recently one of your clients, who is still in fairly good health, tells you that he is having sex with women and purposefully not telling them of his condition. Nor does he want to take protective measures. What should you do?

7) You observe that one of your colleagues, with whom you are friendly, is faking her records. She is recording interviews that have not occurred and taking time off from work to go shopping. You have expressed to her your concern with this unethical behavior. But you see that she is persisting. You don't like the idea that you would be the one to get her in trouble, but you are concerned that clients are not being served and that the agency may be greatly harmed by her actions. What should you do?

8) You work for an agency that provides day services for mentally challenged adults. The agency's main purpose is to teach these adults living skills, such as cooking and housekeeping. But you learn soon after you arrive that most of their time is spent in watching TV cartoons. Instead of teaching them cooking, the counselor takes them to a restaurant. You question the ethics and practices of the agency. What might you consider doing?

Chapter Notes

[1]Thomas, R.R. (1990). "From Affirmative Action To Affirming Diversity." *Harvard Business Review*. W, 2, p. 109.

[2]Thomas, p. 109.

[3]Thomas, R.R. (1991). *Beyond Race and Gender: Unleashing the Power of Your Total Workforce By Managing Diversity*. New York: AMACOM, pp. 10-15.

[4]Thomas, pp. 15, 167.

[5]Thomas, "From Affirmative Action to Affirming Diversity." pp. 107-117. Solomon, C.M. (1990). "Careers Under Glass." *Personal Journal*, 4, pp. 96-105. Copland, L. (1988, May). "Learning to Manage a Multicultural Work Force." *Training*, pp. 1-5. Geber, B. (1990, July). "Managing Diversity." *Training*, pp. 23-30.

[6]Popple, P.R. & Leighninger, L. (1993). *Social Work, Social Welfare & American Society*. Boston: Allyn and Bacon, pp. 73-78. - pp. 148-50.

[7]Barker, R.L. (1995). "NASW Code of Ethics." *Dictionary of Social Work*. Washington, D.C.: NASW Press, pp. 431-437.

[8]Loyd, K.L. (1991). *Sexual Harassment: How to Keep Your Company Out of Court*. New York: Panel Publishers, Inc. p. 7.

[9]Alexander Hamilton Institute, Inc. (1991). *What Every Manager Must Know to Prevent Sexual Harassment*. Maywood, N.J. pp. 10-11.

[10]Alexander Hamilton Institute, Inc. p. 20.

[11]9 to 5 Brochure, 1990.

[12]NASW Standards for Social Work Personnel Practices, 1992. Thomas, R.R. (1990). "From Affirmative Action To Affirming Diversity." *Harvard Business Review*. w, 2, p. 109.

CHAPTER 11

Organizational Structures and Processes

All organizations—whether professional agencies or grass roots and whether large or small—require structures and processes to get their work accomplished.

FUNCTIONS RELATED TO STRUCTURES

The purpose of structure is to allow the organization to divide its work into various units and then provide ways to integrate this work. No one structural format is appropriate for all organizations because structure should fit unique needs and should emerge out of an organization's goals and objectives.

In his classic analysis of major corporations, Alfred Chandler showed how the form of the organization follows its function.[1] This same concept can be applied to human service organizations. For example, if the organization provides services over a large geographic area, it will likely decentralize its delivery of services. If agency services need to be coordinated with other integrating programs, then staff teams could be established. Form should always follow function.

Structure also can be affected by the composition of the staff. In some instances, the structure emerges out of special strengths or weaknesses that staff possess. For example, a manager with strong interpersonal skills may be weak in handling administrative details. Elaborate structures are

153

sometimes built based on special qualities of the staff, and when certain staff leave, restructuring may be necessary. Hence, structure takes into consideration both the organizational tasks and the attributes of staff available to fulfill them.[2]

Structuring Staffing Patterns

An organization can have a variety of staffing patterns on which to develop a structural framework. Jobs can be organized by: 1) **specialization**, where all similar jobs are placed in one department (e.g., financial activities), (2) **service programs**, with all positions clustering around a particular service (e.g., counseling), or (3) **site location**, with different positions being coordinated at the site (e.g., outreach offices).[3] These different formats can be combined depending on what an organization must accomplish. Sometimes only through a process of trial and error will the proper structure emerge, and even then there may be tradeoffs since no structure is likely to work optimally under all conditions.

Ex - Change in CHS from State Supervisors of programs to sites

Coordinating the Work of the Organization

Every organization develops one or more structures to help carry out its functions. Usually one structure is predominant, but it is possible that several coexist. Moreover, a structure suitable at one time may be altered to meet a special situation at another. Effective managers continually assess their organization's structural emphasis to maximize its use of scarce resources and the productivity of staff.

The _bureaucratic_ or _hierarchical format_ is commonly used in large human service organizations. Hierarchy is an organizational structure that is shaped like a pyramid to reflect different levels of authority. A director is at the top of the pyramid, a level of managers below that position, and staff below that. Staff have specialized jobs, are accountable to a higher authority, and are promoted on the basis of competence.

Despite the negative connotation attributed to the term "bureaucracy," the bureaucratic format persists because it has a number of advantages. For one thing it facilitates and coordinates the work of many people. For another, it provides continuity and can process large groups of people efficiently. In some organizations, standardizing procedures through a bureaucratic format helps reduce friction and ensures predictability of response.[4] Then, too, a bureaucratic structure allows for staff to develop expertise in special areas.

Although bureaucracies can be impersonal and limit decision making and autonomy of staff there are ways that staff can experience fulfillment from their jobs. An effective staff person working in a bureaucracy can make discretionary decisions if he/she is aware of which behaviors in the organization are prescribed, which are permitted, and which are proscribed or prohibited.[5] Further, a successful organizational member will not expect that her actions will be constantly rewarded but instead develops an internal sense of pride based on the knowledge that the job is well done.

An effective staff member recognizes that a bureaucratic organization operates at both a formal and informal level. At the formal level decisions are conveyed through the hierarchy, and people operate under a division of labor. At the informal level ideas are transmitted by word of mouth and people may have degrees of power unrelated to their formal roles—as for example, secretaries can control access to administrative decision makers. Finally, an effective staff member in a bureaucracy will continually ask how can she add value to the work of the organization and how to become indispensable by developing a skill or competence that the organization needs.[6]

The *market format* allows staff to move in and out of assignments based on changing needs. High turnover is normal. A particular assignment or compensation can attract staff. Considerable negotiating and bargaining occurs between the organization and employees. In human service organizations, an example of this approach would be staff brought on to fulfill the requirements of a two-year proposal, with no commitment for permanent employment. Staff function with a high degree of independence and autonomy, as if they were individual entrepreneurs invested in their own business.

The *matrix* or *cross-functional format* provides an opportunity within a hierarchical structure for staff from different units to work as a team on a goal-oriented project on an ad hoc basis.[7] Once the project is complete, participants return to their functional units. Staff, for example, from the departments of counseling, fiscal management, public information, research, and child care might convene to carry out new ways of reaching potential clients.

The advantage of this approach is that it fosters coordination and stimulates staff to focus on problems from different perspectives. Of course, the fact that members of the team continue to have ongoing responsibilities within their own units and have dual lines of accountability can cause problems. By anticipating problems and yet making the expectations of a temporary or focus assignment clear, the matrix approach can be an effective way to deal with issues that cut across functional areas of responsibility.[8] Increasingly, organizations are relying on the matrix or cross-functional approach to heighten commitment, encourage collaboration, and engender creative thinking.[9]

Structural emphasis, then, may need to be modified with changing circumstances. During times of fiscal contractions or periods of innovation, the market approach may be suitable. If implementing routine tasks is needed, then a hierarchical emphasis makes sense. On the other hand, certain structures can interfere with an organization's goals. For instance, a task force designed under the matrix plan for a particular purpose may strive to exist beyond its original intent because staff enjoy working together, and what was once an asset to the organization becomes an impediment to the usual flow of work and should be abandoned. Obviously, the issue of structure should periodically be revisited to ensure that organizational needs are being met.

MAKING MEETINGS MATTER

The processing of ideas, information, and decisions frequently takes place in organizational meetings. Poorly planned and poorly managed meetings waste staff time and can cost the organization a great deal of money. It is generally not a good idea to hold a meeting when one or more of the following situations exists:

- When you can communicate better by telephone or memo;
- When the issue is so confidential that it cannot be shared with others, e.g., hiring, firing, or negotiating salaries;
- When there is inadequate data or poor preparation; or
- When there is no compelling reason to hold a regularly scheduled meeting.

On the other hand, holding a meeting is a good idea when:

- You want to reinforce the organization's essential values (e.g., emphasizing cooperative efforts) or relate staff efforts to the organization's mission, goals, or objectives;
- You are dealing with a complex problem involving several options, and you consider staff interaction essential to solve the problem or make a decision;
- You need the expertise or advice of selected individuals;
- You need to share concerns or clarify an organizational issue;

- You want to share with or obtain information from group members about a current project or event, and you want to improve the accuracy of information so that everyone receives the same data in the same way;
- You want to coordinate activities of various units;
- You want to provide training or use the session for questions and answers;
- You want to publicly recognize an achievement, build morale, or encourage teamwork; or
- You expect resistance from some individuals and think their participation in a group process will ameliorate their concerns.

To enhance the effectiveness of the meetings, make sure you have considered these questions:

- What do you want to accomplish by the end of the meeting?
- Based on your expectations, who should attend and what kind of involvement do you want from them?
- What will be on the agenda? How much time should be allowed for each item?
- What specific tasks, deadlines, and responsibilities will you communicate?
- Who will be responsible for decisions?
- Whom should you meet with before the meeting?
- What materials must be prepared in advance of the meeting?[10]

USING MEETING TIME PRODUCTIVELY

You cannot control the outcome of a meeting without being perceived as manipulative, but you can guide possible outcomes and plan accordingly. Have a definite reason for every meeting. Think, "reason" first, then "meeting." By doing this, you can avoid the malady of "meeting-itis"—the tendency to have regularly scheduled meetings whether they are necessary or not. By letting the participants know up front what you are hoping to achieve by the end of the meeting, you will be able to more easily facilitate the discussion.

You should also plan the meeting in detail. Think in advance about who, what, when, why, where, and how. Send out in advance any pertinent reading material, such as minutes of previous meetings or special reports. Print out the agenda so everyone knows what will be discussed. Set a specific ending time and violate it only under extraordinary circumstances. Normally meetings should last no longer than one to two hours. If a meeting is extended beyond that, the group runs the risk of cutting into others' schedules. As a result, staff who must leave before the meeting ends may feel that their departure prevents them from participating in significant decisions. Set a time limit for each topic on the agenda and stick to it. Under exceptional circumstances, the group could agree to extend the time period of one item by subtracting time from another.

In some agencies, the need for continuous and current information is essential for the smooth implementation of treatment plans. In a health-care facility, for example, it may be necessary for personnel from different floors to meet briefly each day to confer about their patients. The meetings are purposefully kept short so that staff can return to their workstations. Replacing prolonged, unstructured meetings with shorter ones with focused agendas leads to improved productivity and higher morale.

It is better to delay a proposed agenda topic until you have the appropriate staff to deal with the issue. If, in a children's treatment center, for example, a meeting is called to handle discipline problems among the children, and the group inadvertently excludes the recreation counselor and the night supervisor, not all of the appropriate staff are present to address these concerns.

Functions of Meetings

It is critical that both the chairperson and the group understand the central function of a group session. Among the functions are the following:

Coordinating: Gather several participants to work on the same issue and develop ways to complement their efforts.

Distributing Work: Clarify and distribute assignments to group members.

Team Building: Establish an esprit de corps and mutual support among participants. Emphasize working cooperatively.

Reporting Information: Provide the necessary background that later may become the basis for decision making. Reports can include facts and other findings gathered in recent studies.

Studying a Problem: Undertake precise problem analyses.

Making Decisions:	Make a decision or recommendation from among alternatives. Group members may or may not be the same as those who study the problem.
Ratifying Decisions:	Propose a recommendation to a decision-making body.
Monitoring:	Review progress toward resolving the problem.

A group can be established to undertake only one of these primary functions, but most carry out more than one, although not necessarily at the same time. That is, a group may study a problem, then gather facts, then choose recommendations, then act on a decision, and finally monitor results. Moreover, identifying, analyzing, and solving problems can take several weeks or even months. In the meeting itself, it is important that the group always be aware of its primary function(s), for by doing so, discussions will be kept on track and irrelevant or peripheral issues can be dealt with in an objective manner. Be mindful that some participants may have "hidden agendas." Make certain that individual needs do not dominate the discussion. Private discussions may be necessary to deal with those whose special needs interfere with the group process.

FORMING A CONSENSUS

A group arrives at a consensus after all members have had an opportunity to voice their opinions. A consensus is a solution that everyone can live with—one that does not violate any strong convictions or needs. The process of arriving at a consensus is a free and open exchange of ideas that continues until the group reaches a conclusion based upon criteria, agreed-upon in advance, that will guide the decision.

This process ensures that each individual's concerns are heard and understood and that the group will make a sincere attempt to take everyone's ideas into consideration while searching for a solution. The final resolution may not reflect the exact wishes of every member, but since it does not violate the concerns of any one participant, it can be agreed upon by all.[11] In fact, some members may even "agree to disagree" and are willing to cooperate because their differences are not tremendously deep, and they are committed to the spirit of working together.

Decision making by consensus works best when members of a group trust each other. In a trusting climate, disagreements are a natural and acceptable means of fostering opinions and ideas rather than a reflection of inter-personal hostility or rivalry.

The need to arrive at a consensus thus encourages group members to listen to each other and try to understand viewpoints that may differ from their own. It also encourages people who disagree to continue hammering out their differences. A consensus discourages an "I win/you lose" mentality and promotes a climate that allows everyone to come out ahead.

Conformity Through "Groupthink"

Sometimes the quest for consensus goes too far. Some members of a group feel they must show loyalty by agreeing with the group's position even though they inwardly have serious concerns with the direction of the meeting. This "groupthink" occurs when members want to avoid what they fear will be harsh judgments by their peers. Consequently, they keep criticism of the position to themselves. "Groupthinkers" choose acceptance over their wish to express fundamental differences. "Groupthink" is most likely to occur in strongly cohesive groups where criticism is not the norm. Members suppress their differences of opinion and may minimize, even to themselves, their own misgivings. As a result, the group develops the illusion of unanimity.[12]

One danger of "groupthink" is when members are pressured to give in, and the resulting diluted decision greatly weakens what might otherwise have been a strong stand, position, or program. Another danger is that unvoiced criticisms may later result in some form of sabotage because of their deep-rooted reservations. A third danger is that the desire for conformity may squelch a valid criticism that could prevent a poor decision. Ways to prevent "groupthink" include:

- Propose alternative choices presented to the group;
- Establish the ground rule that ideas are to be based on their merit, not on who presents them;
- Recognize there are many appropriate paths that can lead to desired results;
- Encourage members to play "devil's advocates" to ensure positions are defensible from a variety of angles;
- Talk with people who are not part of the deliberations, including knowledgeable people outside the organization who can suggest other options and ideas;
- Think through scenarios about how different people would react to the ideas under discussion;
- Encourage "groupthink" members to express reservations if they have them.[13]

INVOLVING PEOPLE IN DECISION MAKING

An ancient Chinese proverb states, "Tell me, I forget; show me, I remember; involve me, I understand." Involving people, whether community residents or professional staff, in organizational problems or decisions that affect them and their performance not only enhances their understanding but also engages them so they become invested in a positive outcome.

When people are involved and have a stake in their work, they feel enthusiastic about and committed to it. Effective leaders recognize that when staff have a say in decisions that affect the work environment in general and their jobs in particular, the result is greater job involvement and satisfaction.[14] In short, when staff have been part of the problem-solving process, the implementation process will flow quite naturally. Shared decisions work because of authentic collaboration.[15]

For example, one organization, concerned that clients were not showing up for scheduled appointments, formed a task force of outreach staff to explore possible solutions. After a number of discussions, the staff concluded that the agency should borrow a vehicle to transport clients three mornings a week from a nearby agency that needed its minivan only in the afternoons. Staff also agreed to be available on a rotating basis two nights each week to see clients who found it difficult to make day appointments.

Genuine people involvement does exact a price from both management and employees. Supervisors may feel that traditional prerogatives are being undermined and that staff involvement dilutes their authority. Effective managers accept the tradeoff of diminished control for increased staff involvement because employee ideas are needed to improve the quality, service productivity, and efficiency of the organization.[16] Another concern is that staff may have to invest considerable time in meetings that take them away from other assignments. In the long run, time invested in the process of work improvement will likely increase their ownership in the organization's work and a commitment to be more productively engaged in their jobs.[17]

Task Forces

Sometimes special staff groups can be commissioned to review particular policies or conduct in-depth analyses with recommendations on specific issues. The advantage of an ad hoc task force (sometimes known as an "action team") is that it has a clear mandate to handle a particular problem and goes out of business once it is solved. Usually members are asked to participate voluntarily, based on their experience and expertise.[18] They may establish their own timetable and set their own pace. The supervisor can be team leader or, preferably, the role may be assigned to different members of the staff for different issues.

If task force members are drawn from different units of the organization, then problem analysis has the advantage of different perspectives. Moreover, there is the possibility of developing a network as task force members communicate back to their home base units.

Five caveats should be kept in mind to keep task forces from becoming counterproductive. First, the staff who develop an idea may not necessarily implement it. The group formed to carry out the plan may need to be reconstituted with top management and participants from other units.

Second, there is always the possibility that staff will identify so much with their task force that they become elitist and exclusionary in their outlook. Others in the organization may become resentful because they perceive this task force as a clique. Members of the group must understand that they have a responsibility to share their experiences with others. Time limits and rotation to different groups help diminish cliques.

Third, in establishing the task force, it is important to clarify roles, responsibilities, and ground rules under which it will function. Otherwise the group will be unclear about its function and decision-making boundaries. Is it only advisory? Is it responsible for carrying out its own recommendations? Is it designed to initiate ideas or react passively to ideas being generated by management? Can its decisions be overridden and, if so, by whom? It is also important to clarify the role of the "task master." Is the chairperson responsible for following through, or is his or her role limited to facilitating the group discussion process?

Fourth, staff involvement on task forces can be superficial when staff appear to have an input into the organization's decision-making process but management ultimately ignores or belittles their ideas. If staff are limited to making trivial decisions, they will consider their participation to be pseudo-involvement.[19] People sense when their ideas are genuinely desired and when the organization is resorting to gimmickry.

Fifth, we need to distinguish between groups that are formed in an organization to furthering team spirit and those designed to accomplish a task. If your purpose is to address the establishment of cliques or divisions that occur that invite a "we-they" attitude then you would organize people into groups where these concerns can be discussed.

If, however, the intent is to accomplish tasks, then organizing people in teams for their own sake is not sufficient. Each member of the team or task group must feel a sense of responsibility and share a common sense of being accountable for results. The task group has a sense of urgency, a high degree of autonomy and agreed upon performance goals. While the charge to the task group could come from top management, the group has plenty of room for setting its own objectives and determining its own approach and timing.[20] An example would be a team brought together to mount a foster care recruitment campaign. Each member of this team would feel a sense of responsibility and a commitment to each other to get the job done.

Finally, unless the various parts of the organization coalesce on certain issues, serious problems could result from efforts to engage staff. If some members, for example, are working to change the agency's reward system, others the way tasks are organized, and still others certain personnel practices, they are likely to be out of sync with each other. Changes proposed by one group may have repercussions in other parts of the organization that must be considered. Having a number of staff committees making recommendations independent of each other can produce chaos and organizational turmoil.

Total Quality Management (TQM)

Total Quality Management has become quite popular in industry as companies discover that involving their staff in decision making can lead to more productive enterprises. While leaders in human service agencies may have been fostering staff involvement for many years, there are some interesting techniques now being developed in industry that non-profit organizations could benefit from. Of special importance to the human services field are those efforts designed to help agencies take corrective action that will enhance client satisfaction.[21] Some of the principles and processes being developed include the following:[22]

1) The organization promotes a working environment of teamwork, trust, and a quest for continuous improvement.

2) Employees strive to make the organization the best at what it does. Staff focus on operational problems, want to improve the way the organization performs its functions, and are encouraged to correct errors.

3) Typically staff are brought together for identifying common concerns. If the organization is small enough this would include the entire staff; if staff cannot be gathered around a table, then

segments of staff would be convened to identify problems and issues that prevent the organization from being effective and efficient.

4) Some organizations elect to identify several issues on which to apply TQM at the same time; more often, only one or two are identified and the organization expands into other areas as it experiences success with the initial few issues it has selected.

5) The team that is chosen to work on the problem is composed of both those who have primary responsibility as well as those who ordinarily are not involved with the issue. This cross-functional team approach is based on the assumption that those outside the function can bring a fresh perspective and may be in a better position to suggest ways to overcome barriers.

6) The team goes through a process of identifying the nature of the problem (with base line data) and the impediments to its resolution. It then proposes solutions, sees that implementation steps are carried out, and monitors results. The team can then move onto another issue or be discontinued. Meanwhile, another team may be created so that the organization is continually experiencing the TQM process.

Suppose, for example, that the staff of an agency is concerned that their phone system is not operating properly. Phones are not answered properly, messages are lost, and callers experience delays. A TQM team consisting of the office manager, a manager of one of the departments, the receptionist, a support staff member, and the counselors would determine the specific issues that need to be addressed. Then they might conduct a survey of staff and clients before developing possible solutions. If proposed remedies cost money, they might check with administrative staff about the feasibility of their ideas so they would know under what constraints they must operate.

The key, then, to TQM is the involvement of staff at *all* levels of the organization. It is a commitment that all staff—not just managers—have the responsibility to make the organization as productive as possible.

SUMMARY

One of the most important ingredients to successful organizations is the capacity to foster positive and constructive staff interactions. In part this will occur as a result of the way an organization is structured, in part in the way staff interact in meetings, and in part the way staff are engaged in meaningful projects through task forces. In their interactions, staff need not always agree; in fact, striving continuously to arrive at a consensus may create blind spots that could eventually have negative consequences. TQM is the latest (but probably not the last) tool being developed by organizations to promote interactions and involvement.

QUESTIONS FOR DISCUSSION

1) What organizational format is used by your agency (bureaucratic, market, or matrix)? What do you see as the advantages or disadvantages of your structure?

2) How are meetings conducted in your agency?

3) What two positive or negative experiences have you had in working with staff teams, committees, or other groups?

Chapter Notes

[1]Chandler, A. (1966). *Strategy and Structure.* Garden City, NY: Doubleday.

[2]Cohen, S. (1988). *The Effective Public Manager: Achieving Success in Government.* San Francisco, CA: Jossey Bass, p. 54.

[3]Crow, R.T. & Odewahn, C.A. (1987). *Management for the Human Services.* Englewood Cliffs, NJ: Prentice-Hall, p. 10.

[4]Crow & Odewahn, pp. 26.8. Beer, et al., 1984, pp. 178-9.

[5]Macht, M. & Ashford, J. (1991). *Introduction to Social Work and Social Welfare,* New York: Macmillian Publishers, pp. 228-229.

[6]Macht, & Ashford, p. 229.

[7]Sarri, R. C. (1995) "Administration in Social Welfare." *Encyclopedia of Social Work* (19th ed. Vol. 3, pp. 637-639). Silver Spring, MD:, National Association of Social Workers.

[8]Crow & Odewahn, pp. 28-9.

[9]Peters, T.J. & Waterman, R.H. (1982). *In Search of Excellence: Lessons from America's Best Run Companies.* New York: Harper & Row, pp. 270-77.

[10]Doyle, M. & Straus, D. (1976). *How to Make Meetings Work.* New York: Berkley Publishing Group, p. 84.

[11]Schein, E.H. (1970). *Organizational Psychology*. New York: Prentice Hall.

[12]Janis, I.L. (1971, November). "Groupthink." *Psychology Today*, pp. 43-46, 74-76.

[13]Brody, R. (1982). *Problem Solving: Concepts and Methods for Community Organization*. New York: Human Sciences Press, Inc., p. 68-69.

[14]Schuler, R.S. (1987). *Personnel And Human Resource Management* (3rd ed.). St. Paul, MN: West Publishing Co., p. 437.

[15]Doyle & Straus (1976). p. 243.

[16]Stayer, R. (1990). "How I Learned to let my Workers Lead." Harvard Business Review, 6, pp. 66-83.

[17]*Commitment Plus* (1988). "What is Culture." pp. 1-4.

[18]Campbell, R.B. (1982, May). "The Process." Public Address at Higbee's Annual Meeting, Cleveland, OH.

[19]Lawler, E.E. (1986). *High Involvement Management*. San Francisco CA: Jossey Bass, pp. 53-59.

[20]Katzenbach, J.R. & Smith, D.K. (1993). *The Wisdom of Teams: Creating the High-Performance Organization*. New York: Harper Collins Publishers.

[21]Moore, S.T. & Kelly, M.J. (1996, January). "Quality Now: Moving Human Services Organizations Toward a Consumer Orientation to Service Quality." *Social Work*, V 41, pp. 33-40.

[22]TRW. (1993). Workshop Notes. (unpublished).

CHAPTER 12

Skills in Running Meetings

Managing the flow of ideas in meetings is an art that professionals can learn. In this chapter we provide some specific techniques you can use to evoke good discussion and come to group resolution.

QUESTIONS THAT FACILITATE DISCUSSION

If participants feel their ideas and thinking will contribute to common objectives, they are more likely to address the problem at hand and participate in its solution. One of the most useful techniques to enrich discussions is to elicit responses through targeted questions. Although the group facilitator is primarily responsible for directing the flow of ideas through questions, any member of a group can ask questions. The following kinds of questions can stimulate discussion:

If you want to:	Then ask:
Focus the group on an issue	What information do we need to explore the problem?
Redirect the group's thinking	Are there other ways we can go about this?
Stimulate the group and bolster their arguments	What makes you think this will work?

Inject your own ideas	What do you think would happen if we did this...?
Encourage alternative solutions	What other options should we consider?
Focus on one idea	Which approach do you think is best?
Clarify an issue	Could you explain your position further?
Make an abstract idea more understandable	Would you walk us through this process?
Shift from the details to the essence of an idea	Before we get into the details, shouldn't we consider our main objective?
Stimulate new ideas	Are there new approaches we can consider?
Encourage participation	What does each of you think about this idea?
Consider next steps	Where do we go from here?
Come to closure	Have we agreed upon the following..?
Assist the group in assessing itself	How can we improve our discussion process?

These questions do not exhaust all the possibilities. They illustrate that, through the questioning process, you can guide the discussion without being perceived as manipulative. One of the main attributes of a good discussion leader is the ability to continuously pose questions that help the group with its decision-making process.

FACILITATING THE GROUP PROCESS

Situation #1: You have been asked to conduct a group process that can assist the ongoing chairperson and community organization members to develop creative ideas that can help the group move forward on an issue that concerns them.

Situation #2: You have been asked by your agency director to conduct a staff meeting to come up with recommendations on an issue that has been stymieing the agency.

Both these situations require you to be in the role of facilitator, a neutral person who can help the group think creatively and arrive at an agreed upon course of action. Here are specific steps to keep in mind:

Preparing for the Session

Determine who is the owner of the issue to be discussed. This initiator (or client) is the person who presents the problem to you, the one who will want to ensure follow-up, the one who has an itch to want to get something done (e.g., the chairperson of the organization or the director of the agency). Suggest to this person that the group size be kept small enough so that everyone will have a chance to participate (5-12) persons. Your goal is to elicit the group's best thinking while encouraging complete participation. Indicate that your approach is to creatively explore a wide variety of ideas and then focus on a manageable and feasible few for concentrated follow-up.[1]

Determine whether this is to be a one time meeting or part of a series. If the group is to meet only this one time, clarify what the product of the meeting is to be. Similarly, if this meeting is part of a longer-range project, determine what you want to have in place by the end of the series and how this first meeting fits into the overall plan. Assuming for now that you have been invited to facilitate a one time meeting, consider the following:

1) Be explicit about the purpose of the meeting. Here are some examples that illustrate the kinds of issues that can be focused on:

- To develop three doable ideas that will help us decrease "no-shows" by 25 percent.
- To identify critical steps we must take to improve communication.
- To attract more publicity for our agency targeted to our funders.
- To heighten staff commitment to their work.
- To identify new sources of funding.
- To resolve open or smoldering conflicts in the organization.
- To determine the least damaging cost cutting procedures.
- To consider ways of meaningfully involving our trustees.
- To consider how we must change to position ourselves better for the future.
- To prepare ourselves for anticipated managed care requirements.
- To identify ways management and staff can work more effectively together.

- To figure out how we can take financial advantage of our staff expertise.

2) Be prepared to spend time reworking the purpose of the session. Can it reasonably be accomplished in the time allotted? Is this the right group of people to grapple with the issue? How does the issue relate to the overall project (if this is one of a series)? What will be indicators of success or failure of this meeting? What specific product is to be produced at the end of the meeting (sometimes called "the deliverable")? By spending time up front in this design phase, you develop a clarity that will help focus the discussion better.

3) Determine how wide open and creative the group can be. Discuss with the initiator what constraints must be considered so that the discussion does not lead the group down unacceptable paths. Sometimes the initiator will indicate that all ideas—even wild, far out ones—can be considered. At times the initiator will indicate that proposed ideas cannot exceed a certain cost factor or not be ones that could potentially offend the organization's major funders.

Setting the Stage

1) Arrange for a room in which the group can sit in a circle with you at the head. Being able to sit around a table would be desirable but not essential.

2) Provide materials for visualizing the ideas that are presented. This is extremely important because seeing ideas will keep the group focused. You can use several ways to do this:

   a) Use a blackboard if one is available. You can erase or change ideas around.
   b) Use an easel with large newsprint paper. Tape sheets to the walls so the group can scan ideas easily. During the course of the discussion you can circle ideas that are similar and cross out ones that are redundant.
   c) You can "story board" ideas. This involves obtaining 4x6 card stock, pins and a wall to which the cards can be pinned. An alternative is obtaining large "post-its" which can be taped to walls—or even using scotch tape to post the cards. The advantage of this is that you can write each idea presented in a word or short phrase and move the ideas around as needed.

3) Establish ground rules. Here are some that will facilitate the session:

   a) Initially every idea is a good one. No criticism or challenge is allowed.
   b) Anyone criticizing can be challenged.
   c) Participants can and should build upon ideas.
   d) The group can alter the major issue before it (in consultation with the initiator).
   e) Initially there is little cross discussion since the purpose is to let individual members express his/her own thoughts.
   f) Ask someone to monitor your neutrality.

4) Discuss the format for the session:

   a) State the overall purpose of the session.
   b) Indicate that planning meetings have been held with the initiator.
   c) Review the purpose of the session (see examples, above). Have this written out.
   d) Indicate what the session will not focus on.
   e) Discuss any constraints that must be considered.
   f) State that the intent is to come out with doable ideas that will be followed-up.
   g) Explain how the session is to be divided up and the projected amount of time for each segment (modify the following times, as appropriate for your situation).
      (1) Background of the issue—10 minutes. The initiator or someone else in the group that is familiar with the situation provides a list of key information items (e.g., what events precipitated the problem, what the consequence is of the problem).
      (2) Generation of ideas—40-50 minutes.
      (3) Action plan—who will do what and by when—20-30 minutes.
   h) Arrange for one of the members of the group to be the scribe and write on the board, newsprint, or cards the word or short phrase that captures the essential ideas of each member.

Stimulating Discussion

In opening up the discussion, indicate there are to be no speeches, that participants are to listen to each other carefully, that they are to suspend judgment, and that if they wish, they can build on the ideas of other participants. Accept that initially ideas may be vague, unusable, unrefined, and off the top of the head.

To stimulate thinking of the group ask such questions as: a) How can we build on this? b) Can we explore this thought further? How can we tighten

(broaden) this concept? c) How can we make this idea workable?   Use
judgment in determining whether the ideas as initially presented should be
written out or whether they could be played with further.

You will likely generate a list of ideas that will require honing down.
Determine with the group which ideas might be merged. Now ask the group
if they particularly like some ideas because they are unique or interesting.
At this point people may want to express their criticisms and even challenge
some of the ideas. The tone of the session is that the ideas do not belong to
any one participant, and therefore challenges are not directed at people but
at the ideas themselves.

Based on the discussion, suppose the original list of thirty ideas have now
been narrowed down to twenty and you determine that you would like to
narrow it further to three to five useable ideas. You are ready to prioritize.
You could do this in several ways: Give each person one vote (or two to four
votes) and by a simple show of hands count the votes for each item.   Or
provide a set of bright colored dots (available at any office supply store)
which participants can stick to the paper. The advantage of dotting is that it
allows people to walk around and make independent decisions.   The
clustering of dots is a good visual way of displaying where there is
consensus.

Be mindful that this is not a final vote. Clearly some items will have a
preponderance of interest. Circle these items and determine whether there
are any major concerns about putting them on the final list of priorities.
Invite further discussion about the feasibility of the ideas that seem
appealing. Some may be prohibitively expensive; some may run against
the culture and style of the organization; some may require staff training
that won't be available until next year. Through this discussion, you will
sort out further whether some of those items with lower votes might be
substituted for the higher rated items. (Incidentally, you will discern that
patently ridiculous ideas will be weeded out either through the voting
process or in subsequent discussion.)   Though in this phase of reviewing
feasibility the initiator (chairperson, director) is a contributor, he or she
does not dominate.

In determining feasibility further you may wish to divide the ideas into
more refined categories, such as the following:
1) feasibility of implementation (easy, medium, hard)
2) time frame (soon, intermediate, long term)
3) cost (small, medium, large)
4) resource requirements (staff, trustees, outside volunteers)
5) homework (information immediately available, easily collected,
requires long time frame)

This refinement can assist the group to consider what is immediately doable and which ideas may need to be delayed or refined further.

Developing an Action Plan

Indicate the following:

Task to be done	Responsible persons	Team leader	Time frame	Accountability

You are not done with the process until you have in place a clear action plan and timetable for implementing the ideas of the session. What needs to be clarified? What further information is needed? What are the costs of the various ideas? Who could be a potential saboteur with whom you must meet so the idea doesn't get derailed? Whatever is required to ensure the implementation should be listed. You may need several people on a committee or only one person to follow up a particular task. Be sure to indicate when they are to report back either to the team leader or someone else in the organization. A communications strategy may need to be developed as part of the accountability process so that you can identify who needs to be informed of what information and who will be the messenger.

If this is one of a series of meetings, you would need to repeat these same processes at each session in order to continually refine the group's thinking.

ENCOURAGING NEW AND DIFFERENT IDEAS

Sometimes a group is faced with a problem situation in which ideas do not flow easily; people feel they are at a dead end and they need stimulation to trigger creative thinking. Under these circumstances, several approaches using analogies, employing a checklist, and reframing the issue can be considered to promote novel ideas.

Stimulating Novelty Through Analogies

Using analogies can help a group to view a problem in a new way. By making a comparison of a problem situation with something else that is in some way like it (and in other ways unlike it), one comes to see the problem from a different perspective. Through the use of analogies, familiar situations become strange because they are temporarily distorted.[2]

Personal analogies require empathy, i.e., putting oneself in the other person's place. The question to be asked is, "How would I react if I encountered a problem experienced by others?" By identifying oneself with a hypothetical person in a given situation, one is in a better position to understand how that person would feel and act. Consider the following examples: You want to convince resistive legislators to increase grants to ADC recipients. If you were in their shoes, what tactics and appeals would be most convincing? Among your answers might be receiving appeals from welfare constituents, from business persons whose business might be affected, and from concerned middle-class constituents.

Direct analogies involve the comparison of a particular situation with similar, but not exactly the same, situations. Frequently, analogous ideas occur to people spontaneously, but sometimes a group may wish to promote analogous thinking by asking members to consider comparable situations in other settings.

If, for example, a group is considering how it could get more people involved in working on a community problem, members would be asked to think of a situation similar in nature. Someone might suggest looking at insects. Then members would be asked, "What insects do we see working together?" There might be a discussion on how bees or ants work cooperatively with some further contemplation on what makes this possible, followed by an exploration of how this could be accomplished with people.

Or if a community organization is concerned with disharmony between two ethnic groups, the organization would be asked to consider what other situation is comparable from which solutions might be drawn. One of several responses could be to compare the situation with a sports game (e.g., football or basketball in which opposing sides live within clearly defined rules). Are there other ideas that can be drawn upon from the sports world that are applicable? Or can analogous examples be drawn from cooking, machine functioning, gardening the seasons? These analogies may seem farfetched and may not in themselves be a solution, but they are mind stretching and offer new perspectives. Thus, group members stray momentarily from the problem, develop one or more analogies that serve to expand their thinking, and then seek to make a connection—to find relevance between the analogy and the problem with which they are grappling.

Using a Checklist to Stimulate Novelty

Another method designed to generate ideas when the group is running out of ideas is to make a checklist. For example, a group has developed some preliminary ideas but is still dissatisfied. So, to expand the groups's thinking, the following list of questions (with verbs designed to trigger thinking) could serve as a stimulus to more and different ideas.

1) Can the idea be *copied*?
   What else is *like* this?
   Are other communities *doing* this?
   Has something like this been *done* before?

2) How can the idea be *modified*?
   Should a new twist be *tried*?
   Should the format be *changed*?

3) Can the idea be *expanded*?
   What can be *added*?
   What can be *done* more frequently?
   Can we *multiply* it?

4) Can this idea be *reduced*?
   Can elements be *subtracted, condensed, made shorter, streamlined*, or *split up*?

5) What could be *substituted* for the idea?
   Who else could *pursue* it?
   In what other place could it be *conducted*?
   What other approaches could be *considered*?

6) Can the idea be *rearranged*?
   Can components be *interchanged*?
   Can the sequence be *altered*?
   Can the pace be *modified*?

7) Can the idea be *reversed*?
   Can roles be *reversed*?
   Can negative aspects *turned* to positive ones?

8) Can ideas be *combined*?
   Can units be *combined*?
   Can purposes be *united*?

The following examples illustrate how the italicized verbs above trigger creative approaches:

Problem: An organization wants to provide a group home for mentally retarded offenders in a middle income, potentially highly resistant community.

Question: How can people in the community become involved in the project so as to soften their resistance?

Trigger   Magnify. What are the ways to involve a variety of
Verb: new people in the issue?

Potential: 1) Involve high school students in an essay contest.
Solutions: 2) Conduct a community carnival sponsored by the Veterans
             of Foreign Wars, Teamster's Union, and the local Chamber of
             Commerce.
             3) Involve grandparents in giving presentations to local
             groups about the mentally retarded offenders.
             4) Involve PTA's in a community bake sale.

Reframing the Issue to Stimulate Novelty

Previously we described a willingness to break out of the usual way of doing
things as one of the important ingredients conducive to creativity.   The
technique of reframing the issue is useful in stimulating new ways of
dealing with a problem situation.   By going through the exercise of
reframing the question, the group inevitably must be prepared to challenge
the underlying premise of the current question or point of view under
consideration. Some examples of the reframing process are listed below:

Original Question: How can we recruit more foster parents for the long
                          waiting list of foster children?
Potential Answers: Conduct an   annual   foster   parent recruitment
                          campaign.
Reframed Question: How can we reduce the number of foster children on
                          waiting lists?
Potential Answers: Work more intensively with natural parents to
                          reduce the need for foster care.

Original Question: How can we get employees to become more
                          productive?
Potential Answers: Increase pay; improve working conditions; give
                          bonuses.
Reframed Question: How can we make work more interesting?
Potential Answers: Rotate jobs; reorient jobs around group decision
                          making.

Original Question: How can we obtain more money for speedier
                          ambulances?
Potential Answers: Special charity drives; work for a tax levy for
                          ambulances.
Reframed Question: How can we prevent more accidents from occurring
                          at the railroad crossing?

Potential Answers: Pass a law requiring a safety light.

Original Question: How can we obtain more medical services for people who need them?
Potential Answers: Obtain more Medicare, Medicaid.
Reframed Question: How can we provide health services geared to the prevention of illness?
Potential Answers: Retrain medical personnel; encourage consumers to keep their own health records; offer special health education courses to people.

Original Question: How can we prevent teenagers from stealing automobiles?
Potential Answers: Provide more social activities, basketball courts, and other recreation.
Reframed Question: How can we prevent automobiles from being stolen?
Potential Answers: Educate people to remove their distributor caps at night.

As can be seen from the above examples, the reframed question changes the fundamental premise. It requires looking at the issue in a new light, a different way of perceiving the problem. The result: a new set of solutions to be considered.

These different approaches to stimulating creative ideas can, of course, be combined by the group. For example, when brainstorming the group could decide to promote additional ideas with analogies. Or the group could agree to reframe the issue to provoke a different list of ideas. What makes creativity possible is not the rigid adherence to any one technique but the attitude of evoking heretofore unexplored ideas.

Cautions

Two cautions should be mentioned. First, organizations in search of ways to solve intractable human problems should not overvalue creative approaches, as helpful as they may be. Organization members should not expect tremendous breakthroughs from one or two sessions using analogies. For such difficult problems as teenage pregnancy, inner city unemployment, and inadequate housing tremendous odds work against significant resolution. Even efforts to deal with less demanding problems require considerable trial and error. Hard work and a willingness to persevere after hitting dead ends will need to accompany creative thinking.

Second, although initially innovative ideas are stimulated by holding back critical judgment, eventually the ideas must be subject to critical review to be certain that they are in fact feasible and that they do not produce too great negative side effects.

USING PARLIAMENTARY PROCEDURE

Parliamentary procedure is based on the democratic principle of majority rule, which requires that the minority abide by the will of the majority. In turn, the acceptance of majority rule by the minority is based on the willingness of the majority to permit the minority to express its views before action is taken. Parliamentary procedure also assures that deliberations will proceed in an orderly fashion so that discussion can be crystallized into group action. Decisions must be made in the face of conflicting interests among members. For parliamentary procedure to work effectively, there must be a basic belief in the organization, despite major differences. Thus, parliamentary procedure provides the rules under which group discussion and group action can occur.

This section on parliamentary procedure is a digested version of one developed by O. Garfield Jones entitled *Parliamentary Procedure at a Glance.*[3] It is based on the assumption that, for most organizational meetings, exhaustive knowledge of parliamentary procedure is not necessary but that an understanding of basic concepts can facilitate group discussions and action. Those interested in more extensive examination of parliamentary procedure should consult the basic, *Robert's Rule of Order.*[4]

For most organizations involved in making decisions about service and community problems, parliamentary procedure is not a preferred method because it is much too formal and intensifies adversarial, win/lose relationships. It tends to solidify opposing forces, to lower the losing faction's commitment to the decision (unless those in minority have very strong investment in the organization), and to set in motion future competition over other issues. It also discourages exploration of innovative ideas in a free and open manner because people tend to take sides early in the discussion.[5] For organizations that require a formal way of conducting business or for large assemblies, the following pages should cover the salient points about parliamentary procedure.

Clarification of the Procedure of Motions

The main motion is the principle resolution that the organization is discussing. Because having more than one primary idea before the assembly at any one time would cause confusion, the main motion has the lowest rank or precedence. It can be moved only when there is nothing else before the group.

The most commonly made motions are ranked in order or precedence. Note that the main motion and the motion to repeal are ranked lowest. They yield to all the motions above them.

When a main motion is before the assembly, any motions above it may be moved. For example, motions may be made to amend the main motion, postpone consideration, close debate, rise for information, or to adjourn. These motions also take precedence over the main motion because they either apply to it, or, as in the case of the motion to adjourn, are of such urgency to the assembly that they must be voted on immediately regardless of what else is before the group.

It is possible, of course, to have many motions before the assembly at any one time, provided they are offered in the correct sequence. For example, if a main motion has been moved, then an amendment can be made to that motion. Also, a motion to postpone to a certain time, a motion to close debate, a motion to table, and, finally, a motion to adjourn can all be made. While technically this could happen, the chairperson and the majority may be concerned that this is a result of manipulation by the opposition, and the chairperson may choose to ignore some of the motions until other motions before the assembly are voted upon. Of course, if members are dissatisfied with the chairperson's decision, they can appeal it.

Classification of Motions

Motions can be classified as follows:

1) **Privileged motions** are of such importance to the assembly that they must be acted upon immediately. They are undebatable because of their high rank. The reason the motion to adjourn is privileged is that in the event of an emergency it can be acted upon at once.

2) **Incidental motions** are of two kinds: either they arise out of a pending motion and must be decided before any business is taken up or they are connected with that business of the assembly that must be attended to immediately. Most incidental motions are indubitable. Points of order, parliamentary inquiry, and requests for information do not require group action but are usually decided by the chairperson.

3) **Subsidiary motions** are intended to affect the main motion by modifying it, delaying action on it, or otherwise disposing of it. They supersede the main motion and must be dealt with before the main motion.

4) **The main motion or question** is the primary idea before the group. Often an idea will be presented to the group and discussion will take place before a

motion is made. Sometimes this helps to identify and refine the main issue. But frequently this procedure results in unusually long meetings and a vague attempt at consensus. It is usually better for a motion to be made early in the discussion so that members have a specific, concrete proposal to which they can react. As was stated previously, there can only be one main motion before the group at any given time.

Discussion of Common Parliamentary Procedures

Common parliamentary procedures are discussed below:

Adjournment. When the time for the next meeting has been determined (as is usually the case in most organizations), then the motion to adjourn can be moved at any time and must be voted upon at once because it is not debatable. If, however, no time has been set for the next meeting, then it is not a privileged motion, can be moved only when there is no other business before the group, and is debatable. In this circumstance, it yields to a motion to fix the time for the next meeting.

Question of Privilege. Usually questions of privilege (not to be confused with privileged motions) are related to the rights and comforts of the group. Accordingly, they are given immediate consideration, regardless of what else is before the assembly. For example, a member may even interrupt another speaker to complain about the lack of proper ventilation or request visitors to leave because of the confidential nature of the discussion. The chairperson decides immediately whether or not the special privilege is to be granted.

Rise to a Point of Order. When a member believes the chairperson has made a mistake or a wrong decision, the member may rise to a point of order without waiting to be recognized by the chairperson. The member may even interrupt another member who has the floor. The chairperson then decides whether or not to accept the point of order.

Appeals. If any member is dissatisfied with the chairperson's decision, the member may rise and, without waiting to be recognized by the chairperson, appeal the decision to the assembly. This requires a second. The chairperson then states the reason for the decision and calls for a vote.

Out of Order. A motion is out of order when it is moved while a motion of higher precedence is pending. For example, after a motion is made to refer to committee, an amendment to the motion could not be considered. A person is out of order when speaking without being recognized by the chairperson. Remarks are out of order when they are insulting or not germane. The chairperson must explain the reason for the ruling.

Amendments. Amendments are designed to change the motion before it is finally voted upon. Sometimes amendments are intended to obstruct rather than facilitate business, or they may be well-meaning but absurd. Therefore, the chairperson may sometimes have to rule amendments out of order or help the member reformulate them.

Amendments can be made not only to change the main motion but also to fix the time of the next meeting, to refer to committee, to postpone consideration to a certain day, and to the motion to limit debate. When amendments are made to these particular motions, they must be considered and voted upon before discussion of the motion to which they refer. Although amendments have low precedence, this is only for amendments to the main motion. Amendments to the other motions listed above take precedence in relation to the motion to which they refer. Hence, an amendment to fix the time of the next meeting must take precedence over all other motions.

An amendment made to another amendment has precedence over the original amendment. The first amendment is called the primary amendment; the second, the secondary amendment. For example, a motion is made to request a stop sign for a particular street corner. An amendment could be made to replace the stop sign with a caution light, an amendment to the amendment could be to replace the caution light with a stop light. The stop light would be discussed and voted upon first, the caution light, then the stop sign. No more than two amendments are permitted; otherwise, the deliberation becomes too complicated. If the two amendments are voted down by the assembly, then other amendments can be made. A member may alert the assembly of intentions to make an amendment if the two pending amendments are defeated.

Motion to Limit Debate. To prevent discussion from going on endlessly, a motion can be made to limit each speaker's time, to limit the number of speakers, to limit the overall time of debate, or to close debate at a set time and vote. These each require a two-thirds vote.

Motion to Table. A motion to lay on the table means to temporarily put aside one motion to consider another. A motion can then be made to take from the table either at the same or next meeting.

Withdrawal of a Motion. A motion may be withdrawn unless there is an objection by any member: in that case, withdrawal requires a majority vote.

Motion to Rescind (repeal). Any member can move to rescind a motion. It requires a majority vote with previous notice or a two-thirds vote without notice. The motion to rescind reopens the whole question for discussion.

Substitute Motion. This is a motion of similar but different intent than the pending motion. Usually this involves changing an entire sentence or paragraph. If a substitute motion carries by majority vote, then the original main motion is now modified. The new substitute motion may be amended and voted upon in its entirety.

Unanimous Consent. Occasionally, suggestions are made which the chairperson determines do not require a vote by the assembly. For example, a request to close or a suggestion to make a slight correction in the wording of a motion could be accepted by the chairperson. The chairperson would say, "If there is no objection, then we will proceed with the discussion." Of course, an appeal could be made to challenge the chairperson's decision, in which case a formal vote would be put before the assembly.

"PARLIASENSUS"

The term, "parliasensus," is not in the dictionary; it is a term coined to reflect the idea that meetings often combine parliamentary procedure and consensus. Generally, group decision making is informal and characterized by consensus, although a superficial form of parliamentary procedure is also used. Among the ingredients of parliasensus are the following:

1. The chairperson encourages a free flow of ideas but, instead of remaining neutral, inserts personal opinions into the discussion.

2. Usually ideas evolve from an extended discussion. After the ideas begin to crystallize into a position, the chairperson entertains a motion.

3. Amendments are made informally, e.g., "I suggest this modification..."

4. Group members speak to each other and interrupt with points or questions without being called upon by the chairperson.

5. Sometimes votes are taken only after the group has appeared to have exhausted an idea; the chairperson senses when the group is ready for a vote.

In general, this hybrid approach works well for most organizations, particularly if the group is no larger than fifteen to twenty persons. The natural inclination is to arrive at decisions through consensus, but the semblance of parliamentary procedure gives enough structure to expedite the group's business. Formal, although limited, parliamentary procedure is thus imposed upon informal discussion to control or expedite the traffic of ideas and actions. Most meetings could be facilitated if the major idea before the group could be made explicit as early in the discussion as possible.

RECORDING GROUP DISCUSSIONS

Because ideas can easily become lost in group discussions, it is wise to record them. During the course of the meeting large flip chart paper can be used. Following the meeting, either minutes or a group record can be prepared.

Writing down ideas that occur in the course of the meeting on flip chart paper (or newsprint easel pad) enables the group to keep track of the discussion. As each page is completed, it can be separated from the pad and hung up with tape. The advantage of this technique is that the group can 1) communicate many ideas at the same time; 2) visualize all the ideas at all times; 3) make changes in the wording of ideas; 4) easily determine gaps in, and overlap of, ideas; 5) focus, if the group wishes, on one idea at a time; and 6) prevent the same idea from being stated over and over again. These ideas recorded on the flip chart can be written up and transmitted to group members so they become part of the group memory.

Many groups have someone taking minutes as a way of preserving the ideas and actions agreed upon during the meeting. Then at the next meeting the chairperson insures that the minutes accurately reflect the essence of the session by providing an opportunity for corrections. Because the action of the group sometimes can be buried in the text, it is suggested that every group action be underlined for emphasis. Another way of highlighting actions taken by the group is to distinguish discussion from action taken, as shown below:

Discussion: Juvenile court staff expressed interest in developing a formal procedure process for mentally retarded offenders.

Action: Mental retardation staff agreed to prepare, in writing, procedures by April 15. An alternative to minutes is the group record, which is used when only one or two major topics are discussed. It contains three sections:

Figure 12.1
Group Record

NAME OF GROUP:	Day Care Coalition
DATE:	May 1
CHAIRPERSON:	Dottie Lor
PRESENT:	Buce, Ander, Berg, Gray, Spoon
MEETING PURPOSE:	To consider ways to pass legislation in the state assembly on funding for day care for mentally and physically handicapped children.
PROBLEM/ISSUE:	Legislation on special needs day care is encountering considerable resistance in the Human Resources Committee of the House.
MAJOR POINTS OF DISCUSSION:	Major opposition appears to be those legislators who are pressing to keep a lid on spending for human services.
	General agreement was reached that committee members must undertake a vigorous advocacy campaign between now and June 5 when public hearings are held.
NEXT STEPS:	Group to be divided into task forces.

Assignments By Responsible Person When

(1) Undertake letter writing campaign	Roz Buce	May 20
(2) Obtain editorial support of local papers.	Alex Ander	May 25
(3) Have newspaper reporter write a human interest story.	Rose N. Berg	May 28
(4) Have a busload of people appear before hearings.	Les Gray	June 5
(5) Steering Committee to meet.	Gail Spoon	May 26

1) the issue—how the group analyzed it and alternatives considered.
2) the decision of the group.
3) the tasks to be carried out, by whom, and within what time period.

Figure 12.1 illustrates a group record format. The special advantage of this kind of recording is that it captures the essence of the meeting and pinpoints responsibilities for follow up, without requiring people to read extensive narrative.

SUMMARY

This chapter has provided a variety of ways organizations can foster a good flow of ideas leading to resolution. Asking question, facilitating a group process, encouraging new and different ideas, and making decisions using parliamentary procedure. Consider using these methods based on the group context.

QUESTIONS FOR DISCUSSION

1) What issue in your organization or community would you select for discussion? How would you arrive at a resolution: Consensus? Creative thinking? Parliamentary procedure?

2) How would you record the meeting?

Chapter Notes

[1]McNellis, J. (August, 1995). Creative Specialist Workshop at Oberlin, OH.
[2]Kiritz, N.J. (May-June, 1979). "Program Planning and Proposal Writing." *The Grantsmanship Center News*, pp. 60-61.
[3]Jones, O.G. (1949). *Parliamentary Procedure at a Glance*. New York: Appleton-Century.
[4]Robert, General H.M. (1943). *Robert's Rules of Order*. Chicago: Scott, Foresman.
[5]Glidewell, J.C. (1976). *Choice Points*. Cambridge, MA: The MIT Press, p. 77.

CHAPTER 13

Managing Time and Stress

PLANNING THE USE OF TIME

Because employees typically feel they have too much to do in too little time, working harder or longer is not an answer. Effective staff limit the amount of unproductive time and place greater emphasis on those activities that have the greatest importance in relation to mutually agreed-upon objectives. It is easy to get caught in the "activity trap" where time is filled with busy work that is not focused on the highest priorities and is not goal-directed.

The best advice is to plan your use of time. In doing so, you may experience a paradox: you may not have enough time to plan and yet you cannot get more time until you do. Certainly planning takes time, but planning saves time. In general, those who do not plan sufficiently end up devoting too much time to correcting, controlling, and monitoring staff activities. Take time to plan!

Setting Priorities

How do you determine priorities? Identify those activities you judge to have the greatest return on your investment of time. You must be quite clear and focused on what you must accomplish in order to achieve your primary objectives.

Determine your major responsibilities—those things you must do in order to competently carry out your job. These include prescribed tasks—work that is required by your own supervisor or by the organization's work flow, such as attending weekly staff meetings or completing monthly reports.

Also, determine whether someone else is depending on your activities—a client waiting for your services, a colleague waiting for your analysis to incorporate it into a report, or your boss waiting for a reply to an important question.

Setting priorities initially requires your making a random list of activities—some being more important than others. Now determine which items are most important—and which are least. To establish priorities (most important) you must have posteriorities (least important). These are activities that need not be done now as well as items that should be done by others.

Setting priorities means making an **ABCD** list, broken down as follows:

Priority	Explanation
A. Highest Priority	An activity that is both important and urgent because it provides the best payoff in accomplishing the organization's mission.
B. Medium Priority	Important, though not urgent. It is necessary to achieve a significant objective.
C. Low Priority	An activity that contributes only marginally to the achievement of an important objective.
D. Posteriority	Neither important nor urgent. It could be delayed, minimized, delegated, or even eliminated.

To refine your priorities further, assign numbers to each lettered category, e.g., A-1, A-2, A-3, B-1, B-2, etc. By designating priority categories to your list of items, you can discipline yourself to concentrate on the A and B items and minimize time spent on C and D items. If you have such items as "read a report for next week's meeting" or "straighten out files" on your C list and on your A list you have "write an introduction to a 30-page report due tomorrow," you know where you must give your time and attention.

To make time for priorities, you must give special attention to eliminating D items. These are time wasters that detract from your ability to carry out major assignments. Attending unproductive meetings called by other organizations, reading junk mail, going to unproductive conferences, or accepting assignments that could easily be delegated elsewhere are examples of time wasters. If you can answer the question, "What would happen if I did not undertake these activities?" with the reply, "Nothing of consequence," then you should not be doing them. Weed out D items.

It is possible that what was previously on a C or B list may, as time passes, now be on your A list. The thank-you letter that should have been written ten days ago now must be written. Be prepared, therefore, to re-order priorities each day. Constantly ask this question: **WHAT IS THE BEST USE OF MY TIME RIGHT NOW?**[1] By forcing yourself to ask this question, you will keep uppermost what your most important priorities are and you will discipline yourself to put aside less important (but perhaps more enjoyable) activities.

Setting a list of priorities can be useful in structuring time, but, particularly if your job is not routine, expect the unexpected to occur. Leave room for emergencies that may require immediate attention. Troubleshooting may be a standard part of the position, for you may have to deal with the responsibilities of your subordinates in addition to your own. Their concerns become yours and therefore must be added to your A list.[2] The list is a tool in increasing productivity, but it must be used flexibly.

Prepare a priority list each day and, as you complete tasks, check them off. If you do not complete the major activities scheduled for the day, determine whether the time frames you have established for them are realistic. Ideally, you should feel a sense of accomplishment in completing the priorities you set for yourself. Some managers prefer making a priority list the night before so that they start with it first thing each morning.

Restructuring Time: The 80/20 Principle

The 80/20 time rule is derived from the principle developed by Vilfredo Preto, a 19th century Italian economist who analyzed the distribution of wealth in his time (80 percent of the wealth was held by 20 percent of the people). The concept has been modified as applied to time management to mean that if all activities are arranged in order of their value, 80 percent of the value would come from only 20 percent of the activities, while the remaining 20 percent of the value would come from 80 percent of the activities.

The 80/20 rule suggests that out of ten things to do, doing the most important two will yield most (80 percent) of the value to you or your organization. The key to effective time management is to focus on the right 20 percent instead of on low-value activities where the payoff is small. In other words, do not become bogged down on low-value activities (priority C's and D's). Develop the ability to say "no" to organizational requests that are on your C and D lists. Of course, the 80/20 rule should not be taken too literally. Percentages are a way of conceptually illustrating that more time could profitably be spent on a few highly critical issues or activities.

COMBATING TIME GOBBLERS

In the course of a given workday, certain endeavors tend to waste time and produce limited results. The following suggestions are no doubt more than any one person can implement in trying to combat time gobblers. They will not work for every person all the time. Consider the following items as a smorgasbord of suggestions from which you could select those that fit your working style.

Handling Incoming Paperwork

- Never handle a piece of paper more than once. If it is a paper that requires a reply, do it now. If a short report is required, do it now. The main objective is to get the report off the desk.
- To handle the tremendous flow of paper, discipline yourself to see that each piece of paper is handled by a) acting on it immediately, b) referring it to someone else, c) filing it, d) discarding it, or e) under special circumstances delaying action pending other necessary events.
- Arrange to have a place for every piece of paper you save.
- Consider whether you can handle communications through phone calls or face-to-face contact rather than through long written reports.
- Sort your mail based on your guidelines on routine materials that can be discarded without opening it, filed, or rerouted.
- Carry reading material with you to take advantage of "deadline time," such as waiting for a meeting to begin, waiting for transportation to arrive, or sitting in a large meeting in which some of the items do not require your attention.

- Respond to incoming correspondence by writing a reply directly on the letter.

Organizing Paper Flow

- Clear your desk of clutter periodically so that you do not waste time trying to find materials. Arrange, if necessary, to work occasional evenings or weekends to clean up.
- Use stick on note tags to indicate what needs to be done with each item, especially for filing. Stack items in priority piles to make sure you deal quickly with "A" items.
- Develop a tickler file that sorts, by days or months, projects that must be accomplished in the future.
- Establish at your desk a few working files you are likely to need in the next few days. These are projects you are currently working on that require your continuous attention.
- Schedule time to clean out files once or twice a year.
- Divide incoming items into four categories: dump it; delegate it; delay it; or do it.
- Color-code your files, for example:
      red folder: mail/memos-primary, contains items for immediate attention;
      orange folder: mail/memos-secondary, contains items of lesser importance;
      green folder: contains items requiring signature;
      yellow folder: easy reading; contains everything that could be ignored for a week without causing problems.
- Remember that there is a place for everything and everything should be in its place.
- Be choosy about what to read. Practice the art of skimming materials, looking for the most significant and relevant aspects. Concentrate on the introduction and conclusion.
- Get off unnecessary mailing and circulation lists.
- Learn to use a word processor so you can more easily revise drafts.
- Organize e-mails into designated files for easy retrieval.

Managing Conversations

- Keep a small notebook to jot down names of people you met and a brief record of issues discussed with them.
- Organize your thoughts before beginning a conversation or a phone call. Know what you want to say, say it, and omit everything else.
- While socializing is enjoyable, remember to limit it so you can get your tasks done.

- Drop-in visitors present a special problem. While they are important for relationships in and outside the organization, they can detract from accomplishing certain responsibilities. Be courteous and friendly but also maintain control. Of course some spontaneous conversations may prove to be highly productive so be flexible about this guideline.
- If another staff member asks to meet with you, consider going to his or her office instead. It will be easier for you to leave when the business is concluded.
- If possible, meet drop-in visitors outside your office so that you can easily end the conversation.
- Request a brief summary of issues you can review before a meeting or discussion.
- Keep a clock in full view for yourself and visitors so you can be aware of the passing of time.
- Have a file card with agenda topics available for each person with whom you are likely to meet so that you are prepared to discuss specific items with them.
- Establish a time limit when a visitor arrives and be candid about the time pressure you are feeling. If your time is limited ask the visitor to set up another appointment.
- Allow time each day for interruptions and unscheduled events.
- Learn how to say "no" diplomatically if someone asks you if you have a minute.
- Stand up and move the visitor toward the door when you are ready to conclude the discussion.

Managing Telephone Calls

- Instead of using separate telephone memos, use an 8 by 11 inch chart that provides column for date, caller, time, and message. Place the charts in a notebook so you can track infrequent callers. This will save you time looking for separate memos.
- Sometimes callers tend to ramble. They go into great detail about a situation before getting to the point. Encourage them to state the "bottom line" issue and then go back to fill in the details. This will help focus the discussion.
- If most of your work interruptions come from your boss's calls, do not assume that you must put up with them. Pick a judicious time to explain that you are trying to get better control of your time and would appreciate a mutually agreeable time to discuss routine matters.
- To make a phone message brief: a) Tell the person in one sentence why you're calling, b) explain it briefly, and c) say what you plan to do or what action you want the other person to take.
- When you leave the office, indicate when you will be back so callers know when to reach you.

- Rely on phone mail and, if feasible, cell phones.
- Indicate to the caller your time constrains: "I only have 3 minutes because of an important meeting I have to prepare for. Will our discussion take longer?" Usually it will not, and your announcement will push the caller to get to the point.
- Consider faxing your ideas in advance of a phone call to better focus the conversation.
- Keep a list of frequently called numbers by your phone. If possible program your phone for those you call often.
- Don't play "telephone tag." Indicate in your phone mail message when you will be available again.
- Certain times are generally better for returning calls: early morning (8:00 a.m.—9:00 a.m.) and at closing (4:00 p.m—5:00 p.m.).
- If you find that you must stay on the line to prevent telephone tag, have available material that you can read while waiting.
- Establish quiet hours during which you will not accept calls except in an emergency or from special persons you designate.
- If you are in a tremendous time bind, try to limit the time you will accept calls, such as from 2:30 p.m. to 3:00 p.m.
- Outline topics to discuss before calling.
- Set aside a particular time for calling. Make as many calls as you can at one time.

BLOCKING OUT TIME

Now and then, you need to find time to undertake long-range projects that require sustained periods of concentrated attention. One hour of time will be worth more than four 15-minute time slots scattered throughout the day. You should mark the time blocks on your calendar and generally try to protect them, making exceptions only for special situations or emergencies. Reserve the time block as if it were an important scheduled meeting, canceling it only as you would cancel the meeting.

Use your time block for these kinds of activities:

- writing an outline or draft of a major report
- thinking about a major problem
- completing difficult assignments
- taking the time to visit branch offices
- developing better relationships with significant staff, inside or outside the organization
- working on a major project, such as a fundraising campaign or legislation.

To block out time, you must prune activities; some things have to be let go to make room for other activities. Also, in scheduling time blocks, determine the rhythm of the organization. If, for example, the organization annually requires a heavy investment of time to prepare the budget in November, this would not be an appropriate time period to set aside a time block for a major new project.

If a project requires concentrated attention, schedule a time block in a quiet room away from the office to prevent telephone interruptions or unexpected visitors. You may have to use weekends, evenings, or early mornings to make time blocks available. You may not want to do this on a regular basis, but on occasion, to get the job done, you may have to work extra hours. An hour spent from 7:30 - 8:30 a.m. or 5:00 - 6:00 p.m. may be far more valuable than trying to snatch small intervals during a hectic day. You may also need to establish "availability hours" so that staff and others trying to reach you won't feel shortchanged. By making yourself available at certain times, you can more easily set aside a time block. Of course, this must fit your management style; some managers prefer an open-door approach, in which case they may need to block out evening or weekend time.

Set deadlines and sub-goals within the period you have allocated for your time block. By setting these deadlines, you discipline yourself to complete discrete pieces of work. Sub-goals provide a target and keep you on track. Thus, within each block of time, you should achieve a specific sub-goal: complete an outline, write four pages of a report, finish an analysis of a staff problem.

If the task is too large to complete within a limited time period, then segment the tasks into smaller, more manageable portions, and discipline yourself to complete action on one segment before stopping. This way, you will avoid leaving loose ends when you put the task aside. You will have completed one phase of the project and will be ready to begin the next. The emphasis is not on putting in time but on completing tasks. Develop a compulsion for closure.[3]

MANAGING ORGANIZATIONAL STRESS

The fact that such terms as "job stress" and "job burnout" have become so prevalent is a reflection of the tremendous pressure and demands that staff involved in the delivery of human services must endure. Because stress has become an increasing concern, there may be a tendency to focus attention on trying to get rid of it altogether. This should not, however, be your objective. It is not only unrealistic, but some degree of stress actually contributes to productivity.

Many employees do work well under pressure; anxiety and tension mobilize their energies. These staff experience "positive stress."[4] In high performance organizations, staff are expected to function under pressure. They are held accountable for getting results and are constantly pushed to do better. Offsetting this pressure is a sense of accomplishment and of being part of a staff team whose needs are considered important. Hence, the goal of human service organizations is not to be stress-free but to provide a work environment in which the pressures of the job are not so demanding that they immobilize staff.

Certainly, the work of many human service organizations is inherently stressful. Staff who make critical decisions regarding whether children should be removed from their homes because of neglect or abuse experience tremendous stress. So do welfare or Red Cross staff whose work entails finding emergency housing or employment staff who are responsible for finding jobs for school dropouts. Frustration and tension are, unfortunately, an integral aspect of these jobs, and learning to manage stress is essential.

To be sure, some organizationally caused stress can be controlled enough to reduce the harmful impact on staff.[5] Organizations should be aware of—and do something about—the following stressors:

Role Ambiguity

If staff are unclear about their objectives and tasks, they will be confused about what is expected of them. Job descriptions and mutually agreed upon objectives can reduce this great sense of uncertainty.[6]

Overload (or Underload) of Work

Some organizations are addicted to work. This is a particularly insidious problem because we value dedication so highly. But when the demands of the job regularly require 60 or 70 hours a week to complete assignments properly, the workload has gotten out of control, not unlike a disease. An organization fostering this problem needs to analyze and seek ways to address its unusually heavy workload demands. Conversely, an organization may provide professional staff with too little to do; the resultant under achievement engenders feelings of uselessness and boredom among those directly affected—and a sense of inequity among other staff members who resent the way work is distributed.

Contradictory Expectations

Some organizations state one kind of promise or expectation in their mission, but staff experience something quite different in their daily professional lives. The incongruity between the ideal and the reality leads staff to become disillusioned and deflated. For example, the organization may espouse the ideal of wanting to improve the lives of poor people but then may require staff to impose layers of regulations on clients before they qualify for services.

Contradictory expectations also create stress when staff have to report to multiple lines of authority and juggle the demands of different supervisors. This occurs especially when staff are encouraged to participate on ad hoc, problem-solving teams while still maintaining home-base responsibilities. Under these circumstances staff have the awesome responsibility of reconciling the different priorities of their managers.

Poor Preparation

If the agency does not prepare carefully, small problems can be exacerbated, eventually causing undue stress on staff. For example, because of inadequate preparation, a computer entry in a public assistance agency results in clients receiving checks in the amount of $3 instead of $300. As a result of the system foul-up, staff have the extra burden—on top of their already demanding schedules—of handling these new complaints. The tremendous feelings of frustration could have been avoided with better preparation.

Laid Back Atmosphere

An overly permissive atmosphere can also cause undue stress. Take, for example, an agency that provides outpatient counseling for teenagers. In its quest to establish a family feeling of warmth and informal relationships, the agency permits a two-hour lunch break, unfocused supervisory sessions in the park, and "shooting the breeze" with teenagers. Because of this commitment to an informal, relaxed atmosphere, clients are not required to notify the agency when they must miss their appointments. Moreover, staff are not held accountable for their work, nor do they set objectives. There are no guidelines for handling crises such as suicide attempts. The results: work does not get done, and staff feel that they are overworked because they have to put in 60 hours each week. The laissez-faire atmosphere, paradoxically, causes the staff to feel tremendously burdened and "burned out."

Poor Match Between Staff and Jobs

Stress can occur as a result of staff being assigned work that is beyond their abilities, as, for example, when an effective staff person promoted to a supervisory position finds the job too demanding. Conversely, stress can occur when employees are assigned a job that only minimally uses their skills, for example, highly motivated college graduates being assigned menial, routine work.[7]

Reducing Stress

Here are some suggestions you can use to handle stressful situations:

- Find ways to reconnect with those aspects of your work you truly enjoy. By doing so, you can balance the problematic parts of your job with those that give you satisfaction. Strive to rediscover what attracted you to the field and to your job in the first place. Identify your "sources of joy" and work with your supervisor to accentuate these activities.

- Get in touch with a support group of staff who are having similar experiences. This could take the form of an informal communication network with colleagues who are undergoing similar kinds of stress or with others outside the organization who are good listeners and who may be able to provide suggestions based on their experiences.

- Identify and change whatever might be causing stress. If, for example, time pressures are becoming extraordinary, then develop methods for managing time better. Similarly, if clients or coworkers evoke excessive feelings of anxiety, identify the specific causes of your stress as a first step to gain control of it.

- Recognize that sometimes you may be over-investing in your work to the point of near exhaustion. Your passion for your work and commitment to your clients, while at first a blessing, can become a curse. For periods of time you may fly high with extraordinary energy and verve but then may become worn out and crash to the ground. Determine how you can better pace yourself.

- Sometimes the cause of your stress may originate from outside the job. A very sick child or a stormy relationship can put special pressures on you that spill over to your work performance. Be cautious about using your supervisor as your therapist. You may need to seek outside counseling to help you deal with outside pressures that affect your ability to do your job.

- Develop work habits that can help reduce unnecessary tension and anticipate crises. For example, anticipate work assignments so that you do not experience last minute, extraordinary pressures on top of your already demanding schedule. If handling crises is a natural part of the workload, develop an "inoculation" to stress. By discussing a crisis plan with your supervisor, you will be more likely to handle problems that arise with more skill and sensitivity. Request training sessions that simulate difficult situations to enhance your skill and sensitivity.

- Take time to care for yourself. Develop a good support system, including a caring family and friends with whom you can share some of the burdens of the job. Just being able to talk about your concerns and anxieties can help relieve some of the pressure. Also, find an outside hobby or recreational pursuit. Participate in an exercise program, yoga, or meditation. Some people find inspiration in participating in a religious experience. The important thing is that you get away from the job, be with people who matter to you, and have an opportunity to refresh yourself.

- Develop realistic expectations about yourself and the results of your work. Some people demand more of themselves than the situation will ever allow. For example, given the nature of a particular target population of young cocaine addicts without family supports, the recidivism rates are likely to be quite high. You would need to measure "success" not in relation to "curing" your clients but in helping them achieve some limited degree of progress with their educational, employment and social goals.

- If all else fails consider leaving the stressful situation. You could work with your supervisor to change your assignment or even consider transferring to another unit better suited to your abilities and interests.

In conclusion, manageable stress is a natural part of a productive organization. It is only when staff find that they have the inability to cope with the pressures of the job that negative stress becomes an issue. The best antidote for handling stress is to have high expectations within a supportive organizational climate. Staff should address those factors that cause stress, and management needs to take time to mitigate unnecessary organizational stressors.

SUMMARY

Because of tremendous demands most staff experience, they must make decisions on the best use of their time. This involves purposely establishing priorities, which includes what activities may need to be put aside. It also involves blocking out time to accomplish long term projects. Breaking large tasks into smaller, more manageable ones is a useful technique. Managing stress should be a high priority for both staff and management.

QUESTIONS FOR DISCUSSION

1) Review your activities for the past week. What two examples can you provide in each of the following categories:

   Highest priority

   Medium priority

   Lowest priority

   Posteriority

2) What are ways that staff use their time efficiently or inefficiently in your agency?

3) What kinds of stress occur in your organization and what approaches do you or your organization take to alleviate stress?

Chapter Notes

[1]Lakein, A. (1973). *How to Get Control of Your Time and Your Life*. New York: New American Library, p. 96.

[2]Uris, A. (1986). *101 of the Greatest Ideas in Management*. New York: Wiley & Sons, p. 292.

[3]Bliss, E. (1976). *Getting Things Done*. New York: Bantam, p. 180.

[4]Herman, R.E. (1990). *Keeping Good People: Strategies for Solving the Dilemma of the Decade*. Cleveland, OH: Oakhill Press, pp. 160-162.

[5]Middleman R.R. & Rhodes, G.B. (1985). *Competent Supervision: Making Imaginative Judgments*. Englewood Cliffs, NJ: Prentice-Hall, pp. 132-5;

Schaef, A.W. & Fassel, D. (1990). *The Addictive Organization.* San Francisco, CA: Harper and Row.

[6]Moss, L. (1981). *Managing Stress.* Reading, MA: Addison-Wesley, pp. 101-2.

[7]Crow, R.T. & Odewahn, C.A. (1987). *Management for the Human Services.* Englewood Cliffs, NJ: Prentice-Hall, p. 144.

REFERENCES FOR CHAPTER 13

Coscia, S. (Mar. 2006). " How to Respond to Call Center Stress." *Call Center Magazine*, Vol. 19. No. 3. pp. 45-47.

Dodd, P., Sundheim, D. (2005). *The 25 Best Time Management Tools & Techniques: How to Get More Done Without Driving Yourself Crazy.* NL: Peak Performance Press, Inc.

Goulson, M. (2005). *Get Out of Your Own Way at Work... and Help Others Do the Same: Conquering Self-Defeating Behavior on the Job.* NL: Putnam Adult.

Harvard Business School Press (2005). *Time Management: Increase Your Personal Productivity and Effectiveness (Harvard Business Essentials).* Harvard: Harvard

Jaskyte, K. (2005). "The Impact of Organizational Socialization Tactics on Role Ambiguity and Role Conflict of Newly Hired Social Workers." *Administration in Social Work*, Vol. 29. No. 4. pp. 69-87.

Karatepe, Osman, M., (Jan. 2006). "The Effects of Antecedents on the Service Recovery Performance of Front Line Employees." *Service Industries Journal*, Vol. 26. No. 1. pp. 39-57. Business School Press.

Menzies, H. (2005). *No Time: Stress and the Crisis of Modern Life.* Vancouver, British Columbia, Canada: Douglas & McIntyre.

Morgenstern, J. (2005). *Never Check E-Mail In the Morning: And Other Unexpected Strategies for Making Your Work Life Work.* New York: Fireside.

CHAPTER 14

Organizational Leadership and Supervision

THE INTERACTION OF MANAGER AND SITUATION

The key to effective leadership is to function in a way that is an appropriate match to the situation. There are two frameworks that can help one understand leadership styles within an organizational context: (1) the way in which a manager exerts influence and (2) his or her leadership orientation toward managing staff.

Leadership Influence

Managers may exert influence over staff in several ways:[1]

Legitimate influence is derived as a result of the manager's position and degree of authority, as bestowed by the organization. A program director, for example, is expected to give general direction to staff.

Coercive influence results from the capacity to impose punishments on those staff who do not comply with work requirements.

Reward influence attempts to motivate staff by providing them with valued outcomes. These could include both financial and symbolic rewards.

Expertise influence is exerted by the manager who has special knowledge that can be imparted to staff.

Psychological influence can take various forms: personal magnetism or charisma, instilling a sense of loyalty, or fostering identification with the manager's goals and philosophies.

Communication influence results when the manager is the source of critical information and has the power to determine whether to share or withhold it from staff.

Managers selectively determine which of these influences they will use and under which circumstances. A manager may decide, for example, to use coercion and authority for staff who are under performing. A different manager faced with the same problem might determine that rewards, participation, and communication were preferred methods of improving productivity.

Leadership Orientation of the Manager

A second framework related to leadership style involves the dynamic interplay among managers, the behavior and attitudes of their employees, and various situational factors.[2] Some managers prefer *a controlling leadership style,* feeling that they must assume personal responsibility for making major decisions and then acting as a taskmaster to get things done. Although they may occasionally ask questions or allow limited dialogue, there is no doubt that the decision is essentially and primarily theirs. They prefer to "take charge." They see themselves authoritatively functioning as an orchestra conductor, calling on staff to harmoniously achieve a desired result.

Other managers choose a *participative leadership orientation* in which they present ideas and invite feedback from staff. They want to retain final decision-making authority, but they also want their employees to consider alternative solutions.

Still others prefer a *delegative style.* These managers derive considerable satisfaction from giving decision-making responsibilities to their staff. If they participate in the decision-making process, they are comfortable in assuming no more authority than other members in the group. An extreme form of the delegative style is sometimes referred to as "laissez faire" (meaning hands off). Managers rely entirely on their subordinates to determine and carry out their assignments.

Managers have their own predisposition toward one of these three orientations. Which is best to effectively manage? The answer is that it all depends on the nature of the staff and external and internal situations.

Factors Operating Within Staff

The way staff respond to organizational tasks and decision making can greatly influence managerial leadership style (directive, participative, or delegative). It is likely, for example, that a manager would delegate responsibilities and decision making to those employees who have the needed education and experience to do the job properly. Likewise, a supervisor would likely delegate if staff are motivated to be involved in their work, if they identify with the goals of the organization, if they can manage unstructured work situations, and if they have the self-confidence and self-reliance to work independently.

If, however, staff are inexperienced, feel reluctant to take additional responsibilities, require structured and unambiguous assignments, or resist making decisions, then a more directive management style may be required.[3] This kind of staff presents a challenge to those managers who value staff participation in decision making.

Situational Factors

Certain forces operating outside the manager and employees will affect the managerial style. The organization itself may perpetuate certain values, work habits, traditions, and expectations around managerial behavior. Some organizations, for example, operate under a high degree of pressure and crisis, thereby requiring a more directive management style. Moreover, an organization's size and structure will influence the nature of leadership styles. An organization with offices in different locations, for example, will tend to promote autonomous decision making because of the decentralized nature of its operations.

The problems an organization has to deal with may themselves affect leadership style. If a problem is complex and compels the involvement of staff with different types of knowledge and experiences, then a participative leadership style would be appropriate. On the other hand, if a problem requires the expertise of the leader only, then staff may be involved in more supportive functions.

The pressure of time is another key ingredient affecting the leadership style. The more immediately a decision must be made, the more difficult it is to involve other employees. Agencies operating under emergency conditions (e.g., handling housing needs in the aftermath of a flood) require expeditious decision making. Many decisions that might ordinarily and appropriately involve staff are made unilaterally because of limited time.

Managers must be flexible in their leadership style. At times, a directive approach may be more appropriate than a delegative or participative one because of organizational context or the nature of the situation. Where a crisis exists or where difficult budget or personnel decisions must be made, a "take charge" (directive) leadership style is appropriate. Managers sometimes need to combine approaches based on the circumstances. For example, in setting up a phone system, a manager might ask a staff committee to recommend a system even though their role will be advisory only. By alerting them in advance to the constraints on their participation in decision making, the manager conveys respect for their thinking and at the same time alerts them to their boundaries—reflecting both a delegative and a directive approach. Unless the manager is clear about the staff role, confusion and dissatisfaction might occur.

Although flexibility in leadership approaches is desirable, certain leadership styles are realistically more responsive to the needs of a professional staff and more conducive to productivity in human service organizations. Today's professional staff expect to be consulted and to exert influence, especially on those areas that have a direct impact on their own work. Most want the manager to hear and consider their ideas. They will tend to become resentful if their manager treats them as if they were easily manipulated machine parts in a factory.

MAJOR ASPECTS OF GOOD LEADERSHIP

Administrative staff of human service organizations will reflect certain competency qualities. They can identify and articulate future directions, persevere in the face of obstacles, treat staff with dignity, communicate well, engender trust, and inspire top level performance.

Identify and Articulate Future Directions. Effective managers constantly seek out trends—possible changes in demographics, funding, or political alignments—and determine how these trends might influence their organization. They work at formulating a vision of the future either within their own mind or by mobilizing the organization to think strategically. (See Chapter 4.) They have the ability to get everyone who should be involved, whether it be staff, board of trustees, or even public officials, to focus their attention on issues leaders consider significant.[4]

Persevere. Effective managers persist in accomplishing goals even in the face of setbacks and failures. They take risks, knowing that failures may occur, and they learn from their mistakes.[5] They assume that if something does not work, they will try something else until they ultimately succeed. This combination of perseverance and tenacity in the face of obstacles and adversity is what sets effective managers apart from their less intrepid counterparts.

Treat Staff with Dignity. Effective managers minimize the use of command language and maximize the language of persuasion and request. They understand that they cannot coerce staff to excel; true motivation must come from within.[6] They create a climate in which staff feel so positive about how they are being treated that they willingly perform at their best.

Communicate Well. Effective managers are able to articulate concepts, ideas, and philosophies in such a way that staff understand both intellectually and emotionally how they are involved. These messages are clear and uncomplicated; they speak to the heart as well as to the mind. Managers help staff see the relationship between what they are doing and the mission of the organization—how they are a part of the whole .[7]

These managers work to shape ambiguous ideas into operational programs with clear guidelines, thereby giving structure and clarity to them. Without patronizing their staff, effective managers clarify what the work is for, why it needs to be done in a particular manner, and what constitutes successful performance. One of their major messages is that everyone must work together to achieve the organization's goals .[8]

Engender Trust. Effective managers have a deep sense of integrity. They are honest with themselves and are aware of both their strengths and limitations. Staff respect and trust effective managers who take steps to either address their own limitations or find ways to compensate for them.[9] Staff know what values their leaders are committed to and what positions they stand for and know they can count on these managers. Competent managers are careful to promise only what they can deliver, and they expect others to do the same. The trust that effective managers earn is not based on blind faith. It is built upon a give-and-take interaction, which might sometimes include some degree of doubt.[10] The manager and staff feel committed to each other, but they both can also raise questions and challenge issues within a relationship of mutual respect. Maintaining this balance of respect and willingness to challenge is the essence of the implicit compact between the managers and staff.

Inspire Performance. By establishing high, but achievable, expectations, successful managers infuse in their staff a standard of excellence.[11] They create a positive and productive working atmosphere within which staff are stimulated to perform at their best. Even as they expect high performance, at the same time they are realistic. They attempt to stretch people, not overwhelm them. The words that best describe this kind of leadership are "elevating," "uplifting," and "cheerleading." Their optimism, confidence, and "can-do" demeanor mobilizes staff to take on the toughest of challenges. They lead best by their personal example.

Survey results of business organizations could just as meaningfully apply to human service agencies: "In more than 550 original cases that we studied, we didn't encounter a single example of extraordinary accomplishment that occurred without the active involvement of people."[12] Simply put, no leader can accomplish results alone; it's a team effort. Getting things done in an organization must be everyone's business.

Aspiring To Be In A Leadership Role. There is no substitute for learning by doing. Take advantage of opportunities to facilitate team meetings, lead a task group, chair a fund raising drive, or head up a student or professional conference. The more you do the more learning experience you'll have to deal with failures and successes.[13]

Once you attain the leadership role, be mindful of the problem of hubris. People can easily become seduced by the power, self-importance, and the glory of the leadership role. Watch for becoming bloated with an exaggerated sense of self, or using the office to pursue personal needs.[14] Leaders sometimes get in trouble, having given significantly of themselves to an organization, come to feel that the organization now owes them more rewards and perks than is appropriate for their contribution.

SUPERVISION

Supervisory staff face a tremendous challenge in dealing with different supervisory aspects of their jobs, among them: reconciling the expectations of superiors with the needs of subordinates, integrating the many roles they must play, and determining when and in what ways to delegate assignments.

Reconciling Expectations

Managers are frequently the "pickle in the middle," sandwiched between the conflicting expectations of their bosses and those who work under their supervision. They are often called upon to reconcile the expectations and policies of the organization with the concerns and needs of their subordinates.[15]

Whether a supervisor in a local welfare office, a director in a mental health clinic, or a unit head of a foster care program, the effective supervisor must deal with value conflicts and differing perspectives. To handle this diversity, these middle managers must be able to truly understand and accept that there is validity in different points of view. If, for example, middle managers understand and are committed to the mission and goals of the organization, they will appreciate why it has regulations to restrict some client services. At the same time, they understand that staff often want to "bend the rules" to increase eligibility of those with whom they come in contact.[16]

Through this appreciation of different perspectives, managerial loyalties can be pulled in several directions. Managers' abilities to connect the needs and requirements of one level of the organization to those of another ultimately determine their effectiveness. Effective managers work to diminish a "we-they" atmosphere, replacing it with an emphasis on teamwork. Managers could explain to staff, for example, why they must complete the monthly reporting forms that top administration requires and at the same time work with the administration to modify these report requirements so that staff can complete the forms with greater ease.

Certainly, being part of a team is not always easy for middle managers. At times they will be caught in a conflict and want to advocate for staff because most middle managers have moved up through the ranks and so naturally identify with their former peers. Or they may feel that in order to sustain staff loyalty they must be willing to advocate for staff concerns. As a result, managers may try to persuade the administration to make changes based on the experiences of their staff.

On the other hand, even if middle managers question a particular change made by top administrators, after making their case they are obligated to help staff understand why the change is necessary and help them implement the new arrangements. Hence, middle managers are the ultimate facilitators of communications between different staff levels of an organization.

Playing Multiple Roles

Supervisory staff must often take on different roles, which are not necessarily compatible with each other.

The Role of Coach. One of the most demanding roles a manager has is that of coaching staff. As a coach, a manager's primary responsibility is to train staff to help attain the goals of both the organization and the unit. The coach must recognize that each employee has a different array of strengths and weaknesses. He or she provides feedback to staff, encourages them to devise their own plans for performance and improvement, and supports their growth. As the situation demands, the coach may provide support and counseling or confront staff with the consequences of their behavior. Throughout all of this, the coach conveys a combination of genuine concern for the employee and an expectation that tasks will be accomplished well.[17]

The Role of Judge. As judge, the manager must evaluate the extent to which staff achieve their goals. If they are not achieved, the manager must diagnose whether the problem lies within the staff, the work environment, or the nature of the task itself. Moreover, if the problem lies within staff, the judge must determine whether the solution is skill training or other measures.

To carry out this role, subordinates should be monitored through formal review procedures (e.g., computerized data or evaluation sessions) or informal, but purposeful, contacts with staff. Closely linked to this judging role is the ability to evaluate and then influence the distribution of resources. Pay increases, promotions, or symbolic rewards are connected to employee assessments. In this role of judge, a manager may also be called upon to handle disturbances and resolve differences between staff and units of the organization.[18]

Evaluating staff is one of the major roles of a supervisor. To carry out this role well, the supervisor should keep the following principles[19] in mind:

- Staff should be involved in establishing the criteria that will be used to assess them. This ensures the use of relevant criteria, clarifies expectations, and intensifies commitment.

- Evaluation should be continuous, rather than a one-time event. The formal evaluation should be an opportunity to review previous discussions.

- The evaluation should be communicated in the context of a positive working relationship.

- The focus of the evaluation should be on the work performance of the supervisee rather than any evaluation of the worker as a person. Of course, where personal traits affect work performance these should be acknowledged.

- Both strengths and areas of growth should be articulated.

- Evaluations should be conducted in a manner that provides a balanced picture of performance.

- The evaluation procedure should be a mutual, shared process with supervisee participation encouraged.

The Role of Explorer. The manager frequently engages employees as partners in searching for solutions to problems. By involving employees in this process of mutual problem solving, managers build the confidence and commitment of their staff. As an explorer, the manager seeks to understand the basis of the problem but resists jumping prematurely to final answers, encouraging staff instead to search out constructive options. By encouraging staff to develop their own ideas and communicating genuine belief that staff are capable of developing creative solutions, the explorer fosters a commitment to exploration throughout the entire staff.[20]

Communication with staff is a major part of the explorer's job, and so this manager must seek out and disseminate information to staff. To be an effective communicator, therefore, the explorer must have a network of contacts both within and outside the organization.[21]

The Role of Warrior. The term "warrior" is a metaphor for the manager as a person of action. If productivity is decreasing, this alerts the manager to take aggressive action to improve it. To be an effective warrior, the manager must persevere in the face of obstacles to get the job done. He or she must often deal with others in the organization, whether subordinates, colleagues, or top administrators, who are involved with their own agendas and must be coaxed to correct their end of the problem. The warrior must continually encourage staff to do better. If certain operations are inefficient or unproductive, the manager may have to make the painful decision to discontinue them. If the organization or the unit experiences a crisis, the warrior must respond without hesitation.[22]

Each of these roles must be handled judiciously and not be carried to such an extreme that it interferes or becomes incompatible with other roles.[23] For example, managers should not be so focused on the encouraging and supportive functions of the coaching role that they are unable to fulfill the roles of objective judge and distributor of resources. When sorting out problems, the explorer role is appropriate, but when dealing with a crisis, a manager may need to become a warrior, able to make intrepid decisions.

DELEGATING ASSIGNMENTS

If managing is the art of getting things done through working with others, then delegating is the process of giving others assignments to complete. But delegation is no simple matter; it requires considerable thought, planning, and follow-through.

Both managers and staff can be resistive to delegation. Some managers do not delegate because they fear that their subordinates may upstage them. These managers have an inordinate need to reap full credit. They may fear losing control, or they do not want to take the time to guide the process, or they prefer doing the assignment themselves (even when they are pressed for time), or they do not want to invest in developing their subordinates. These problems reside in the delegator. On the other side, staff may resist responsibility because they lack the necessary experience or training, are overloaded with work, or are poorly organized.

These problems must be addressed if staff are to grow in their capabilities and the work is to get done. By developing staff, effective managers increase the organization's flexibility. By shifting responsibilities from one level of the organization to another, managers can free up staff to take on new assignments and expand their skills.

It is not, of course, desirable to delegate every task. Some responsibilities are simply too complicated or controversial to pass along. Some tasks require such advanced technical knowledge and judgment that they cannot be easily delegated. Some are so sensitive, such as budget information or disciplining staff, that delegation is inadvisable.

So the issue, "when to delegate," is clearly a delicate one. Delegation must be used judiciously and with careful consideration of the criteria listed below:

- Select the right people: delegate according to realistic assessments of strengths, limitations, and task preferences.[24]

- Ensure that assignments are fair and realistic by maintaining continuous communication with staff.

- Make the assignments clear.[25] Staff must understand what the organization expects of them. They should have a clearly detailed work plan complete with deadlines.

- Delegate tasks to the lowest possible level that they can be performed satisfactorily to make the most efficient use of organizational resources.[26] Resist making a decision that your staff could make just as easily—even though it might be different from yours—if the result is likely to be a positive one.

- State the constraints (if any) within which staff must operate. An example might be a budgetary constraint.

- Determine criteria for selecting employees to take responsibilities on the basis of who can best do the job, who can use time most productively, who wants more responsibility, and who would experience the most professional growth.

- Give staff a voice in the assignment. The delegation process should be a dialogue, not a monologue.[27] Being sensitive to staff preferences is more likely to ensure their enthusiasm in completing assignments.

- Determine how thoroughly staff understand the task, and, based on that understanding, communicate all necessary knowledge to assist them in completing it. Provide specific instructions about what the result should be, and clarify the limits of the employee's responsibility. Anticipate where problems are likely to occur, such as requests for more funding or more staff to carry out the assignment, and establish ground rules for what resources are available (or not) to carry the project forward.

- Convey your expectation that if staff encounter problems, they will consider one or more solutions before coming to you. This conveys your confidence that they will work hard to resolve problems and will not become unduly dependent upon you as their ultimate problem-solver. On the other hand, make yourself available in the event they encounter particularly difficult challenges. Find the right balancing point between letting staff work out their problems and interceding when vexing problems arise.

- Grant authority to get the task done. Responsibility without authority never works. You may have to give your imprimatur to the employee who is carrying out the assignment so that others are aware of your backing.

Since managers who delegate assignments are ultimately responsible for the work of those under their supervision, it is vitally important to maintain control without limiting the freedom of staff to think and act. If managers have made assignments clear and have mutually determined outcomes, then tracking progress should be fairly easy. Moreover, if they have developed a method of feedback, including a reporting schedule and checkpoints, then they help ensure proper control of the project. On the one hand, managers should not "micro manage" the project or overindulge their own need for information and data. On the other hand, they must not assume too passive a role so that needed information comes too late to take corrective action. They must clarify that staff must tell them of any unexpected developments, delays, or problems.

ELEMENTS OF GOOD SUPERVISION

Effective supervisors are those who can help their staff be highly productive in meeting the goals of their agency. First and foremost, good supervisors have a keen understanding of themselves, including their assets and their limitations. Self-awareness is a prerequisite to helping others.

In addition, good supervisors recognize that the supervisory process is not designed to provide personal therapy for staff. Sometimes staff will have personal difficulties that could interfere with their work and may want to talk in depth about these personal problems. It is important that supervisors stay focused on the goals that need to be accomplished. Staff may need to be referred elsewhere to deal with their personal problems.

Effective supervisors are purposeful in the way they critique staff performance. They use their authority purposefully and selectively. They do not ventilate their anger or denigrate staff, especially in front of others. When possible, critiquing staff is done within a context of a trusting and positive relationship.

BEING A PRODUCTIVE SUBORDINATE

Newly hired staff sometimes wonder how they can function in the best way possible under the administration and management of an agency. Here are some suggestions that can help you be a productive member of the staff.

1) Understand the general context within which you must operate. You need to know what is important to the organization by being aware of the mission statement, the general goals that the agency wishes to achieve in the next few years, and the specific objectives that it seeks to accomplish in the coming year. Review the annual report and recent newsletters of the agency. Request a list of priorities. By understanding the essential commitments you can become a more useful employee.

2) Be clear about what is specifically expected of you. In your discussion with your supervisor, determine not only what you must do but also how you will be assessed. Ask, "What do you look for in the performance and outcomes of an excellent employee?" In effect, develop a contract between you and your supervisor about what you can mutually expect from each other. Ask to see the evaluation form that will be used to judge your performance at the end of a specific time period. Request that your supervisor assess your performance throughout the year so that you can take corrective actions.

3) Consider that you are entering a life-long pattern of learning. Expect that initially you may be overwhelmed with the amount you have to absorb: new procedures and policies to learn, new colleagues to get to know, new concepts of practice, new clients to understand. Be prepared to make mistakes; you will rarely be faulted if you are perceived as genuinely trying and if your attitude is one of growing and learning from your errors. Develop an ability to be introspective, asking, "What can I learn from this new experience?"

4) Communicate openly with your supervisor and colleagues. Accept that at times you will be uncertain and even anxious about a particular assignment. Share your concerns with your supervisor so that she or he can better tune into when they need to give you necessary counsel. Use your supervisory conference proactively, by thinking in advance about the issues and questions you need to raise. If an assignment is unclear, request clarification in the spirit of wanting to achieve the best possible results.

5) Demonstrate that you are a contributor. Managers welcome staff who take initiative, who volunteer to pitch in. Keeping in mind the

results that the organization is expected to achieve, staff must continually ask, "How is my work adding value to helping the organization achieve its mission?" During the evaluation process be explicit about what you have done to contribute to the overall results of the agency.

6) Develop a network of professional relationships. Working with others in the agency is usually a valued trait. Most activities require cooperative relationships. Staff often team up to work on projects that cannot be achieved by individuals working alone. Besides, there is much to learn from co-workers. Sometimes staff can be used as informal consultants because of their experience and expertise. Not all learning will be derived from your immediate supervisor.

DEALING WITH A PROBLEMATIC SUPERVISOR

Unfortunately not all supervisors have good management (or even good human relations) skills. Some are incapable of providing proper directions, and you are left to float. They reflect a "laissez faire" (hands off) attitude that the best supervision is no supervision. At the other extreme are those who micro-manage and become unduly involved in the details of their staff's work. Some may not be knowledgeable about resources of the community or about how to handle challenging situations that you encounter. Some are poorly organized and therefore are no help to you in organizing your time and work. To be sure, there are no easy remedies. You are in a vulnerable position, whether as a student intern or as a new member of the staff. Here are several options to consider:

1) Determine whether the supervisor's limitation is confined to a specific trait in which case you can still experience growth. A poorly organized supervisor may nevertheless evidence a caring quality and a commitment to help you grow. Look for strengths.

2) Consider whether you can obtain good advice from other colleagues, both in your agency and those that work elsewhere. Think about where else you can obtain good consultation and advice to augment what your supervisor has to offer.

3) If you feel secure enough, communicate directly to your supervisor how he or she can provide you with better supervision. Explain not what is wrong with him or her, but what you need. Use the phrase, "I'd like you to know that for me to grow as a professional, I could benefit from this kind of supervision." You need to consider

whether your supervisor is the kind of person that can respond to this approach.

4) If you are a field student, discuss the situation with your faculty advisor who can intercede on your behalf. Often, a discussion about expectations, if held early on, can prevent later problems. Suppose, for example, that your supervisor is continuously unavailable. A joint meeting with your faculty advisor could impress the supervisor that you have to be among his or her priorities.

5) If previous options do not work out satisfactorily, then you may have to arrange through your faculty advisor or agency administrator to change supervisors. Because of the seriousness of this step, carefully examine whether you have played a part in the problem.

SUMMARY

Organizational administrators continually seek to harmonize their various strengths. As managers, they work to bring order and consistency to complex organizations. As leaders, they challenge the status quo and work to meet new demands.[28] They strive to achieve their vision and simultaneously facilitate the staff's input in the direction-setting process. They are oriented to accomplishing tasks and are sensitive to the needs of their staff. They set their sights on the future while making certain to give proper attention to everyday details. They are both conveyers of messages and consummate listeners. They engender trust by respecting their staff and treating them with dignity. This blend of vision, sensitivity, and high moral purpose makes for inspiring leadership.

QUESTIONS FOR DISCUSSION

1) Identify a supervisor or manager in your organization or another agency that you are familiar with. What is the predominant style of leadership?

2) What two or three special competencies does this manager reflect?

3) Normally Agency X fosters a highly participative style. When major decisions have to be made, staff are invited to participate on committees or to let their views be known in staff meetings. Now the agency is faced with a crisis that it has never experienced before—a 25% cut in funding and the likelihood is that 20% of the staff will have to be laid off.

- Should staff be involved in determining the criteria for who stays and who goes?
- What particular staff should be let go?
- What action could staff take to soften the lay-offs?

4) The leadership style of Ms. Bossy is clearly directive. She readily acknowledges her style: "I'm a strong willed person." In fact, it is this very quality that got her the job because her board of trustees wanted someone with a vision and with a track record of getting things done. But now the director has come to the staff, saying that she believes the organization must develop a housing program for marginal people. She observes in the staff meeting, "I know that I've tended to be somewhat domineering in the past, but I sincerely recognize that for this project to be successful, I'm going to need your support and cooperation." She has asked you to prepare suggestions on how this—and future projects—can be implemented in such a way as to secure your enthusiastic participation.

- What are your suggestions?

5) What are the multiple roles that your supervisor assumes?

6) What are instances in which your supervisor has had to serve as an intermediary between management and staff?

7) How are tasks delegated in your agency?

Chapter Notes

[1]Seltzer, J. (1989). "Developing an Effective Leadership Style." In L.E. Miller (Ed.), *Managing Human Service Organizations* (pp. 41-44). New York: Quorum.

[2]Tannenbaum, R. & Schmidt, W. (1993). "How to Choose a Leadership Pattern." *Harvard Business Review*, 3, pp. 162-80.

[3]Stanton, E.S., (1983). "A Critical Re-evaluation of Motivation, Management, and Productivity." *Personnel Journal*, 3, pp. 5-6.

[4]The National Assembly of National Voluntary Health and Social Welfare Organizations, 1989, pp. 36-44.

[5]Bennis, W. (1989). *On Becoming a Leader*. Wilmington, MA: Addison-Wesley, pp. 95-96.

[6]Townsend, R. (1970). *Up the Organization*. p. 124.

[7]The National Assembly of National Voluntary Health and Social Welfare Organizations, pp. 36-44.

[8]Cyert, R.M. (1990). "Defining Leadership and Explicating the Process." *Nonprofit Management and Leadership*, 1, p. 33.

[9]Bennis, pp. 40-41.

[10]Bennis, p. 140.

[11]Garner, L.H., Jr. (1989). *Leadership in Human Services: How to Articulate a Vision to Achieve Results*. San Francisco: Jossey-Bass, pp. 151-2;

Schultz, W.N. (1984). "What Makes a Good Nonprofit Manager?" *Nonprofit World*, 3, p. 32.

[12]Kouzes, J.M. & Posner, B.Z. (1995). *The Leadership Challenge*. San Francisco, CA:Josey-Bass Publishers.

[13]Kouzes & Posner, p. 326.

[14]Kouzes & Posner, p. 338.

[15]Havassy, H.M. (1990). "Effective Second-Story Bureaucrats: Mastering the Paradox of Diversity." *Social Work*, 2, pp. 103-9.

[16]Kadushin, A. (1985). *Supervision in Social Work* (2nd ed.). New York: Columbia University Press, pp. 117-33.

[17]Kadushin, pp. 145-64.

Lauffer, A. (1987). *Working in Social Work*. Newbury Park, CA: Sage Publications, p. 278.

Middleman, R.R. & Rhodes, G.B. (1985). *Competent Supervision: Making Imaginative Judgments*. Englewood Cliffs, NJ: Prentice-Hall, p. 6.

[18]Herman, R.E. (1990). *Keeping Good People: Strategies for Solving the Dilemma of the Decade*. Cleveland, OH: Oakhill Press, p. 192.

[19]Pecora, P. & Austin, M. (1987). *Managing Human Service Personnel*. Newbury Park, CA: Sage, pp. 250-51.

[20]Kirby, T. (1987). *The Can-Do Manager*. New York: AMACOM, p. 49-54.

[21]Mintzberg, p. 169.

[22]Brown, R. (1979). *The Practical Manager's Guide to Excellence in Management*. New York: AMACOM, p. 113.

[23]Martin, D.C. (1989). Performance Appraisal, 2: Improving the Rater's Effectiveness. Reprinted in *Performance Appraisal*, American Management Association, p. 25.

[24]Cohen, p. 72.

[25]Drucker, P. (1985). *The Effective Executive*. New York: Harper & Row, p. 182.

[26]Brown, p. 11.

[27]Cohen, p. 72.

[28]Kotter, J. (1990). "What Leaders Really Do." *Harvard Business Review*,
  3. pp. 103-11.
  Bennis, pp. 46-7.

REFERENCES FOR CHAPTER 14

Biggs, D., and Swailes, S. (2006). "Relations, Commitment and Satisfaction in Agency Workers and Permanent Workers." *Employee Relations*, Vol. 28. No. 2. pp. 130-143.

Bray, Ilona M. (2005). *Effective Fundraising for Nonprofits: Real-world Strategies that Work.* Berkeley, CA. (1413300944).

Brooks-Young, S. (2006, January). Show your work: Your grant proposal's success lies in the details. *Technology & Learning,* p 34.

Coleman, A. (Apr. 2006). "Does Your Style Translate?" *Director*, Vol. 59. No. 9. p. 31.

Dolgoff, Ralph. (2005). *An Introduction to Supervisory Practice in Human Services.* Boston: Pearson/Allyn and Bacon.

Howell, Jon P. (2006). *Understanding Behaviors for Effective Leadership.* (2nd ed.). Upper Saddle River, NJ: Pearson Prentice Hall.

Edles, P. (2006). *Fundraising: hands-on tactics for nonprofit groups.* (2nd ed). New York: McGraw-Hill.

Fracaro, K. (Jan. 2006). "Releasing the Power within Your Employees." *Supervision*, Vol. 67. No. 1. pp. 14-16.

Kanter, R.M. (2005). *Confidence: How Winning Streaks and Losing Streaks Begin and End.* New York: Crown Business.

Maxwell, J.C. (2005). *Developing the Leader Within You.* Nashville, TN: Thomis Nelson, Inc.

McBain, R. (Winter 2005). " Leadership- Influences and Outcomes." *Henley Manager Update*, Vol. 17. No. 2. pp. 23-32.

Neff, T.J., & Citrin, J.M. (2005). *You're in Charge--Now What?* The 8-Point Plan. New York: Crown Business.

Preston, C. (2006, January). Guide to Winning Proposals. *Chronicle of Philanthropy,* p. 43.

Protch, O. (Apr. 2006). "Delegation of Authority." *Supervision*, Vol. 67. No. 4. pp. 12-14.

Wheatly, M.J. (2006) *Leadership and the New Science : Discovering Order in a Chaotic World.* San Francisco, CA: Berrett-Koehler Publishers, Inc.

Zeigler, Kenneth (2005). *Getting Organized at Work: 24 Lessons to Set Goals, Establish Priorities and Manage Your Time.* New York: McGraw-Hill.

CHAPTER 15

Searching for Funds

Because there are potentially thousands of funders, you must be highly selective in finding those few that are appropriate for your organization and your proposal. Initially you may have to identify many funding sources and then undertake a process of elimination to determine which ones are right for you. To avoid a time-consuming and often futile approach, it is best to select initially a core of foundations that match your interests. The ease of word processing might tempt you to send out indiscriminately "boilerplate" proposals. But this kind of diffused distribution is generally ineffective. Through research, you can pinpoint those foundations whose patterns of giving over the past several years reflect an interest in your area.

Having decided to secure special funding, it is important to determine what type of funding is practical. Initially explore whether you think funding can best be obtained from private or governmental sources. Private sector funding may allow you considerable freedom in developing your own project, but you may not be able to receive as much funding as you need. The government sector may provide you with a sizable grant but you may have to abide by specific conditions of the grant. Furthermore, you may experience much more competition compared to private sector funding.

MAJOR SOURCES OF PRIVATE FUNDING

Each year approximately seven billion dollars are spent by religious congregations on donations to organizations, both within and outside sectarian denominations. According to a special survey commissioned by the Independent Sector, *From Belief to Commitment: The Activities and*

Finances of Religious Congregations in the United States, some $6.6 billion of the $47.6 billion in expenditures reported by congregations (14 percent) was spent on donations to organizations both within and outside specific denominations.   Congregations contribute about 20 percent of their donations to organizations outside their denomination for activities they wish to promote. These activities include education, human service, grass roots, and advocacy programs.[1]

By far, most private philanthropic contributions are derived from individual giving—about $120 billion annually. This represents about 80 percent of all charitable giving.   Organizations use a variety of ways to attract individual donations including direct mail, membership campaigns, fund raising events, and deferred giving (endowment).   In 1996 foundations contributed about $12 billion annually (7.8 percent) and corporations about $8.5 billion (5.6 percent); approximately $10.5 billion (6.9 percent) was given by bequests.[2]

Foundations

The best way to learn about foundations is to write to the Foundation Center, 79 Fifth Avenue, NY, NY 10003. The Center will send you a publications catalogue that describes major sources of information about foundations. These sources, which include summary statements of each foundation's requirements, are available for purchase or through the facilities of the Center in New York or its offices in Atlanta, Washington, D.C., Cleveland, or San Francisco. The Center also has a network of Cooperating Collections in all fifty states and some foreign countries. For information, call 1-800-424-9836. The names of the Cooperating Collections can also be found on the Foundation Center Web Site: **www.fdncenter.org.**

Human service organizations are likely to request funds from three types of foundations: community foundations, independent foundations, and corporate foundations.

Community Foundations

Community foundations are publicly supported organizations that make grants for social, religious, educational, or other charitable purposes. They are supported by, and operated for, the benefit of a specific community or region. They receive their funds from a variety of donors, both living and those who have made bequests in their wills to establish endowments. Their endowments are frequently composed of a number of different trust funds, some of which bear their donors' names.   Their grant-making activities are administered by a governing body or distribution committee representative of community interests.   Investment funds are managed professionally, usually by trustee banks.   You can find out about community foundations through their IRS 990 tax return, which is available to the public. Many publish guidelines or annual reports.[3]

A community foundation has such a broad charge—it has to be concerned with the charitable concerns of the community in which it is located—that almost anything fits within that charge.   Still, even community foundations develop priorities. You can determine what they are through their 990 tax returns, their annual reports, foundation directories, or the **CD-ROM**, which will be discussed later. Because community foundations are primarily concerned with local needs, indiscriminately mailing requests for funding throughout the country is usually a waste of time.

Independent Foundations

Private, independent foundations are established to provide funds for community, educational, religious, or other charitable purpose. Their funds are generally derived from an individual, a family, or a group of individuals.   They may be operated under the direction of the donor or members of the donor's family, a type often referred to as "family foundations," or they may have an independent board of trustees or directors that manages the foundation's program. Decisions are made in several ways: by the donor, members of the donor's family, by independent directors, or by a trust official acting on the donor's behalf.   Because independent foundations can be inundated with requests, many have specific guidelines and priorities. Frequently they limit their giving to the local area; in many instances they may not wish to have applications submitted to them.

Information about independent foundations can be determined by contacting them directly. Only a small percentage issue separately printed annual reports. Annual information can be obtained from the IRS tax returns (990-PF) that must be made available to the public. These can be found at the Foundation Center offices.   The following are good directory sources of information: The Foundation Grants Index, the Foundation Directory, The Foundation Directory Part II, and the Guide to U.S. Foundations. (Specific directories will be discussed later in this chapter.)

Corporate Foundations

Corporate foundations, also called company-sponsored foundations, are created and funded by business corporations for the purpose of making grants and performing other philanthropic activities, which they do as separate legal entities. Generally, they are managed by a separate board of directors composed of corporate officials, although the board may also include individuals with no corporate affiliation. (In some company-sponsored foundations, local plant managers and senior officials are also involved in grant making and policy decisions.) Their giving programs usually focus on communities where the company has operations and in areas related to company interests. A corporate foundation makes it possible for a company to set aside funds for use in years when earnings may be reduced and the needs of charitable organizations may be greater. Some corporations maintain both a company-sponsored foundation and a direct-giving program, with the two often coordinated under a general giving policy.[4]

But company-sponsored foundations should not be confused with corporate contributions or direct-giving programs that are under the full control of the corporation, with funds drawn solely from the corporation's pretax earnings. Direct-giving programs may also encompass noncash "in-kind" contributions, such as donations of equipment, office space, supplies, or the labor of volunteer employees, as well as monetary grants. In contrast, a company-sponsored foundation, despite its close ties to the parent company, is legally an independent organization. It is classified as a "private foundation" under the Internal Revenue Code and is subject to the same regulations as any other private foundation. The foundation receives funds from the parent company's pretax earnings, which it then "passes on" to non-profit organizations in the form of contributions. It may also maintain its own endowment, however small.

In some instances a corporation may choose to make charitable contributions to the same non-profit organization through both its foundation and its direct-giving program. In this instance there may be little difference in the giving interests and procedures of the two vehicles, and they may even be administered by the same staff and board. There are significant differences, however, in the type and amount of information available to the public about these two funding vehicles.

By law, corporate foundations must report annually on their activities and grant programs to the IRS on the same Form 990-PF used by all private foundations. Many corporate foundations also issue annual reports or informational brochures detailing their program interests and application procedures. Corporations are not required, however, to inform the public about contributions and grants made directly through the corporation. As a result, even with a growing number of corporations choosing to publicize their giving interests, restrictions, and application procedures, it is generally much more difficult to research direct corporate giving programs.

Information on the more than 1,700 corporate foundations and the 600-plus direct-giving programs is provided in the *National Directory of Corporate Giving*. Many of the Foundation Center's other directories and guides also highlight corporate giving.

To find out about corporations in your community and/or in a specific industry, check with the business reference department of your local public library for sources such as *Standard and Poor's Register of Corporations*, the *Dunn and Bradstreet Reference Book of Corporate Management*, Chamber of Commerce directories, and corporate annual reports. Another readily available, but commonly overlooked resource, is your local yellow pages. Also many communities have business newspapers, such as *Crain's Business*, that provide good information.

Increasingly, corporations are integrating their contributions management into their overall strategic planning. Because of increased global competition, many corporations have limited dollars for philanthropy. Nevertheless, because of their responsibility to address social problems, companies are focusing more resources on fewer social issues and on those that can have an impact on their communities and ultimately on their business success. Companies are making contributions that benefit relations with their communities, the general public, and their employees.

Faced with justifying philanthropy, corporate decision makers are increasingly expecting grant receivers to provide measurable program results. Corporate contributions must be shown to result in direct and tangible benefits to strategic business objectives. Programs that can document success in improving community services and racial harmony, for example, are attractive to corporate donors because of their potential to benefit community relations.[5]

As corporate budgets become leaner, many companies will increase their donations of goods and services to offset reduced cash support. These "in kind" contributions can include product overruns or obsolete models manufactured or distributed by the company, office space or furniture and equipment, paper and printing service, and management or technical advice from company employees.

GOVERNMENT FUNDING

Over 40 percent of funding for social service agencies comes from governmental (local, state, and federal) sources. Despite recent declines in public funding, this clearly constitutes a significant resource.

Tracking governmental funds can be a daunting challenge. The payoff can be great but, then, so are the restrictions. To be chosen over many competitors, you will have to conduct careful research and have tremendous perseverance. Despite a general decline in support, the federal government is still the largest resource for external funding. Government funding information can be obtained from a variety of major sources:[6]

The *Federal Register* is published each weekday. For those who are interested in a variety of grant possibilities and who are able to respond to short deadlines, the *Federal Register* should be read daily. The "highlights" section in the front lists major topics. The "notices" section describes grant availability. Announcements are made of rules governing programs, so that even though money is not immediately available, you gain some idea of which grants are likely to be funded later. The Federal Register is available at most major public or university libraries, or write to Superintendent of Documents, U.S. Government Printing Office, Washington, D.C. 20402 for subscription information. You can also write to the Office of the Federal Register, c/o National Archives and Records, 8th and Pennsylvania Avenue, N.W., Washington, D.C. 29408. (Later in this chapter we will discuss how you can obtain information from the Internet.)

The *Commerce Business Daily* lists all potential contracts. Unlike grants, which give grantees more latitude over the use of funds, contracts require activities specified in advance by funders. The federal agency determines the type of program, format of activity, expected outcome, costs, and length of time. This is a good resource if you are interested in marketing your goods and services to the government. Write to the Superintendent of Documents.

The *Catalog of Federal Domestic Assistance,* published annually, is the most comprehensive source of government grant programs. It provides detailed information on how to apply, who is eligible and deadlines. The financial section describes monies available for the past and current year and indicates the pattern of grant giving. Descriptions of each program provide detailed information on the purpose of the program, eligibility requirements, and application procedures. Indexes by sponsoring agency, subject, functional programs categories, and eligible applicant groups enable users to identify the most appropriate funding programs. Call the Government Printing Office (202) 783-3238. Because it is not absolutely current—changes may have occurred since it went to print—check with the appropriate program officer for updated information. Or you can write to the Superintendent of Documents. It is also at the General Services Administration Web site: **http://www.gsa.gov/fdac.**

The Federal Assistance Program Retrieval Systems (FAPRS) is a computerized question-answer system designed to give rapid access to information provided in the catalog. Contact: Federal Assistance Catalog, General Services Administration Reports Building, 3007 7th St., S.W., Washington D.C. 20407.

Based on readings and general contracts with officials, you should be able to determine what is being funded. Your next step, then, is to make alterations in the framing of your original issue or problem area to fit government priorities. To obtain federal funding, you must conform to the federal requirements rather than expect that the federal government will make changes to meet your agency's particular needs. Federal agency priorities are published in the Federal Register and usually include the specific population to be served, the application deadline, and the type of proposal document to be submitted.

It is generally a good idea to communicate with the program officer responsible for the grant in your regional office or in Washington, D.C., through the name and number listed in the Federal Register. The program officer will be able to provide you with selection criteria. These criteria are extremely important because they indicate on what basis the proposal will be judged by impartial readers. Since proposal reviewers subtract points when a proposal does not measure up to selection criteria, your proposal should be as responsive to these as possible.

Besides these regular sources, every federal agency will periodically announce funds available for specified projects. These announcements provide detailed guidelines. It is useful to contact the appropriate federal agency to get on its mailing list for an application packet. You will be sent a Request for Proposal (RFP) kit that contains details of the grant, the average award amount, the possibility of renewal, eligibility requirements, required format, restrictions, and role of local or state government. This information should serve as your guidelines for preparing the proposal.

DESCRIPTION OF DIRECTORIES

Directories on community, corporate, and private foundations are available at the four Foundation Center offices (mentioned earlier) in Cleveland, Atlanta, Washington, and San Francisco or at the Cooperating

Collections, usually located in libraries serving urban communities.[7] For the location nearest you, check with the Foundation Center Web site: **www.fdncenter.org** or write to the Foundation Center, 79 Fifth Avenue, New York, NY 10003-3076 for the latest catalog. The following directories are available:

National Directory of Corporate Giving gives reliable and up-to-date entries on over 2,700 foundations and direct giving programs. Corporate funders often make grants that reflect the priority interests of their parent companies. The National Directory provides detailed portraits of over 1,800 corporate foundations and an additional 900+ direct giving programs. It features the following essential information: application procedures, names of key personnel, types of support generally awarded, giving limitations, financial data, and purposes and activities statements. Many entries include descriptions of recently awarded grants and program analyses to further indicate the grantmaker's interests.

The Foundation Grants Index is the most current and accurate source of information on recent grantmaker awards. The Grant Index covers the grantmaking programs of over 1,000 of the largest independent, corporate, and community foundations in the U. S. and features over 73,000 grant descriptions of $10,000 or more. Designed for quick grants-based research, its descriptions are divided into 28 broad subject areas, such as health and social services. Within each of these broad fields, the grants are listed geographically by state and alphabetically by name. The *subject index* targets grantmakers by thousands of key words, so you can identify programs similar to the one you are interested in having funded. *The geographic index* directs you to foundations that have made grants in various geographic areas. The *recipient category index* helps you find foundations that have supported your type of organization (community organizations, human services, etc.). The *recipient name index* allows you to discover the foundations that have funded specific non-profits that share your goals.

The Foundation 1000 provides the most comprehensive information available on the 1,000 wealthiest foundations in the country. These foundations hold over $168 billion in assets. They award close to 200,000 grants worth $8 billion to non-profit organizations each year. It describes which major foundations support projects like yours in your geographic area, what projects they have recently funded, how much of their budget they have earmarked for your interest area, and the names and affiliations of the foundations' key personnel. You can target potential funders by using subject areas preferred, types of support favored, and geographic areas typically funded.

The Foundation Directory features current data on over 7,900 grantmakers that have assets of at least $2 million or annually distribute $200,000 or more. The Directory provides fund-raisers with insight into foundation giving priorities by describing over 38,000 recently awarded grants.

The Foundation Directory Part 2 is designed specifically for non-profit organizations that want to broaden their base to include mid-sized foundations that hold assets between $1 and $2 million or with annual grant programs from $50,000 to $200,000. It includes over 20,000 grant descriptions.

Guide To U. S. Foundations provides current information on over 40,000 foundations. The comprehensive trustee, officer, and donor index will be useful to determine possible foundation affiliations of your board members, donors, and volunteers. This is a good guide to use for identifying smaller foundations. Arranged by state and total giving it can assist in pinpointing where to concentrate your search for local grant dollars. And you can also check the trustee, officer, and donor names to learn more about the giving choices of local families. The Guide uses codes to show if another Foundation Center reference book includes more detailed information on the grantmaker you are researching. Using this guide, you can note the employer identification number that will help you locate the foundation's IRS information return (990-PF) which is the best source of information for foundations too small to be included in the Foundation Directory Part 2.

Grant Guides provide you with current information on the grants recently awarded in your field. It gives descriptions of hundreds of foundation grants of $10,000 or more recently awarded in your subject area. The subject index lets you search for grantmakers by hundreds of key words. The geographic index directs you to foundations that have funded projects in your state or county. The recipient index lets you track grants awarded to similar organizations in your field.

The following guides are relevant to human services:

> *Aging*—Grants for legal rights, housing, education, employment, health and medical care, recreation, arts and culture, volunteer services, and social research.

> *Alcohol & Drug Abuse*—Grants for counseling, education, treatment, medical research, residential care and half-way houses; and projects on alcohol and drug abuse prevention.

> *Children and Youth*—Grants to support neonatal care, child welfare, adoption, foster care, services for abused children, research on

child development, pregnancy counseling and adolescent pregnancy prevention, rehabilitation of juvenile delinquency, and youth clubs.

Community/Economic Development, Housing & Employment—Grants to community organizations, government agencies, and universities for a wide range of social services, housing and urban development programs, including business services and federated giving programs.

Crime, Law Enforcement & Abuse Prevention—Grants for crime prevention, rehabilitation services for offenders, courts and the administration of justice, law enforcement agencies, and protection against and prevention of neglect, abuse, or exploitation.

Health Programs for Children & Youth—Grants to hospitals, social service agencies, and educational institutions for research, program development, general operating support, education programs, treatment for drug and alcohol abuse, pregnancy, and handicapped children.

Homeless—Grants to shelters and temporary housing services, legal rights, food services and health care; and to services for homeless families, and youth.

Literacy, Reading & Adult/Continuing Education—Grants to organizations supporting literacy, reading, and adult basic education and continuing education programs.

Mental Health, Addictions & Crisis Services—Grants to hospitals, health centers, residential treatment facilities, group homes and mental health associations; for addiction prevention and treatment; for hotline/crisis intervention services; and for public education and research.

Minorities—Grants for minority populations, including African Americans, Hispanics, Asian Americans, Native Americans, gays and lesbians, and immigrants and refugees.

Physically & Mentally Disabled—Grants to hospitals, schools, and primary care facilities for research, medical and dental care, employment and vocational training, education, diagnosis and evaluation, recreation and rehabilitation, legal aid, and scholarships.

Program Evaluation Grants—Grants to non-profit organizations to establish formal measures of the impact and efficacy of their programs.

Social Services—Grants to human service organizations for broad range of services, including children and youth services, family services, personal social services, emergency assistance, residential/custodial care; and services to promote the independence of specific population groups, such as the homeless and developmentally disabled.

Women & Girls—Grants for education, career guidance, vocational training, equal rights, rape prevention, shelter programs for victims of domestic violence, health programs, abortion rights, pregnancy programs, athletics and recreation, arts programs, and social research.

THE SEARCH PROCESS

For a more manageable process of searching for funds through one or more of the directories noted above, consider conducting your search in several phases:

Phase I

Prior to beginning your search, you should formulate a description of what you want to accomplish, including the problem you want to deal with, your target population, and your specific outcomes. The more focused you are, the easier your grant seeking search will be. Although at this point in the process you need not have developed a complete proposal, it is highly desirable that you have gone through the process of writing your ideas on two or three pages. (See Chapter 16 for a more expanded discussion of proposal writing.) The discipline of writing will encourage you to think through who you want to reach and what you want to do. Your quest at this phase is to develop a focused, easily searchable idea.

Phase II

In phase II you want to develop a broad list of potential supporters. Think of the search process as being an inverted pyramid. You want to identify as many possibilities as you can and then work towards refining the list to a few of the most appropriate ones. Initially, your thought may, in fact, be too broad. So even in this initial phase you may want to be focused. Your two or three page document should be helpful in providing you with this focus. For example, if your broad idea is social service counseling, you could potentially have hundreds of possible funders. By narrowing your idea to counseling teenagers who are involved in substance abuse you can embark on a more productive and manageable search.

Be mindful, however, not to be too narrow in your initial selection of topics. The search process involves a truly creative exploration of different possibilities. Our example of trying to find funds for counseling teenagers could include this variety of different subject categories:

> Adolescents
> Alcoholism
> Mental Health
> Drugs
> Suicide
> Pregnancy Prevention

By scanning the subject indexes in the *Foundation Directory* and the *Foundations Grants Index* you will get some ideas of relevant subjects for your grant proposal. During this phase it is important not to focus your search too narrowly, for it is possible, on the one hand, that those funders who have previously funded projects identical to yours may not want to repeat their funding. On the other hand, you may be able to locate funders who have similar, though not identical, interests to yours. They may be looking for fresh ideas.

Phase III

In phase III you will begin to narrow down your broad list of possibilities to as many as 10-20 or so potential funders. Assuming you have access to various previously discussed directories, you would consider using one or more of the following:

1. If you are seeking a grant over $10,000 you would go to the following sources:
   Indexes of Foundation Grants provide information on actual grants of $10,000 or more by the largest foundations.
   Grant Guides identifies foundations in other states that might fund organizations in your specific subject area and geographic location.
   The Foundation 1000 gives detailed information on major foundations in your state or nationally.
   The Foundation Directory is a major source for foundations that give out sizable grants.
2. If your grant is likely to be under $10,000:
   The Foundation Directory identifies smaller grants, as well as large ones.
   The Foundation Directory Part 2 provides information on those foundations that annually give totally between $50,000 and

$200,000. Also check the subject index for foundations in your state.
3.   If you are interested in applying for a corporate foundation grant:
The National Directory of Corporate Giving is an essential resource.

Phase IV

In this phase your interest is in narrowing the list of twenty or so possible foundations down to three to five. You do this by identifying various criteria: the geographic focus, contact information, limitations, range of donations, trustees, and pertinent information contained in the 990 Forms. You can find out most of this information from the directories or the **CD-ROM**, which will be discussed later. You may wish to keep a worksheet of your findings, as shown at the end of this chapter.

Focus primarily on those foundations that fund grants in your local area. Do not, however, limit your search only to those whose address is limited to the central city. You can probably scan foundations listed by your state to determine those that could fund programs in your local community. Most foundations restrict their giving to a specific community, state, or multi-state region. If you are seeking a relatively small grant with a purely local impact, you need to identify foundations that fund primarily in your local area. Most corporations will provide resources in communities where they have facilities. Review the location of these facilities for possible connections to your community.

If you are seeking corporate support, it is a good idea to obtain an annual report or printed guidelines that will contain the company's philosophy and its plans for the future. Determine whether you need to send a letter of inquiry or a full proposal. Some corporations have established separate foundation offices. Others may implement their giving programs through their marketing department, in which case their corporate giving is more closely tied to marketing products of the company. Always call to determine where your letter of proposal should be sent.

Typically, descriptions on foundations located in the various directories will indicate limitations. Read this section carefully to determine what the specific foundation will not fund. For example, some foundations will not provide funds for ongoing operations, or new projects, or capital campaigns, or certain subject categories. In addition, some foundations will not provide funds for equipment or conferences. Descriptions also indicate what the highest, lowest, and average grants have been. You may conclude that your grant request may be inappropriate based on your funding needs.

Another method of determining prospective funders is to review the list of trustees connected to the foundation and to consider whether members of your board have a relationship with them. In the case of corporate foundations, access to trustees who are employed by a corporation that could fund your project might possibly put you at an advantage.

To find out more about specific foundations, you should check their publications, including annual reports, guidelines, and newsletters. Many community foundations produce these, and even large private foundations will provide you with copies. If you have access to Foundation Centers or Cooperating Collections, you can obtain detailed information on private and corporate foundations by examining their **IRS 990-PF forms**. Contact your local Internal Revenue Service or nearest Foundation Center Library for the latest **990-PF**, which includes a list of all their funding interests, restrictions, application procedures, and deadlines. Some libraries also keep a news clippings file on foundations.

In summary, the sequence of the foundation search process involves two major steps. First, through the *Foundation Directory*, *Grants Index*, and other specialized directories (including, in some instances, state foundation directories), identify foundations that make grants in subject areas similar to yours. Second, research the foundations you have identified by checking their source book profiles, published annual reports, and tax returns. It is imperative that you try to ascertain their funding priorities.

APPROACHING FOUNDATIONS FOR FUNDING

After identifying a list of foundations whose funding patterns appear to match your interests, the next step is to determine how to approach them. Before submitting a proposal to a foundation, find out from information supplied in the directory or call or write to determine exactly how the grantmaker wants to be approached. Although there is no universal rule—each foundation has its own preference and style of operation—in general, small, private foundations require a brief (two or three page) letter telling who you are, what your concern is, what you propose to do, and how much funding you seek. A letter to small private foundations suffices because they rarely have full-time staff and have limited funds and scope; they can therefore readily indicate whether the proposal is within their area of interest.[8]

This same procedure can be used when approaching corporate-sponsored foundations. After sending a letter, it is important to make a personal contact with the person responsible for the corporate foundation (sometimes the president of the company, a person in public relations, or a specially designated program officer). In considering corporate support ask the following questions:

- Does the firm have significant business or employees in the community?

- Is the business related in any way to the type of project you are developing?

- Does your organization deal with issues that are of unique importance to the firm?

- Is there a special benefit to be gained by the firm for being associated with the project, including publicity or visibility with key consumers?

- Does the firm sell substantial products or services to your primary constituents?

Positive answers to these questions will enhance your chances of securing funding.[9] Besides providing grants, corporations can give other valuable resources, including the expertise of their personnel, gifts from their inventory, company facilities, and released time of employees.

Community foundations in large urban areas typically have program officers who are inundated with many proposals each year. They must screen these and determine which ones will be submitted to their Distribution Committee for final approval. Some community foundations prefer that you first submit a proposal and then arrange to come in and discuss it. Others encourage you to discuss a proposal with the program officer before investing considerable time and energy in it. If you can manage to submit a proposal several weeks ahead of the deadline, you may have the opportunity to meet with the program officer enough in advance to be able to make revisions. Meeting with staff is crucial because although not everything they recommend to the board of the foundation passes, their opinions and recommendations are highly regarded.

A general rule of thumb proposed by the Foundation Center is that you should approach three funders for every grant that you need. Because competition for funding is so great, be prepared to be turned down by several foundations before finally succeeding. If you send your proposal to more than one funder, be sure to indicate in the cover letter where else you are requesting funds.[10]

USING THE COMPUTER TO ACCESS INFORMATION

The Internet is a valuable source of information. Here are some important web sites worth browsing:

Foundation Center Links

In the private sector, the Foundation Center (**http://fdncenter.org**) is a major Web site to explore. This site provides links to other non-profit home pages. Unfortunately, only about 200 private, corporate, or community foundations—out of a potential of several thousand—have their folders connected to the Foundation Center Web site at this time. On this site you can find grantmaker information and funding trends, take a short course in proposal writing, or read summaries on recent newspaper articles about philanthropy. The Foundation Center's web site is updated and expanded on a daily basis and provides a wide range of philanthropic resource information. You can learn about the following:

- The *Philanthropy News Digest*, which provides weekly news abstracts in the philanthropy field.

- Free proposal writing short course

- Funding trends based on excerpts from the Center's research publications

- Online Library—direct access to an online librarian who will e-mail answers to research questions within forty-eight hours. (Subscription costs involved).

- Location of the closest Cooperating Collection where you can use the Foundation Center's publication and **CD-ROM**. (To be discussed later in this chapter.)

- Grantmakers accept a common grantmaking form and download this form from the web site.

Government Funding Sources

The Grants and Awards Site dealing with multiple/single government agencies is located at
www.access.gpo.gov/su_docs/dpos/topics/grants.html

At this site you will see a number of government references related to health and human services. Click "Grants and Awards" and then go to a category (listed below) that you are interested in. You will be taken to a grant's page that will provide you with a wealth of information on funding possibilities.

Federal Domestic Assistance Catalog,
Department of Health and Human Services GrantNet,
Department of Education,
Department of Housing and Urban Development,
National Institute on Aging,
National Institute of Health,
Economic Development Agency,
Justice Department

Another site is the *Federal Register* Online via GPO Access. The Federal Register, as the official publication for rules from federal agencies, will provide the first published notification for federal grants.
www.access.gpo.gov/su_docs/aces/aces140.html

Proposal Writing Suggestions

A Guide to Proposal Planning and Writing by Lynn E. Miner.
www.oryxpress.com/miner.htm

"Best Grant Tips of 1997." Reprinted from *Mental Health News Alert.*
www.cdpublications.com/cdpubs/news/97mhtips.htm

"Tips for Grantseekers from Grantscape."
www.grantscape.com/omaha/grants/services/tips.html

Corporate and Foundation Funding. Dick Olsen and Chris Murray of the University of Southern California provide examples of an introductory letter and proposal to a foundation. An outline for effective proposal writing takes the guesswork out of this process. It includes a step-by-step methodology for securing corporate support and foundation funding.
gopher://cis.edu/11/LibraryResearch/Research/Funding

A Proposal Writing Short Course. An excellent how-to guide that defines proposal structure is excerpted from *Guide to Proposal Writing,* published by the Foundation Center in 1997. This site provides recommendations for additional reading.
http://fdncenter.org/2fundpro/2prop.html

Private Funding

Internet Prospector
http://plains.ewyo.edu/~prospect/(especially the people section)

David Lamb's Prospect Research Page
http://weber.u.washington.edu/~dlamb/research.html

Forbes 400 List Generator
http://www.forbes.com/Richlist/richquer.htm

Internet resources for grants and foundations
http://nonprofit.miningco.com/msubfou.html

University of Idaho Education Grants Directory. Includes federal grant sources, foundations and private grant sources, grant directories, and education resources.
http://radon.chem.uidaho.edu/percent7Epmits/grants/homepage.html

Best Starting Places/Mega Sources:

CARDE'S Other Grant and Funding Pages on the Web. Produced by the Center for Applied Research and Development in Education at the University of Texas at Austin, this site has links to federal and private sector grants, general resources for grantseekers, and resources for grantwriters.
http://ed518g.edb.utexas.edu/default.html

Charity Village. Bilingual links to Canadian and U.S. sites for non-profit organizations.
www.charityvillage.com/charityvillage/main.html

Links to corporations' charitable giving interests
http://weber.u.washington.edu/~dlamb/research.html#corp

Council on Foundations. Includes Foundation News and Commentary and Council Columns Newsletter, publications of books and videos, general information on foundations, how to start a foundation, legislative and public policy watch, and foundation homepages.
www.cof.org/

The Grantmanship Center. Non-profit resources, TGC Magazine, today's Federal Register grant information, and links to grantmaking foundations—arts, community, corporate, international, private foundations, and public charities.
www.tgci.com/

Foundations On-Line: A Directory of Charitable Grantmakers. Sponsored by the Northern California Community Foundation, this site has directories of foundations and information on fundraising software, consultants, and products.
www.foundations.org

IAN Web Resources: Grant Opportunities. Links to individual foundations, organizations, and grant collections. Some listings have full or partial text.
www.pitt.edu/~ian/resource/grants.htm

U.S. Foundations and Fundraising Coalitions Resources. Links to organizations, foundations, publications, guides, and directories.
www.contact.org/usfound.htm

Data Base Access

The Foundation Center has another database information available online in two **DIALOG** files through Knight-Ridder Information Services, Inc. It provides access to hundreds of databases covering a wide range of subject areas. There are two online files managed by **DIALOG** Information Services; (1) The comprehensive *Foundation Directory* file includes descriptions of almost forty-thousand grantmakers, including foundations, corporate foundations and giving programs, and community foundations. (2) *The Foundations Grants Index* provides information on grants of $10,000 or more made by approximately 1,000 foundations. Updated five times yearly this index file corresponds to the following publications; *The Foundation Grants Index, The Foundation Grants Index Quarterly*, and *The Grant Guide Series*. Many libraries subscribe to **DIALOG** and perform computer searches for patrons, usually for a fee.

To use the computer data base files more efficiently, you should refer to the *User Manual, Thesaurus for Foundation Directory*, and *The Foundations Grants Index*. The user manual provides useful advice and examples of search strategies. Call the Foundation Center at (212)620-4230. To become a subscriber for the **DIALOG** services call 1-800-334-2564.

CD-ROMs

Several CD-ROMs that provide data on foundations are on the market. Their advantage over hard copy directories described earlier is that they can save you a tremendous amount of searching time as you seek to pinpoint the proper match. The most comprehensive **CD-ROM** is called **FC Search**, which covers over 45,000 U. S. foundations and corporate givers. This one disc also provides about 200,000 associated grants and identifies over 183,000 trustees and donors.

FC Search includes data found in previously described sources:

> *The Foundation Directory*
> *The Foundation Directory Part 2*
> *The Foundation Directory Supplement*
> *The Guide to U.S. Foundations: Their Trustees, Officers and*
>   *Donors*
> *The National Directory of Corporate Giving*
> *The Foundation Grants Index*
> *The Foundation Grants Index Quarterly*

The cost of the **CD-ROM** is expensive for most organizations that only occasionally need to undertake a search ($1,200 annually). It is updated semi-annually, which is important because foundations are constantly being added or dropped. If your organization frequently searches for grants, this may be a good use of organizational funds. Otherwise, you may wish to convince your local university or public library to purchase one. To locate the 200 Cooperating Collections that have the **CD** available, use the **WEB** site for the Foundation Center (**www.fdncenter.org**). Click on "Cooperating Collections," and then note which ones nearest you have the **CD** icon next to its name.

Using FC Search

The **CD** provides information on both grantmakers and grant files. By browsing through these two files you can determine the kinds of grants awarded by different grantmakers and then obtain more detailed information on the grants themselves.

FC Search has a browse function that allows you to review lists of records in each data base. You can browse the entire list or concentrate on specific states. By browsing the grantmaker file you can quickly locate a specific grantmaker and then go directly to a list of grants previously made by that foundation. Browsing the grants' file lets you scan a list of grants given to organizations, and then you can review the individual grants given to that organization.

The search function lets you pinpoint grantmakers or grants meeting your specific criteria. Such criteria can include the following:

> Geographic focus (nationally, state, or local)
> Fields of interest (e.g., social services)
> Types of support (capital, seed money, etc.)
> Total assets
> Total giving
> Subjects

Annual dollar amount

Text search (based on specific words you select that can be in the grant record)

In the Advanced Grants mode you can conduct an in-depth search of grants, the grantmakers that awarded them, and the specific organizations that received them. This is especially helpful if you want to determine which grantmakers provide grants in a specific subject area for a specific population group in a specific locality. One of the benefits of this search process is that it contains an index that is especially helpful in guiding in your search. Among the general fields of interest that are appropriate for health and human service agencies are the following:

civil rights
community development
crime /law enforcement
education
employment
environment
health care
health organization
housing/shelter
human services
mental health/crises services
mutual aid societies
philanthropy/volunteerism
recreation
social sciences
social services
youth development

Within each field of interest is a listing of subject categories. Become familiar with these categories since your search can be matched more directly with key words from the index. For example, if you were interested in searching for fund programs for ex-offenders you could search for this subject under the crime/law field of interest.[11]

Illustrations of Searchable Items

In a matter of seconds you could locate information on a wide list of topics. The following items are illustrative of the searches you could undertake:

- The address and telephone number of specific foundations
- An alphabetical listing of all non-profit organizations in your state or community
- All the grantmakers in your state that fund social services

- Foundations in your state that have given grants relating to aging and Alzheimer's disease (as an example)
- Names of the trustees of a particular foundation
- Foundations that give over $100,000 for capital grants
- Corporate foundations in your state that have given funds for specific purposes, such as building equipment
- Foundations that provide basic operating funds in your local community
- Foundations that have given money for specific purposes such as workshops or technical assistance
- Foundations that have given to organizations similar to yours (e.g., Boy Scouts, YMCA's, Red Cross)

Suggested Search Strategies Using the FC Search

The search strategies described earlier apply as well in using **FC Search**. The obvious advantage in using the CD over the directories is the speed with which you can conduct your search.   If you plan on using the CD, the following suggestions may prove useful:

1. Your primary objective is to locate foundations that will be amenable to funding your project, based on past giving patterns. For example, you assume that a particular foundation that previously funded a foster care recruitment program will be receptive to your foster care recruitment proposal. This may or may not be the case; having funded a previous foster care program, the foundation may be looking for other kinds of programs to help vulnerable children. Through an inquiry letter or a phone call you may be able to determine whether the proposal you have in mind is still a priority for the foundations you have identified.

2. Conversely, foundations that may not have previously funded a program similar to what you have in mind may now be open to considering an innovative foster care recruitment effort. Knowing that these foundations are interested in vulnerable children in general may be a good starting point for exploration.

3. The search process thus entails a certain amount of risk of being too broad or too narrow. For this reason expect to use the **FC Search** as a tool for exploration. The search process can involve a certain amount of trial and error. Suppose, for example, you are interested in establishing drug free zones in your community. Perhaps very few foundations have funded such an effort. That need not deter you from exploring foundations that have an interest in substance abuse, prevention, alcoholism, or neighborhood development.   You

can explore all of these subjects to determine your initial list of subjects. Be prepared to broaden your search if you identify too few "hits"; be prepared, on the other hand, to narrow your search if you identify too many "hits."

4. You need to learn the specific techniques for using the FC Search. It is worth your time to take a workshop if one is offered by your Cooperating Collection, or at least to study the manual that is available with the CD. You will learn specific techniques and vocabulary for expanding or narrowing your search.

5. Assume you have a particular topic in mind. In conducting a search you can either (1) scroll through a field of interest, and you will have available a preselected index or (2) you can use Text Search, which will search for words appearing anywhere within the grantmaker records. Using text search will require some degree of experimenting and time to understand the rules, but mastering it will provide useful payoff in being able to explore vast amounts of data.

Studying the manual will show you how focused your query can be. For example, putting quotes around the first three letters of a local zip code would narrow the list to local foundations that fund grants in your community and nearby suburbs. Another example: By typing in "applications not accepted" you would eliminate from the search process those foundations that do not accept outside grant requests. There are a number of other techniques discussed in the manual that will greatly enhance your search process.

6. Check the "Types Of Support Index" to limit your search to the types of support various grantmakers make. The following list can be useful in determining how foundations categorize their support:

Annual campaigns	Equipment
Building/renovation	General/operating support
Capital campaigns	In-kind gifts
Conferences/seminars	Internships
Consulting services	Loaned talent
Continuing support	Matching funds
Debt reduction	Program development
Donated equipment	Public relations services
Donated products	Publication
Emergency funds	Research
Employee volunteer services	Seed money
Endowment funds	Technical Assistance

7. In considering foundations that might give funding to your community, focus not only on those foundations located in your community or your state but also those located elsewhere that have given grants to your state.

8. With **FC Search** you can print or save the search results lists or grantmaker records you have specifically marked for later examination.

SUMMARY

Searching for funds requires considerable amount of creative ingenuity. The availability of directories and **CD-ROMs** now makes it possible to explore a wide variety of possibilities in a fairly short time period. Expect to do a great deal of trial and error. Above all, be persistent in your quest.

QUESTIONS FOR DISCUSSION

1. Identify several projects for which you might seek funding. What sources would you consider?

2. Assuming you could reach a funder on the phone, what questions might you ask in seeking possible funding?

3. Select a possible funding project. What resources would you use in identifying possible funders?

**Worksheet
on Potential Funders**

Information Source:

    Name
    Address

Contact Person   **Phone Number**

Financial Data:
    Total Assets
    Grant Ranges
    Single Year _____ Multi Year ___

Subject Focus Priorities:

Target Populations:

Special Limitations:
    Geographic
    Funding Restrictions
Types of Support:
    Program Development
    Ongoing Support
    Other

Trustees:

Application Information:
    Printed Guidelines
    Application forms

Initial Approach (letter of inquiry, formal proposal, phone call)

Deadlines:
    Proposal submission dates
    Trustee decision times

Follow-up notes

Chapter Notes

[1]Nauffts, M.F.(ed.) (1994). *Foundation Fundamentals: A Guide for Grantseekers* (5 ed.). New York: The Foundation Center.

[2]Kaplan, A. E. (ed.) (1997) *Giving USA 1997.* New York: AAFRC Trust for Philanthropy, p.1.

[3]Nauffts, p. 4.

[4]Ibid, p. 3.

[5]Marx, J.D. (Jan. 1998). "Corporate Strategic Philanthropy: Implications for Social Work." *Social Work, pp. 35-41.*

[6]Borden, K. (1978). *Dear Uncle: Please Send Money—A Guide for Proposal Writers.* Pocatello, ID: Auger Associates.

[7]The Foundation Center (Fall 1997) *Fundraising & Nonprofit Development Resources Catalog.*

[8]Geever, J.C. & McNeil, P. (1997). *Guide To Proposal Writing.* New York: The Foundation Center.

[9]Ibid, p. 140.

[10]Morth, M. & Collins, S., eds. (1996) *The Foundation Center's User Friendly Guide: A Grantseeker's Guide to Resources.* New York: The Foundation Center.

[11]The Foundation Center (1997) *FC Search Manual.* New York, p. 27.

REFERENCES FOR CHAPTER 15

Alexander, G.D., & Carlson, K. (2005). *Essential Principles for Fundraising Success: An Answer Manual for the Everyday Challenges of Raising Money.* Somerset, NJ: John Wiley and Sons, Inc.

Bey, D.M. (April 2006). "Authority and Issues to Consider Prior to Entering into Funding Agreements with the Federal Government." *Intellectual Property & Technology Law Journal*, Vol. 18. No. 4. pp. 10-16.

Browning, B.A. (2005). *Grant Writing for Dummies.* Somerset, NJ: John Wiley and Sons, Inc.

Coffman, S. (Jan. 2006). "Building a New Foundation: Library Funding." *Searcher*, Vol. 14. No. 1. pp. 26-34.

Hinds, M. (2005). *Grant Writing Made Easy.* Grand Rapids, MI: Frank Schaffer Publications.

Hood, K., & Matsko, J. (2006). *Grant Writing: a Basic Guide.* Spokane Valley, WA: Whispering Pines Press, Inc.

CHAPTER 16

Preparing Effective Proposals

PRELIMINARY CONSIDERATIONS

The process of obtaining funding for important projects or programs can be both enriching and overwhelming. Preparing proposals disciplines thinking and simulates more purposeful fund seeking endeavors. But the process can also be awesome because of the many details you have to focus on and the many decisions you have to make. The purpose of this chapter is to identify those aspects of the proposal preparing process that will make your grant seeking activity more effective.

Conducting a Preliminary Assessment

Because you will be investing a considerable amount of time, energy, and organizational resources in a proposal, you should conduct a preliminary assessment. During this pre-proposal phase, review the following fundamental questions:[1]

First, is the project idea desirable and feasible? Conduct a preliminary review of the literature and contact persons who have undertaken similar projects. Judge whether the problem to be addressed is truly solvable. Clarify during this exploratory period whether the project idea is unique or, if a similar project has been done elsewhere, why there are compelling

245

reasons to duplicate it. Assess the urgency of embarking on the target population at this time. Determine who might support the project. Make a preliminary assessment about the feasibility of the project, given anticipated difficulties in implementation.

Second, is your organization able to carry the project forward? Analyze the project in relation to the current mission and goals of the organization. Review whether there is sufficient organizational will and staff capability to take on a new endeavor. Consider your competitive position in relation to other potential applicants. Assess your ability to take on the demands of the project considering other pressing priorities. Will taking on a new project divert funds and staff time away from ongoing projects?

Third, are there funders who might be interested in the project idea? Determine through preliminary direct contacts or through descriptions of funding sources whether their priorities match your proposal idea.[2] (See Chapter 15 on searching for funding.)

Fourth, what are the potential financial consequences of obtaining funding? Examine whether the likelihood of new funding will limit your autonomy and curb your decision making regarding people to be served or ways of functioning. Consider the impact of discontinued funding at the end of the grant period. Review whether funding is likely to be sufficient to carry out the program adequately.[3]

These issues contain cautions that must be weighed against the almost irresistible attraction of seeking funding for new projects. The clear message: anticipate as much as possible before you formally begin writing your proposal. Do your homework!

Prior to Writing the Proposal

Because foundations will give grants only to organizations that are incorporated as non-profit agencies, you will need to obtain this designation from the Internal Revenue Service. An attorney can help you obtain the designation, 501(C)(3) status. To achieve this status, you will need to have a board of trustees. The Secretary of State or the state's Attorney Generals Office can provide you with the 501(C)(3) application. Once completed, your organization is eligible to receive tax deductible gifts. While you are waiting for approval, it is still possible for you to receive tax deductible gifts if you have made arrangements with another organization to serve as your fiscal agent. This organization serves as a conduit of funds and may need to give assurances to the grantor that the budget will be monitored.[4]

Assuming that you either have 501(C)(3) or a creditable fiscal agent, you should strive to insure the funder that you have an organization worthy of investment. In some instances funders may be willing to take a chance on a brand new organization if they are excited about the idea and they have confidence in the leadership. Your strategic plan should convey a sense of direction and an ability to implement programs.

You must also have a clarity about your priorities. Since it is impossible for organizations to meet all the needs of their clients or the community, it is vital that the organization, through its trustees, staff, and volunteers, determine its priorities. Then the organization can be pro-active in searching out funding for programs around which consensus exists. This approach is far better than selecting programs that fit priorities of funders but are not in keeping with the mission of your organization or the commitment of your constituencies.

As you are about to do the actual writing of the proposal, make sure that you have gathered all the information you need to document your case. You may need to assign several people to gather the necessary data. Make sure that you are prepared to discuss in clear terms your goals, objectives, implementation plan, timetable, and staffing requirements. Since you are only at the beginning of the process, details around the budget may have yet to be worked out. But you should have some general idea of the expenses involved so that you can decide whether you can realistically pursue funding—or whether you have to reduce the magnitude of your projected program. Create a preliminary outline that will help you sort out your main ideas from subordinate ones. To add human interest to your document, be prepared to discuss actual situations of need and how people could benefit. Grantmakers prefer real life experiences to enhance the text of a proposal. Human interest stories will help humanize your program.

How Fundable is Your Project?

If your idea is brand new, expect foundations not to be immediately receptive. Even though foundations are in the business of providing risk capital, they nevertheless generally like to feel that there has been some experience or track record that indicates the feasibility of the idea. If you can start your program on a small scale pilot project before requesting funds, you can increase your chance for funding considerably. At the very least identify programs similar to yours that have succeeded somewhere else. Your search process of grants similar to yours could reveal successes elsewhere.

Generally, foundation and corporate funders prefer specific projects over general operating requests. This reality can be frustrating for organizations that require ongoing support. Your search process may identify those foundations that are amenable to general support. Generally, however, funders prefer to know exactly how their money is being used and the specific impact it could have.

To increase your chances of funding, you would be wise to demonstrate to potential funders that you have embarked on ways to raise your own resources. Funders are impressed to learn that 100 percent of your trustees contribute to your annual fundraising campaign. Knowing that you are raising money in various ways gives them confidence that your organization and the specific projects, like the one you are proposing, can be sustained. Consider seeking funding for general operating purposes from non-foundation sources, such as local United Ways, fundraising events, or membership campaigns.

PREPARING PROPOSALS

Proposal formats and length may vary depending on the requirements of funders. Government proposals use a highly structured format. Proposals for foundations are not usually as structured but generally all will want to know what you intend to accomplish and how you propose doing so. The following format is offered as a guide, to be modified if the funder requests a different outline:

> Summary Statement
> Statement of Need
> Goals and Objectives
> Program Components: Activities and Tasks
> Evaluation
> Organizational Capability
> Program Continuation
> Budget
> Appendices

SUMMARY STATEMENTS

Normally a summary statement should appear first because readers need an overview to orient them to the project and to prepare them for the details that are to follow.[5] The summary should be less than one page and contain the following elements:

- what the need is
- what will be accomplished

- who you are and why you are qualified
- what activities you will perform
- what it will cost
- how long it will take

The summary should be prepared after the full proposal is written because it should accurately reflect its major elements.

STATEMENT OF NEED

The purpose of this section of the proposal is to define precisely what condition your organization wants to change. Focusing on local conditions would likely appeal to a local foundation. Dealing with a problem or issue that has implications beyond your own community may appeal to a large national foundation or a federal agency. Whether you approach a local or a national foundation, focus on the people who will be served, not on how funding will be used to benefit the organization.[6] Specify who the target population is, what specific problem will be addressed, where the problem is located, what its origin is, and why it continues to exist. If the problem is multifaceted, then all the significant aspects need to be identified. For example, a problem statement about out-of-school, unemployed, adolescent ex-offenders living in poverty would need to describe their life style, educational lags, and need for income.

Distinguish here the difference between risk, target, and impact populations.[7] The risk population is the total group needing help or at risk, for example, eight hundred ex-offenders in the community. The target population is that subset toward whom the program is aimed; for example, seventy ex-offenders are to be served. The impact population is the subset likely to benefit from the program; for instance, forty-five of those served will obtain jobs. If possible, the theoretical basis for the problem should also be discussed. You should review the literature on the target population's needs to develop a conceptual understanding of the factors causing the problem. Avoid circular reasoning. It is not enough, for example, to say that the problem is the lack of the service you intend to provide.[8]

To demonstrate your grasp of the problem, provide prospective funders with data from a variety of sources: national studies and their local applications, testimony from congressional records, surveys, or quotes from authorities. Give special attention to provide local data on the issue. Use information that is most relevant to your project. Document as best you can through data obtained through local sources (e.g., United Way, Department of Human Resources, Juvenile Court). Be as specific as possible when describing the need.

Unless a funding group requests detailed information in the narrative, do not inundate it with pages of statistics; summarize the data and place detailed, statistical tables in an appendix. Because many problems are chronic, the statement of need should convey why there is a special urgency to seek funding now. What new crisis has arisen? For example, are the kinds of crimes being committed by adolescents more serious than before? Does new state legislation place a special burden on the local community to deal with delinquency? Are local institutions more prepared now than before to deal with delinquency? A description of special circumstance makes the importance of funding the project more compelling. The potential funders must see the problem as both timely and critical.

Where feasible, indicate how the community constituency or client group has been involved in defining the problem. Such involvement is obviously desirable if the proposal relates to community improvements, for the clients are in the best position to comment on their special needs. Even those who normally do not participate, such as mentally retarded offenders or recently released, mentally ill patients, can be consulted. Their participation in the problem-defining process conveys the message that you have a more profound depth of understanding.

Although the statement of need is presented before the section on goals and objectives of the proposal, it should be written with objectives clearly in mind. Because needs and objectives must be consistent with each other, it might even be desirable to write the latter section first. This would be especially necessary if the prospective funder has specified what the proposal should accomplish, which is usually the case with federal.[9]

If your program is to be considered a model, show how your model can be replicated. If, on the other hand, your own program is itself a replica of another project done elsewhere, document the success of that program and show how it can be of benefit to your community.[10]

GOALS AND OBJECTIVES

As discussed in Chapter 6, organizational or program goals represent broad statements of what the organization wants to accomplish. They provide a general direction for commitment to action. They are global descriptions of a long-term condition toward which the organization's efforts will be directed. Goals are ideals, they are timeless, and they are rarely achieved. Examples of goal statements are the following:

"Reduce crime in the community" ... "upgrade housing" ...
"improve interracial relations" ... "provide information to low

income clients" ... "prevent illegitimate births by teenagers" ... "eliminate child abuse and neglect."

Although goal statements are inspiring, they are not amenable to clear definition and measurement. Objectives, in contrast, represent relevant, attainable, measurable, and time-limited ends to be achieved. They are relevant because they fit within the general mission and goals of the organization and because they relate to problems identified in the proposal. They are attainable because they are capable of being realized. They are measurable because achievements are based upon tangible, concrete, and quantifiable results. They are time-limited because the proposal specifies the time frame within which results can be achieved. Objectives provide the funder with clear-cut targets for organizational accountability. Be aware that while objectives are intended to be realistic and achievable, their accomplishment may not necessarily eliminate a problem described earlier in the proposal. Obtaining jobs for forty-five ex-offenders will not solve the high rate of recidivism in the community.

Four kinds of objectives can be prepared. They are operational, process or service, product, and impact objectives.[11]

Operational objectives convey the intent to improve the general operation of the organization. Examples include the following:

> to sponsor four in-service training workshops in the next three months for 40 staff;
> to increase the size of the membership by 150 within the coming year (and thereby put the organization in sound financial shape).

Operational objectives enhance the functioning and survivability of the organization. Achieving them puts the organization in a better position to help its target population.

Service objectives (sometimes called process objectives) are based on the organization's quantifying units of service rendered. Examples:

> to serve 300 clients in the program year;
> to conduct 680 interviews;
> to provide 17 neighborhood assemblies;
> to refer 125 clients to agencies in a year.

Product objectives relate to a tangible piece of work that will be delivered at the end of the funded period. Examples:
> to prepare a resource directory;
> to create a case management system;

to produce a videotape that will provide clients with information about the agency's services.

Impact objectives specify outcomes to be achieved as a result of process activities. Whereas service objectives reflect the amount of effort to be expended, impact objectives detail the return expected on the investment of time, personnel, and resources. Impact objectives focus on results. Examples include the following:

to place 50 percent of the youth enrolled in the vocational training program in full-time jobs within 18 months;

to increase educational attainment of a school's two hundred entering students; 80 percent of whom will complete at least one full year of school;

to obtain a commitment from the board and the youth commission to incorporate the program, by the end of the third year, into the regular school program.

The advantage of each of these objectives is that they alert the funders to expect a clear-cut outcome from the project. Stating the objectives in measurable terms disciplines you to set realistic achievements, not ideal ones. While considerable flexibility can be used to prepare impact objective statements, the following criteria are suggested:

1) Generally use a strong verb that describes an observable change in a condition. "To reduce," "to improve," "to strengthen," and "to enhance" are examples.

2) State only one aim with one specific result. An objective that states two aims may require two different implementations, and confusion could later occur about which of the two objectives was achieved. "To reduce the recidivism rate by 10 percent and obtain employment for twenty former delinquents" is an example of an objective with two aims.

3) Be certain that the objective is realistic. Do not, for example, promise to reduce significantly unwed teenage pregnancies through a program designed to work with one hundred youngsters in a community that experiences two thousand unwed births a year. Furthermore, although the format presented here separates Goals and Objectives from Program Components (next section), they may be combined so that specific activities and tasks are listed under each objective.

PROGRAM COMPONENTS: ACTIVITIES AND TASKS

This aspect of the proposal presents a work plan of how the organization intends to accomplish its objectives. To convey the logic and continuity of the project, the proposal should describe, in relation to each objective, what will be done, by whom, and by when. To discipline your thinking about planning the work that needs to be accomplished, undertake reverse-order and forward-sequence planning, as discussed in Chapter 6. For a project designed for ex-delinquents where one of the objectives is to obtain jobs, a simplified work plan would be formatted as follows:

Objective: To place 50 percent of previously delinquent youth in the vocational training program in full-time jobs within 18 months.

Activity #1: Develop a pool of not less than 40 potential jobs.
Tasks: 1. Have employers' sign contractual agreements
        2. Follow up letters with personnel contacts
        3. Mail letters of inquiry
        4. Devise contractual forms
        5. Hire job recruiters
        6. Train job recruiters

Activity #2: Provide orientation for youth
Tasks: 1. Prepare training materials
        2. Obtain facility
        3. Recruit staff
        4. Train staff

Besides a visual time line chart (See Chapter 7), you should describe in detail how the program would actually function. When relevant, state in the narrative, for example, how the proposed work has been successfully used elsewhere, how it will relate to existing programs in the community, and what current resources of the organization will be used. The determination of activities and tasks will typically involve a group process because knowledge is not usually concentrated in one person, and a consensus may need to emerge if organizational members are to be involved in implementing the proposal. But the actual proposal writing itself cannot be done by a committee; one or two people have to take primary responsibility. The group can react to a draft, and their suggestions can then be incorporated.

EVALUATION

The essential value of evaluation for most proposals is to be able to compare intended results with actual outcomes. Objective statements should be written to foster subsequent evaluation by incorporating measurement indicators, as indicated below:

> To improve school performance (as indicated by teacher evaluation) of past offenders in 50 percent of the cases served in one program year.

> To improve personal adjustment (as determined by specifically constructed psychological tests of ex-mental hospital patients) in 75 percent of those served during one program year.

> To reduce the rate of recidivism of juvenile offenders (as measured by official police re-arrest data) by 50 percent during the next program year.

> To develop ongoing funding for the innovative delinquency prevention project (as indicated by letters of commitment from the Youth Commission and the United Way) by the end of the second year.

In some instances it is necessary to devise instruments, called performance indicators, to measure results. In the objective statements illustrated above, these might be teacher assessment forms or psychological tests. Each organization will have to determine whether it will create its own or adopt existing performance indicators. When the information has been collected, the organization can compare planned with actual performance. Process evaluation (sometimes referred to as monitoring) examines the internal processes and structure of the program to determine whether it is functioning as planned. Is it achieving its objectives in a timely manner? Is it keeping an accurate record of who is being served and under what conditions? Are clients being processed as expected? What administrative problems are being encountered? The major value of process evaluation is that it helps the program staff review whether they are going off course and allows them to take corrective action before the end of the funding period.[12] Process evaluation assures funders that proper feedback is being built into the project.

To carry out process evaluation, a local advisory committee could be appointed to judge the effectiveness of the effort and report back to the funder. Another possibility is to identify an expert in the field to visit periodically the project and furnish reports to the donor. A third possibility is for the project staff to report on its monitoring to the results of the project, particularly when objectives are measurable. Regardless of the design model, the proposal should explain the questions to be answered and the details of the evaluation plan, including who will perform it, how evaluators are to be chosen, and what instruments are to be used.

CAPABILITY OF THE ORGANIZATION

Funders want to know that the organization is capable of implementing the project.[13] Because they must be convinced of your competency to accomplish what you promise, you need to demonstrate your credibility for undertaking the project. Describe briefly how and why the organization was formed, past and current activities, the support you receive from other organizations, and your significant accomplishments. Especially if your organization is unknown to funders, provide evidence of your involvement and competency in the area in which you are requesting funds. Indicate what financial or other resources are available. Letters of endorsement are desirable, but letters committing actual resources (staff, equipment, funding) are even more impressive. (Note: You have an option of discussing the organization's capability as part of a general introduction or in a separate section after discussing program evaluation. Review the funder's guidelines for the specific format.)

Because the proposal itself must be concise, you may want to refer to the competency of staff in the appendices and provide a list of positions, titles, qualifications, chain of responsibility, salary levels, and responsibilities. If appropriate, describe the selection process for key personnel. Funders appreciate knowing that your board of trustees is actively involved in decision making and fully supports the proposal. List trustees and their identifying information in the appendices. Testimony from key figures in the community is also useful if their endorsement letters are sincere and reflect genuine support. Indicate the role and names of an advisory committee, if appropriate. If requested, include in the appendices an annual report, documentation of your organization's IRS non-profit status, latest audit statement, and a copy of your agency's affirmative action policy.

PROGRAM CONTINUATION

In this section of your proposal, indicate the feasibility of the organization continuing the program beyond the grant period. Foundations that give time limited funding want assurance that the project will be sustained. Among the options for continued revenue are the organization's operating budget; revenue from client fees; third-party payments, such as insurance; special fundraising drives; application for membership or special funding in a United Way or other federated fundraising programs; and an assumption of costs by a voluntary organization or government agency.

Although it may be difficult to anticipate sources of funding two or three years hence, it is of such crucial importance to funders that you should make a concerted effort to explore other funding options as part of the proposal preparation process. If you intend to have a scaled-down version of your program absorbed by other community agencies, indicate how you plan to have it incorporated into their programs.

THE BUDGET

The budget is important, but unless it reveals major weaknesses or is obviously overinflated, it will not be the primary reason for the rejection or acceptance of a proposal. If your idea is sound, the budget is generally negotiable. Consider the following general guidelines in preparing the budget:[14]

Different funders require varying degrees of detail in the budget. Most governmental agencies require a great deal of detail and usually provide budget forms and instructions for their completion. Foundations and corporations are less structured in their requirements but will want a budget that is well thought out and complete. Some governmental agencies have special instructions for preparing the budget that are in the regulations. These instructions are continually being revised. Use the most recent instructions available rather than delaying the preparation of your budget. Allow time to make necessary changes if you find that a new set of instructions is to be issued shortly before the final application is due. Grant application instructions generally include information regarding budget forms, examples of how to calculate specific budget items, agency formulas for determining the maximum allowance in major budgetary categories, and allowable rates for consulting fees, per diem expenses, and travel. Be prepared to document your needs when costs exceed the agency formula.

As an aid in developing the budget, prepare worksheets. They provide a structure for budget planning so that no type of expense is overlooked. Make detailed records of each budgeted item, and be prepared to discuss the potential impact of budget cuts during negotiations. The worksheets will provide a plan for use in actual project operation. A good budget will relate directly to the objectives and activities. Each budget item should be justified on the basis of its potential contribution to the project. To prepare a budget, review each major activity and estimate its expenses. There should be a clear connection between activities and budget items.

The budget is an estimate of what the program's costs will be. Generally, you will have a degree of flexibility in spending, as long as you do not exceed the total amount of the grant. Requests for budgetary changes should be made in writing to the funding source and, if approved, become formal budget modifications that change the conditions of your grant. Adequately planning your budget reduces the number of changes that may be required and also establishes a degree of credibility necessary to obtain permission for needed modifications. Usually, if the grant is to cover more than one year, funders want a breakdown of the year-by-year budget and then a total amount. Also, if more than one funder is being asked to contribute to the costs, indicate the expected income from each different source. If the organization can make inkind donations to the project, such as staff time and building space, then the budget should reflect this.

In the narrative that accompanies the budget, be as specific as possible about unusual costs. This is particularly necessary if the funder is not familiar with the nature of the project. Be able to document exact costs for each major item. When it is necessary to create new positions, survey other agencies with similar jobs to justify salary scales. If you include items in the budget that you cannot fully support, the integrity of your project may be open to question. Regarding salaries, provide a detailed breakdown of each position and percentage of time that would be allocated to the program. Include fringe benefits, worker's compensation, state unemployment insurance, social security, retirement, and other such items as a separate category in the budget.

Other direct costs would include space costs; rental, lease, or purchase of equipment; supplies; travel in and out of town; telephone; copying; and printing. Add other categories if expenditures are significant. Give details for the basis of cost estimates. Indirect costs are more difficult to determine than are direct costs, but they are important to the financial well-being of your organization. Indirect expenses may include estimated portions of time spent on the project by other staff members, such as the director, accountant, and maintenance personnel. Such costs can also encompass expenditures that are difficult to account for with precision, such as the depreciation of office equipment. Indirect expenses may or may not include such items as office rental or office equipment, depending on whether they can be isolated or are an integral part in the administration of your organization.

Indirect costs may be included in the grant request (if they are allowable) by adding a certain percentage for indirect expenses to the direct costs of the grant. That percentage is usually determined after an analysis of your overall financial operations by an experienced accountant. Many organizations that carry on extensive grant activity within federal agencies negotiate an acceptable percentage with one governmental agency and are then able to use the same rate in contracts with other governmental agencies. The federal government will allow indirect expenses arrived at either as a percentage of total salaries involved in the project or as a percentage (much lower) of the total direct costs of the grant. Some foundations are becoming more accepting about including indirect costs, but depending upon the policies of a particular foundation, you may have to absorb indirect costs in other parts of your budget. Check with your funder on its policies on indirect costs.

If you intend the program to serve a certain number of people, divide this number into the costs to see if the cost of service per client is reasonable. Funders often calculate this figure; so if you have not provided it in the proposal, be prepared to defend the program's per capita cost. Do not accept less money than is needed for a successful effort just to obtain the grant. You receive no credit for good intentions if they are not accomplished. Accepting the accountability for a project without having the essential resources to follow through with it is irresponsible. If you decide to accept fewer dollars, be sure you revise your anticipated achievements.

Any earned income (e.g., fees, special events, use of endowment income) anticipated should be included in the budget. The funder will appreciate your acknowledgment of anticipated revenues that will offset anticipated expenses.[15]

APPENDICES

The proposal appendices provide information that is not essential to making the case but lends reliability and understanding to the organization and its request.[16] Include the following items: a list of your board of trustees, documentation of your agency's 501 [c][3] tax-exempt status from the IRS, audit, job descriptions, affirmative action policy, statistical charts, letters of support or agreement, evaluation instrument, and other items that bolster your proposal or that may be required by the funder.

THE PROPOSAL IS ONE PART OF THE PROCESS

Proposals by themselves—even well written ones—do not necessarily insure that funding will be forthcoming. The best chance for a grant request to succeed requires not only a well thought out plan (the proposal) but also a meaningful connection with a potential funder.

Those who give away money want to be inspired and feel that their funds are going to a good cause that will result in meaningful impact. Funders want their grants to be used by an organization that can implement a worthwhile program. Expect, therefore, that your potential grantors will be greatly interested in your program if they anticipate a dynamic collaboration.[17]

Ideally, the proposer should strive to develop a partnership with the potential donor. Building the relationship is an essential part of the funding process. While it is true that funders look to the track record and the reputation of the organization, fundamentally they are investing in people, not the organization as an abstract entity. The old adage, "people give to people," is certainly appropriate.

In keeping with this idea of developing a relationship with potential funders, it is generally a good idea to contact a foundation staff person (assuming there is one) to determine whether there is a good fit between your proposed ideas and the foundation's priorities. This contact provides an additional opportunity to obtain input from the funder about the criteria that will be considered. You could determine, for example, the time period, the amount of the request, the need for evaluation, and the expectations of results.

Depending on the initial interest of the foundation and its style of operating, you will determine various ways of contacting the funder: phone calls, face to face meetings, and possibly foundation trustee contacts. (Note, however, that some foundation officers may be offended that you are "going over their heads" to influence voting trustees.) These efforts are designed to help the funder understand your organization and its programs. Even if you do not succeed in obtaining funds for your current project, you lay the groundwork for possibly succeeding with future proposals.

CRITERIA FOR EFFECTIVE PROPOSALS

Funders will obviously vary in the criteria they use for judging a proposal. As indicated previously, government agencies will have specific and unique criteria for each grant. Foundation funders will tend to be more flexible in using criteria to judge proposals. The following criteria should be kept in mind when preparing your proposal:

Competency of the Individuals Involved

Are those who have prepared the proposal considered highly competent?

Are they dedicated to making their ideas a reality?

Do they have a successful track record?

Do they demonstrate a depth of knowledge about what is happening in their community and across the country?

Are they sufficiently aware of the complexity of the problem?

Participation of the Organization's Membership

Are board members familiar with the proposal? Have they approved it?

Is the board composed of the best possible combination of members of the community, client representatives, and others who can be effective resources for the organization?

Is the board willing to provide some of the organization's own resources?

If applicable, has provision been made for client or consumer participation in the design and implementation of the project?

Desirability of the Project

Does the proposal make a strong case for the urgency of funding?

Is it clearly a high priority for the requesting organization and for the community?

If similar programs already exist, does the proposal acknowledge this and strongly convey why, nevertheless, one more program is necessary?

Is the project creative in proposing an innovative approach to dealing with a community problem?

If asking for renewal of a grant, has the project adequately demonstrated accomplishments?

If the project has fallen short of its accomplishments, does the proposal adequately explain why and what the organization intends to do about it?

Is the proposal in keeping with the funder's own priorities?

Feasibility of the Project

Does the proposal illustrate how it will adequately cope with the problem it has identified, neither being too limited in its objectives nor too grandiose in its claims?

If it proposes to meet a long-standing problem, does the proposal have a well-conceived rationale for how it expects to succeed?

What specific ingredients and talents can it bring to bear on the problem?

If the project is to continue, what assurances are there for ongoing funding?

On the basis of research of programs in other communities, does the proposal indicate why it can succeed in the same way as others have?

If others have failed, what modifications are proposed to insure success?

Possibility of Leveraging Funds

Will the project draw on other private or public funding?

If the request for funding is large, has the organization explored combining this request with requests to other funding organizations?

If several funders are involved, can each funder's contribution be separately identified?

Continuity of the Project

If funds are being requested for a startup project, what are the assurances of the requesting organization or another group to continue it?

If the proposal is a demonstration project, what is the likelihood it might be replicated if it proves successful?

Impact Potential

Are the results likely to be transferable to other programs and other communities?

Will the results have a significant impact on the community?

Does the organization have a record of being able to involve other organizations and outside individuals to work together to achieve objectives?

If the proposal purports to make institutional changes, what assurances can it offer that it will be able to succeed?

Dedication

If the proposal was previously rejected, has it been resubmitted with necessary modifications made?

Does the organization demonstrate a willingness and ability to obtain resources from its own community or constituency?

Clarity of Proposal

Is the proposal written clearly with professional jargon used selectively?

Are subheadings used to guide the reader?

Is the proposal concise?

Fiscal Soundness

Is the budget adequate to do the job but not wasteful?

Are there contingency plans if income or expenses do not turn out as expected?

Does the operational budget of the organization appear sound?

Does the organization have a 501(c)(3) tax-exempt status with the IRS?

Record of Results

Will there be accurate recording of results to demonstrate the project's success?

Has appropriate evaluation advice been considered?

Will the funder be kept informed through written or verbal reports?

SUMMARY

To summarize, funders are looking for a proposal that reflects the following:

- a match of the funder's priorities with the grantee agency's purpose
- a committed board of trustees
- a competent staff and a good track record
- a compelling need that will be met in a creative and resourceful manner
- a program that is neither too grandiose nor too limited
- a clear, measurable set of objectives
- a capacity to continue beyond the grant period
- the potential for the funded activity being replicated or expanded upon
- a clearly written document that is free of professional jargon

- an appropriate evaluation
- an organizational capability to produce tangible results

Following these guidelines can both enhance your competitiveness and provide a foundation for a well thought out plan that can be implemented effectively to achieve your objectives.

QUESTIONS FOR DISCUSSION

1) What do you consider the most important aspects of a good proposal?

2) If your agency has recently prepared a proposal, what do you consider the strongest elements of it?

Chapter Notes

[1]Brody, R. (1974). *Guide for Applying for Federal Funds for Human Services*. Cleveland, OH: School of Applied Social Sciences, Case Western Reserve University.

Brody, R. (1982). *Problem Solving; Concepts and Methods for Community Organizations*. New York: Human Sciences Press, Inc., pp. 170-172.

Hall, M.S. (1988). *Getting Funded: A Complete Guide to Proposal Writing*. Portland, OR: Portland State University, pp. 15-20.

[2]Hall, pp. 15-20.

[3]Brody, R., pp. 170-172.

[4]Geever, J.C. & McNeill, P., eds. (1997) *The Foundation Center's Guide to Proposal Writing*. (Revised Ed.) Washington, D.C.: The Foundation Center, pp. 1-4.

[5]Jacquette, L.F. & Jacquette, B.I. (August, 1977). *What Makes a Good Proposal*. Washington, D.C.: The Foundation Center, pp. 1-7.

[6]Gooch, J. (1987). *Writing Winning Proposals*. Washington, D.C.: Council for the Advancement of Education.

[7]Brody, R., pp. 41-42.

[8]Kiritz, p. 15.

[9]Brody, R., p. 179.

[10]Geever & McNeill, pp. 111-120.

[11]Drucker, P.F. (January-February, 1976). "What Results Should You Expect? A Users' Guides to MBO." *Public Administration Review,* pp. 12-39.

Elkin, R.& Vorvaller, D.J. (May, 1972). "Evaluating the Effectiveness of Social Services." *Management Controls*, pp. 104-111.

Raia, A.P. (1974). *Managing by Objectives.* Glenview, IL: Scott, Foresman, pp. 24.

[12]Rossi, H. & Freeman, H.E. (1989). *Evaluation: A Systematic Approach.* Newbury Park, CA: Sage Publications, p. 141.

[13]Steiner, R. (1998). *Total Proposal Building.* Albany, NY: Trestletree Publications, pp. 121-122.

[14]Brody, R., pp. 185-187.

[15]Geever and McNeill, p. 54.

[16]Burns, M.E. (1989). *Proposal Writer's Guide.* Hartford, CN: Development & Technical Assistance Center, p. 18.

[17]Geever and McNeill, pp. 111-120.

CHAPTER 17

Community Problem Analysis

THE EMERGENCE OF A COMMUNITY PROBLEM

Staff and volunteer leaders involved in social planning must initially devote time, energy, and thought to articulating a social problem. Although some individuals in a community may be dissatisfied with a given situation, this by itself does not constitute a community problem. A condition may be troublesome, but people may adapt to it, alter their community institutions and practices to cope with it, and even change their values to accommodate it. Take, for example, alcohol abuse. For a number of years this was not considered a community problem, although many adults and youngsters individually suffered the consequences of this disease. Similarly, individual women privately experienced inequality until the women's movement articulated it as a public issue. Private troubles experienced by certain unemployed individuals, pregnant teenagers, or poor elderly do not necessarily become community problems.

A community problem exists when ordinary citizens can convince high profile individuals (public officials, agency executives, business leaders) that a condition experienced privately by certain people in the community deserves to be changed. Obviously, the problem has to have some basis in reality. This is the reason that facts about the situation must be gathered, although different people (and experts) may argue about how to interpret these facts. A problem becomes a community problem when individual discontent becomes a broadly felt concern.[1]

Awareness is thus a first stage in the development of a community problem. Accompanying this growing recognition is the gaining of community legitimacy. The problem moves from a little known group to become more widespread as the public media write and talk about it, foundations become interested in funding pilot projects, politicians endorse proposals to deal with it, and voluntary and governmental funders provide financial support for programs. Examples of current community interests include drug abuse programs, combating teenage gangs, housing for battered women, child abuse prevention programs, group homes for the mentally retarded—all of these programs began with a collection of individuals deeply concerned about a target population. They then formed organizations that worked to influence the broader community and the country, first to be aware of the problem and then to do something about it. The significance of this discussion is that one important, and often difficult, step in the social planning process is that of making individually experienced, latent concerns known to a broader segment of the population.

Understanding the Background of the Problem

A wide variety of factors sustain most community problems, and some are more influential than others. The challenge is to locate the major factor(s) that has an effect on the problem requiring correction. To meet this challenge effectively, it is essential to research the background of the problem and gather relevant facts about it.

Developing a thorough understanding of the problem demands an intensive review of the literature on the conceptual bases of the problem and discussion with those experienced in dealing with it. The following questions should be asked:

- Is it transitory or ongoing?
- Is it limited to a few people or widespread?
- Who in the community defines it as a problem, and who does not?
- Is the problem confined to individuals and families, or is it related to general community conditions?

For example, a group is interested in developing community-based residences for recently released mentally ill patients. The group would need to have a solid understanding of the theories and concepts of optimum living conditions that aid patient recovery. Then, too, in anticipation of dealing with the community, it would need to be aware of sociological and psychological concepts of community resistance. Further, it would have to become knowledgeable about legal precedents for establishing group homes and financial requirements. In short, a community group thoroughly investigates all facets of the problem.

Gathering facts about the community condition is also crucial. In the group home example, it would be essential to know how many people from a locality were likely to be needing the facility, where current group homes were located, how community decisions have been made, and what other attempts have been made to obtain a group home.

Depending on the particular problem under consideration, information can be obtained from various sources, including census data, employment statistics, housing surveys, or records from schools, courts, and human service agencies. Local community planning agencies in health, human services, and mental health usually issue periodic reports. State and federal agencies also issue reports with certain information that has local relevance. Those experiencing the problem may need to be surveyed. And service providers, funders, and academic experts may need to be contacted. Of course, confidential information, particularly involving individuals, must be protected in any kind of survey work.

In gathering data on the problem, the group may be faced with two difficulties: (1) obtaining too much information that may prove to be irrelevant, and (2) identifying too little information from normal sources. Good judgment must be used to distinguish noise (meaningless data) from information that helps in analyzing a problem. Similarly, when data is not easily obtainable, concerned individuals may be required to use ingenuity, functioning like good investigative reporters by checking out leads. With the advice of researchers, special studies may need to be conducted as part of the fact-finding process.

Clarifying the Theoretical Perspectives of the Problem

Those dealing with a problem tend to limit their perspective to the conceptual methods in which they have been trained. The world is viewed through the lenses of a particular academic discipline or body of thought, which then forces any given problem to be viewed and dealt with in a particular way.

In dealing with the problem of alcoholism, for example, psycho-analytically oriented professionals will identify intrapsychic conditions as the major factors to be dealt with; behavior modification proponents will select immediate reinforcement; social psychologists will examine social pressures. In examining the problem of unemployment, to use another example, some may consider the problem as residing in the individuals and therefore propose educational and training remedies, whereas others would see the problem in the structure of the economy, thus seeking alterations in economic policies.

It is no wonder that discussion of community problems is often confused; participants in the discussion use different definitions and assumptions but often fail to make this explicit. Consequently, they talk past each other. It is essential, therefore, that the theoretical perspective be made explicit and that consideration be given to its appropriateness in the problem formulation phase.

Refining Community Problems Within an Organizational Context

In the discussion of community problems, emphasis has been placed on examining a community problem without reference to organizational constraints or realities. The advantage of this initial approach is that it can free people to concentrate on the special needs of a particular population.

Certainly, some situations and some organizations permit a wide latitude in identifying and selecting community problems. Multi-issue organizations, such as community action commissions, neighborhood organizations, health and human service councils, and women's coordinating councils, have a broad mandate to tackle a variety of problems. Normally they do not have the responsibility of administering social service programs, and frequently they are involved in advocating for change. They can be open to a full exploration of a wide variety of community problems.

Other organizations may have a more narrow focus, and they may be constrained by their mission, funding requirements, and bureaucratic regulations. They may have programs to run, services to provide, and political expectations to meet. Mental health centers, welfare departments, and city-sponsored human resource departments all operate under these constraints. Hence, potential problem solvers must be aware of both community and organizational factors that could affect how they deal with a problem.

Regardless of the nature of an organization—whether single purpose or multi-issue, primarily involved in running programs or advocating for problem resolution, functioning individually or joining with other groups—it must be able to develop a clarity and precision about the problem before embarking on a course of action. To achieve this clarity, it should arrive at a refined problem statement that avoids vague and ambiguous terms, answers certain basic questions, avoids too narrow a view, clarifies organizational perspectives, and identifies key factors that could have an impact on the problem.

Avoiding Vague and Ambiguous Terms

Initially, groups tend to express a general problem in vague and ambiguous terms. Vague terms have too little meaning. If a problem definition states that welfare grants are "too low," the meaning is not clear unless "too low" is defined as, for example, being 72 percent of the state-determined minimum level of decency. Ambiguous terms have multiple meanings. If concern is expressed about people on welfare, for example, does this refer to the elderly receiving Supplemental Security Income (SSI) benefits, families receiving Aid for Dependent Children (ADC), or general relief for single adults and childless couples? Unless the terms are defined precisely, one cannot be certain what is meant by "people on welfare."

Figure 17.1 illustrates how problems might have been expressed initially on the left side and then how they might be revised with key words defined. Depending on the particular problem situation and community context, other revised statements are possible.

Figure 17.1 Problem Statements

Initial Problem Statements	Revised Problem Statements
Teenage unemployment is high.	Unemployment for those inner city black youth age 16-20 is 38 percent as compared to 6 percent unemployment for adults.
Sexism in higher education exists.	Women occupy only 10 percent of administrative posts in higher education.

The revised problem statement defines key terms and gives concrete examples of the problem. To achieve precision in a problem statement, add the phrase, "as evidenced by." This is illustrated as such:

The problem is that teenage unemployment is high as evidenced by a 38 percent unemployment rate for inner city black youth aged 16 to 20 compared with a 6 percent rate for adults.

Sexism in higher education exists as evidenced by the fact that women occupy only 10 percent of administrative posts in higher education.

Identifying Key Factors

Because any given community problem is likely to have many contributing factors, social planners must review all the possible factors that could affect it. Consider the following problem statement: In our community approximately 150 abused or neglected children who suffer physical and emotional damage are identified each month.

Below are listed some factors considered as contributing to the problem:

- Parents lack parenting knowledge and skills.
- Parents have severe emotional problems.
- Parents do not know where to seek help.
- Parents feel socially isolated.
- Insufficient foster homes exist to permit temporary placement.
- The public agency is unable to provide sufficient staff to work with parents.
- Staff is inadequately trained to work with emotionally needy parents.
- Parents have inadequate financial resources.
- Parents have unrealistic expectations of children.

Examining Factors

Following the listing of factors (in the example above a dozen more factors probably could be identified), the next step is to examine them to determine which are more crucial than others and which might more easily be affected by the organization. Here a sorting-out process needs to take place. Some factors may contribute to other factors, e.g., lack of knowledge about normal growth and development leads to unrealistic expectations about a child's behavior. Some factors may not be directly related to the organization's mission, e.g., inadequacy of financial resources. Some factors reside in the target population, e.g., parents have emotional problems, whereas other factors may reside in the organization, e.g., lack of staff training. A social planning group considering these various factors would explore their meanings and relationships by combining some with others and omitting duplicates.

Narrowing the Problem Focus

The danger of narrowing a general problem area too soon, thus resulting in prematurely selecting a solution, was discussed previously. Also, the reality that different people will bring different perspectives that can influence problem selection was discussed. Once the general problem area is determined, it is essential to begin sorting it into specific problems that can be dealt with by the group and analyzing those factors that contribute to the problem. An analysis of the general problem area, specific problems, and contributing factors is illustrated in Figure 17.2.

Figure 17.2

Analyzing the Problem

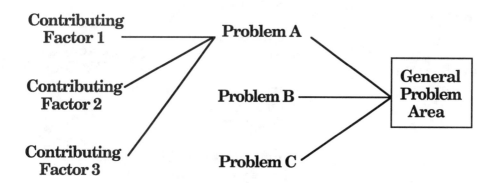

Contributing Factor 1 — Problem A

Contributing Factor 2 — Problem B — General Problem Area

Contributing Factor 3 — Problem C

Suppose, for example, a community committee is composed of volunteer leaders and foster care staff that is concerned about the lack of foster homes, which has been identified as one of several factors related to abused children. Obviously, even this factor is too broad, so the group begins to analyze the general problem and determines that specific problems include the following: (1) insufficient foster homes resulting in monthly waiting lists, (2) insufficient staff to handle large caseloads, (3) payments to foster parents that have not been increased in five years despite inflation, and (4) concern by current foster parents about how to handle problem situations.

Each of these specific problems has in turn contributing factors that affect the problem on which the community committee may wish to concentrate its efforts. The community committee identifies the following factors that contribute to insufficient foster homes: limited public information about foster care, insufficient follow-up of those who do make inquiries, and inadequate orientation for interested potential foster families. Figure 17.3 reflects this analysis.

For the moment, the social planning committee has decided to concentrate on insufficient foster homes and the attending contributing factors. In time, it may decide to also concentrate on one or more of the other specific problem categories.

| Figure 17.3 |

Foster Care Problem Analysis

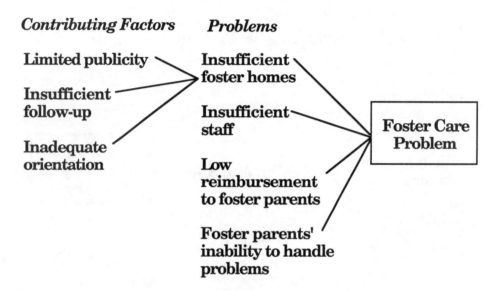

Contributing Factors   *Problems*

Limited publicity

Insufficient follow-up

Inadequate orientation

Insufficient foster homes

Insufficient staff

Low reimbursement to foster parents

Foster parents' inability to handle problems

Foster Care Problem

Expressing the Consequences of the Problem

Sometimes a problem statement clearly conveys the consequences of the problem, but often it does not. If social planning members are developing problem statements only for their own use, then describing consequences may not be necessary, for they have a common understanding of the significance of the problem. If, however, they need to convey their problem statement to others, then it is desirable to indicate the consequences of the problem. Otherwise, they risk being asked what the significance is of such statements as, "More girls who run away are put into institutions than are boys," or "There is not a sufficient number of day care centers."

It cannot be assumed that because those close to a situation know something is wrong, that others outside the process will feel the same way. The consequences of the problem need to be explicitly expressed.

In the problem analysis phase, consequences are defined as unfavorable conditions the organization wants changed. Just as there are likely to be several contributing factors affecting a general problem, so there may be a number of consequences that emerge from the problem, as illustrated in Figure 17.4.

Figure 17.4

Consequences of the Problem

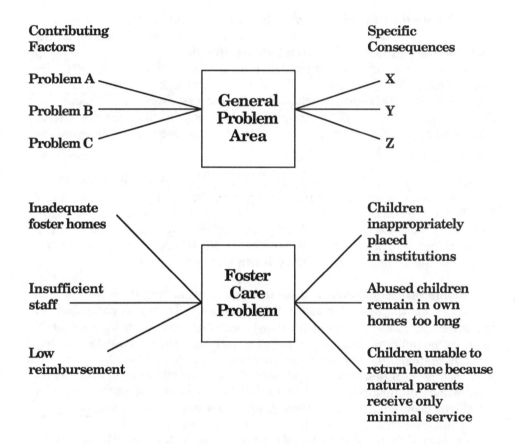

By identifying one or more specific problems and their contributing factors on the one hand and their consequences on the other, the organization is now able to make explicit the target for its efforts to change conditions. It knows precisely what it wants changed. By articulating consequences, the group will know later (after it has carried out its action plan) to what extent it has been on target in resolving the precise problem. As Figure 17.4 illustrates, if an organization has elected to concentrate on the insufficiency of foster homes because of the consequences of children being placed in institutions or remaining in abusive home situations too long, then it is now prepared to establish objectives and consider action plans designed to deal with these consequences. Later, the organization can or will be able to evaluate to what extent its efforts resulted in a reduction of these specific unfavorable conditions.

DETERMINING PROBLEM PRIORITIES

Because an organization involved in social planning has limited time, energy, and money, it must purposefully select which problems and contributing factors it will concentrate on and which ones it will postpone. The organization must select priorities (first things) for focused attention. Since it is unlikely that an organization will be able to give equal attention to all problems, it should explicitly identify posteriorities (last things), i.e., those problems that it will ignore for the present by placing them at the bottom of a list. Of course, at some later time those specific problems initially put aside may become priorities.

By establishing priorities, the organization is faced with a dilemma. On the one hand, by establishing boundaries around its area of concentration, it can focus its resources so as to assure potential resolution. It avoids spreading itself too thin in diverting its members and staff from doing so many things that none of them are done well. It concentrates on the few critical issues or problems on which it can have an impact.

In the illustration on foster homes, the organization might elect to concentrate only on the need for more foster homes. To try to campaign for increased per diem rates and training for foster parents at the same time could result in its not being able to deal effectively with its priority problem. After it successfully concentrates its energies and resources (sometimes called the critical mass) on one problem, it can then move on to other issues. Indeed, an organization may purposefully establish a sequence or phasing process as it moves from one aspect of the major problem to another.

On the other hand, by limiting the priority focus to only one of several problems, a social planning organization may not be able to fully resolve the general problems of the cumulative effect of specific problems. Problems are so often intertwined that, unless they are all dealt with, only limited success can be anticipated. In our example, unless the foster care reimbursement rate is raised, staff are increased, foster parents are given tangible support, and counseling is given to natural parents, concentrating efforts to recruit more foster parents may not be sufficient to cope adequately with the totality of the problem. Similarly, a program designed to deal with teenage unemployment may not prove successful unless simultaneous attention is given to the school system from which a constant stream of new school dropouts is emerging.

There is no easy, simple answer to the dilemma of whether to concentrate on one problem at a time or all problems together. The problem analysis will help the organization to be clear and purposeful about what aspect of the overall problem it is, or should be, addressing. With this realistic appraisal, the organization can determine to what extent it will likely affect the problem, and this in turn will prevent it from overselling the potential impact of its project.

RATIONAL PROBLEM-SOLVING METHODS

Social planning can be based primarily on rational processes of formulating problems, examining causes, weighing alternative means of implementing a course of action, and developing objective standards to assess outcomes.[2] This approach assumes that if enough of the right people have the facts, then they will be responsive to change.

Frequently social planners work on the assumption that the capacity for change resides within those agencies within the community that must deal with problems of their clients (e.g., hospitals, juvenile courts, human service departments) and that if sufficient information is made available then they will make the appropriate decisions. The rational approach relies on an orderly, systematic analysis of facts that leads to the formulation of programs.[3]

But facts by themselves may not be sufficient to prompt a community response. Teenage pregnancies may be high, drug abuse on the increase, AIDS patients growing, and welfare persons being added to the rolls. How is a community to determine which of the many issues to concentrate on?

Formal Needs Assessment

One means of stimulating a community focus is the use of a needs assessment. In order to properly address community problems it is important to determine the size of the population in need of special interventions, often a formidable challenge because need is difficult to define and measure. The assessment of need is undertaken in several ways:[4]

1) **Professional studies of problems**. Examples: studies of school dropouts, delinquency rates, unemployment, unwed pregnancies. Sometimes value judgments are involved in determining the threshold rate of the

seriousness of the problem, need, or objectives to be achieved. For example, The Federal Department of Health and Human Services has issued a report "Healthy People 2000: National Health Promotion and Disease Prevention Objectives." Over ten thousand knowledgeable people participated in the development of objectives relating to such areas as family planning, mental health and mental disorders, violent and abusive behavior, and sexually transmitted diseases.[5] Throughout the decade of the 90's and undoubtedly into the 21st century the Federal Government will continue to refine these objectives, and state and local health and human service organizations will be developing them for implementation.

2) **Surveys of what people perceive their needs to be**. Though costly to conduct, surveys do tap into what people feel about unmet needs. An alternative is to conduct focus groups in which a facilitator is able to explore more in depth the concerns that selected representatives have about their community. A variation of a survey is to conduct public hearings at which time community representatives express their views.

Sometimes surveys are conducted to obtain the opinions of professionals on the assumption that they are on the firing line and their proxy vote can reflect the needs of their clients. Is there a need to provide drug services in the inner city or the suburbs? Should more emphasis be placed on treatment or prevention? Should more services be provided for youth or adults? What service barriers exist? The answers to these and other questions help guide social planners in determining where to place limited resources.

> **Example**: The County Alcohol and Drug Addiction Service Board considers adolescent service a priority and develops a survey to determine gaps and resources for prevention and treatment of drug and alcohol abuse. The purpose of the survey is to help guide where the resources of the organization should be directed.

The survey covers such topics as the following:

- Are there enough treatment services for youth?
- Is the quality of services adequate?
- Are minority and ethnic populations adequately served?
- Are special populations (e.g., mentally disabled, delinquent youth, public housing residents, pregnant teens) being adequately served?

Supervisory and counseling staff categorize the results of the survey, and the results become part of the deliberations of the Board.

3) **Analysis of unmet needs**. Collected by agencies, these data provide some idea of the number of people who are on waiting lists, but they may not

give a full picture since those who learn of long waits before they will be seen may be discouraged from going for services.

4) **Comparing the need for services with their availability.** This analysis involves reviewing how well balanced the distribution of services is by geographic areas or identifiable communities. A public housing authority, for example, may conduct a survey of residents to determine what they perceive to be desired services. Their responses include the following areas: day care, vocational training, GED, recreation services for youth, social experiences for the senior citizens. Different residents express different preferences on different estates. For example, where there is a concentration of senior citizens, needs emerge that are different from those expressed by estates where young families predominate.

The staff then compile services that are either on the estates or easily accessible in the neighborhood. They prepare a matrix that shows the services along the left column of the page and the residents social service needs across the top. Gaps on the graph paper reveal for the policy board and the administration what they must concentrate on.

Frequently a community needs assessment will consist of several kinds of analyses and surveys. For example, consumers and professionals will both be polled, and these results will be compared with the actual statistical data of agency usage.

One of the major problems of a needs assessment is that, for all the cost of time and money involved, it can only provide a "snapshot" of community need at a point in time. To be useful surveys should be conducted periodically. The results should be carefully reviewed to determine how various community constituencies view important issues.

Informal Needs Assessment

Frequently the staff from various organizations come together to share their concerns and discuss the problems faced by their particular clients. Out of these discussions emerges a picture of the status of the individuals and the families with which they work. Their daily and intimate knowledge constitutes a kind of "needs assessment" that must somehow get translated into a case to be made to funders and other community decision makers.

Example: Concerned that the community is not sufficiently tuned into the mental health needs of the Latino community, professionals from nine different mental health organizations decide to form a Latino Mental Health Network. Through data supplied by the local mental health board they prepare the following assessment:

1) The number of Latinos employed in the twenty-three agencies and their specific assignments. They learn that while the numbers of Latino case managers is adequate, there are no Latino mental health counselors available.

2) They identify on a map where concentration of Latino population is located, and then they determine whether the two agencies located in the area actually serve Latinos. They discover that most of the Latinos travel across town to a site that is "Latino friendly."

On the basis of this information, the Latino Mental Health Network prepares a needs assessment analysis and persuades the local mental health board to actively recruit Latino mental health counselors for three of the mental health agencies.

Essential Aspects of a Needs Assessment

Keep in mind several principles when conducting a needs assessment: 1) Involve those affected by the problem because they can help implement action and because they bring valuable information to the process. 2) Keep the technical aspects of the survey in perspective. Remember that what you are striving to achieve is the proper involvement of key decision makers. 3) Find the right balance between conducting an overly ambitious needs assessment that must involve all elements of the community and one that is so limited that it is discounted by those to whom the results will be directed. In general it is better to lean towards a more modest process that produces tangible results.[6]

SUMMARY

To undertake an analysis of a community problem requires that a community consensus be formed. Frequently a small group of people who have an awareness of a problem must convince other community decision makers that the issue is worth the community's attention and resources. Even after a general issue is identified the organization dealing with the problem must set priorities and determine on which specific aspect of the problem to devote concentrated energies. One of the major tools to help get the attention of a community is a needs assessment.

QUESTIONS FOR DISCUSSION

1) Can you identify a major social problem in your community?

   a) How would you define it broadly?

   b) How would you define it narrowly?

2) What are some factors contributing to the problem?

3) How does what you consider to be the three most important problems of the community compare with those of your fellow students? Why are there differences (or similarities) in perception? What does this say about value judgments?

Chapter Notes

[1]Brody, R., (1982). *Problem Solving: Concepts and Methods for Community Organizations.* New York: Human Sciences Press, pp. 17-21.

[2]Gilbert, S, & Specht, H. (1987). "Social Planning and Community Organization." In A. Minihan (Editor-in-chief), *Encyclopedia of Social Work*, (18th ed., Vol.1, pp. 602-619). Silver Spring, MD: National Association of Social Workers, p. 613.

[3]Chess, W., & Norlin, J. (1991). *Human Behavior and the Social Environment.* Boston, MA: Allyn & Bacon, p. 388.

[4]Moroney, R. (1995). "Social Planning." *Encyclopedia of Social Work*, (19th ed., Vol. 1, pp. 598-603). Silver Spring, MD: National Association of Social Workers.

[5]Healthy People 2000: *National Health Promotion and Disease Prevention Objectives.* (1991). Washington, D.C.: U.S. Government Printing Office.

[6]Tropman, J.E. (1995). "Community Needs Assessment." *Encyclopedia of Social Work* (19th Ed.), pp. 563-568.

CHAPTER 18

How Community Organizations Affect Change

MODELS OF COMMUNITY INTERVENTION

Community organization practice continues to evolve as social work practitioners strive to find various ways to be responsive to community needs. To better understand the various forms this practice has taken, community intervention models have been developed.

These models serve a useful purpose of focusing professional activities and stimulating critical thinking about effective community intervention. But some words of caution are in order: By their very nature, models provide an idealized picture of what is believed to be happening in the real world. In fact, structures and processes described by the model may not always occur the way that they are supposed to because of unique situations. Moreover, models can convey a static rather than a dynamic reflection of a continuously changing social environment. In reality, structures, processes, and events are in continuous flux. Be mindful that each organization is unique and responds in specific ways to particular circumstances that may not fit the models to which they are assigned. Still, the development of community intervention models provides a good starting point to examine the attempts to influence change and to bring about improvements in the quality of life of specific target populations.

Building upon the original formulation of Rothman, who provided the standard practice framework for community organizers, we have developed a chart (Figure 19.1) that divides community intervention structures into three primary category models: 1) local level organizations, 2) social issue organizations and 3) social planning and service coordination organizations.[1] Local level organizations relate to specific geographic areas, whereas social issue groups are organized by function and group identity that do not have geographic boundaries. Social planning organizations tend to be organized on a community wide basis and, unlike local level or social issue organizations, may not actively engage consumers or clients. These beneficiaries in local level and social issue organizations are likely to become empowered in the process of improving their lives.

Local level organizations are formed to deal with issues at the neighborhood or local community level. Often they are referred to as "grassroots organizations," implying that they are rooted to a territory. At the neighborhood level, they address such issues as inadequacy of police protection, insufficient street lighting, dilapidated buildings, and lack of swimming pools. Through such different structures as street clubs, area councils, drug free zone organizations, and business and homeowner associations, residents strive to achieve greater control and mastery over their quality of life. Initially, they come together to form a consensus around priorities; then they mobilize to target local officials and businesses to be responsive to their concerns. In one community, for example, they may form a Drug Free Council that focuses on getting rid of drug dealers. They will organize drug marches, actively alert the police about drug dealings, develop drug free zone signs, mount a campaign for residents to sign "zero tolerance pledges," and work with city officials to rid their neighborhood of unsightly, dilapidated buildings that could be used for drug transactions.

In another community, residents may determine that their most important priority involves joining with other communities in fighting state legislation that prohibits local control of predatory lenders. (This is the practice of private loan companies duping residents into making financial commitments that they cannot realistically carry out and then foreclosing on their recently bought properties.) Through their neighborhood organizations residents push their mayor and city council to take political action to influence their state legislature.

In still another community, efforts are focused on economic development. Residents and local business people work together to garner city block grants designed to improve sidewalks in front of businesses, obtain low interest business loans, and provide a special public transportation shuttle for seniors who live in near shopping areas.

Community organizing practitioners work at the local level in various roles. They help residents form their organization, coordinate their working together, assist in identifying issues, and help them mobilize to take action. Typically, the practitioner is not out front advocating but facilitates resident efforts. The community organizer works both to strengthen the capacity of local community residents to address their own issues and helps them accomplish specific objectives and tasks.

(Note: For a fuller discussion of community development and community building initiatives, see Chapter 19.)

Social issue organizations bring together people who share common interests and are committed to achieving social justice. People who have an affinity for one another related to ethnic origin, race, sexual orientation, age, or gender join together to advance their cause. Witness, for example, the proliferation in the past few decades of gay rights groups, women's organizations, civil rights organizations, and senior lobbying groups. Their common backgrounds create natural linkages and a desire to band together to deal with issues that affect their group identity and their quality of life.[2]

A common ideology related to shared values and beliefs can also form the basis of community of interests. People who have the same concerns about their environment, about abortion (for or against), or about drunk drivers form organizations to further their interests.

Some ban together to form action groups because of personal experiences. A group of former mentally ill persons may lobby for increased funding for community-based services. Parents of developmentally disabled children unite to put pressure on their local school board to provide needed resources in the schools. Women who have been battered may organize to seek legislation designed to influence stricter penalties for abusing spouses. A group of physically handicapped adults join together to advocate for legislation to make buildings more accessible. Families with a relative who has been the victim of gun violence form an organization to provide stricter gun control laws. These are examples of people who are emotionally committed because of their own personal experiences and who have a desire to join with others who have been similarly affected. Through their common experiences, they seek remedies to redress fundamental issues.

Social issue organizations thus typically have an agenda—a social concern that they want resolved. They want to gain sufficient power to have a significant impact. They seek to influence public officials and agency administrators to become more responsive to their needs. They rely on a variety of

Figure 18.1
Community Intervention Models

Features	Local level organizations	Social issue organizations	Social planning and service coordination organizations
1. Expected outcomes	-Building capacity -Accomplishing tasks	-Changing policies -Changing power relationships	-Solving community problems -Obtaining funding -Developing programs
2. Target of change	-Local public officials - Local institutions (e.g., banks, schools)	-Public officials -Agency administrators	- Elected officials at the local, state and national levels - Interagency organizations
3. Primary constituency	-Residents in a geographic area	-Issue focused groups	-Volunteer leaders -Elected officials -Human service funders -Coalitions -Welfare Councils and United Ways -General public
4. Scope of concern	Neighborhood quality of life	-Social justice -Resolution of an issue	-Improved services for target populations
5. Change tactics	-Formation of consensus -Advocacy for positions -Mobilizing neighborhood response	- Confrontation - Negotiations - Collaborations - Litigation	-Fact gathering -Technical analysis -Advocating policy and legislative change -Mobilizing community support
6. Empowering constituents	- Building the neighborhood capacity to make decisions - Promoting greater control of their own destiny	-Creating an awareness of constituent rights - Developing capacity to have an impact	-Documenting consumers' unmet needs -Transmitting analysis to the decision makers -Organizing coalitions -Coordinating service delivery
7. Practitioner roles	-Facilitator -Coordinator -Organizer at the local level	-Advocate -Broker -Negotiator	-Researcher -Proposal writer -Planner -Advocate -Facilitator

tactics ranging from confronting and even embarrassing officials to negotiating and collaborating with them to accomplish mutually determined goals. Sometimes they may resort to litigation, seeking a court remedy when public administrators and legislators are unresponsive. The practitioner typically serves as advocate, broker, and negotiator.

A coalition of homeless provider organizations developed to provide services for homeless people is an example of a social action organization. It is successful in creating a joint city/county Office of Homeless Services. As a result, the mission changes from a service orientation to empowering and organizing homeless people to break out of the cycle of poverty through public education and advocacy. It also changes its name to the "Homeless Advocacy Organization" (HAO).

When the mayor of the city orders the police to conduct a series of sweeps to rid the downtown area homeless people, HAO files a lawsuit challenging this position. While the lawsuit is pending, HAO organizes protest marches to bring the plight of homeless people to the attention of the media and the public. Furthermore, it makes a list of local agency administrators who attend a meeting with the mayor but who do not challenge his position. Those attending the meeting are identified on a " wall of shame," which lists the attendees who failed to challenge the mayor for arresting homeless people, and this list is submitted to the local newspaper. The publication of this list is purposefully designed to embarrass the service providers who attended the meeting. The position of the organization is that while the people who are listed on the "wall of shame" are well meaning, they were ethically wrong in not taking a firmer stand against the mayor. In subsequent meetings with the HAO, social service administrators pledge to be more responsive to homeless persons.

(Note: For more discussion of negotiating and advocating positions, see chapter 21.)

Social planning and service coordination organizations focus on such community wide issues as (1) reintegrating former delinquents into the local school system, (2) developing better mental health services for those entering the justice system, (3) providing more adequate day care for working mothers, or (4) developing new programs for the elderly. By obtaining information on unmet needs, social planners hope to influence public officials and other funders to provide the necessary resources. They use technical skills in research and program analysis but also embrace advocacy in working for changes in legislation and administrative practices.

Constituents of social planning and service coordination are health and human service coalitions, United Ways, human service funders, elected officials, volunteer leaders, and service administrators. Through joint planning, problem solving, and technical analysis they hope to devise improved services. Practitioner roles include researcher, planner, proposal writer, advocate, and facilitator. Here is an example of social planning:

> A local health and human services planning council organizes a committee of professional and volunteer community leaders to examine the plight of frail senior citizens in their community who, though they have low incomes, are just above the financial threshold to qualify for public funding. With the data analysis assistance of a staff professional they determine that over 3000 low income seniors do not qualify for public funding for services that could keep them in their own homes. After conferring at length with their elected officials, they determine that neither federal nor state funds are available. Undeterred, they decide to develop a pilot program with a combination of funding from local foundations and county commissioners. They also obtain funding from another foundation to evaluate the program. After two years they revisit their county commissioners with data documenting the value of the pilot program and persuade them to put a "keep seniors in their own homes" levy issue on the ballot. They mount a campaign to get the levy passed and achieve their ultimate purpose of providing services to the frail elderly.

(Note: For more discussion of social planning and service coordination, see chapter 22 "Developing and coordinating human services.")

We emphasize again that while each of these models has distinguishing features, in many ways each also encompasses features that duplicate those found in the others. Neighborhood organizations may join with social planners to develop better service delivery in their community. Social issue organizations may require technical expertise to document their case before embarking on a campaign to change fundamental community attitudes. Advocates can become technical experts on community issues. Social planning organizations may need to mobilize community support to show legislators that they have political power.

INFLUENCING CHANGE

The most profound reason for why these organizations have overlapping features is their common interest in influencing change. This desire for change could involve modifying community attitudes, redressing imbalances in the way resources are distributed, heightening sensitivities of public officials, or altering the way services are delivered. Typically, these interventions are carried out through some form of community organization.

Community organization involves an intervention process to help individuals and groups deal with problems through planned collective action.[3] The key words in this definition are "collective action," for in joining together people develop the strength and resources usually unavailable to individuals who seek to change a problem or improve a situation. Fundamental to community organization work is fostering self-determination, involving the collective struggle of people, acting on their own behalf to improve conditions affecting their lives.[4]

Affecting change, however, is no easy task for a number of reasons. For one thing, factors operating outside the control of an organization can perpetuate a problem. Community groups established to rid their area of drugs, for example, rapidly find out that closing drug houses on one street may only lead to the shifting of operations to another. A group wanting to deal with teen unemployment in their neighborhood can become easily frustrated because teen unemployment is a nationwide problem. Community people have to be convinced that even their small efforts can make some difference in improving their neighborhood. They must have hope that they can do something to accomplish tangible results.

Moreover, problems are interconnected. A group organized to reduce the recidivism rate of former incarcerated convicts must deal with low self-esteem that is reinforced daily by the inability to obtain jobs, that in part is based upon low educational and skill levels. The answer to the question, "Where do we devote our efforts to make an impact?" often is, "everywhere," because problems are so interrelated.

Then, too, change may be difficult to influence because of the dynamic and often inconsistent response on the part of those who could make needed changes. Public officials have multiple agendas, multiple pressure groups, and an attention span that often lasts only as long as the next election. Groups wanting to make changes are coming at them all the time asking—even demanding—that they respond to their requests. At times, for example, the public is sympathetic to the plight of mothers on welfare; at other times these matters are seen as overly dependent on the public treasury. Changes in the public mood undoubtedly influence community policy makers.

Hence, resistance to change can be profound, challenging, frustrating, and even at times seemingly insurmountable. Those involved in community organization work must be mindful that even if people become involved, they may give up when results are not forthcoming. Even so, the quest for improving people's lives is strong and compelling.

Working for Change

What are some of the reasons that allow those engaged in community organization work to take on daunting challenges and influence change?

First, people must be involved in an issue that reflects a deeply felt need. Their commitment must be so profound that they are willing to endure frustration and to persist in the face of continuing roadblocks. Initially, a few who have great conviction that something must be changed will articulate this deeply felt need. Examples of this could include the following:

- a children's advocacy group fights to increase income maintenance funding;

- women are convinced that sexual harassment in the workplace must be stopped;

- gay teachers resent that schools discriminate in their hiring practices on the basis of sexual preferences;

- a small group of community residents is fed up with the lack of police response and wants to set up their own neighborhood patrols.

These examples reflect that a few people are concerned enough to want to become organized into an action group. They then involve a broader circle of those who could become enthused enough to work for the cause. When people are angry, when they feel passionate about an issue, then they will invest. Their personal grievances form the basis of collective action. Community organizers strive to become aware of discontent that can be used to mobilize action.

Sometimes people's grievances lie dormant beneath the surface, and an event or episode occurs that galvanizes them to organize to take action. A speeding driver hits a child, and a street club is organized to promote a street light. A teenager dies from an overdose of drugs sold in the neighborhood, and a group of concerned parents comes together with police officials and school personnel to form a community committee against drugs. Women employees resent that a qualified female supervisor is passed over for what seems to them a less competent male and organize a citywide effort to promote women in leadership roles. In each of these instances concerns were dormant until an episode triggered latent feelings.

Second, people need a target toward which they can direct their energies. It is not enough for them to challenge "the system"—that is too broad and abstract. Specific chief executive officers must be reached about sexual harassment in their work places; specific board of education members must be persuaded to change school board policy regarding the rights of gay teachers; the mayor or the police chief must be confronted regarding the inadequacy of police responses to neighborhood calls. In each of these instances specific decision makers must be identified who become the focal point for encounters.

Third, people must feel a sense of their own power. They must have confidence in the possibility that an organization can accomplish what they as individuals cannot. The empowerment of organization members can be as important as, if not more important than, the accomplishment of a particular result. A neighborhood organization might, for example, know of an influential businessperson who could intercede with the mayor so that police response time improves. This would not be the same as the group developing its own power to influence the mayor. People must, however, feel their own sense of power in influencing change; by doing so they become emboldened to take on other challenges.

Finally, people must be involved in achieving concrete and immediate changes. Because they will inevitably encounter frustrations, they need short term victories, or milestone achievements, that will sustain them for the long haul. Large issues must be segmented into smaller attainable goals. For example, progress toward achieving better recreation for the youth of the community might need to be measured by getting the local swimming pool open during the next two months before the start of the summer season. Once this is achieved, then they can tackle the more difficult issue of building a year-round recreation center. Passion for a cause, clear targets for change, empowerment, and winnable results—these are the basic ingredients for successful community organizing. We turn now to specific ways that organizations can mobilize support of their constituencies, how they can leverage their influence through coalitions, and how they can use strategic thinking and tactics to achieve their goals.

DEVELOPING COMMUNITY SUPPORT

Getting people involved, especially at the neighborhood level, is no easy matter. Those involved in community organization work can take one of three tactics:[5]

1) Conduct an exploratory survey. They can knock on doors and individually inquire about what is on the minds of residents. Through this one-on-one approach they not only get to know the people and their individual concerns but they also have the chance to determine who could possibly be involved in leadership roles. The primary purpose of these expeditions is to determine what are people's genuine concerns.

2) Sell an issue through individual contacts. Those involved in this phase of community organization work come with a predetermined and specific problem that needs remedying and their objective is to galvanize public sentiment to join in an organized effort to deal with the problem. They might, for example, knock on doors to obtain signatures for a petition drive to request local officials to lower the traffic speed limit on their street. The focus is not on general concerns (e.g., poor housing) but on specific targets that need to be changed—for example, a particular run-down house in the middle of the street.

3) Promote attendance at a particular meeting where community action will be taken. Community organizers in this phase actively seek to mobilize community involvement by engaging as broad a degree of participation as possible. At such public meetings the goal is to do more than impart information—it is to conclude with a set of action steps, to make demands on those who have the power to make decisions, and to elicit specific responses from them.

The Interfaith Action Coalition (IAC) illustrates the mobilization process. Consisting of the membership of ten local churches, temples, and mosques, it has brought together three hundred members from the different congregations. Each identified a set of issues and then came together to determine a set of priorities: domestic violence, education, and economic development.

The organization wants the court to provide full-time advocates in the court system to assist and support victims of domestic violence. They also want training to be provided for law enforcement officers. In education, the group is calling for a career initiative to be implemented in the local high schools. Further, they want the schools to have a closer affiliation with the local youth summer employment agency. Finally, in economic development, IAC wants the local community to update the 20-year-old economic strategic plan.

At a mass meeting attended by six hundred community people, task groups report their specific recommendations. Because of the sizable turnout and the clout of the organizations involved, the mayor, county commissioners, and congressperson attend, and each is asked specifically what he or she could do to address the problem. The meeting concludes with each official pledging to follow through.

IAC represents a typical mobilization cycle: Specific needs are identified and articulated through a series of individual and small group discussions. This initial process is consciousness raising designed to identify community issues. Then an organization is formed—committees or task forces come into being to concentrate on specific aspects of the problem(s). As the organization experiences success, it is then reinvigorated to pursue other issues.

The Community Organizer's Role

As reflected in the example of IAC, community organizers use several methods to effect social change: advocating, mobilizing, and organizing.

Advocating assumes that if there are a large number of people suffering there must be something wrong not just with the individuals but with society. Lobbying efforts through NASW or community organizations are designed to change unjust laws or to redress economic distribution of income. Often these efforts are done on behalf of those who are affected by undesirable policies. Advocates represent someone else.

Mobilizing begins the process of empowering vulnerable people to take action on their own behalf. They are organized to protest the closing of a day-care center, or picket in front of a board of education building, or challenge the county commissioners for not providing adequate funding of services. Often, however, mobilizing is focused on an immediate situation and therefore is limited in achieving accomplishments over the long run.

Organizing efforts strive to build ongoing community organizations that can properly address the ongoing needs of their members. People who previously have felt disempowered to express their concerns to the mayor or the school superintendent or the police chief find their collective voice through their organization. They become individually and collectively empowered.

Practitioners engaged in this empowerment process can create tension between their intense zeal to right society's wrongs and their own employment stability. If, for example, they are city employees, they can end up being mistrusted and even disciplined if they try to organize residents to fight city officials.[6]

To carry out these functions, a social worker will adopt roles of *enabler, broker,* and *advocate*.   As enablers, social workers provide guidance without being intrusive. Frequently community organizers will work with potential participants, such as neighborhood residents, to help start an organization. They may, for example, work with a core group to survey the neighborhood in advance of a community meeting. They may provide guidance in the early stages of an organization, raising questions about premature publicity until the organization has had an opportunity to clarify its priorities.

Also as enablers, the community organizers are concerned about developing leadership of the organization and helping members divide their tasks so they can meet their objectives. Community organizers assist group members in defining issues for action and preparing action plans.[7] Furthermore, as enablers, staff are normally in the background assisting indigenous community leaders in presenting their concerns to community decision makers. In the enabling role the social workers discourage participants from becoming dependant upon them. Rather, they work to empower people to take action on their own behalf.

As brokers, social workers help to mobilize resources. Often they are knowledgeable about funding sources in the community, including government contracts, foundation grants, and united fund raising.

Social workers who work primarily with clients may also find themselves in a brokering role, especially in relation to securing resources and services for their clients from other agencies. As generalists performing the brokering role, social workers may assist in coordinating the work of their agency with other organizations. Example: Counselors in a mental health agency are assigned to work with a local community services coalition. They learn that many representatives are not aware of their agency and arrange for their director to meet with them. As a result, their agency develops a much better referral network.

As an advocate, social workers seek to make fundamental changes in the way institutions respond to clients. Example: Residents approach the social worker about concerns that the local school policies have resulted in what they consider to be a poor educational system. The social worker identifies who in the community has the power to make decisions and how they can be influenced. Example: A "safety first" group wants to confront the mayor to get better police protection in their community. The social worker would think through various options with the group.

In the 1990s there has been a moderation of confrontational tactics used by organizations and this in turn is resulting in changes in the social worker's social action role. Grassroots organizations now tend to seek to establish a working relationship between those with and those without power.[8] As grassroots organizations get to the bargaining table, social workers may be called upon to help them more effectively express the concerns and needs of the community.

PREPARING STRATEGIES AND TACTICS

As discussed previously in Chapter 5, strategic planning is essential for the survival of all organizations, and obviously it is extremely important that community groups go through a continuous process of assessing where they are and where they want to go.

Community organizations must come to terms with such fundamental issues as:

- What is our primary purpose for existing (mission)?
- What might we be doing several years from now for which we should be preparing ourselves?
- What are our strengths, weaknesses, opportunities, and threats?
- What are the critical issues facing our organization that must be addressed (e.g., membership, finances)?
- What are our goals and objectives?
- Who are our supporters and what value do we offer them?
- Who are our opponents and what form is their opposition likely to take?
- Who do we need to influence, and how can we go about it?

These are strategic issues because they deal with the broad outlines of what must be done. Specific tactics, those narrow actions that an organization embarks upon, must take place within a strategic framework. Tactics can be divided into three categories: collaboration, campaign, and contest.

When those who seek change and those who are the target of change are likely to agree that change is needed, then collaborative tactics will work. For example, community organizations may join with school officials, representatives of unions, juvenile court, police, and the city recreation department in a mutual problem solving effort to develop school-based recreational opportunities. A spirit of cooperation prevails when all parties want to achieve a common goal and welcome the opportunity to come together to figure out the best way to achieve it.

Campaign tactics involve various forms of persuasion. These could include lobbying legislators, appearing before a public hearing to state the organization's case, initiating petition drives, using the mass media to educate the public on the organization's position, and conducting letter writing campaigns.

Contest or confrontation tactics are employed in a win-lose situation where the intent is to overpower the target of change. Examples include boycotts, lawsuits, legally disruptive tactics (e.g., withholding rent), and civil disobedience. Sometimes the implementation of these tactics or even the threat of using them make the target of the change more receptive to coming to the table to resolve the issue.

WORKING ON COMMUNITY ORGANIZATION ISSUES

Community organizers grapple with specific issues at the organizational level.

1) **Dealing with residents who are reluctant to become involved either because they are apathetic or because they are mistrustful.** Residents may have experienced previous attempts to get them to work on community issues with limited success. The community organizer has to develop trusting relationships, provide a sense of hope that something can be done, and offer compelling reasons for how their contributions can significantly help.

   During this initial period social workers should expect that community residents will be testing them for sincerity and commitment. Are they truly committed to the welfare of the community—even though they live outside the community? Will they side with the establishment against the community's needs? If the social workers are from another ethnic group can they truly be sensitive to the community's needs? In general, the best approach to these concerns is to understand the basis of the hostility and use opportunities to clarify values, attitudes, and commitment that will enable the group to accomplish its objectives.

2) **Determining what residents really want and developing differential strategies to meet their needs and interests.** To avoid being unduly influenced by a few people, it is usually appropriate for the community organizer to talk to as many people as possible or conduct systematic surveys that will document how residents feel about various issues. The challenge, then, is for community organizers to understand their community and its readiness for change.

Not all communities can be organized in the same way. Each has to be inventoried to determine its strengths, its leadership capacity, and its readiness to be organized. In a community where drug trafficking has caused a child to be murdered and where several organizations already exist, the task of structuring a community effort is fairly easy. People are ready to take action. In another community where residents deny (despite evidence to the contrary) that drug dealing is occurring, where ministers do not want to get involved, and where people feel isolated, the challenge is much more difficult. One community may, therefore, be more amenable to action than the other.

3) **Accepting the importance of self determination.** Suppose, for example, you have been asked to work with a group to improve the economic viability of the community. You have come up with several suggestions that you think would attract outsiders to come in and spend money. The group rejects your notions and instead comes up with ideas that you think are unfeasible. Should you yield to their decisions knowing that they are bound to fail and thus may be frustrated in taking further action? In your role as community organizer you can be in a position to identify potential consequences of certain actions, knowing that ultimately the organization must make its own decisions, even if you have questions.

4) **Continually energizing organizations.** Members of organizations that have been in existence for a while may not assist in reviving tired organizations. This is the paradox of organizational life: in achieving a particular goal, an organization can sow the seeds of its own demise. Suppose, for example, that a community organization is formed to fight the placement of a low security prison in the neighborhood. Tremendous energy is generated to resist the prison. Once victory is achieved, residents are likely to withdraw even though there are other significant issues with which to grapple. The organization needs a new challenge to engage its members.

Sometimes, without compelling goals, community organizations shift to emphasizing social relationships and devoting energies to social events. Or, feeling frustrated with the obstacles encountered in achieving a particular program, members may want to divert time and resources to less ambitious, but more doable, efforts. Because of these possibilities, organizations that have been in existence for a long time must continually reexamine themselves and provide opportunities for regeneration.

5) **Helping to develop a clear focus.** Because members come with different agendas and different ideas of what needs to be done, almost all

organizations have difficulty determining where primary energies should be devoted. There always exists the temptation to take on more than an organization can reasonably handle. That is why community organizers constantly work to prevent organizations from spreading themselves too thin.

Setting priorities means essentially setting "posteriorities"—that is, some issues, at least for the time being, may need to be put aside so as to properly concentrate on those issues that matter the most and on which the organization can potentially have the most impact.

An African-American organization, for example, may start out wanting to provide employment opportunities for young male adults in a community and within a short while want to improve educational opportunities. Then it identifies other needs and members wish to tackle cultural enrichment for pre-teen African Americans. Unmet family counseling needs become identified, but instead of seeking other organizations to meet them, the African-American group wants to establish its own social service component.

Soon the organization becomes overwhelmed in trying to meet all its priorities. Clearly, there is so much to be done, and everything seems to have a sense of urgency. Community organizers face the constant challenge of helping their groups develop boundaries that can help them focus resources and improve prospects of doing a few things well.

6) **Seeking a balance between wanting to make a major impact in the community and identifying projects that can be feasibly implemented.** For those who work in central cities, problems cry out for remedy: unemployment of central city youth, drug trafficking, school dropouts—these are among many examples that are a part of the community landscape. If efforts to deal with them are too grandiose, people will give up because results seem so elusive. But if boundaries can be drawn around an issue so that it becomes more manageable, people will be enthusiastic about tackling the next level of difficulty. Obtaining twenty jobs, or getting rid of drug trafficking in a five block area, or working to keep thirty ninth graders in school may represent only a small part of a total problem, but they are, nevertheless, successes that can be built upon.

GUIDING PRINCIPLES

The following principles can serve as a guide for community organizers:

1) Anticipate possible problems and challenges so that you will be prepared to meet them. It is sometimes helpful to imagine what issues a community organization will be facing three months, six months, or a year from now.

2) Start where the group is. You may be hired by the local hospital to reach out to the community to provide information on preventing cancer, but the group you organize may want first to complain about the insensitivity of the hospital in treating local residents. To ignore their concerns and insist on concentrating initially on the hospital's needs would prevent you from gaining their trust.

3) Encourage people in the organization to take on assignments in which they can be successful. Some may be good at fund raising; others at conducting door to door surveys; others at organizing a rummage sale. When the community organizer helps them succeed at their task, people will want to contribute further to the work of the organization.

4) Be aware of organizational dynamics and interactions. Are some members domineering? Are there cliques emerging that eventually will be detrimental? Are some members not fulfilling their responsibilities? As an organizer, you can assist the group's development by tuning into interpersonal relationships and working with the leadership to address these problems. As a facilitator in this organizational process, you listen, question, probe, and search for areas of agreement and compatibility.[2]

SUMMARY

People form community organizations to address a variety of concerns and issues. Sometimes these organizations are based where people live; frequently they emerge from common interests. Regardless of their origin, they have in common the need to influence change, mobilize support, deal with resistance, and see results. To strengthen their power to influence change, community organizations will frequently form coalitions. Through community development processes, some community organizations attempt to have an impact on the economic life of the community.

QUESTIONS FOR DISCUSSION

1) How is your agency attempting to influence change in your community?

2) What tactics for change would you consider especially effective currently?

Note: For additional discussion questions based on case examples, see Appendix B.

Chapter Notes

[1]Rothman, J. "Approaches to Community Intervention" (1995) in Rothman, J., Erlich, J.L. & Tropman, J.E. (Eds.). (*Strategies of Community Intervention* (5th ed.). Itasca, IL: F.E. Peacock. pp. 26-63. See also the following: Meenaghan, T. M. and Gibbons, E W. (2000) Generalist Practice in Larger Settings. Chicago: Lyceum Books, Inc. Chapter 6.Rothman, J. (1968). "Three Models of community organization practice." National Conference on Social Welfare, Social Work Practice 1968. New York: Columbia University Press.Rothman, J. (1974). Planning and Organizing for social change: Action principles from social science research. New York: Columbia University Press.

[2]Weil, M.O., &Gamble, C.N. (1995). "Community Practice Models." Encyclopedia of Social Work (19th Ed.). pp.577-594.

[3]Barker, R. L. (1991). *Social Work Dictionary* (2nd ed.). Washington, D.C.: National Association of Social Workers, pp. 5, 43, 220.

[4]Burghardt, S. (1987). "Community Based Social Action." in A. Minihan (Editor-in-Chief), *Encyclopedia of Social Work* (18th ed. Vol. 2, pp. 292-299). Silver Spring, MD: National Association of Social Workers, p. 298.

[5]Trapp, S. (1986). *Basics of Organizing*. Chicago, IL: National Training and Information Center, pp. 1-4.

[6]Kahn, S. (1995). "Community Organization." *Encyclopedia of Social Work* (19th ed.), pp. 596-576.

[7]Fisher, R. (Fall, 1994), "Community Organizing in the Conservative '80s and Beyond." *Social Policy*, pp. 11-12.

[8]Meenaghan, T.M. (1987). "Macro Practice: Current Trends and Issues." In A. Minihan (Editor-in-chief), *Encyclopedia of Social Work*, (18th ed., Vol. 1, p. 41). Silver Spring, MD: National Association of Social Workers.

CHAPTER 19

Community Development/
Community Building Initiatives

COMMUNITY DEVELOPMENT

Community development is a form of community organization. Typically staff are recruited from outside a community to work with residents to help them improve their community. In the past volunteers have worked through the VISTA program or the Peace Corps. Volunteers interested in pursuing a college career may be eligible to participate in the National Service Trust Program known as Americorps. Citizens of all ages and backgrounds will be able to work on community projects.

Community development emphasizes self-help and voluntary cooperation among members or residents of disadvantaged communities.[1] Staff assist low income residents of an urban community to develop a food bank distribution system. They help residents in the inner city remodel their dilapidated homes. They volunteer to work for Habitat for Humanity to build housing in low income communities. They set up tutoring programs for economically disadvantaged students. They establish a "crime watch" program in a public housing unit for senior citizens. Overseas, they assist rural communities in developing improved sewer systems or reforestation programs.

Economic development often is a crucial aspect of community development work. Since many inner city areas experience the flow of consumer spending moving out to the suburbs, special efforts have to be undertaken to encourage people spending in their own neighborhoods and fostering those outside the community to find reasons to shop. Economic development may involve bringing together local business persons, public officials, the police, the schools, and the banks to develop viable plans for enhancing local businesses. They may focus on such interrelated issues as finding other uses for an abandoned movie theater, developing public funding for crumbling bridges, obtaining low interest loans from the banks, or securing a commitment from the police to provide a more visible presence on the streets. They require the coming together of various elements of the community to seek common solutions.

Several common elements characterize community development work. First, staff have a tremendous desire to improve the lives of vulnerable people. They have chosen to forgo better paying jobs for the opportunity to give expression to their altruism and commitment to others.

Second, they strive to help people to build on their individual strengths and community assets. Their primary purpose is to empower people. The emphasis is on building a grassroots membership or a "bottom-up" approach to community problems. Stimulating citizen participation is the underlying purpose of community development.[2] Staff might, for example, meet with several neighbors in an area known for drug dealings to determine whether there is sufficient interest to form a drug prevention council. Then staff would help convene a meeting, work with the chairperson to set the agenda, and assist residents in developing their strategies and plans. They might, in this example, assist the residents in organizing drug marches or in arranging meetings with the local police chief. Community development staff do not function independently of the residents but work with them in such a way that after staff leave the community, residents will have the confidence and the experience to carry forward.

Third, community development staff identify outside resources that can be tapped. They might, for example, help write proposals that will bring in funds to hire local staff. Or they might make connections with other volunteers in the broader community, such as outside tutors.

Here is an illustration: Increased amount of muggings and robberies so intimidated a senior citizen group living in a public housing unit that they were becoming prisoners in their own homes. One community development staffer organized an attorney's organization to commit over 100 hours each week to participate in joint patrols with the public housing residents. Even in this illustration of outside involvement, the community development staffer ensured that the residents themselves, through their council, remained in control of the program.

Hence, community development work greatly stresses the bottom-up approach to meeting social needs. The premise is that people must be actively involved in the resolution of their needs and that while the outside community developer can facilitate participation and can be a resource person, he or she must not take over or make the residents dependent. The ultimate criterion for success is that after a community successfully completes one project, it is able to function on its own to address other needs.

COMMUNITY BUILDING INITIATIVES (CBIs)

In recent years there has been a rekindling of interest in and commitment to the rebuilding of inner city, distressed communities. Rather than dwell on the problems of these areas, the emphasis has been on enhancing neighborhood capacity for planning, service delivery, advocacy, and implementing a wide range of development strategies. Community building refers to activities, practices, and policies that support and foster positive connections among individuals, groups, organizations, neighborhoods, and geographic and functional communities.[3]

A Community Building Initiative (CBI) involves a process of empowering residents to work together in mutually supportive relationships. Through their active participation, they develop new social mechanisms to help them identify and then achieve their community goals. These relationships form a kind of "social capital" as residents begin to discern how their own well-being and prospects are tied to their neighborhood and their community.[4] Thus, CBI refers to activities, practices, and policies that engage residents in reinvesting in the development of their communities.

The concept of community building has developed naturally out of an understanding of how communities function. In most of our neighborhoods, citizens interact with each other to create institutions, businesses, schools, and social groups. These entities help people achieve their aspirations, strengthen their shared values, and provide a fabric and a network that binds them together. Where these are weak, that is, where people feel a sense of isolation and removal from their local institutions, and where support systems are fragmented, communities invite alienation and deteriorated relationships. Efforts at community building are designed both to offset this decline and to build on the natural strengths that continue to exist no matter how poor the neighborhood is or how vulnerable the people are.[5]

Principles of Community Building Initiatives

Developing in different parts of the country, CBIs differ from previous efforts to deal with community problems in several ways. For one thing, in the past programs tended to focus primarily on how people could overcome their individual problems.   Training and educational programs, for example, emerged from the War on Poverty era in the 1960s to facilitate the movement of people out of poverty. Only incidentally and superficially did these programs give attention to expanding the resources and capacities of the communities in which individuals resided.

A second difference is that in the past efforts have tended to focus on problems one at a time. Funding patterns and services concentrated on such disparate problems as homelessness, mental illness, delinquency, or substance abuse. Service delivery systems were designed to address these specific problems, separate from each other and from the social environment that fostered them.

A third distinction is that programs tended to be agency-driven. Over the past three decades a large social welfare industry has emerged. Now one can see multi-service centers, Salvation Army offices, and food distribution centers in place of viable stores and shopping areas. While it is probably accurate to say that the intention of these organizations was to serve the needs of the poor, the unintended consequence has been a growing dependency on social services.

CBI offers a different set of strategies to deal with urban disinvestment. It looks at a community holistically and acknowledges the inherent connection of people within a geographic area. It offers the opportunity to provide solutions that are tied together in a way that reinforce each other. And it provides a means through which residents who have had limited mastery over their lives can now take greater control.

Several strategic principles form the conceptual framework for CBI:[6]

- A first strategic principle is that efforts to improve the community must be comprehensive. Because poverty is a result of interrelated problems that reinforce one another, a single solution is not possible. Any response will therefore need to factor in a wide variety of interventions. Among the elements that can achieve a synergy are the following: expansion of human services, such as child care, family supports, and senior programs; health care; mental health and substance abuse programs; economic development; housing; adult education; job training; neighborhood security and recreation.[7] Any new development within a community must fit into a comprehensive community mosaic.

- A comprehensive approach also requires linkages among the economic, physical and social life of a community. By linking different spheres of activities, resources can be used more effectively and various efforts can be marshaled synergistically to advance neighborhood change. For example, unemployed persons can receive vocational training as they work on a housing renovation project. Another example: a neighborhood cleanup project can be linked to the development of a recycling facility and the cultivation of a community garden.[8]

- A second principle is that strategies must be tailored to individual neighborhood areas of a manageable size. By targeting specific geographic areas, it is possible to single out specific and unique factors that affect families and individuals. It also permits customizing strategies to the special character and culture of a particular community. This approach can result in different communities arriving at different issues with which they must grapple—even in the same city.

- A third principle is a commitment to build on a community's assets. These include its local buildings and institutions, such as schools, banks, churches, storefront businesses, social agencies, and hospitals. They also encompass such intangible, but tremendously essential, human assets as life experiences, skills, and a willingness to improve the community.

- Finally, strategies must engage residents and other local stakeholders in establishing community goals and plans to address them. This is perhaps the most important strategy, for if people are not involved in a significant and meaningful way, a CBI will not succeed. In the past, efforts at "top-down" programs imposed on communities tended to turn residents into passive recipients. Urban Renewal, Model Cities, and other similar federal programs, although well meaning, could not achieve their desired results because residents were not sufficiently involved.

On the other hand, approaches that are solely "bottom-up" may not themselves produce comprehensive changes needed to address more complex issues. A more successful approach is to involve residents in significant partnerships with the social institutions of their community and with policy makers and public officials outside their community.

IMPLEMENTING A COMMUNITY BUILDING INITIATIVE PROGRAM

If you were a community organizer hired to assist in implementing a CBI, how would you go about fulfilling your role? What follows is a description of how one CBI is stimulating several communities in one city to develop a process of empowering residents to take charge. Established in 1994, the Cleveland Community Building Initiative's mission is to reverse the conditions of poverty, and it is doing this by creating four Village Councils that develop and oversee neighborhood-specific plans.[9] As discussed earlier, this program is based on the four principles of being comprehensive, targeted to specific neighborhood communities, built on assets and other neighborhood resources, and driven by residents. What follows is a review of how a community organizer might undertake a CBI. Consider the following four phases:

Phase I - Understanding the Community

The first task of a community coordinator is to learn about the community, especially its problems and assets. Problems can usually be ascertained through readily available census data, which can include demographic information on income levels, racial composition, unwed births, and welfare recipients. The local juvenile court can supply statistics on delinquency. The county health department has data on premature births and mortality.

Far more important than looking at the limitations of a community is looking at its assets and strengths. Do a "windshield tour" as an initial starting point. Drive through the community to locate major institutions serving the community, such as libraries, schools, churches, and social agencies. Walk through the community and talk with the mailperson, small business owners, and other people walking on the streets. This first phase of getting to know the community can take as long as four to six weeks.

Of special importance are discussions with community leaders. These include the council person, street club presidents, ministers, and school principals. Besides talking with these formal leaders, meet with "invisible" leaders—those who do not have a formal role but who nevertheless are influential in their own circles. You would meet, for example, with informal social groups or with teenagers playing basketball to talk about their concerns and interests.

During this initial phase, you will begin to get an understanding of some of the issues concerning people. One person may express concern about the lack of youth recreation programs, while another about the absence of adequate tutoring for elementary school children. A third might describe the need to support grandparents raising their children.

Then, too, you may sense that different people or institutions have different perspectives about the same problem. For example, several individuals may discuss the lack of affordable housing. Then you learn that a local church may be interested in developing a high-rise apartment, while the local community development corporation wants to build housing for the middle-class at the market rate. As a result of these discussions, you begin to discern a pattern of interests that can be clustered together for possible follow-up.

Although identifying projects or issues in this first phase is useful in your initial exploration, it is absolutely crucial that you do not jump too quickly into becoming project oriented. It is this ability to be disciplined about not moving prematurely into projects, however desirable they may be, that distinguishes community building from other one-shot efforts that may have occurred previously in the community. Because the essence of community building is to develop a process that empowers community residents to participate actively in establishing their own goals, your task as community facilitator is to involve them in this process, rather than immediately formulating solutions.

Phase II - Recruiting People

Having had initial conversations with people will greatly facilitate this next phase of identifying people who can become active participants in the CBI. During this phase, you may encounter resistance from the residents. This is to be expected. The residents themselves may be suspicious, because they may have previously experienced others who have come into their communities—students, outside volunteers, transient staff—who have made promises about helping them only to leave without fulfilling their promises. The first question residents are likely to express is, "Are you committed to working with us in the long run?" Your commitment must be positive, clear, and unambiguous.

A second resistance may come from certain social agency representatives, particularly those affiliated with neighborhood centers or from church leaders who may fear that their leadership may be diverted from their own organizations. You need to convey to them that the CBI program is to supplement, not supplant, their own efforts and that the community will be able to speak in unison as they connect the different parts.

A third form of resistance may come from local public officials. After all, they have built up ward structures and precinct committee persons who have helped them tune into the community and get elected. Council persons are among the first you would contact when entering a community. They need to understand the value of having a neutral organization that transcends politics and at the same time works cooperatively within existing political processes.

During this phase residents will be encouraged to attend community meetings to air their concerns. A common worry of community organizers is not so much that residents will articulate their annoyances at community gatherings but that attendance will be minimal. To counter apathy, special efforts have to be made to reach out to people. Although it is desirable to obtain mailing lists from church groups, street clubs, and other organizations in the community, sending out flyers is probably the least effective way of ensuring a turnout. The most effective approach is through word of mouth. People are most likely to come to meetings when they have been asked face to face to do so. As a community coordinator, you would spend considerable time laying the groundwork by talking with people in small groups or individually. This time spent in developing relationships is well worth the effort.

If the proper groundwork has been laid during the initial phase of outreach, residents will understand that they are coming together to consider a new way of building up their community. At these initial meetings the community coordinator would take primary responsibility to explain how this new effort differs from ward activities, social agency programs, and previous time-limited, project-oriented efforts. The main message will be to create a new spirit of working together to influence change.

To some residents, this will be reminiscent of living in a small town or village. Perhaps people will remember how vital their own neighborhoods were when they were growing up, as neighbors looked out for each other and were committed to caring about all the children in the neighborhood. In Cleveland, the four targeted CBI communities are called "villages" to capture the sense of small town caring.

Some might think that the strategy of not selecting a local leader to run these initial meetings is ill-advised. After all, the fundamental purpose of the ultimate organizing effort is to have the people of the community take charge of their lives. An outsider running a meeting seems to be the opposite of this goal. On the other hand, attempting to select a spokesperson at this stage may itself arouse rivalries among the residents. In addition, all challenges to the CBI concept need to be handled by staff: They, not a "front person," need to respond to the questions and criticisms that might be raised in a town meeting.

Phase III - Creating the Structure and Strategy

Following the initial meetings, the community organizer would work with those enthusiastic volunteers who are committed to a vision of rebuilding their community. Together they would establish an organizing committee, consisting of twenty to thirty people, that would then elect interim officers and identify certain committees, such as finance, nominating, bylaws, and program. Interim officers could serve for several months, until the nominating committee has recruited and recommended candidates who could serve a full term.

During this phase the organization members take on the challenge of developing a strategic plan. They would develop a mission statement and undoubtedly would want to prepare a vision statement of what they will want their community to look like in few years. Furthermore, they would analyze the assets of their community so that when considering potential projects, they can relate these to the community's strengths. As a result of discussing a vision of their future, they may identity two to five long-term goals that will be their focus of attention for the next three years. Finally, they would want to establish specific, concrete objectives that will help them achieve their goals.

In a large urban city if CBIs are taking place in several different communities (as is the case in Cleveland), it is anticipated that each one, through its own self-determination process, may arrive at different issues based on each locale's unique special strengths and concerns. Each will tailor its approach to fit its own community style and culture. One community, for example, may focus on relations with its diverse ethnic populations and may decide to pursue a Cultural Diversity Center. The residents of this area may also want to expand home ownership for low-income citizens.

In a different part of the city, with a different composition of people and with a high level of children and youth, the organization may decide to expand recreation programs and child-care centers. A third community may decide to develop Family Resource Centers where people can enhance their employment skills, reinforce family values, and provide substance abuse and mental health counseling.

Phase IV - Linking and Marshaling Resources

Because low-income communities do not have adequate resources them-selves to achieve their goals, they must develop linkages and partnerships with others. One type of partnership is with institutions both inside and out of the local community. These can include, for example, a vocational guidance agency, a community college, a high school with a GED program, or a neighborhood center with a mental health and drug abuse counseling program. Partnerships can also be arranged with ministerial alliances and with a downtown planning council.

Another type of linkage is with business leaders and policy makers from outside the community. This is important because residents by themselves do not have the resource base to accomplish their goals. They must have linkages with power brokers outside their own communities. An organization, consisting of people from the broader community, as well as representatives of the local CBI would be formed to be a powerful voice in obtaining outside resources and public commitment. This umbrella organization would have direct linkages with the mayor's office, the local United Way, and foundations. The existence of such a board would add credibility to the local CBI. Being able to garner resources can avoid participating in an exercise in futility. The key is finding the right balance involving community control on the one hand and engagement of resource gate keepers on the other. Each complements the other.

The Challenges Ahead for CBIs

CBI is a relatively new approach; it has yet to prove itself as a way of breathing new life into impoverished inner city communities Even as we advance this concept it is important to recognize ongoing issues that must be confronted to ensure its long-term viability. Among the issues and dilemmas to be examined are the following:

1) **The role and expectations of funding sponsors.** In many communities, local, private, or community foundations provide the necessary funding for staff and other expenses for CBI. In some instances, these sponsors establish ground rules for how the various participants can relate to each other. Sponsors set the levels and duration of funding and the frequency and manner with which funds are provided to community groups.

   They can provide grants that are single-year or multi-year and allow for differing degrees of freedom. For example, they can provide a lump sum to a governance group and allow it to disburse funds, or they can retain the right to choose what to fund, project by project. In some instances, the sponsor may play a direct role in the planning and governance of comprehensive Community Building Initiatives. Because a considerable amount of time has to involve the development of the community process, sponsors must develop a high degree of patience that the fruition of this process in the form of tangible results may take several years.[10] Hence, a natural tension will exist between CBI and the funding sponsors. On the one hand, sponsors may want to see immediate results and be impatient about the time CBI needs to take to ensure a proper community process. On the other hand, CBIs may experience disappointment that their funding sponsors are not giving them sufficient resources to accomplish their goals.

2) **Individual mobility**. Many people who can afford to do so want to move out of their impoverished neighborhoods. Paradoxically, a community can lose the very people whom it helps to develop. New educational and training programs designed to improve economic well being of individual families may improve their plight sufficiently that they may want to raise their children outside their community. Under these circumstances individuals have gained but the community has not. Limited community resources become expended on people who no longer continue as residents. Thus, as people increase their capacities and "vote with their feet," there is the possibility that the community as a whole will decline. This doesn't mean that CBI cannot work. It does mean, however, that strengthening community capacity allows residents pathways out of their community.[11] The antidote for preventing flight is to develop an infrastructure of special job opportunities, decent housing, good schooling, and excellent crime prevention measures that will make the community attractive to those who have an option of leaving.

3) **Competition with public officials**. One of the problems encountered by community organizers of the "War on Poverty" in the 1960s was that in seeking to develop maximum feasible participation of residents they encountered tremendous resistance from local public officials. So far, this does not seem to be happening in the CBI movement. In general, CBIs are accepted by and acceptable to local government officials. Presently, representatives of local government do not see them as a fundamental intrusion on the roles or prerogatives of elected officials. Nor are they seen as a threat.

Because CBIs are targeted to specific areas, public officials have seen them as a conduit of information and as a broker between neighborhoods and them. At least until now, CBIs seem to have worked out partnerships with local government. They must, however, be clear on their boundaries in not making city policy and not assuming certain responsibilities, such as dealing directly with criminal activities that are the statutory responsibilities of the city.[12] Moreover, as a result of CBI experience and training, new community leaders may emerge, and CBIs may be perceived as training grounds for those who would oppose elected officials. How these real or perceived threats will be handled is a challenge that has yet to be confronted.

4) **Relationship with resource power brokers.** Earlier, we discussed the issue of linking the local community with resources outside the community. A major concern is finding the right balance so that on the one hand people can take control of their lives and, on the other, recognize that they must be part of an interdependent partnership with those who control outside resources. Successful CBIs need to draw on outside resources, including both public and private funds, professional expertise, and new partnerships that bring influence. Many problems experienced by inner-city residents arise from powerful economic forces and from deficiencies in public and voluntary systems that originate beyond their own borders. They must, therefore, be able to draw upon funding, expertise, and influence from the outside. Residents from distressed neighborhoods cannot entirely rely on their own resources.

At the same time, the CBI cannot permit "top-down" decision-making to accompany outside resources. Effective interventions designed to transform neighborhoods require a new set of dynamics between insiders and outsiders.[13] The challenge of CBIs will continue to be to preserve that right balance of self determination while gaining a commitment from those who control resources outside their community.

SUMMARY

Community building is not a program or an activity or a series of newly funded projects. It is, rather, a process of transforming a community, a commitment to empower people to revitalize their own lives. It changes the way residents relate to each other and to people outside their community. It is based on the fundamental belief that inner-city residents and their organizations must take primary responsibility to solve their own problems. CBI is a process that organizes a community to identify key resources and to develop and train local leaders to become full partners in strengthening their community.

QUESTIONS FOR DISCUSSION

1. What neighborhoods in your city would you consider for a CBI? On what would you base your decision?

2. What specific assets or strengths would you attribute to your hometown community?

3. In a small group discussion, assume that you represent different perspectives of a hypothetical community (e.g., homeowner, small businessperson, parent, teenager). What issues would you identify that will require developing a CBI?

4. Select a community with which you are familiar. What resources, assets, or strengths would you identify?

Chapter Notes

[1]Spergel, I. A. (1978). "Community Development." In A. Minihan (Editor-in-Chief), *Encyclopedia of Social Work* (18th ed. Vol. 2, pp. 299-307). Silver Spring, MD: National Association of Social Workers.

[2]Spergel, pp. 300, 304.

[3]Weil, M. O. (Sept. 1996) Vol. 41. No. 5. "Community Building: Building Community Practice." *Social Work*, 3. pp. 481-498.

[4]Goodman, H., Chrmn. (1997). *The Cleveland Community-Building Initiative: Four Neighborhoods Begin to Address the Conditions that Maintain Poverty*. Cleveland, OH: Cleveland Community Building Initiative.

[5]Dooley, D. (Nov. 1997) "A Major New Strategy for Reversing Poverty, and the Man Who Shaped It." *Northern Ohio Live*, pp. 21-23& 71.

[6]Naparstek, A.J. & Dooley, D. (Sept. 1997). Vol. 42. No. 5 "Countering Urban Disinvestment Through Community-Building Initiatives." *Social Work*, pp. 506-514.

[7]Chaskin, R.J., Joseph, M.L., Chipenda-Dansokho, S. (1997). Vol. 42. No.5. "Implementing Comprehensive Community Development: Possibilities and Limitations." *Social Work*, pp. 435-444.

[8]Ibid., 438.

[9]Goodman, pp. 1-3. (Material for this section was also provided by R. Register, Executive Director, and G. L. Brown, Associate Director of Village Operations, Cleveland Community Building Initiative. Feb. 4, 1998.)

[10]Stone, R., ed. (Feb. 1996). *Core Issues in Comprehensive Community-Building Initiatives*. Chicago, IL: Chapin Hall Center for Children, University of Chicago, pp. 32-35.

[11]Ibid., 84-85.
   See also Cohen, C. S. & Phillips, M. H. (Sept. 1997). Vol. 42. No. 5. "Building Community: Principles for Social Work Practice in Housing Settings." *Social Work*, pp. 471-481.

[12]Chaskin, R. J. & Abunimah, A. (March 1997). "A View From the City: Local Government Perspectives on Neighborhood-Based Governance in Community-Building Initiatives." Discussion Paper from *The Chapin Hall Center for Children at the University of Chicago*.

[13]Schorr, L. (1997). *Core Issues in Comprehensive Community-Building Initiatives*. Chicago, IL: Chapin Hall Center for Children, University of Chicago. p. 393.

REFERENCES FOR CHAPTER 19

Austin, Sandra. (2005). "Community Building Principles: Implications for Professional Development." *Child Welfare*. Vol. 84, Issue 2. April 2005. pp. 105-122.

Dale, Ann & Onyx, Jenny. (2005). *A Dynamic Balance: Social Capital and Sustainable Community Development*. Vancouver, Canada: UBC Press.

Kubish, Anne C. (2005). "Comprehensive Community Building Initiatives—ten years later: What have we learned about the principles guiding the work." *New Directions for Youth Development*. Vol. 2005, Issue 106. Summer 2005. pp. 17-26.

Shaffer, Ron, Deller, Steve, and Marcouiller, Dave. (2006). "Rethinking Community Development." *Economic Development Quarterly*. Vol. 20, Issue 1. February 2006. pp. 59-74.

Zimmerman, Julie., & Meyer, Alissa. (2005). "Building Knowledge, building community: integrating internet access to secondary data as of the community development process". *Journal of the Community Development Society*. Vol. 36, Issue 1. January 2005. pp. 93-103.

CHAPTER 20

Grassroots Organizing:
Empowering the Needy

Grassroots organizing from the ground up reflects a long and proud tradition in our society. Neighbors, school children, parents, service organizations, political and faith-based groups, self-help groups, women and youth groups, welfare groups, community project committees—all of these and more—have for hundreds of years provided opportunities for local people to participate in efforts to improve people's lives through collective action. These organizers may not label their actions as "grassroots level organizing." Inspired by the German word "Graswurzel," the movement allows people to organize through a *bottom-up* approach with voters demanding change, rather than existing political leaders directing the process in a "top-down" fashion.

This chapter is based on the idea that grassroots organizing can become more effective and sustainable. It is based on the idea that it can be a powerful force for empowering people to take charge of their lives by engaging in a process of democratic participation.

Consider this a work in progress. As you read it, you may agree with some ideas and disagree with others. This can be used as a self-study guide for members of your small formal or informal organization.

Our approach has been to identify the best practices used by grassroots organizations as we answer four basic questions:

1. How can we make our organizations more effective?
2. How should we develop strategic and project planning?
3. How can we go about seeking resources for our organization?
4. How can we develop income-generating activities?

CREATING AN EFFECTIVE GRASSROOTS LEVEL ORGANIZATION

A GLO is an organization whose members voluntarily support each other and work on behalf of projects that benefit a majority of the members. Formation and operation is confined to a particular geographic area, such as neighborhood associations or religious-based committees.

This sometimes evolves from small self-help groups involving 4 or 5 close friends or families who meet regularly to enjoy each other's company and contribute to a shared pool of money, commonly referred to as merry-go-rounds. The money is then distributed once a week or once a month on a rotation basis to various members for purposes agreed to by the group, such as school fees and home improvement. This process encourages trust among members and is a way of disciplining them to save. At some point the members may decide to move beyond their small group to involve others on projects that benefit the community. Some of these networks are known as Co-operative Societies whose purpose is to directly serve their own members, such as credit unions.

In general, a GLO has three primary purposes:

1. To provide benefits only to their members.
2. To provide primarily for the benefit of a community project.
3. To provide a combination of benefits for their members and for the community.

Elements of an Effective GLO

The following guiding principles can ensure that the GLO runs democratically and with good governance procedures:

Member participation. The GLO's leaders encourage members to work together to strengthen the organization so that they can accomplish their agreed-upon goals. When members actively participate they feel that their input and involvement is taken into consideration and can make a difference. Members then have the will and the commitment to keep the organization going.

Clear focus. The GLO must make explicit its reason for existence. To do so requires a strategic plan that has a mission statement, a vision statement describing its future, and a value statement that conveys what it believes in. Members are thus clear on what the GLO is trying to achieve.

Transparency. A GLO that is transparent shares information with others, discusses ideas openly, and freely debates policies. It should be willing to conduct self-reviews and should be willing to have its finances carefully monitored.

Accountability. Accountability involves the right of the organization's members and others to hold members of the governing body responsible. The governing body (sometimes referred to as the management committee) is required and expected to justify its actions and decisions related to the running of the GLO. When members express concerns, the governing body would genuinely evaluate them and consider modifying its policies.

Constituency representation. A GLO gains trust when it reflects the interests and concerns of the group it represents. If, for example, the GLO consists of men and women, but women's concerns are inadequately represented because women tend to defer decision making to the men in the group, then a major constituency is not adequately represented.

Clarity of member roles. It is important that the GLO clearly defines roles and responsibilities of members, the management committee, and staff management. For example, managing committee members should not interfere with the staff management on day-to-day operations. Also, the chair of the management committee should not have a concentration of power but be willing to share decision making with the management committee and the GLO membership.

Rotation of power. Good governance requires that elections be fair and based on the active participation of GLO members. The rotation of leadership should be encouraged and new leaders should emerge over time.

Preparing a Constitution

To become a recognized Grassroots Level Organization, a group must register with the government (to be discussed) and before it can do this, it must have a constitution. Each group must devote time and energy to preparing its own constitution and not automatically copy those of other groups. Investing in developing your own constitution heightens a sense of ownership and makes it more meaningful and relevant.

Often a group will invite resource people who have previously developed a constitution with the understanding that their own constitution will not be a direct copy. A small committee is appointed to prepare a draft, which is then reviewed and revised by the rest of the members. The following are elements that are generally included:

> Name of the group
> Aims of the group—what it wants to accomplish
>> Example; provide extra income for its members
>> Example: provide awareness of the AIDS epidemic
>> Example: provide clothing, food and shelter for homeless children
> Membership
>> Criteria for becoming a member
>> Number in the group
>> Determine how members can resign
> Officers (governing body)
>> How elected and how long they can serve
>> Duties
>> How often management meetings are to be held
> General meetings
>> Frequency (for example, monthly, quarterly)
>> Quorum (the number required to conduct the business of meetings—usually a majority)
> Group funds
>> Entry fee and ongoing fees
>> Handling of money, borrowing and lending conditions
>> Bank accounts—who can sign
>> Audits
>> Procedures for handling financial disputes
>> Procedures for dissolving the GLO
>> How funds or property would be distributed
>> Who will make decisions in disputes?

Registering the GLO

To become a formal, official GLO, you must register your group at the state level. Your state representative's office will be more than happy to assist you with proper information about the registration process. The group must elect members of the management committee, including the chair, vice chair, treasurer, secretary, and, if desired, other members. The organization is expected to provide annual reports. Upon registration the group must open an account with the bank of its choice.

Registering your GLO has several advantages:

1. Helpful consultation

2. Commendations and Letters of Support

3. May qualify to receive small grants from the governmental entities

4. Allows your organization to receive non-profit status with the Internal Revenue Services (IRS)

The Role of the Leader in an Effective GLO

The chairperson plays a vital role in helping the GLO run smoothly and achieve its purposes. Because the leader's role is so crucial to sustaining an effective organization, we identify some of the skills needed:

1) Sets the purpose of every meeting. The chair would say at the beginning of each meeting, "This is the agenda at today's meeting." The chair would then allow other members to suggest agenda items they think would need to be discussed.

2) Is keenly aware of how members feel about important matters. The leader is sensitive about members who are unhappy or are hesitant to speak. These persons are encouraged to express their ideas. The chair works to reconcile differences and is also aware when the group is ready for a consensus decision.

3) Encourages open discussion in which members are treated with dignity. Leaders may at times express their own views, but they try not to impose their will on the group. They establish ground rules of how people are to interact with each other. They treat everyone with equal dignity and do not take sides in personal conflict. They make members feel that they are making a meaningful contribution. Also, they help members focus on the issue and prevent them from attacking each other's integrity or character.

4) **Keeps the discussion on track.** While effective leaders encourage an informal, relaxed atmosphere, they keep the focus on the agenda topic under discussion. They continually review the points that have been discussed and identify where there are differences of opinion and where there are agreements. Sometimes leaders will have to delay action if members can not come to agreement. Leaders summarize points that have been discussed and identify what next steps need to be taken. Meetings start on time and end on time.

5) **Encourages meaningful action.** After summarizing the discussion, the leader identifies what next steps need to be taken and makes assignments. The leader keeps in touch with people to determine what can be done to further the agreed-upon action plans.

Conducting Meetings

GLOs work best when they provide an opportunity for socializing, for promoting a sense of being part of a community, and for conducting important business of the organization.

The Order of the Meeting

- Call a meeting to order on time.
- Review and adopt the minutes from the previous meeting.
- Propose an agenda for the meeting and obtain additional agenda items from group members.
- Receive reports from members who have been assigned responsibilities from the previous meeting.
- Receive and approve the treasurer's report.
- Receive report on attendance of members, with focus on those who need special follow up.
- Focus on each agenda item. When desired, determine how much time will be devoted to various topics.
- Summarize and record decisions.
- Adjourn the meeting on time.

MAJOR ISSUES AFFECTING A GLO

Many grassroots level organizations are likely to face important issues that could have a major impact on how well they will be sustained. Some of the more common issues are listed below:

Communication Among Members

Either because they are fearful of expressing their views or for other reasons, some members are reluctant to speak up, even when they disagree with how the discussion is going. For example, the chair may suggest that monthly fees need to be raised and those who disagree with this position remain silent only to complain afterwards or even to withdraw from the group. It would be far better if people would voice their concerns. Open and honest communication may at times cause tension, but it is better that concerns be expressed and dealt with rather than be ignored and allowed to feed member discontent.

Small Group Domination

Some organization's leaders may not encourage full participation, preferring instead that the major decisions are be made by a small clique. Or the chair may not be willing to delegate responsibilities, feeling that only a few are capable of following through. While this may work in the short run, in the long run the vitality of the organization will be strengthened only if people feel they are sharing in the decision making and in carrying forward programs.

In some organizations members of one family may come to dominate the organization, for example, the chairperson's brother is the treasurer and his or her niece is the secretary. Often in these instances the statement is made, "There is no one else qualified and willing to assume responsibilities besides another member of my family." While there may be some truth to this assertion it could lead to the perception that one family is trying to dominate the organization and there could be a sense of unfairness. For these reasons GLOs should be very careful about concentrating decision making in the hands of one or two families.

Decision Making

The least effective decisions are those that are decided only by one individual or a small group. This can occur when a small group of powerful individuals tend to dominate the group and then wonder why others are so uninterested and uninvolved.

The preferred decision-making approach is to achieve consensus. This usually involves letting all opinions be heard, combining various possibilities, and perhaps compromising on certain positions to achieve a general agreement. This can best occur in a climate in which all members are able to express their ideas and at the same time are open to the ideas of others. Further, it means that members will make a sincere attempt to take everyone's ideas into consideration while searching for a common solution. The final resolution may not reflect the exact wishes of every member, but the differences are not deeply felt and people are committed to the spirit of working together.

Not everyone can be involved in decision making. Large groups may require at times that decisions be made by a smaller management committee. A good rule to observe is that the more deeply people are affected by a decision the more important that they participate in making it. In the case of the pre-school, issues around school fee payments would clearly need to be brought to the larger assembly for approval.

Transparency

If decisions are made by only a few and if people operate with a degree of secrecy and reluctance to share, then members will feel manipulated and used. By being open and transparent people convey respect for each other and trust builds. Certainly there will be times when complete consensus is not possible and decisions will have to be made by the majority members, but even then those in the minority must feel they have had the opportunity for their ideas to be heard.

Rotation of Officers

Some GLOs have committed leaders who provide the organization with a strong sense of direction and focus. This can be especially true when the leadership resides in the organization's founder. When an organization has a strong leader, it could take one of two approaches:

1) It could place a time limitation in how long officers, including the chair, can serve, thus providing rotation of leadership.
2) It could continue the leadership for as long as people are willing to vote the leader in office.

In the later instance it is conceivable that the chair could be in that position for ten or more years. Sometimes this can present problems in that the leader begins to assume more power and control as the result of being in office so long. On the other hand, the organization may not be able to provide a strong alternative leader.

There is no right or wrong answer as to whether to provide time limits. Each organization needs to debate the issue and come to its own resolution. If the organization is concerned with who will eventually replace the current leadership, then steps should be taken for people to assume leadership responsibilities. They may be given leadership assignments to test out if they can assume responsibilities.

Membership Participation

When they are first organized, most GLOs generate member enthusiasm and involvement. Over time, participation may decline. Some organizations handle this by fining latecomers and observers. This conveys how serious the organization takes member involvement. If absenteeism seems to be widespread the organization has a serious problem. The group's leaders may need to emphasize with individual members the importance of their attendance and work to make the meeting agendas interesting and compelling.

Inability to Take Action

A number of factors can affect whether a GLO can move from discussing ideas to taking concrete actions. Discussions in meetings may lack focus in which case participants and the chair may need to encourage greater concentration on the topic at hand. Goals may be unclear, and as a result, members want to cover too many issues—and not do justice to any of them. In this case members need to develop a set of priorities. Another reason for inaction is that members do not take responsibility for following through on their assignments. This is a serious issue, and a GLO faced with this problem needs to have frank discussions about member commitment to the goals of the organization.

STRATEGIC AND PROJECT PLANNING

GLOs are formed because members are eager to do something about a concern they share. But before you rush into developing a program for finding solutions you must have an adequate amount of planning. You want your efforts to reflect the idea of, "Ready, aim, shoot," not "Ready, shoot, aim." The more your GLOs undertake the thoughtful preparation the more likely you are to achieve success.

This section will discuss two major forms of planning, strategic planning and project planning. Each is important and necessary for helping the organization achieve its goals.

Strategic Planning

The primary purposes of strategic planning are to improve the way the organization functions in your community and help it to make adjustments to changing circumstances.

Good strategic planning involves both (1) a process of involving people actively participating together and (2) preparing policy directions that can be realistically implemented. Participation of GLO members and key people in the community is essential because their involvement will lead to enthusiastic support and follow through. Preparing direction help members envision where the organization is going and how it can get there.

In the absence of good strategic planning the organization may drift away from its primary purposes. For example, a GLO formed to provide housing for homeless children may gradually shift its emphasis to providing economic development primarily for the benefit of its members, thereby losing it original reason for being. Through strategic planning the organization becomes more purposeful in what it will do and what it will avoid taking on. As members explore new projects, they will refer to their mission and to their strategic plan to determine whether these projects are consistent with the overall direction of the organization.

Generally it is a good idea for an organization to conduct strategic planning when it is created and every three to five years after that. By going through the review process, the organization takes a step back from concentrating on current activities to view the "big picture." Members assess where they have been, where they currently are, and, most importantly, where they are going. For those organizations that have been in existence for awhile it can prevent becoming stale and give members a sense of renewed purpose.

DEVELOPING THE STRATEGIC PLAN

To develop a good strategic plan it is important to develop a process that will
- Engage members
- Develop or review the mission statement
- Prepare a vision statement
- Develop a values statement
- Review both internal and external forces affecting the organization
- Identify critical issues requiring follow up

Engage Members in the Planning Process

Strategic planning should involve as many members of the organization as possible. Staff or volunteers, members of the GLO, the local councillor and business leaders should be asked to contribute their ideas. We emphasize that participation itself is as important as whatever formal plan emerges. Working together helps educate members and others in the community, builds commitment, and mobilizes participants to take action. It builds enthusiasm for going forward.

Develop a Mission Statement

The purpose of a GLO is to meet a need. Addressing that need is the mission of the organization. The mission provides a purpose without which the organization will lose its direction, support, legitimacy, and resources. A good mission statement should be inspiring, yet concise and capable of being easily understood and remembered.

Examples of mission statements from different organizations:

- To ensure that people living in poverty in our community will have access to income-generating activities.

- To provide schooling for preschool children whose parents can not afford to pay school fees.

The mission establishes boundaries for GLO activity and guards against the tendency to chase unrelated opportunities. Each organization should spend time and thought in preparing a mission statement that reflects the essence of the group.

Prepare a Vision Statement

A vision statement expresses the dreams or aspirations of an organization. It should be short and inspiring. It is a picture of an ideal future and deals with the question, "What kind of organization would we like to be in the future?" In summary it is an expression of the hopes and dreams of GLO members. Though the vision may never be realized, it proclaims a call to action.

A vision statement would express lofty ideas, such as the following:

> "We visualize the future where all people have access to resources and rewards for their hard work."

> "We desire to build a community where government agencies are responsive to the concerns especially of children and those most vulnerable."

> "We envision a community in which fundamental human needs are being met, including sanitation, education, and adequate food.

Vision statements can focus on aspirations for the future of the community, as the above statements indicate, or they can relate to a vision of the future of the organization. It could reflect a dream of what the organization could become as in this statement: "We envision that our organization will eventually be able to generate sufficient income from our own resources that we will not have to rely on outside donors."

Make Explicit the Values of the Organization

Some groups have found it helpful to develop ways of dealing with each other that set the overall tone of behavior. Sometimes this is called a "Values statement" that begins with the words, "We believe..." or "We are committed to..." For example:

- We believe that everyone in our organization should have the opportunity to voice his or her opinion about what we should do.

- We believe in majority rule, but the minority should be heard.

- We believe that the chairperson should allow full and complete discussion before the vote it taken.

- We believe that no one person or small group should control decisions.

- We believe in working with other organizations to gain strength in what we want to achieve.

- We respect differences in our community and strive to understand different viewpoints.

- We are committed to improving our community so that our children will have a better way of life.

- We strive to meet those in great need and are willing to give of ourselves to improve the lives of our beneficiaries.

- We want to build on the strengths of our community and look for strengths in everyone we serve.

- We know that we may not be able to meet all the needs in our community and so will have to develop priorities of what we most want to concentrate on.

- We exist primarily for the benefit of the community. Benefits to the members are an important, but secondary, benefit.

We suggest that each organization review these value statements and then write one for itself, with values that best reflect the organization's position. Merely copying this list is not enough. Take the time to develop your own values statement so that you develop conviction about the rules you want to operate by. In sharing how you want to proceed and operate with each other, you will be able to address matters as they come up. Then when conflicts occur, as will likely happen, members can be in a better position to resolve them.

Moreover, the act of formulating a values statement will make everyone clearly understand what the organization stands for. It will also permit the group to periodically examine whether the practices of the organization are living up to what the members say they believe in. For example, if the members stress the idea of open communication and this is not in fact observed, then members can use the review of values as a way of getting the organization to implement what members feel strongly about.

Review Both Internal and External Forces (Conducting a SCOT Analysis)

As part of the planning process, members will want to analyse both internal (organizational) and external (environment) factors that could affect the organization's future. The term, SCOT, conveys the following for the internal analysis review:

> Strengths (organizational)
> Challenges (organizational)
> Opportunities (environmental)
> Threats (environmental)

(Note: Sometimes the term SWOT analysis is used. The W stands for weaknesses in the organization. We prefer using a C for challenges.)

In looking at your organizational strengths, list the things that you do well. For example, you might have a strong volunteer component. Be sure you can answer the question: What value are we adding to our community? In looking at your internal challenges, have a candid discussion about your limitations and concerns. For example, you might be concerned about the low level of attendance at meetings.

In looking at environmental opportunities, such as changes in governmental policy that might provide funding for the beneficiaries of your program, you might want to conduct an indepth review. Similarly you may want to examine current or potential external threats, such as a new GLO competing for the same beneficiaries and resources in your community. Again, you would make a list of potential external threats that could require special follow up.

Identify Critical Issues

Concentrating on *critical issues* is especially important for GLOs seeking to update the current strategic plan in response to new developments. Review the lists developed under the SCOT process and ask which of these cry out for resolution. If you have identified two or three critical issues then you need to determine how you are going to address them over the next period of time. You might ask the following questions:

1. What changing community needs are of special interest to our GLO?
2. Can we improve our program by expanding services to the beneficiaries of our program?
3. Should we consider phasing out programs that are declining or are not as vital as they once were?

4. Should we modify out funding?

5. Should we network with other organizations to achieve our purpose?

These questions illustrate the kinds of issues that could be raised. It is essential that each organization identify its own unique critical issues because each GLO has a limited amount of resources. It is likely that only a few critical issues can be addressed at any one time. Priority decisions must be made. Trying to be everything for everyone can only guarantee being ineffective.

Later we will discuss project planning. In this discussion it is important to recognize that selecting a project will depend on its relevance to achieving the organization's mission and whether it is seen as a primary project related to a critical issue identified through the strategic planning process.

Implementing the Strategic Plan

After determining what should go into your strategic plan (or what should be revised from your last strategic plan), then you must be committed to implementing an action process. People need to be assigned specific responsibilities with a specific timetable for reporting to your strategic planning group.

During this implementation phase, people will be assigned to do homework or to implement plans that were developed. For example, if you decide that your mission or value statement needs to be revised, you might select a small group to work on this. If you want to explore indepth government policy changes that might impact your organization, you might assign a special group for this purpose. It is extremely important that you assign specific people to follow up and report their findings and recommendations.

SUMMARY OF THE STRATEGIC PLANNING PROCESS

1) Determine what benefits you see from embarking on an intensive strategic planning process.

2) Ensure that your GLO's leadership and its members are committed to doing strategic planning.

3) Form a strategic planning group consisting of representatives from your GLO, volunteers, staff, and key community leaders.

4) Analyse your situation including strengths, challenges, opportunities, and threats (SCOT).

5) Prepare or revise your mission statement.

6) Develop a vision of the community and the organization.

7) Develop a value statement that reflects the beliefs of the organization.

8) Identify the most critical issues facing the organization.

9) Prepare an action plan with assignments for specific participants to follow up.

10) Implement the plan with the intent of modifying it as circumstances change.

PROJECT PLANNING

Selecting and implementing projects involves:
- Conducting a needs assessment and determining priorities
- Identifying goals and objectives
- Determining activities that must be implemented
- Delegating assignments
- Reviewing projects for self-correction.

RAISING RESOURCES WITHIN THE COMMUNITY

Preconditions for Conducting Fundraising

Whether you rely on local fundraising or reach out for external funding, your organizations should first get your house in order. A well-run organization is an essential requirement for raising money. As discussed in Sections #1 and #2, make certain that you have the following in place:

1) A clear and inspiring mission
2) A strategic plan that provides direction for where you want to go in the next few years
3) A focus on one or more community issues or problems
4) Strong volunteer involvement
5) A track record of accomplishments
6) A clear list of the objectives you want to accomplish
7) Transparency of finances and operations

Community people are more likely to work for an organization that values their input. Outside donors are more receptive if they see that your organization shows a commitment to helping beneficiaries and demonstrates the capacity to do so.

Reasons to Seek Internal Resources

GLOs should seek to raise resources from within their own communities for several reasons. First, a primary source of funding projects is most likely to come from within the community. While it is tempting to rely on donations from outside the community, with so many GLOs competing for outside donors, the chances of obtaining outside funding are limited.

Second, your chances of receiving outside donations increase considerably if you can convey that you are developing internal resources. Outside donors like to know that you are not entirely dependent upon them for your programs and are committed to raising funding within your own community.

Third, your own sense of pride and dignity should encourage you to contribute your own resources in the development of your programs. By making contributions you begin to master your own destiny and gain confidence that you can benefit your community. Working to achieve your own dreams will make you and your community stronger.

Fourth, if you only rely on outside funding you foster a heightened sense of dependency. When the donor funding is withdrawn from a project that is entirely dependent on external resources, the likelihood is that the program will not be sustained. When people become dependent on outside funders, they wait for things to be done for them. They assume that they have nothing to contribute to their own welfare, cannot be masters of their own fate, or do not have an impact on decisions that affect their lives and the lives of the people in their community. They lack a belief in themselves and what they can do. By taking initiative to raise their own resources, people achieve a heightened sense of dignity and accomplish community improvements based on their own efforts.

DIFFERENT APPROACHES FOR RAISING LOCAL RESOURCES

Community Members Contribute

Some GLOs require their members to pay a small registration fee for office expenses and contributions to projects.

Merry-Go-Rounds

This is a common way for village groups to provide informal savings for close friends. Members contribute equal amounts of money regularly (weekly or monthly). The proceeds are given to one member at the end of a given period (for example, weekly) until the rotation is completed. Sometimes the group will dictate the purposes for which the money will be used, such as payment of school fees. This procedure provides a way of saving and loaning money to members. It ensures collective responsibility and disciplines members to save regularly. A caution is that some members may be inconsistent with their contributions and some may be forced to withdraw because they can not keep up with the payments.

Volunteers

In many communities, GLOs provide volunteers to meet special needs. Voluntary efforts reflect significant ways GLOs contribute to their communities and stimulate other to give. In the past, GLOs may not have tracked this kind of contribution, and this may have been taken for granted. In the future, outside donors and funders may want more evidence of volunteer input, and GLOs will have to keep better track and report these efforts.

When negotiating with donors, it is important to note the number of volunteers and their various tasks and then highlight how much it would have cost the organization if it were to pay for the same services.

Cautions about Focusing only on Internal Fundraising

Although there are clear advantages for striving to raise money from internal resources, you should be aware that devoting a considerable amount of time to raising funds could divert energy from the major purposes of the GLO.

Also, recognize that internal funding by itself will have limited success in sustaining most projects. In reality, few local organizations can go it alone, especially if they want to expand their programs. While GLOs may not want to avoid becoming overly dependent on outside funders, in reality they may need to seek resources from outside the community.

CULTIVATING DONORS

Reaching Out to Donors

It is understandable that GLO members may have been reluctant to seek out potential donors in the past. Because GLO members may lack natural and informal relationships with those whom might make contributions, they are uneasy to reach out for contacts that could be of help. For those that want to reach out, we offer these suggestions:

Make a personal contact. If at all possible try to establish a personal relationship with a donor. People are more likely to give a donation if they have been personally contacted—either directly by a member of your group or by a friend of your group. They are least likely to make a donation based on a letter or contact from an unknown person. There are several ways relationships can be developed:

> a. Someone in your group knows a retired businessperson who is willing to volunteer with your group. In turn, this outside volunteer knows other people, both working and retired, who could be solicited.

> b. Your ward councillor may have outside contacts, either within the country or with potential donors in other countries.

> c. Your members attend a church or mosque where they meet people who might be encouraged to visit your program. A social action committee might be invited to take on the cause of your program.

> d. Business people might be asked to individually volunteer or serve on committees to give suggestions on how you might improve the running of your organization. Later, after they have gotten to know about your organization, you can solicit them and ask them to solicit others.

What all of these have in common is that they provide opportunities for outside donors to become acquainted with your program—before you ask for a donation. Donors need to be cultivated, encouraged to find out what you do, and see first hand, if possible, the benefits your organization provides. At least they should be contacted by someone they know and respect who has seen your program first hand. People give to people. **Fundraising is friend raising.**

Communicate an emotional message to donors. Whether in person, in a letter or in a brochure, donors need to feel an emotional tug on their heartstrings. Talk about one family or one child that needs help. Communicate a poem or essay from a child (you may have to be their scribe) that describes his or her difficulties and conveys a heartfelt request.

Indicate in concrete terms what a difference their donation will make. Donors like to know that they can make a meaningful difference in the lives of people.

Describe your local efforts to make your program work. Donors want to have confidence that while you may need to depend on outside help, you are making special efforts to draw upon your own internal strengths for resources. Let them know that you have a strong volunteer component, that people in the community are willing to pitch in, and that you are working to raise funds within the community, as limited as resources may be.

Convey an inspiring message. "It is more blessed to give than to receive" makes clear that Christian values have a place in fundraising. Appealing to religious values provides a powerful motivation for people to make a contribution.

Involve local donors in your program. One of the best ways of developing an interest in your program is to actively engage potential donors in a meaningful way. There are several ways to do this. You could request outside individuals to provide you with technical assistance. You could involve attorneys, accountants, and business people to provide you with specialized technical assistance as part of their charitable good will commitment. Often professionals will be willing to provide a free service, sometimes referred to as a *pro bono service*, because they appreciate the work you are doing on behalf of your beneficiaries.

Another approach for generating involvement is to ask outside business leaders and professionals to serve on a specialized committee, such as a strategic advisory committee. This committee might only meet two or three times a year to give you guidance on strategic planning. After the group becomes familiar with your organization, they might be willing to undertake fundraising. We know of examples of current or retired business people who have taken on specific responsibilities, such as selling the organization's products when they go abroad or getting their friends to join them in sponsoring needy children.

Communicating with Contributors

The first and most important rule about working with donors is that you must stay in communication with them. This means keeping the donors informed continuously after you have received the donation. Even if your organization is dealing with a negative situation (for example, one of your members has stolen money), donors need to know directly from you, rather than hear it from somewhere else or be surprised at a later date.

Follow directions. If the donor requires a five-page report, make sure you comply with this request. If another donor prefers to receive a brief email every three months, respond to this request. If a donor prefers not to fund ongoing operations but instead wants only to fund special projects, then you must honor this request.

Keep your promises. To maintain credibility with your donors be sure to follow through on using the money the way you said you would. If, for example, you said you would spend the money for purchasing chickens, then that is what you must do. If you find that you can not follow through with your promise, it is extremely important that you request permission to use the funds in another way. If you decide, for whatever reason, that purchasing a dairy cow would a wiser decision than buying chickens, ask the donor for permission to make the switch.

Communicate successes and failures. Certainly, donors will want to hear about your accomplishments. But they also expect to hear from you about your failures and your challenges. Problems will likely occur along the way and when they do, it is important to be transparent and open with your donors. It is most helpful to indicate how you plan to deal with the challenges you have encountered. If, for example, a drought is affecting the grass where the cows feed, inform your donors. Also tell them what alternative plans you have for feeding the cows.

Plan for future requests. Suppose your donors have contributed to particular project, such as dairy cows, and you have come to the end of the donation period. Let the donors know what you have accomplished—the purchase of the cows, which has resulted in X number of litres of milk for the year and an income of Y amount. Now is the time to convey your hopes and plans for the future. If you have been successful with two cows, maybe you could use two more to expand your income. Or maybe you are ready to raise chickens. Donors will be receptive to supporting your program when they sense they can build upon your successful track record.

More information about proposal writing can be obtained from the chapter under this title in this book.

QUESTIONS FOR DISCUSSION

1. In your residential neighborhood, make a list of several types of grassroots organizations and write a brief description of each.

2. Contact one of the GLOs' officers and collect their history, mission, goals, and present activities.

3. Identify the strengths and weaknesses of this GLO.

4. Any suggestions to improve the working of this GLO?

REFERENCES FOR CHAPTER 20

Epstein, Paul D. (2006). *Results that Matter: Improving Communities by Engaging Citizens, Measuring Performance, and Getting Things Done.* San Francisco, CA: Jossey-Bass.

Nitzerg, Joel (2005). *Putting Youth at the Center of Community Building.* San Francisco, CA: Jossey-Bass.

Procter, David E. (2005). *Civic Communion: the Rhetoric of Community Building.* Lanham, MD: Rowman & Littlefield Publishers.

Rahman, Hakikur. (2006). *Empowering Marginal Communities with Information Networking.* Hershey, PA: Idea Group Pub.

Staples, Lee (2004). *Roots to Power: A Manual for Grassroots Organizing.* (2nd ed) Westport, CT: Praeger.

CHAPTER 21

Negotiating and Advocating Positions

Eventually all community organizations will be involved in a negotiating process. Wanting something from someone else—whether a banker, a politician, another organization, or a funding body—requires staking out a position and entering into a give-and-take discussion. In successful negotiations both parties ideally perceive that they have given up something of limited value to gain something of major value. The goal of negotiators is to achieve as strong a position for their organization as they can, or at least to minimize the potential loss for their weaker organization when negotiating with stronger opponents.

Often, one party may gain more than the other; there may not be equal exchange. Even in less than ideal negotiations, both negotiating parties must feel that some of their needs are satisfied, that something was gained from the process. If the members of one side suffer a humiliating defeat, this leaves open the possibility of their wanting to return someday to even the score. If one side feels it must make a great sacrifice, with minimal gain, it has no stake in making the agreement a stable one and may be provoked into laying plans for future retaliation.

CLARIFYING OBJECTIVES

Before the negotiating process begins, the community organization must have a clear understanding of what it intends to accomplish, both in the short run and the long run.[1] Little is to be gained if a community organization wins a short-run gain that could jeopardize its long-term interests. For example, a community organization committed to improving the education experience of its children will weigh carefully whether to use possible pressure tactics to force teachers to provide tutoring. If these tactics antagonize the faculty so much that they go through the motions of complying but reduce their involvement with students in other ways, then, to repeat an old cliché, "the battle may be won but the war is lost." Before negotiating commences, therefore, the community organization must clarify its goals and objectives. It must ask how the negotiations will serve to advance its short- and long-term interests.

Setting the Agenda

Part of the preparation of negotiations will also involve establishing an agenda for discussion. The agenda reflects both the power of the two parties and the importance of issues. It is the first step in which both the community organization and the other parties' expectations, attitudes, and values are formally identified. Agendas can be used to clarify or hide motives. They can keep negotiations on track or permit digressions. They also can contain issues that are meaningful to both parties or can serve as a smoke screen for latent problems.

Obtaining Information on the Issue

Knowledge is power. The more information a community organization has available, the more likely it will be able to present its case forcefully and with conviction. One way of obtaining the data is through gathering it systematically. If an organization is concerned with low-paying jobs for women, it must research how many women are in menial jobs. If an organization is concerned that minorities are not represented in administrative positions in proportion to their numbers, then it must document its case. Data can be obtained from census material, county court house records, community or national studies, or through specially designed research.

Sometimes data cannot be collected, in which case a community organization may need to rely on less systematic procedures. For example, if a community organization was concerned with the redlining practice of banks (drawing a red boundary line on a map to indicate where mortgage loans will not be given), then volunteers might need to make informal inquiries in the neighborhood or with real estate companies to determine where people were denied loans.

Sometimes knowledge is gathered informally from employees who work for the institution being challenged. For example, if a community organization was concerned with decisions regarding a city's community development fund, a well-planned informant could provide it with advance information. Informants serve as one of the best sources of inside information, and their identity should always be protected.

Knowledge experts are another source of information. Attorneys, accountants, economists, and businesspersons can provide both information and insights on issues. These experts can be particularly valuable when dealing with technical matters.

Although logic and reason alone will not sway decision makers whose self-interests are at stake, an essential minimal requirement of negotiations is preparing a sound case. Arguments supporting a position must include a good definition of the problem, a clear statement of what ought to be changed, and a proposed solution for what could be done. Since the natural tendency for most organizations and communities is to resist change, the burden of proof falls to advocates to document that something is wrong with the status quo. It is essential to present facts and figures that substantiate the organization's position.

In defining a need, considerable thought should be given to framing the issue in a way that is easiest for the negotiators to agree. For example, in an effort to raise welfare grants, a community organization would try to arouse positive sentiment by concentrating on the benefits to children.

There is a difference of opinion about the extent to which a community organization should develop methods for solving the problem as part of the preparation of its position. Some would argue that a detailed proposed solution impresses the negotiants and will go a long way to moving them to accept the community organization's position. Advocates appearing before county commissioners to obtain more day-care funding, for example, would show precisely where funding could be located in the budget. By offering a concrete, feasible solution, the group helps decision makers to justify their position.

There may be tactical reasons, however, for not proposing a solution. If the community organization becomes involved with locating additional revenues or changing legal mandates, then it may be detoured into unfamiliar territory. So another approach often taken, especially by neighborhood groups, is manifested in the expression, "We have identified the problem—now you find the solution." This approach could, of course, turn a negotiant into an adversary.

ANTICIPATING RESPONSES OF OPPONENTS

In addition to developing general background information about negotiants, it is necessary to anticipate their reaction to the particular proposal and to develop a response and alternatives to their potential reactions. In this regard, negotiation is like a chess game in which one needs to consider not only one's next move, but also the opponent's response to that move and one's subsequent responses, and so forth. This approach requires mentally working through the possible scenarios.

In anticipating possible responses to the negotiant, it is particularly useful to consider what might have special value or appeal to the other side's self-interest, such as enhancing its prestige or stature if the proposal were adopted. In addition, the community organization will want to anticipate how it will respond if objections are raised. What responses can be prepared in advance if the other party says that it does not have sufficient staff or funds to implement the proposal, or that there is insufficient support for the proposal, or that the opposition is too strong? Through this kind of anticipation, the community organization can avoid being caught off guard in negotiations.

Often opponents will agree that a change is needed, but then argue that the proposed solution is worse than the problem. One way of dealing with this resistance is for the community group to prepare the opponent's case as it prepares its own. The advocacy organization raises as many harsh objections and questions as it can about its proposal and then develops its response to them.

> **Example**: A community organization is concerned with an extremely difficult issue: how to develop more group homes for recently released mentally ill patients. It has decided to concentrate on five suburban areas that have previously resisted group homes. The organization has embarked on a campaign to persuade the legislators from each municipality to modify their zoning laws. The next page lists some of the anticipated objections to change as they might be expressed by the legislators and how the organization tends to deal with them.

Anticipating Objections

Objection: Property values will decline.

Response: *Our research of other communities where there are group homes shows homes have maintained their values in proportion to rising inflation.*

Objection: Why should we change zoning that would open up group homes? Residents would not be from our communities.

Response: *We can document that each year approximately 120 to 250 people from your communities need special living arrangement, until they are able to move out on their own.*

Objection: Our constituents will be hostile if they learn we have altered zoning.

Response: *In other communities across the country where group homes have been installed, the initial reaction is fear, but this usually gives way to confidence that neighborhoods will function normally. In addition, we can identify key community leaders who will support your efforts.*

Objection: Current zoning laws are adequate, why change?

Response: *If you do not change your zoning laws, you may experience what has happened in other communities: the possible concentration of group homes in less desirable neighborhoods. Our proposal provides a formula that insures that homes will not be located closer than one-half mile to each other.*

Objections: If we change our zoning, then group homes will be attracted to just our community.

Response: *We are working with four other contiguous communities; all have expressed similar concerns. They have agreed to sign a joint pledge that if four out of five agree to our proposal, they will introduce legislation into the communities.*

Through the exercise of listing all the anticipated resistances, the community organization can begin to prepare its case.

Developing a Fall-Back Position

Some community organizations have a tendency to express their concerns through moral self-righteousness. Indeed, their profound sense of indignation and sincere commitment to their cause greatly contribute to their power at the negotiating table. Since, however, the negotiation process will often involve compromises, the community organization needs to think out in advance what it is willing to compromise on—what its fall-back position is. At the same time, the community organization needs to determine what its minimal, bottom-line requirements are. Hence, it must be clear on what it is, and is not, willing to compromise.

Communicating with Constituents

Because there always exists the danger that the negotiating team could take a position different from the group it represents, it is crucial that reporting procedures and mechanisms for decisions be worked out in advance. Such procedures could include periodic meetings where group consensus process or votes would take place either with the entire membership or a body representing the membership.

BEING WATCHFUL ABOUT NEGOTIATING MANEUVERS

The negotiating process often fosters situations in which parties try to out-maneuver each other. These maneuvers or gambits (in chess, a gambit is an opening in which a pawn is sacrificed to get an advantage in position) are intended to manipulate the negotiating situation to special advantage of one party over the other. By being aware of the most common maneuvers that could be attempted by the opposition, community organizations can be in a better position to deal with the negotiating process.

Using the Pressure of Timing. There are two ways that time can be used as a maneuver: stalling or pressuring deadlines. Opponents who stall do so with the intent of preventing quick resolution of the issue in exchange for the expectation of gaining more in the future. They deliberately decide to extend negotiations over a long period of time in the anticipation that they can hold out longer than their opposition. An example of this would be a landlord who deliberately delays negotiations in the hopes that the renters will be unable to sustain the consequences of a long rent strike.

Sometimes the position will use the pressure of time to precipitate action. The urgency of a deadline for legislative bills or year-end funding decisions can push both parties to compromise.

Slicing. This maneuver (sometimes called "slicing the salami") is designed to get the community organization to agree to a relatively innocuous position, with the intent of obtaining more and more later. The small concession made at one point opens the door for larger concessions.

Fait Accompli. This means "accomplished fact" and is used as a surprise maneuver by the opposition to take action that produces a result so as to make any negotiations meaningless. For example, community groups are invited to a mental health hearing to discuss potential models for psychiatric emergency services, when a decision has already been made. Or, at a state budget hearing, community groups are invited to present their views only to discover that the budget has already been established. In both instances, the hearings are a charade. To remedy potential fait accompli situations, it is desirable to determine in advance whether a decision already has been made. Negotiating should make explicit that decision making would be open to options. If it appears that the decision has already been made and therefore the negotiations are a sham, then negotiants have to be challenged or an appeal made to a higher authority.

Limited Authority. In this maneuver, when negotiators are asked to make concessions, they plead the need to check with a higher authority. They are unable to make final decisions. To prevent this from happening, it is important to clarify in advance the extent of the authority of the opponent. If necessary, community organization members may need to go directly to the higher authority under which the negotiant's team is operating, such as the director of an agency, the governor, or a board of trustees.

Co-optation. Sometimes opponents bring into the decision-making process out-spoken and antagonistic community organization members with the intent of getting them to soften their position. When those advocates who formerly took a strong position are invited into the decision-making process of those they once attacked, the advocates tend to lighten their demands. An example of this would be a school board that requests that vociferous community leaders serve on an advisory committee. Although being invited to participate in the decision process may offer opportunities for influence, the chief danger is that such participation may be illusory.

Quid Pro Quo. The Latin term quid pro quo (something for something) describes how each party makes a concession in exchange for the other party's concession. While the quid pro quo process is a common part of negotiations, two aspects require special vigilance. First, the opponent could concede relatively minor points with the expectation that the community organization will concede on major items. Second, the opponent may take significant concessions but then propose to offset these with other actions, thus nullifying the original concessions. Negotiators deliberately make an enticing offer, an inducement that is difficult to refuse. This is like a grocery store that attracts customers with "loss leader" below normal market costs but makes up the loss by charging customers regular or higher than normal prices on other items. An example of this would be a funding body agreeing to pay for a special request but then reducing funds in another part of the community organization's budget.

Pleading Powerlessness. Public officials sometimes plead that they are powerless to act on a request. For example, state mental health officials may claim that their facilities are incapable of dealing with persons who are both mentally ill and retarded. But then state retardation officials claim the same thing. Both want the other administration to deal with dually diagnosed people, with the result that neither does.

Public officials often claim that they have no control over funding. Obviously, funding organizations do not have monies to fund all requests. They have to make priority decisions. But when they say they have no power to provide funds for a particular community organization's request, what they really mean is that they have made a decision (based on past or current commitments) to give priority to other funding requests.

Ambiguity. Ambiguity is often used as a way of facilitating the negotiation process to come to a resolution on a difficult or complex issue. At times, negotiants may purposefully use ambiguous words as a possible basis for reopening discussions later if they are not satisfied with the results of the negotiations. Vague words or escape clauses are purposefully written to permit self-serving interpretations later. If the ambiguity leaves basic issues unresolved, they could flare up again.

Escalation. Some negotiators purposefully appear to work out agreements with the intent of introducing last minute requests. Although the community organization thinks it has reached an agreement, suddenly, as time appears to be running out, it is faced with new and different demands. It then has the difficult choice of accepting the new demands or renegotiating.

Final Offer. At times, the opponent may make a take-it-or-leave-it-offer. This is likely to occur when opponents feel that the preponderance of power is in their hands. Negotiations can then result in an impasse, capitulation, or an open fight.

Stonewall. As the name indicates, the purpose of this maneuver is to place an obstacle in the way of the discussion so that important issues are not fully discussed. An opponent will ignore or deny that a problem exists, as illustrated by school officials who say that children are as well educated as any in the county or state. Employment services administrators may claim that services are quite adequate for funding people jobs, despite unemployment figures being to the contrary. This approach is introduced to prevent negotiations from occurring.

Diversion. An opponent may attempt to shift the issue away from the original concern. For example, a community organization may want to discuss how unresponsive and inefficient staff is, but the negotiator will shift the discussion to the lack of adequate staff.

Another form of diversion occurs when, faced with mounting community criticism, some institutions create a community relations unit to work with advocacy groups to reduce tension and improve perceptions. A police department will create a community relations division; private industry, a community affairs unit to improve communication. A community organization has to determine whether the new unit is a sincere effort to alter institutional practices or a means of diverting the discussions from focusing on its immediate concerns.

Repudiation. At times an agreement may appear to have been consummated when the opponents retract or repudiate their positions. Because this is an ever-present danger, it is wise to make agreements public. Witnesses should be present. To avoid repudiation it is helpful for both parties to sign drafts of agreements. If repudiation does occur, the community organization may have, as its only recourse, the publicizing of the bad faith of its opponents.

Thus, by being aware of these maneuvers community organization representatives can be in a better position to bargain and advocate on behalf of their concerns and interests.

ADVOCATING LEGISLATION

Increasingly, community organizations are aware that they must develop the ability to influence legislative changes in order to obtain the resources needed to meet special needs of people. Day care, mental health, health services, programs for the elderly, resources for the homeless or for those with AIDS—all these require that legislators develop the will and the commitment to adequately fund programs geared to vulnerable populations. Since typically most local organizations depend upon and are most likely to want to influence their state legislature, we will focus our discussion on this level of government, though the approaches to legislative advocacy can apply as well to the city and county government and to federal officials.

Developing an Advocacy Capability

Community organizations would do well to appoint one committee or at least designate one person to give concentrated attention to the legislative process. These legislative advocates would track pertinent legislation, educate members about the process, and develop contacts with relevant legislators.

Community organizations are likely to participate in a coalition (discussed previously) because legislation is rarely passed or funds allocated based on the energies of only one organization. A good working relationship within a coalition entails members sharing information and developing common strategies. It is essential that coalition members be involved through creating ad hoc committees, scheduling information meetings, and establishing a good communications network. By engaging and informing members, the coalition can stimulate a ground swell of support among grass-roots groups.

Most experienced advocates recognize that persistence is one of the most important traits needed to eventually achieve desired results. Only a very small percentage of bills introduced in the legislature are enacted the first time around. The process of gaining converts to a new program or putting together a winning coalition often requires more than one session of the legislature.

In every state invaluable information can easily be obtained to enhance a community organization's capacity to deal with the legislative process more effectively. Below some of these resources are listed:

- The state legislature typically provides a toll free number and can provide information on any bill. Other sources include the League of Women Voters, the Democratic and Republican headquarters, and the state citizens' council.

- Most states provide a guidebook on the legislative process. Citizens' councils in most states print a legislative bulletin and directory.

- Typically the legislator in the organization's district will respond to requests for keeping track of particular bills.

Developing a good "intelligence system" is essential. It is important to build a file on the positions legislators are likely to take on issues important to the organization. Community organizations would do well to collect such background information as special interests, committee assignments, current and potential supporters, and previous votes.

Implementing Legislative Advocacy

The best approach in communicating with a legislator is to arrange for a face-to-face contact. While it is difficult to make generalizations about how to relate to legislators, what they seem to appreciate most is specific information on how a particular piece of legislation will affect their constituents. They also want facts and figures in addition to anecdotal information. They want to hear directly from those constituents the proposed legislation would affect.

Frequently legislators hold public hearings at which advocates can testify. These hearings provide an opportunity to educate and influence legislators, spotlight issues, educate the public, arouse public opinion, and test reactions to positions. These hearings are extremely important because legislators rely on testimony in formulating their positions. Advocates can also benefit from learning where the opposition is and what gaps in information need to be filled.

Maintaining ongoing contact with legislators is highly desirable. By persevering and continuing to be in their universe, community organizations have a better chance that their issue will be given priority consideration. If at all possible, arrange for legislators to address the organization. They welcome the platform and exposure, and in turn they can become impressed that the organization can turn out a committed audience.

In addition to meeting with legislators, letter writing campaigns can be influential. This is especially true if the letters reflect a reasoned analysis of why a decision one way or the other would be desirable. Letters that are "canned," where it is obvious that a large number of people have been instructed to use the same wording, are of limited value.

As is shown in Figure 20.1, timing is crucial in influencing the legislative process. For example, if you want to have a major impact on a budget item, it is essential that you begin to meet with department administrators when they are in the process of preparing their budgets, usually about six to nine months before the state general assembly convenes for the new biennium. This is also the time to communicate with the governor's office. Inclusion of your budget request in the governor's submission to the legislature will give it a boost.[2]

Also, meet with legislators immediately after the November elections in order to convince them of your cause before they are likely to take hardened positions. Within the first six months of the biennium, most state legislators devote considerable time to the budget.

TIMING OF THE LEGISLATIVE PROCESS

Figure: 21.1 Summary of Legislative Advocacy: When To Do What

---

Approximately Six to Nine Months Before the Legislative Session

Discuss with key members of your group the specific legislative proposal.

Begin drafting the legislation or at least outlining ideas so that you can transmit them to a legislator.

Approximately Four to Six Months Before the Legislative Session

Recruit a legislator to take either draft or outline of your bill.

Identify key decision-makers in the legislature (legislators, officials, party leaders) and learn how to reach each of them.

Access the numbers, resources, time and energy of your citizen's groups.

Approximately Two to Four Months Before the Legislative Session

Select sponsors for your legislation, and obtain early commitments from other legislators.

Arrange visits with key legislators. Let them know about your interests and to ascertain their viewpoints.

If it is an election year, arrange meetings with candidates.

Obtain commitments from allies and from coalitions.

If a coalition has been formed, have a general briefing session for members, and set up a communication network.

Concentrate on the opposition you will be facing. Prepare statements to counter expected arguments from the opposition, and publicize them before the opposition surfaces publicly.

Develop your grassroots advocacy strategy.

Establish media contacts.

Line up community supporters.

Approximately One Month Before the Final Vote in the Legislature is Anticipated

Pursue your grassroots advocacy activities.

Update your head count at least weekly.

Go after further media coverage if you feel it will benefit your cause.

If you have recruited prominent endorsers, keep them in the public eye.

Stage a big event if you feel it will help.

Keep in close touch with others on your side of the issue.

Organize your grassroots advocacy blitz.

Meet with legislators on a one-to-one basis.

Update your head count daily.

Intensify public information efforts through the media.

In some instances, when the stakes are high enough and the ability exists to raise a "campaign chest," it may be desirable to hire a lobbyist who can guide the process and pinpoint how organization members and others affiliated with organizations across the state can be marshaled to meet one-on-one with key legislators.

MEDIA ADVOCACY

Frequently organizations want to communicate their story in order to pass important legislation or challenge business practices that harm the community. They want to create a shift in public opinion and mobilize the necessary resources and community influences to either oppose or support a particular policy or issue. Media advocacy is a way to combine community organization with use of the media to pressure political and business decision makers to make desired changes. Through media advocacy organizations can increase the volume of their public voice; they hope to be loud enough to make their presence felt.

Media advocacy should be distinguished from using the media for educational purposes. When organizations or policy makers use the media to educate the public about a particular issue, usually the intent is to influence individual behavior. In the public health arena, for example, publicizing the use of seat belts or the dangers of smoking take the form of educational messages.

By contrast media advocacy shifts the focus from changing individual behavior to changing policies and practices of government and corporations. It concentrates, for example, not on the behavior of the smoker but on the behavior of the tobacco industry. Billboard advertising, tobacco vending machines, and industry sponsorship of community activities become targets for the tobacco-control movement.[3]

Suppose your community organization is concerned that billboards in the inner city display advertisements for alcohol. Here are some of the specific action steps you might consider.

1) You could develop data on the extent of the problem, including the number of billboards in specific geographic areas as compared with other areas in the suburbs.

2) You could conduct an analysis of what your organization wants to accomplish with focus on the specific endpoint. The organization would be clear on what constitutes victory. Is it the abolition of all billboard advertising or some reduction in number? As part of this analysis the organization would determine its assets and limitations: its clout in the community, its support from residents, its ability to raise necessary funds.

3) You could determine a way to speak with an authentic voice. You could identify those in the community who had been affected by excessive drinking and would be willing to speak out.

4) You could determine who has the power to change the advertising. In this instance a large beer distributing company or its advertising firm could be the target for change.

5) You could develop an action plan with a timetable and a campaign that could be easily understood by the general public. In our example this could involve boycotts, informational packets, public shaming, and letter writing campaigns.

6) You could take advantage of situations that could stimulate visual, lively, and compelling media coverage. That is, you would create events to capture the news media's attention or take advantage of an existing event for communicating the organization's message. People with powerful and personal stories would be involved. A tragedy involving a drunken driver killing a young mother and her small children would dramatize the

message. A protest march at the creation of a new billboard would also invite media attention.

7) You could proactively create interest on the part of TV or newspaper journalists. For example, the organization could send an information packet to a journalist about the extent of alcoholism among young people in the community. Further, you might write letters to the editor or arrange to meet with the editorial staff to alert them to the nature of the problem.

The value, then, of media advocacy is that it amplifies the community's voice. It sets up a situation that appeals to the media through an event that is dramatic and interesting and at the same time furthers the community organization's goals and benefits the community.

SUMMARY

Because community organizations typically are involved in efforts to bring about change, they inevitably will engage in negotiating and advocacy activities. An essential part of this process is to understand the resistance to change and to formulate positions and strategies that take into account ways to overcome obstacles. Whether dealing with a state legislator, a local public official, or agency administrator, community organization volunteers and staff must prepare a persuasive case. Further, they must be purposeful in the timing of their presentation so as to have the maximum impact on the decision making process. Finally, community organizations need to become more sophisticated in using media advocacy.

QUESTIONS FOR DISCUSSION

1) Take a position on a social issue. (Example: why the state legislature should raise taxes to pay for more day care slots for working women.) What case can you make for adopting your proposal?

2) What objections can you anticipate and what is your response to them?

3) In regard to the position you have taken, what alliances would you form? What other ways would you use to demonstrate your strength?

Chapter Notes

[1]Rubin, J.R. & Rubin, I.S. (2001). *Community Organizing and Development*. Needham Hts., MA: Allyn & Bacon, pp. 328-335.
[2]Brody, R., Goodman, M, & Ferrante, J. (1985). *The Legislative Process: An Action Handbook for Ohio Citizen's Groups*. Cleveland, OH: Federation for Community Planning, pp. 65-81.
[3]Wallack, L., Dorfman, L., Jernigan, D., & Themva, M. (1993). Media *Advocacy and Public Health; Power for Prevention*. Newbury Park, CA: Sage Publications.

REFERENCES FOR CHAPTER 21

Avner, Marcia. (2002). *The Lobbying and Advocacy Handbook for Nonprofit Organizations*. Amherst H. Wilder Foundation.

Borut, Donald. (2006). "Now's the Time to Tell Congress About Our Priorities." *Nation's Cities Weekly*. Vol. 29, Issue 16. April 2006. pp. 2.

Gormley, William T. Jr, & Cymrot, Helen. (2006). "The Strategic Choices of Child Advocacy Groups." *Nonprofit and Voluntary Sector Quarterly*. Vol. 35, Issue 1. March 2006. pp. 102-122.

Higgs, Joy. (2005). *Communicating in the Health and Social Sciences*. Oxford, NY: Oxford University Press.

Hoefer, Richard. (2005). "Altering State Policy: Interest Group Effectiveness among State-Level Advocacy Groups." *Social Work*. Vol. 50, Issue 3. July 2005. pp. 219-227.

Hoefer, Richard. (2005). *Advocacy Practice for Social Justice*. Lyceum Books, Inc.

Jackson-Elmore, Cynthia. (2005). "Informing State Policymakers: Opportunities for Social Workers." *Social Work*. Vol. 50, Issue 3. July 2005. pp251-261.

Lens, Vicki. (2005). "Advocacy and Argumentation in the Public Arena: A Guide for Social Workers." *Social Work*. Vol. 50, Issue 3. July 2005. pp. 231-238.

Lerbinger, Otto. (2006). *Corporate Public Affairs: Interacting with Interest groups, Media, and Government*. Mahwah, NJ: Lawrence Erlbaum.

CHAPTER 22

Developing and Coordinating Human Services

As agencies become more specialized, one of the unfortunate results is that services within a community become more fragmented. With the expansion of federal, state, and local agencies, potential clients often are confused by the "smorgasbord" of services and don't know where to turn for their specific concerns. Because each service has its own eligibility requirements and operating methods, potential clients are bewildered and often are turned away, not because they don't need assistance but because they don't know how to "manage the system."[1]

As agencies focus on limited and narrowly defined services, they tend to define their service boundaries in relation to their own offerings rather than to the expressed needs of consumers. A newly divorced mother seeking financial help, for example, will not likely get mental health assistance for her emotionally disturbed child at a public assistance agency. Agency function, not necessarily the client's situation, determines the nature of services provided.

Some clients face extreme problems that are a consequence of fragmentation. Those clients, for example, who have been deinstitutionalized, face a large and diverse system of services that they often have difficulty in negotiating on their own. In a health-care setting persons with

AIDS must weave through a maze of inpatient, outpatient, and community-based health-care services. In addition, they may need such other services as housing, food, transportation, and legal care. The result is discontinuity of services, conflicting eligibility requirements, and haphazard care.[2]

Constellation of Services/Continuum of Care

Two perspectives on service coordination can be useful in understanding how services are organized and delivered: "constellation of services" and "continuum of care." A constellation of services suggests a bringing together of a collection of programs that can be customized for a particular individual or family to meet a variety of needs. This presupposes that an inventory of preventive, supportive, and restorative services exists and is available to be drawn upon. For example, a constellation of services for elders could involve the following:[3]

Access services
- Information and referral
- Outreach
- Case coordination
- Transportation
- Escort

Health services
- Hospital services
- Nursing home services
- Physician services
- Rehabilitation therapists' services
- Health education services
- Home health services

Nutrition Services
- Congregate meals
- Home-delivered meals
- Nutrition education

Housing services
- Independent residential nursing home facilities
- Assisted residential facilities
- Personal care at home services
- Home repair services
- Adult day care

Income maintenance services
- Old Age and Survivors Insurance (Social Security)
- Supplementary Security Income

To provide this constellation of services, several organizations dealing with older persons would come together to identify what was already available in the community and what gaps need to be closed.

The term, "continuum of care," suggests a different view of service delivery in that it emphasizes the degree of intensity along a range of services from preventive care to limited care to highly intensive care. For older persons a continuum might first involve a coordinated program to provide in-home services (e.g., meals on wheels and house keeping) for those seniors who can live on their own. For those seniors who need more help but who can still live fairly independently, an independent living facility would be available. For those frail elderly who need more intensive care, assisted living and nursing home facilities would be available.

A continuum of care approach with children could involve several agencies joining together to provide a range of services. One agency might provide an educational training program for parents on how to meet the normal developmental needs of their children. Another agency could provide therapeutic counseling for parents and children. For those children or youth who require being away from their families, another agency could provide intensive institutional care homes. Thus, clients would have the full sequence of services available as needed.

Similarly, persons with AIDS experience a chronic, debilitating disease that requires a variety of different agencies offering services: community care resources, intermediate care facilities, and skilled nursing facilities. The principle involved in continuum of care is based on the individual's functional capacity—from those who are most independent to those that are least independent. Programs that are guided by this philosophy provide services in the least restrictive environment. Those persons who can manage to function fairly independently are encouraged to do so and resources are made available to foster this independence.[4]

FACTORS INFLUENCING ORGANIZATIONAL COLLABORATION

Providing a comprehensive array of services will only occur when representatives of different organizations come together to form a consensus about goals and means to get to them. The fundamental assumption of a collaborative process is that common community interests exist that compel people to transcend their special interests for the common good of meeting community needs.

Collaboration does not always easily occur. Many organizations concerned with community problems have a tendency to operate in a highly independent, autonomous manner. This is because organizations generally want to control their own decision-making process, develop a sense of identity among their members, and convey to the world their particular efforts and accomplishments. Their need for autonomy and identity is so profound that many community organizations pursue their goals without relating to other organizations. They avoid interaction to preserve their independence, reduce the risk of possible loss of support or resources, or keep from having to expend unnecessary energy on the concerns of other organizations. They think they can achieve their own limited goals without having to relate to others.

Some organizations will even maintain that cooperation among organizations is not necessarily a preferred way of relating; under some circumstances tasks and efforts are better accomplished by a single, unencumbered organization. An overemphasis on cooperation and coordination could compromise the very reason for the existence of these organizations. Other organizations in the coalition may not be as intensively concerned with an issue, and the resulting coordinated effort could be bland and ineffectual. A strongly partisan welfare rights organization, for example, may fear that, by joining with other community groups, its aggressive advocacy becomes diluted. A child advocacy organization may decide not to participate in a cooperative community effort to improve foster care because it wants to preserve its own advocacy "gad fly" role in relation to human services agencies. If the danger exists that, by combining with others, an organization will reduce its effectiveness in accomplishing its goals, then avoiding collaborative attempts may be appropriate.

Despite this tendency to be independent, organizations that work on complex community problems find it necessary, even essential, to deal with other organizations. A collaborative approach requires organizations to harmonize ways of working together on many community problems, such as unemployment, inadequate housing, and delinquency, that are complex and interrelated. Often organizations become highly specialized and concentrate on a given aspect of a problem. As specialization has increased, so too has the need for interaction among organizations. Establishing an employment program, for example, requires more than setting up training programs—health services, transportation, day care, counseling, and housing services all become necessary components. Hence, while many organizations strongly desire to preserve a high degree of decision-making authority and power, the complexity of problems and the need for funds, skills, staff, community support, and other resources may compel them to interact cooperatively with other community groups.

Collaboration occurs when one or more organizations perceive that their own goals can be achieved most effectively and efficiently with the assistance and the resources of others. This collaborative relationship includes a commitment to a mutual relationship, a jointly developed structure and shared responsibility, mutual accountability, and the sharing of resources and rewards.[5]

COALITIONS

A coalition is an organization of organizations. Groups come together so that they can accomplish their mutual goals. The systems term, "synergy," conveys that the sum is greater than the parts, meaning that more clout and power can emerge when groups work together than when they go their own separate ways. By forming alliances, they increase the availability of people power. Not surprisingly, politicians and other public officials discern the difference between a group of fifty and one that represents a coalition of five thousand.

In addition, alliances of organizations offer the possibility of pooling funds, sharing staff and volunteer time, and involving talent and expertise that may not be available in one group.[6]

Example: An organization that provides social and recreation services to seniors determines that a major deterrent to its clients coming to its twelve satellite offices is the lack of adequate transportation. But the Senior Center knows that by itself it is not able to get the public transportation authority to provide Community Responsive Transport, a system of mini buses designed to serve the needs of the elderly and the handicapped. By forming a coalition with the mental health agency, the public housing authority (where many elderly and handicapped persons live) and the mental retardation board, it is able to garner sufficient support to achieve its goal of making its services more accessible.

Goals of different organizations can be similar, as when several of them decide to work together to reduce crime in a neighborhood. Goals also can be complementary, as when one agency decides to serve clients it ordinarily would not serve because it will be paid by another agency for doing so. Sometimes goals can even be dissimilar, as "strange bedfellow" organizations harmonize their efforts to achieve their respective goals.

Collaborative efforts among organizations are also likely to be enhanced when sufficient resources exist to reduce competition or when organizations can work out agreements to divide resources. Sometimes organizations are willing to offer their resources (e.g., staff time) to other organizations without being compensated. Sometimes, however, they cooperate because they expect to receive something in exchange.

Resources that organizations exchange can be tangible, involving funds, facilities, personnel, clients, information, and services, or they can be intangible, involving prestige and good will. Sometimes the exchange is immediately reciprocal: Organization A agrees to serve the clients of Organization B in exchange for funding. Sometimes the exchange is initially unilateral: Organization A agrees to assist Organizational B on child welfare legislation in anticipation of Organization B assisting Organization A in passing a human services levy the following year, though this expectation may not be explicitly stated. Organizations thus often weigh anticipated costs of the exchange against potential benefits.

As shown on Figure 22.1, a number of factors can deter collaboration or advance it. Compromises have to be arrived at, inequalities of power must be worked out, and issues of autonomous vs. joint decision making must be resolved. The individual identity of the partners may need to be submerged under the banner of the coalition.

Factors influencing collaboration among organizations include whether
1) organizations discern that they can achieve their respective goals by working together;
2) they feel that resources are sufficient and that they mutually benefit from an exchange of resources;
3) the respective national organizations or funding bodies are encouraging collaboration;
4) all participating organizations have clear expectations of the performance and products of their efforts;
5) a way of dealing with potential conflicts exists;
6) the organizations have distinctive and complimentary roles in relation to the same population or they serve different populations;
7) good feedback is provided to the participating bodies;
8) all participating organizations sense their prestige is enhanced by the collaboration; and
9) influence is shared.

Perhaps the most intangible factor, yet the one that is most indispensable, is that members of the respective organizations basically trust that others will live up to their commitments. This trust is most likely to grow over time as

Figure 22.1
FACTORS INFLUENCING ORGANIZATIONAL COLLABORATION

Factors	Facilitating Conditions	Impeding Conditions
Goals	Simultaneously maximize their goals	One organization maximizes its goals at the expense of others
	Similar goals/ complementary goals	Divergent goals
Resources	Resources are sufficient for organizations to benefit or agreement on how resources are to be divided	Competition over scarce resources Perception that costs of the exchange exceed benefits
	Reciprocity in exchange of resources	No exchange
Role of higher authority	State or national organization encourages local coordination	State or national organization sets up procedures and funding arrangements that discourage local coordination
Expectations of performance	Clear expectations of performance and products	Ambiguity about performance and products
Conflict resolution	Mechanism developed for dealing with conflict	No procedures for resolving differences
Domain of activities and target population	Complementary roles and different roles in relation to target populations	Perception of encroachment on activities and target population
Feedback	Essential information available to all participating organizations	Limited or no exchange of essential information
Prestige	All parties feel their prestige enhanced	Perception that prestige is reduced in favor of other participating organizations
Influence	Perception that each can preserve its autonomy Influence is mutual	Perception that one organization will have undue influence over others
Trust	High degree of trust	Low degree of trust

relationships are established. As organizations have opportunities for successfully conducting joint programs, there is greater willingness to accept new forms of interdependence. A health center, for example, may be willing to accept clients from a senior citizen center if previously the two organizations had participated in collaborative programming. Figure 22.1 summarizes the conditions that facilitate or impede collaboration.

COLLABORATIVE STRUCTURES

The structure developed as a result of the need for collaboration can vary, depending on the desired ends. Where the situation requires autonomous agencies to retain a high degree of independence while linking temporarily on a specific issue, the collaborative process is ad hoc and limited. A special crisis, e.g., a hurricane, may require organizations to temporarily mesh their programs, but once the crisis recedes (and in the absence of provisions for an ongoing structure), organizational relationships will likely vanish as autonomous groups return to their independent ways.

Sometimes organizations with different goals will work together informally through a loose coalition on a temporary basis. Coalitions emerge from the joining of two or more parties who discover they have more to gain by collaboration on a given issue or activity than by pursuing independent courses of action. As soon as the issue is resolved or the activity is completed, the coalition is dissolved. Example: You form a coalition to pass a mental health levy. For a period of three months the ten mental health agencies send representatives to meet weekly to develop strategies for the campaign. Then the group is dismantled when the campaign is concluded. Four years later, in time for the next levy campaign, a new coalition is formed.

Organizations may also establish a formal ongoing relationship through a federation. Each organization is self-directing, neither is entirely dependent upon nor completely responsible to the federated body. Organizations within the federation remain primarily accountable to themselves and only in a limited way to the federation. Usually actions proposed by a federation must be approved by the constituency groups. Since one of the major purposes of the federation is to harmonize and integrate different groups, controversial issues that might cause a breakup are often avoided.

If a collaborative effort is ongoing, as one problem is resolved, be prepared to move on to the next. Suppose, for example, that you form a coalition to combat neighborhood crime. Your first project is to obtain better street lighting for your various neighborhoods. But that is only the beginning and there are many projects that you feel compelled to address and you can either work on them sequentially—one after the other—or simultaneously.

COLLABORATIVE SERVICE DELIVERY AT THE LOCAL LEVEL

To meet the various needs of their clients, agencies often find they must develop coordinating structures at the local level. Below we describe four kinds of structural arrangements: 1) Consortium Partnerships, 2) Multi-Service Centers, 3) Coordinating Structure Based on Target Populations, and 4) Neighborhood Family Network.

Consortium Partnerships

Two or more agencies may form formal partnerships to undertake joint activities or programs. These include the following:

- Joint planning to coordinate services
- Joint evaluating of program effectiveness
- Combined fund raising
- Centralized purchasing of equipment
- Joint outreach of clients
- Lend lease staff from one organization to another for a specified time
- Purchase of service agreements to give priority to another organization's clients
- Joint funding of a program

Through these kinds of linkages organizations can leverage their own resources to accomplish their goals. By joining with others in this synergistic manner, the sum of the parts can contribute to a more powerful and effective effort than if the organizations were to go their separate ways.

Multi-Service Centers (Co-Location)

In the 1960s local anti-poverty programs (community action agencies) created multi-service centers that sought to provide a variety of programs under one roof where residents could experience "one-stop shopping." Under this structural arrangement, each agency operates with its own complete autonomy and reports to its main office, which will be located elsewhere. Thus, the legal aid office in a multi-service center would report to its main office, as does the local department of human services.

Although some coordination may take place, agencies tend to operate as if they were located in a shopping mall, each with its own separate, autonomous service. Just as a shopping mall offers its customers the ease of moving from one store to another, so presumably clients of a multi-service center have the convenience of being able to go to more than one service. Food stamps, day care, housing referrals, job finding, and neighborhood organization are all located in the same facility. Because of their close physical proximity, agencies may find it easier to refer clients to various services. Co-location, however, does not inherently result in formal coordination among various organizations.

Coordinating Structure Based on Target Population

Frequently agencies develop formal structural arrangements to deal with special target populations. In many communities, for example, the school system, mental health board, mental retardation board, local hospitals, United Way, substance abuse board, and other major organizations will establish a "Children's Cluster" or "Children's Council" so that funds can be pooled to provide for multi-need children who may tend to fall between the cracks. In Chapter 2, we described "Wraparound Services" for children who can better be serviced by a coordinated approach.

Another variation of this arrangement is school-based services in which the local school becomes the natural hub for coordinating agencies (e.g., child guidance center, health clinics, outside tutoring services). Agencies work out collaborative agreements with the school to focus on the target population.[7] A coordinator from any one of the agencies or the school facilitates coordination of services.

Neighborhood Family Network

The neighborhood family network concept is based on the following features: First, representatives from the neighborhood school, recreation centers, block clubs, youth clubs, head start, community development corporations and religious institutions come together to identify the positive resources in a specific neighborhood/local community that can help families to grow and develop. The emphasis is on bringing together family and neighborhood assets. Organizations will be offered the opportunity to exchange information and support and facilitate public and private partnerships. Second, the staff from various agencies respond to family needs flexibly and comprehensively. Public and private funders are encouraged to collaborate in funding family and neighborhood strengthening efforts. Third, staff provide an opportunity for parents and children to be involved in workshops, support groups, and other family related activities, and access to schools and community agencies. Fourth, they focus on the unique aspects of a particular community. In one area, for example, efforts are designed to assist neighborhood foster parents and the families of children placed with them. In another community, foster grand parents may be organized and supported. These efforts have in common locally developed, culturally sensitive neighborhood-based programs designed to preserve the family and provide positive growth experiences for children.

Occasionally, federal or state legislation will be developed to foster neighborhood partnerships. For example, legislation might be created to develop a system of care for children and their families to provide a comprehensive spectrum of mental health and other services organized into a coordinated network to meet the needs of emotionally disturbed children and their families.[8]

Figure 22.2 shows a diagram of a neighborhood family network. Linked together in this local community would be the schools, recreation center, neighborhood association, health clinic, head start program, and such community agencies as the mental health center or the Salvation Army. The "neighborhood family resource center" could either be located in one building or more likely could be an association of representatives from these various local institutions coming together to focus on the special needs and interests of the families in their communities.   Of course, the Neighborhood Family Network may include other organizations unique to a particular community. For example, a community might have a special Community Policing program underway, in which the police are engaged in working with local community institutions.

Mobilizing Resources in the Local Community

In an environment in which organizations that serve people in need are themselves suffering from the lack of adequate funding, agencies can pull both inward and outward.

As resources become increasingly scarce, services tend to become frag-mented, and some staff can experience a degree of futility when attempting to coordinate resources that do not exist.[9] The local mental health board may decide to reduce its services only to those who are in danger to themselves or to others; the local county department of children's services may determine that it will limit its programs only to children the law mandates it to serve. The local board of education may cut out the social service department because of lack of funds. Scarcity fosters a tendency to look inward.

Figure 22.2

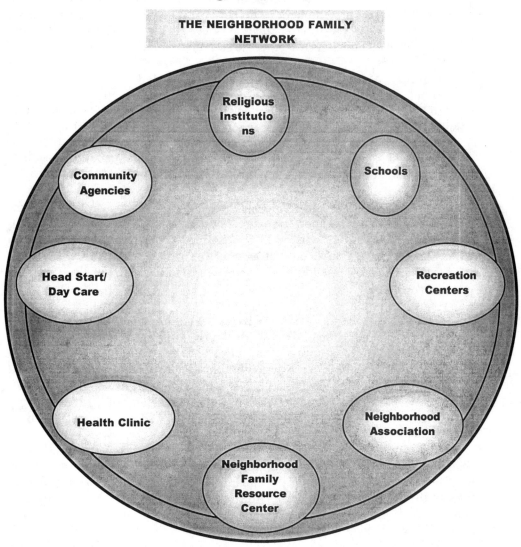

THE NEIGHBORHOOD FAMILY NETWORK

Religious Institutions

Community Agencies

Schools

Head Start/ Day Care

Recreation Centers

Health Clinic

Neighborhood Association

Neighborhood Family Resource Center

Scarcity can also stimulate organizations to look outward based on the realization that no one agency can achieve results alone and that by pooling resources much more can be accomplished.

Example: Ten human service agencies that provide counseling services to families, mentally disabled children, and residents in neighborhoods are brought together by the local social planning organization to coordinate their services in the local schools. They work out common referral procedures and evaluation protocols.

Example: A local children's cluster is formed, consisting of the alcohol and drug addiction board, juvenile court, mental retardation and disabilities board, public schools, and youth services for the purpose of assuring service for children who have multiple needs and for whom appropriate local services are not accessible. The organization develops individual service plans, assures proper management, and arranges for shared funding.

Example: With the assistance of a social planning agency a neighborhood center arranges for three outside organizations—day care, vocational training, and youth counseling—to co-locate their services in their agency. This is part of a general strategy to revitalize the local neighborhood by providing integrated services in a family friendly environment.[10]

Example: A county-wide citizens drug prevention organization sponsors a "Red Ribbon Week" designed to promote awareness of the importance of drug prevention. The citizen volunteer chairperson learns that certain inner city neighborhoods desperately want to build a playground so their youth can have wholesome activities. Contacts are made with the mayor, the city planning commission, and, interestingly enough, the local national guard, which is willing to use its engineering equipment to build the play ground.

These examples all have in common the coordination of services at the local level. The agencies benefit because they are not involved in an undertaking that is bigger than they can handle separately. The community benefits from the renewed involvement of organizations that might not ordinarily work together.

SOCIAL PLANNING: COORDINATION AT THE COMMUNITY-WIDE LEVEL

Coordinating efforts at the community-wide level uses approaches similar to those employed by counselors in their treatment of individuals. Just as a professional working on a one-to-one basis must employ the framework of study, diagnosis, and treatment, so the social planner uses a process of identifying and analyzing a social problem, developing a plan of action, implementing the plan, and reviewing the outcome.[11]

Social planners help a community action system—composed of individuals, groups, or organizations—address social problems. Intergovernmental bodies or social planning organizations employ social planners; often those who participate in social planning are social work administrators or line staff who are responsible for representing their agency and the clients they serve in some endeavor to improve the delivery of services in their community. Social planning consists of two interrelated components. On the one hand it involves a community process, encouraging citizens to participate in a problem-solving process so that they can articulate and advocate for changes. The social planner functions as a facilitator and mobilizer of a community process. On the other hand, social planning involves such analytical skills as data collection, quantifying problems, problem formulation, and strategic planning. The social planner issues reports and analyses that can influence community decision makers.

In the past there existed the temptation to overemphasize the analytic function over the importance of engaging citizens in the process of determining their own destiny. Now there is a general sense that comprehensive planning on social problems cannot succeed without the involvement and participation of the community.[12]

There is a certain amount of overlap between community organization and social planning work. Both deal with serious social problems. Both seek to formulate plans and then to influence policy makers. Though the distinction may be somewhat artificial, in general community organizers tend to function at the neighborhood level and to emphasize grassroots participation on the assumption that those effected by social problems must be empowered to influence outcomes.

Social planners, on the other hand, tend to work with business and civic leaders who are removed but still vitally concerned with the plight of the vulnerable people of the community. These leaders often have the clout and credibility to affect change. The social planner assists these civic groups to document and validate social needs in order to influence the direction and the funding of policies, programs, and services. Sometimes the grassroots and the civic leaders join and complement each other's strengths, as when, for example, civic leaders participate in a local community's efforts to strengthen the neighborhood schools.

Social planning can deal with a wide range of social issues, including homelessness, family instability, unemployment, and school dropouts. It endeavors to address such questions as the following:

- How can we keep more frail elderly in their own homes?

- How can we better integrate formerly institutionalized delinquent youth into the regular school system?

- How can we provide more adequate health care to those who are living on the streets?

- How can we better coordinate human services in certain localities?

- How can we increase the number of foster homes for abused and neglected children? Or, operating under different assumptions, how can we develop the kind of services that will permit more abused and neglected children to remain in their own homes?

These are issues that transcend the concerns of any one neighborhood; they affect the entire community, and therefore organizations must address and deal with these community-wide issues.

SOCIAL PLANNING ORGANIZATIONS

Social planning is a rational approach to community issues and problems involving a series of logically related steps: 1) becoming aware of the problem 2) identifying goals and objectives that relate to a realistic assessment of resources 3) considering alternative programs, and 4) implementing the program design and evaluating results.[13] These steps are similar to those applied in addressing agency problems and in community organization work.

Although reason and logic strongly influence directions in social planning, community values do play a predominant role. How a community goes about dealing with employment, homelessness, or other issues depends in great part on the values of the community. Hence, social planning is influenced greatly by subjective forces, including instincts, political interests, and self interests.

Social planning functions under a number of different structures.[14] In some communities there may only exist one organization with the responsibility to provide planning; in others, several organizations undertake this function. Here are some models.

Local Planning Councils

Known as federations, planning councils, or community alliances, these are free-standing, non-profit organizations that receive their local funding from their United Ways, foundations, and county and state governments for specific planning projects. Some have developed special funding sources, such as endowments, consultation fees, and special events.

The common characteristic of these planning councils is that they are citizen-led, independent organizations that take on a variety of community problems: older persons, juvenile justice, family integration, school dropouts, mental health, AIDS, homelessness—to name a few. Typically they organize citizen committees to identify specific problem areas, gather necessary data, and formulate an action plan. Normally they do not provide direct services to clients—unless they sponsor a time limited demonstration program that will eventually be spun off as an independent organization or become part of another agency.

Here is an example: A group of volunteer leaders and professionals are brought together to concentrate on the problems of the elderly. The chairperson is a manager of one of the units of a local company who has a general interest in the elderly but does not consider herself an expert on their problems. The group determines that, as a high priority, action should be taken at the state level to obtain legislation and funding to help older persons remain in their own homes, rather than have to go into nursing homes when they become slightly impaired. They prepare legislation to expand the number of home visitors, which they help pass as a result of mobilizing groups throughout the state to support. Then they work at persuading the governor to allocate funds in the budget for the next biennium.

Their feelings of elation are short-lived because, although funding is eventually available, rural counties in the state appear to receive a disproportionate share of the funding. The committee then mobilizes the political forces in their own community to persuade the governor to override the state office on aging so that more funds can be made available to the local community. The entire process, from problem formulation to ultimate results, takes four years.

Local planning councils play an important role in bringing together different organizations to work cooperatively on common problems. For example, they will convene the local public housing authority and the city health department to develop better ways of delivering health services to residents in public housing. Or they may bring the mental health board and the department of human services together to improve counseling services for emotionally handicapped children who are in the care of the department. Or they may develop a planning project to help agencies in the community work together to assist African-American males obtain training and employment.

Planning councils have varying degrees of expertise that their staff can bring to bear on community issues, including the following:

- demographic analysis
- pilot project design
- grant writing
- policy research and development
- legislative analysis
- program analysis
- budget analysis
- fiscal management
- media relations

These technical competencies can be made available to state and local governments, health-care organizations, law enforcement agencies, non-profit agencies, and public-sponsored agencies.

United Ways

Encouraged by their national office, many local United Ways (UW) are becoming involved in social planning, known as community problem solving. Their roles include those of catalyst, convener, facilitator, and coordinator, rather than central problem solver and funder. This approach recognizes that no single organization has the resources or expertise to solve a major community problem.[15] Sometimes the local UW will take a leadership role in identifying a problem and implementing action. Examples include coordinating food collection and distribution for homeless persons, aggressively promoting businesses to provide employment opportunities to teenagers during the summer, and conducting a community needs assessment to affect the UW budget process. At other times the local UW will participate with other organizations in a partnership arrangement, as for example, joining with the mental health board and the substance abuse board to develop a common reporting form.

Coalitions

In every community, organizations come together for a specific purpose, frequently without the need for an intermediary organization like a planning council. An organization may be formed, for example, to deal with the high crime rate in the community. Consisting of representatives of the courts, schools, and agencies, the group may develop ways to work with gangs, encourage substance abuse educational programs in the schools, and work with residents in public housing to make their areas more secure. Sometimes these coalitions are long-lasting and multifaceted, as in committees to fight crime; less frequently they are ad hoc and disband when their objective is accomplished.

Government Planning Efforts

As described in the above examples, government bodies are frequent participants and leaders in local planning. In addition to the partnership arrangements, increasingly public officials often create citizen advisory committees or include professional and citizens on special commissions designed to articulate policies. For example local criminal justice agencies, involving juvenile court, the police, the school system, and social agencies would coordinate their efforts to provide youth resource centers in the school system for youngsters who had gotten into difficulty with the law.

SOCIAL PLANNER'S ROLE

Whether working in planning councils, United Ways, coalitions, or in governmental organizations, social workers functioning as social planners must be able to relate to a number of constituencies. Although social planners seek to educate the public about the directions for health and social services, they mainly seek to influence the perspectives of community leaders to develop, fund, evaluate, or change particular programs.

Their primary constituencies are elected officials, leaders of social agencies, and interagency organizations. They seek to coordinate or integrate services. Excellent communications skills are essential to carrying out these roles, because social planners often have to make presentations before political and business leaders, and prepare proposals and interact with a diverse network of organizations and individuals. Often they become spokespersons for human service coalitions.[16]

Social planning is an essential part of every community. Thoughtful, concerned citizens need a community forum through which they can explore and identify problems, analyze their causes and consequences, develop and execute a plan of action, and monitor results. Social workers who want to influence the outcome of social issues must be willing to participate in the social planning process.

PUTTING IT ALL TOGETHER: A COORDINATED SERVICE DELIVERY SYSTEM

Ideally services should be provided with minimal delay and red tape. Clients should not have to wait to receive services.   Nor should they be denied services because of inefficiency or rigidity.   Moreover, clients should be able to obtain the full range of services to which they are entitled, regardless of where they enter the service network.   In a coordinated service delivery system clients would receive all of the essential services regardless of which agency they started with.

In reality clients do face obstacles. Serious gaps can occur because of poor coordination, unclear program communication, inflexibility, and lack of services. Because of these obstacles social workers must give concentrated attention to how well services are coordinated. Then, too, what an agency does or does not do and who may receive its services must be made clear to avoid inappropriate referrals.[17] Clients, like all of us, do not want to experience a "runaround." They should not be made to do so because of professional ineptness. Nor should they experience excessive formalization and inflexibility. Social workers who rely on an overly complex set of rules are likely to lose sight of the needs and humanity of their clients.

Components of the Service Delivery System

A good delivery system provides services that are accessible, comprehensive, efficient, effective, and accountable.[18]

Accessible services means that services are easily reached and available. This might involve satellite offices so clients do not have to travel long distances. Or it could mean providing bilingual staff for those who do not speak English.

Comprehensive services involve a number of agencies to meet all the needs of the clients. Case managers often work with clients to determine which programs their clients need and then make appropriate referrals. Follow up insures that the services were delivered as planned. In a comprehensive system professionals work together in a coordinated way to insure that clients receive what they need and that they do not experience duplication of unnecessary services.

Efficient services are those organized to enable agencies to produce the greatest output and benefits in relation to input or resources. Unit costs of a program (e.g., a child care day or a treatment interview) are kept low in relation to the benefits.

Effectiveness relates to the ability of a particular program to meet its objectives. As discussed in other parts of this book, it is important to be able to measure the impact services have on clients.

Accountability can easily be diffused because different constituencies may have different expectations. Social workers are accountable to their profession, to their administrator, to their funders, and to their clients. A good delivery system at least clarifies what these different expectations are and keeps a focus on client needs.

SUMMARY

Coordination and coalitions work best when all parties feel an urgency to come together, both out of self-interest and a sense of community betterment. In the example of a mental health levy campaign, the agencies recognize that if it fails, they would be in desperate financial trouble. Of course, the fact that their clients will continue to benefit from the results of the campaign serves as an additional incentive.

Organizations typically participate in coordination efforts because this is often a way to enhance their organization's capacity and improve the community. Perhaps in the past some may have had the luxury of having sufficient funding to maintain their independence. In a period when agencies suffer from the devastation of limited funding from all levels of government and from the private sector, they are finding that it is imperative to collaborate with each other. Increasingly, collaboration is a means of survival and a way of sharing resources so that clients can benefit the most.

QUESTIONS FOR DISCUSSION

1) What are some examples of how your agency coordinates its work with other groups in the community?

2) What are some examples of clients benefiting from good coordination and suffering when coordination has been poor or non-existent?

3) You are a neighborhood advocacy group dedicated to changing poor conditions within your community. Normally you do not affiliate with other organizations because you prefer not to have your efforts diluted, nor do you like being encumbered with a lot of community process. Recently a staff member of the local neighborhood center has approached you to join a coalition of organizations from the broader community to address the problem of lead poisoning in young children

who sometimes eat peeling paint from the walls of their homes. This is an issue of long-standing concern to your members.

What are the pros and cons for joining this proposed coalition? If you decide to join, how would you preserve your autonomy?

4) What are the pros and cons of having one organization in your community determine what the major social issues should be vs. having multiple organizations determine the community's social issues agenda?

Chapter Notes

[1]Rosenberg, M. & Brody, R. (1974). *Systems Serving People: A Breakthrough in Service Delivery*. Cleveland, OH: Case Western Reserve University.

[2]Austin, C. & McClelland, R. (1996). *Perspectives on Case Management Practice*. Milwaukee, WI: Families International, Inc. p. 154.

[3]Wilson III, A. (1984). *Social Services For Older Persons*. Prospect Heights, IL: Albert J.E. Wilson III, (1988 reissued by Waveland Press, Inc.)

[4]Vourlekis, B. & Greene, R. (1992). *Social Work Case Management*. New York: Walter de Gruyter, pp. 1-25.

[5]Mattessich, P.W., & Monsey, B.R. (1993). *Collaboration: What Makes it Work*. Saint Paul, MN: Wilder Research, p. 7.

[6]Rothman et al, (1976). *Promoting Innovation and Change in Organizations and Communities*. New York: Macmillan, p. 314.

[7]Morgan, G. (Nov-Dec. 1995). Vol. LXXIV. No. 6. "Collaborative Models of Service Integration." *Child Welfare*, pp. 1329-1342.

[8]Homonoff, E. & Fineman Malts, P. (Oct. 1991). Vol. 27. No. 5. "Developing and Maintaining a Coordinated System of Community-Based Services to Children." *Community Mental Health Journal*, pp. 347-358.

[9]Moore, S. (1992). "Case Management and the Integration of Services: How Service Delivery Systems Shape Case Management?" *Social Work*, 37(5), pp. 418-422.

[10]McLellan, N. (1993,Summer). "Collaborating with Settlement Houses, Public Systems, and Neighborhood Efforts." Family Resource Coalition Report, 12 (2).

[11]Gilbert, S., & Specht, H. (1978). "Personnel Management." In A. Minihan (Editor-in-Chief), *Encyclopedia of Social Work* (18th ed. Vol. 1, pp. 602-619). Silver Spring, MD: National Association of Social Workers.

[12]Austin, M.J. (1987). "Personnel Management." In A. Minihan (Editor-in-Chief), *Encyclopedia of Social Work* (18th ed. Vol. 2, pp. 244-255). Silver Spring, MD: National Association of Social Workers.

[13]Meenaghan, T.M. (1987). "Macro Practice: Current Trends and Issues." In A. Minihan (Editor-in-Chief), *Encyclopedia of Social Work* (18th ed. Vol. 1, p. 41). Silver Spring, MD: National Association of Social Workers.

[14]Brilliant, Eleanor, L. (1987). "Community Planning and Community Problem Solving: Past, Present and Future." *Social Service Review*, 1986, pp. 568-585.

[15]Wencour, R. (1987). "Social Planning in the Voluntary Sector." In A. Minihan (Editor-in-Chief), *Encyclopedia of Social Work* (18th ed. Vol. 1, pp. 620-632). Silver Spring, MD: National Association of Social Workers.

[16]Weil, M.O. & Gamble, D.N. (1995). "Community Practice Models." *Encyclopedia of Social Work* (19th Ed.), p. 587.

[17]Macht, M. & Ashford, J. (1991). *Introduction to Social Work and Social Welfare*. New York: Macmillian, p. 233.

[18]Macht & Ashford, pp. 236-239.

REFERENCES FOR CHAPTER 22

Cooper, T.L. (2005). "Neighborhood Councils and City Agencies: A Model of Collaborative Coproduction." *National City Review*. Vol. 94, Issue 1. Spring 2005. pp. 43-53.

Darlington, Y. (2005). "Interagency Collaboration between Child Protection & Mental Health Services: Practices, Attitudes, and Barriers." *Child Abuse & Neglect*. Vol. 29, Issue 10. October 2005. pp. 1085-1098.

Healey, Patsy. (2006). *Collaborative Planning:Shaping Places in Fragmented Societies*. (2nd Ed). Hampshire: NY: Palgrave Macmillan.

Parker, Jonathan. (2005). "Collaboration in Social Work Practice." *Journal of Social Work*. Vol. 5, Issue 2. August 2005. pp. 249-250.

Speer, P.W. (2005). "Participatory Decision-Making Among Community Coalitions: An Analysis of Task Group Meetings." *Administration in Social Work*. Vol.29, Issue 3. (2005). Pp. 61-77.

Weil, Marie. (2005). *The Handbook of Community Practice*. Thousand Oaks: Sage Publications.

CHAPTER 23

International Social Work Practice

Because of growing global interdependence, social workers are increasingly developing international contacts and collaboration.[1] Trained to understand the macro practice aspects of organizations and communities, social workers are uniquely qualified to work in various parts of the world. Social workers from all over the world are coming to the United States to study social service practices and apply these to their own localities. American social workers are also traveling abroad to volunteer and take professional positions in health and human services to learn about ways to address social problems. Such issues as AIDS, unemployment, social dislocation, inadequate health care, and the consequences of severe poverty know no country boundaries. These profound problems require professional leadership that understands how global issues are linked to local communities.[2]

Working overseas to improve the quality of life of vulnerable people and a willingness to tolerate discomforts requires special dedication. The experience of working to improve people's lives, however, can be truly rewarding. The exposure to people from different cultural backgrounds can help social workers understand and respond to the unique social-cultural forces that shape human needs.[3] In short, working at the international level can be a life transforming opportunity.

This chapter will highlight international issues in social welfare, cultural exchange opportunities, professional organizations, the role of nongovernmental organizations (NGOs), and volunteer experiences abroad. At the end of the chapter we provide useful websites for volunteering and working in foreign countries.

INTERNATIONAL ISSUES IN SOCIAL WELFARE

At the international level, social workers are involved in many issues and services. Among them are the following:

Social Work with Refugees: A Growing International Crisis: Presently there are about 20,500,000 refugees worldwide, a figure that has grown considerably in the past four decades. (www.unhcr.ch) Social workers provide much needed counseling to refugees, especially to elderly people and abandoned children. Social workers also facilitate the empowerment of refugees through advocacy and lobbying.[4]

International Social Development: Social or community development provides social advancement of both individuals and communities by harmonizing economic and social policies designed to improve people's welfare.[5] Social development seeks to improve human capital through educational and training programs.[6]

The Environment and Sustainable Growth: Community organizers challenge human rights violations and environmental plundering.[7] In Nigeria, for example, under the International Association for Impact Assessment-Nigeria (www.iaia.org) environmental activists have stimulated awareness of the need to preserve communities and protect the environment. Especially in the southern part of Nigeria where foreign oil companies are developing oil refineries, communities are concerned about the impact on their environment, as oil seepage and fires destroy large tracts of farmland. Moreover, people are upset and angry about the fact that money derived from the oil taken from their land is benefiting foreign oil companies and is used by their central government to provide governmental services elsewhere in the country. Community activists work to empower local people to demand responsible business practices and governmental action that will help protect their land or compensate them for damage.

Women's Rights: On a global scale feminist networks reveal the interdependence that exists among women throughout the world.[8] Feminist social actions and campaigns demonstrate that political and social values that undermine equal rights for women can be challenged. For example, human rights organizations have initiated training programs designed to reduce domestic violence, they are working to amend laws concerning adultery by requiring men and women to be treated equally, and they are fighting to prohibit female genital mutilation.

Health: Although social workers generally play an ancillary role in health care services, they can provide administrative, organizing, and planning support.[9] Nongovernmental agencies have been effective in reaching a large number of people and coordinating local leadership. This has been especially important in responding to the HIV/AIDS pandemic. Social workers empower vulnerable people to promote their own self care and protection, and they work with such special populations as prisoners and intravenous drug abusers to help them develop healthier life practices.

Employment and training: Social workers provide guidance and leadership to community organizations to develop special education and training programs. Organizers also help communities achieve economic independence through the development of small businesses such as poultry farms or crafts cooperatives. These microenterprise efforts enhance the well being of individuals and promote their economic development.[10]

CULTURAL EXCHANGE OPPORTUNITIES

To foster a keen awareness of international social welfare issues and to expose students to the rich diversity of foreign cultures, many universities provide travel abroad opportunities. As participant observers, students learn about cultural practices involving family relations, religious beliefs and rituals, and response to vulnerable people. They learn to live, dress, eat, and socialize as indigenous people do. By being immersed in the culture of another country, students learn at a much deeper level than they would by simply reading about local customs and practices.

Program participants interested in social work practice also have the opportunity to learn about how human services are developed and provided in a foreign culture. This, in turn, can trigger ideas for improving services in their own communities. Figure 23.1, The India Experience, demonstrates how study abroad social work participants become immersed in a culture different from their own and are exposed to different human service delivery practices.

Figure 23.1
The India Experience

Program participants experience the Indian culture by having the opportunity to dress in local clothing, which for the women means wearing sarees and for the men wearing jubas. They become accustomed to eating the spicy native food of rice, curries, roti, papaya and coconut. People eat without utensils, instead using their right hand to mix the food on a banana leaf before eating it. Program participants also have the opportunity to live with families and talk with them about facets of their lives.

Student participants also have opportunities to learn how local social services develop and sustain their programs through a series of observational visits. For example, they learn how these agencies receive private funds, government donations, religious contributions, and donations from such civic organizations as the Rotary Club or Lions Club. Students also learn the art of how nongovernmental organizations manage with limited resources and unlimited needs. They see first hand that an orphanage raises money by encouraging wealthy donors to celebrate a birthday or anniversary by providing a dinner, buying clothes, purchasing furniture, or building a room and that by so doing contributors achieve good dharma (good deeds), as encouraged by the Hindu religion.

Participants typically also have a mini internship. For example, they may become involved with a women's empowerment center where women in a neighborhood come together to make handcrafts for sale. Participants learn about the background of the women and how they have benefited from these microenterprise efforts. They see how women weave the clothing and how they market their wares.

As another example, they learn that the high rate of literacy in southern India, despite the prevalence of poverty, occurs because learning to read and write is part of the everyday living experience. For example, women joining together at a ceramics class are taught to read about the skills they are learning. Moreover, reading is promoted even for very young children. A special celebration ritual (called Vidyarambam) occurs when three-year-olds can begin to read and write simple words. The people in the state of Kerela, located in southern most India, take pride in having the United Nations confirm its having the highest literacy rate in the world,[11] and participants learn the way this occurs.

In addition to seeing how services are provided, participants see how local democratic institutions are advanced in India. High school and university students are encouraged to come up with creative ideas to keep their community clean, reduce pollution, improve literacy, and develop formal and informal ways to take care of children after school. (For information see www.csuohio.edu/india experience).

The study abroad experience works best when participants enter any new culture with a sense of adventure, a desire to learn, and an ability to respond with flexibility to new situations. Above all, they learn that despite differences in cultures all people have the same fundamental human needs and desires. They feel better equipped to pursue their own social work career when they return to the United States.

For social work students interested in a study abroad program, a directory (www.studyabroaddirectory.com) lists thousands of international and academic programs and internships at colleges and universities around the world. It also provides scholarship resources for foreign study and social work related employment.

INTERNATIONAL ORGANIZATIONS

The following organizations operate at an international level and are of special interest to social workers:

Professional Organizations

The International Federation of Social Workers (www.IFSW.org) is the international organization of professional social workers. Among the goals of the Federation are to promote communication among social workers throughout various countries and to present the views of the profession to government agencies and other NGOs. *The International Council on Social Welfare* (www.icsw.org) provides a worldwide forum for discussion on a variety of social welfare topics. Conferences are held biannually and attract hundreds of delegates from around the world.

These international organizations, along with others in the fields of mental health, aging, and child welfare, provide opportunities for international social work involvement and action. Some international professionals have proposed that more involvement from social work's national organizations and from individual members is needed in the international field.[12]

United Nations' Agencies

The United Nations and its agencies are major contributors to international social welfare. By sponsoring a variety of social welfare programs, they emphasize maximizing human potential, fostering self-reliance, and promoting community decision making. Of special interest are the following U.N. agencies:

United Nations Children's Fund (www.UNICEF.org) operates in 137 countries. Its major programs include child health, emergency relief, education, and community-based services for children and women. UNICEF is also concerned with child abuse, neglect, and exploitation. It issues an annual report, *State of the World's Children.*

World Health Organization (www.WHO.int/en) works to control communicable diseases and engages in efforts to solve health problems and strengthen national health systems. WHO has taken the lead to control the spread of HIV and provide AIDS prevention and research. Africa, which has about 50 percent of HIV infection cases in the world and grossly inadequate health resources, is of special concern.

U.N. Fund for Population Activities (www.un.org/popin/) helps countries collect statistics and conduct family planning projects.

U.N. High Commission for Refugees (www.UNHCR.ch/) provides protection and services by aiding refugees in transit and helping with their resettlement.

U.S. Government Agencies

The U.S. government implements international programs through its agencies and through participation in multinational organizations. *U.S. Department of Health and Human Services* (www.HHS.gov) conducts significant international work and has made grants to support the transfer of international advances in social services between countries. Under DHHS, the Office of Refugee Resettlement works to resettle refugees in all the states.

The Agency for International Development (www.usaid.gov) administers foreign aid projects in more than 100 countries. USAID focuses on AIDS, child survival, population planning, basic education, agriculture, and the environment. USAID also provides funding to nongovernmental organizations.

The Peace Corps provides volunteer projects, some which are related to social welfare, such as the promotion of primary health care services and community development. To find out how to submit an application, go to the Peace Corps website (http://www.peacecorps.com)

VOLUNTARY INTERNATIONAL PROGRAMS

International exchange programs provide important ways for social workers to relate to the global community. Exchange programs foster experiential learning and expand social workers' commitment to international social welfare. Moreover, exchange programs transfer knowledge, provide a means for transcending cultural barriers, and develop true understanding of diversity.

The Council on International Programs USA (www.CIPUSA.org) is foremost among those agencies, promoting an exchange of social workers. Since its founding in 1956, CIPUSA has brought to the United States over 10,000 social workers from over 100 countries. These visiting social workers are placed in agencies throughout the country. They not only have an opportunity to learn skills developed in the United States but also teach their U.S. counterparts ways of providing services based on their experiences from their home countries.

The alumni of the CIPUSA have now formed their own organization, the Council of International Fellowship, (www.cifinternational.com). Social workers from all over the world meet biannually to discuss their programs and review what can be done to alter global practices.

Hundreds of religious institutions of all denominations provide support throughout the world. They sponsor hospitals, orphanages, and training programs. International Partners in Mission (www.IPM-connections.org) is an example of an interfaith organization that promotes community building, health, and environmental development, and justice through empowering women, children and youth. Among its twenty or so projects is sponsoring programs for remedial school for teenagers in Nicaragua, a hospice center in Rwanda, a sanitation program in the Dominican Republic, health care in Nepal, and promoting economic opportunities in Uganda.

InterAction (www.InterAction.org) is a coalition of more than 150 U.S. NGOs that coordinate their work in disaster situations.

NONGOVERNMENTAL ORGANIZATIONS (NGOs)

Although governmental agencies play a major role in providing health and human services, nongovernmental organizations carry a major responsibility for the development and delivery of social services at the local level in foreign countries. The term, nongovernmental organizations (NGOs), is generally used in place of what, in the U.S., would be referred to as private nonprofit organizations. They are also known as civil societies. NGOs provide health, family planning, and educational programs that encourage beneficiaries who are expected to participate in program implementation. NGOs assist local people to identify their own needs and empower them to take control of their lives.[13]

Thousands of NGOs have emerged throughout the world and especially in developing countries, often because governments cannot meet the tremendous demand for services and because people within the country and at the international level feel a special responsibility to provide care for those in need. Their local efforts could include, for example, literacy programs for adults, homes for orphaned children, and day care programs for preschoolers.

Frequently, NGOs seek outside funding from their religious bodies, national, or international organizations of which they are a part. Some of the larger NGOs write proposals to international foundations. For example, Madrasa Day Care Programs in Kenya and Uganda receive funds from the Aga Kahn Foundation to support literacy training for preschoolers. Well-established NGOs may be able to obtain funding from their government. For example, The Red Crescent in Egypt receives considerable support from the government.

One of the major challenges facing NGOs (as in the United States) is that after obtaining outside funding for a period of time, the outside funder expects that the NGO will be able to develop its own internal capacity for acquiring resources needed to continue the programs of the NGO. Because NGOs are invariably located in communities with limited resources, the challenge of raising their own funds is exceedingly difficult and dependency on outside resources is an ever-present reality.

The following are some examples of NGOs in different countries:

The Amrita Organization (www.amrita.org) has branches throughout India that offer many services to individuals and families. Founded in 1999, it now provides housing for orphans, financial support for the aged and disabled, health care for those with AIDS, and skill training for the unemployed. It relies on volunteers from within the country and from foreigners.

The Alliance for Arab Women (www.allianceforarabwomen.org) is a voluntary organization in Cairo, Egypt with branches in various parts of the country. As the coordinating body for 350 member organizations, its purpose is to raise the quality of life of women, through helping them gain employment, raise community awareness about women's issues, and facilitate women's participation in decision making.

The Centre for the Development of People (http://cedepghana.tripod.com) is an organizing and advocating organization in Ghana. Its mission is to support, facilitate, and build the capacity of marginalized and vulnerable groups and influence policy in pursuit of sustainable human development.

The Madrasa Preschool Association provides consultation and materials to 40 communities around Mombasa, Kenya. Initially funded by the Aga Khan Foundation, it relies on strong support of the village communities to sustain daycare programs. Children learn to read the English language and are prepared to enter primary schools.

Though widely separated by distance and culture, these organizations all reflect extraordinary commitment and vitality. Each relies to some extent on outside support and funding, but each is sustained by the investment of dedicated staff and volunteers.

Community-Based Organizations (CBOs)

Community-Based Organizations (spelled Organisations in British English) function at the grass-roots level and their members participate on a voluntary basis, providing support to each other, and working on behalf of selected beneficiaries. Typically they are village-based groups, neighbour-hood associations or church or mosque-based committees. CBOs pay a registration fee that is considerably less than that of NGOs in their countries.

CBOs sometimes evolve from a small self-help group involving 4 or 5 close friends or families who meet regularly to enjoy each other's company and contribute to a common pool of money. This money is then distributed once a week or once a month on a rotating basis to various members for purposes agreed to by the group, such as school fees. This process encourages trust among the members and is a way of disciplining members to save. At some point the members may decide to move beyond their small group to involve others on projects that benefit the community, at which time they register as a CBO. Sometimes several CBOs will join in a network, called

Associations or Societies, to develop a credit union for the benefit of the members.

CBOs develop programs either by themselves or as part of larger nongovernmental organizations. Some examples of CBO-sponsored programs include volunteer health care for AIDS victims, providing schooling for a local orphanage, or digging a small well for several families. As part of an NGO, several CBOs may receive funding and technical assistance under the umbrella. For example, an NGO may bring several CBOs together to work on a community-wide water system.

In summary, CBOs have three primary purposes:

1. To provide benefits only to their members. An example would be an income-producing cooperative, in which members join together to do joint purchasing of materials and tools. A group of women could develop a craft's cooperative. Proceeds from the sale of crafts would benefit the person who made the products.

2. To provide primarily for the benefit of a community project. For example, a community group may decide to purchase a cow that could provide milk for the orphanage. They would collect money from the community to purchase the cow and group members would rotate the collecting and selling of surplus milk for the benefit of the orphanage.

3. To provide a combination of benefit for the members and for the community. An example would be for the CBO to take a project of building a well.

VOLUNTEER OPPORTUNITIES

For both social work professionals and students, volunteering abroad can provide a way of temporarily immersing oneself in another culture, meeting people who are as committed as you are to improving the human condition, and making a genuine contribution to those in need. By interacting daily with indigenous people, you will gain a depth of understanding that can only come from direct experience. Most importantly, you will learn a great deal about yourself and your ability to live and work in a different environment. Such an experience can have a powerful impact on your professional career.

Volunteer programs abroad can be limited to one or two weeks or extend to several months or longer. Some will require special skills; others may need only a willingness to work hard. Almost all projects require volunteers to arrange and pay for their own transportation to the project site. Most projects arrange for housing and provide for meals. Volunteers should expect to spend time in close contact with a group of strangers. At the end of this chapter we provide a list of volunteer organizations and how you can contact them.

An excellent source for learning about a variety of volunteer opportunities abroad is the book, *Volunteer Vacations*.[14] It provides detailed information, including costs, contact information, and, in many instances, website information. A cross referenced index can help you choose the right project based on cost, length of time required, location, season, and type. Thus if you were looking for a social action project in Africa for the summer months, the index can help you narrow your search.

The International Volunteer Programs Association (IVPA) is another excellent source of information on international volunteer organizations. The website is www.volunteerinternational.org. It has a list of important questions that you should consider in determining which volunteer organization is right for you:

> 1. What do you hope to get out of the experience?
> 2. What are you able to contribute as a volunteer, e.g., knowledge, skills?
> 3. How long are you able to volunteer abroad? At what time of year?
> 4. Where do you want to volunteer?
> 5. Is there a language requirement?
> 6. What type of volunteer organization are you interested in: health, environmental, educational, religious, other?

Here are some examples of volunteer projects:
(Note: See websites at the end of this chapter)

> *International Red Cross* volunteers are the backbone of all Red Cross/Red Crescent activities assisting millions of vulnerable people in need.

> *Care International* serves individuals and families in the poorest communities in the world. Its focus is on providing direct subsistence to needy people and conducting advocacy.

> *Amigos de las Americas* conducts projects in South American countries teaching dental hygiene, developing community sanitation, and promoting general health education.

Amizade Limited builds vocational training centers for street children in Brazil and health clinics in Bolivia.

Global Citizens Network encourages participants to live with local families while working on community development projects, such as renovating youth centers or teaching in a primary school. Countries include Belize, Guatemala, Kenya, and Nepal.

Association for all Speech Impaired Children has projects in North Wales and other parts of the United Kingdom. Experiences include camping activities and working with children who have difficulty with the basic elements of language.

Operation Cross Roads Africa operates a seven-week summer program on education, community health, and women's development.

International Partners in Mission (mentioned previously) is an interfaith organization that promotes community building and health and environmental justice through empowering women children and youth.

InterAction is a coalition of more than 150 U.S. NGOs that are joined to coordinate their work in disaster situations.

United Nations Volunteers offers volunteer opportunities through its headquarters in Bonn, Germany.

FACTORS TO CONSIDER IN WORKING OR VOLUNTEERING ABROAD

Although working or volunteering to provide human services in a foreign country can be a fulfilling experience, it can quickly turn sour if certain factors are not taken into consideration.

Developing the Right Mental Attitude: Do not be motivated solely on the basis of wanting to solve other people's problems; this attitude can have a negative effect on local people. Forcing your own agenda and initiation projects without full participation of local community residents can be disrupting. Consider them the experts on issues affecting their community. Approach working with local people with the attitude of helping them carry out their objectives and encouraging them in their efforts. By being respectful and fully understanding the culture of the community, you can be genuinely supportive and effective.

Health and Safety: It is important to determine what vaccinations you will need while abroad. Meet with your local health facility that specializes in local travel diseases. Contact the Center for Disease Control and Prevention for information to enhance health decisions and to learn about special environmental conditions, such as cautions about drinking water and malaria. It has a hotline for international travelers where you can obtain country specific health advisories: (888) 232-3228. (It is also advisable to obtain health and accident insurance, as well as coverage for emergency evacuation. http://www.cdc.gov/travel/destinat.htm.)

Safety, especially for American citizens, is of special concern because of the possibilities of a terrorist attack. In countries where terrorism has occurred, take extra precautions. In Egypt, for example, Americans are frequently provided with special police protection, especially as they go to communities outside Cairo, and, in some locales, the visibility of police and solider is apparent. The U.S. Department of State issues travel warnings for those countries that American citizens should avoid or exert extra caution in potentially dangerous situations (http://travel.state.gov/).

Additional Considerations:

At the end of this chapter a wide variety of resources are provided to help you explore organizations that are most appropriate for you. Consider these questions:

1. What role, if any, does religion and spirituality play in the work and style of the organization?

2. What level of skill is required that may or may not match your particular skills?

3. Are there costs for volunteering or working (airfare, room, and board) that need to be factored in?

4. Will the experience help you grow as a person and as a professional?

5. Will you accept a physical environment that has less than modern comforts?

By communicating with your potential work or volunteer placement, you can gain a good understanding of how best to prepare yourself.

SUMMARY

Because of growing human service needs throughout the world, international efforts to improve living conditions will continue to expand. Many countries realize that they cannot solve its social problems only through its own efforts. Countries know that to provide health care, education, and social services they must look to outside assistance and, within their own countries, rely on the help of nongovernmental organizations. U.S. social workers, both professionals and volunteers, will undoubtingly play a continuing and expanding role in international social welfare in the 21st century.[15]

Resources for Volunteering and Working in International Social Work

ACDI/VOCA
> www.volunteeroverseas.com
A Directory of Third World and U.S. Volunteer Opportunities
> foodfirst@igc.apc.org
AFS International
> www.afs.org
American Friends Service Committee Staff Openings
> http://ourworld.compuserve.com/homepages/GlobeR/
American Jewish World Service
> www.ajws.org
Amigos de las Americas (partnerships to advance community development)
> www.amigoslink.org
Amizade Volunteer Programs (teachers in the Brazilian Amazon)
> www.amizade.org
Association for all Speech Impaired Children
> www.afasic.org/uk
BRIDGES to International Community Based Organizations
> www.grassrootsbridges.org
CARE Corps
> www.careusa.org
CARE International
> http://www.care-international.org
Cross-Cultural Solutions
> www.crossculturalsolutions.org
Foundation for Sustainable Development
> www.interconnection.org/fsd
Global Citizens Network
> www.globalcitizens.org

Global Exchange
        info@globalexchange.org.
Global Humanitarian Expeditions
        www.humanitariantours.com
Global Opportunities
        www.volunteer.org.nz/
Global Routes
        www.globalroutes.org
Global Service Corps
        www.globalservicecorps.org
Global Volunteers
        www.globalvolunteers.org1
Habitat for Humanity International
        www.habitat.org
How to Live Your Dream of Volunteering Overseas
        info@volunteeroverseas.org
Human Rights Internet
        http://www.hri.ca/index.html
Idealist (international job listings)
        http://www.idealist.org
Institute for International Cooperation and Development
        www.iicd-volunteer.org
InterAction
        http://www.interaction.org/jobs/index.html
International Employment
        www.jobsabroad.com & http://www.teachabroad.com
International Employment Gazette
        www.intemployment.com
International Employment Hotline
        www.internationaljobs.org
International Fourth World Movement
        www.atd-fourthworld.org
International Partners in Mission
        www.ipm-connections.org
International Red Cross
        http://www.ifrc.org/voluntee/
International Volunteer Directory
        www.VolunteerAbroad.com
International Volunteer and Internship Opportunities
        www.volunteerinternational.org
Japan-U.S. Community Education & Exchange
        www.jucee.org
Mobility International USA
        www.miusa.org

Opportunities Abroad
        csouth@cabroad.u-net.com
Operation Crossroads Africa
        www.igc.org/oca
Overseas Jobs
        http://www.overseasjobs.com
Peace Corps
        http://www.peacecorps.com
Service Leader
        www.serviceleader.org
Study Abroad Opportunities for Social Workers
        www.studyabroaddirectory.com
Study, Working, and Volunteering Abroad
        www.transabroad.com
Unitarian Universalist Service Committee
        www.uusc.org
United Nations (Volunteer Opportunities)
        www.unv.org/volunteers
USAID
        www.usaid.gov
University of Minnesota Learning Abroad Center
        www.iste.umn.edu
Volunteers Abroad
        www.volunteerabroad.com
Volunteer Opportunities Directory of the Catholic Network of Volunteer
Service
        cnvs@ari.net; http://www.cnvs.org.
Volunteers for Peace
        www.vfp.org
World Neighbors
        info@wn.org
World Teach, Inc.
        www.worldteach.org
Youth ACTion for Global JUSTice
        info@justact.org

Chapter Notes

[1] Hokenstad, M. C. & Midley, J. (1997). "Realities of Global Interdependence." *Profiles in International Social Work*. Washington, D. C. NASW Press. pp. 1-7.

[2] Ife, J. (2001). *Human Rights and Social Work*. New York: Cambridge University Press. p. 165. George, V. & Wilding, P. (2002). "The Future of Global Social Policy." *Globalization and Human Welfare*. pp. 186-211.

[3] Estes, R. J. (ed.) (1992). "Modeling and Models of International Education in Social Work." *Internationalizing Social Work Education: A Guide to Resources for a New Century*. Philadelphia: University of Pennsylvania School of Social Work. pp. 23-30.

[4] Mudpedziswa, R. (1997). "Social Work with Refugees." *Issues in International Social Work: Global Challenges for a New Century*. Washington, D. C. NASW Press. pp. 110-123.

[5] Midgley, J. (1997). "International and Comparative Social Welfare." *Encyclopedia of Social Work*. Washington, D. C. NASW Press. pp. 1490-1498.

[6] Lowe, G. R. (1997). "Social Development." *Encyclopedia of Social Work*. Washington, D. C. NASW Press. pp. 2168-2173.

[7] Hoff, M. D. (1997). "Social Work the Environment and Sustainable Growth." *Issues in International Social Work: Global Challenges for a New Century*. Washington, D. C. NASW Press. pp. 27-41.

[8] Dominelli, L. (1997). "International Social Development and Social Work." *Issues in International Social Work: Global Challenges for a New Century*. Washington, D. C. NASW Press. pp. 74-89.

[9] Mancoske, R. J. (1997). "The International AIDS Crisis." *Issues in International Social Work: Global Challenges for a New Century*. Washington, D. C. NASW Press. pp. 125-143.

[10] Midgley, J. (1997). "Social Work and International Social Development." *Issues in International Social Work: Global Challenges for a New Century*. Washington, D. C. NASW Press. pp. 11-24.

[11] McKibben, B. (1995). *Hope, Human and Wild: True Stories of Living Lightly on the Earth.* Saint Paul, MN: Hungry Mind Press. p. 119.

[12] Hokenstad, M. C. & Midley, J., "Realities of Global Interdependence", p. 1-7.

[13] Claiborne, N. (April 2004). "Presence of Social Workers in Nongovernmental Organizations." *Social Work.* Washington, D. C. NASW Press. pp. 207-218.

[14] McMillion, B. (1999). *Volunteer Vacations: A Directory Of Short-Term Adventures That Will Benefit You and Others.* (7th ed.). Chicago: Chicago Review Press. See also: Collins, J (2004) How to Live Your Dreams of Volunteering Oversees. London, Eng: Penguin Publishers.

[15] Healy, L. M. (1997). "International Social Welfare: Organizations and Activities." *Encyclopedia of Social Work.* Washington, D. C. NASW Press. p. 1499-1510.

REFERENCES FOR CHAPTER 23

Briskman, L. (2005). "Reclaiming Humanity for Asylum-Seekers: A Social Work Response." *International Social Work.* Vol. 48, Issue 6. November 2005. pp. 714-724

Jackson, Jeffrey T. (2005). *The Globalizers: Development Workers in Action.* Baltimore: Johns Hopkins University Press.

Lacroix, Marie (2006). "Social Work with Asylum Seekers in Canada: The Case for Social Justice." *International Social Work.* Vol. 49, Issue 1. January 2006. pp19-28.

Margaret, Lynn (2006). "Discourses of Community: Challenges for Social Work." *International Journal of Social Welfare.* Vol. 15, Issue 2. April 2006. Pp. 110-120.

Smith, Stephen C. (2005). *Ending Global Poverty: A Guide to What Works.* New York: Palgrave.

Appendix A

Web Site Directory

ADVOCACY

Ballot Initiative Strategy Center
http://www.ballot.org

Contacting Congress
http://www.visi.com/juan/congress/

Conference on Community Organizing and Development
http://comm-org.utoledo.edu/

Handsnet Human Services Community Online
http://www.handsnet.org

IdeaLIST Action Without Borders A directory of 8,000 nonprofit websites.
http://www.contact.org/ or **http://www.idealist.org**

Legislative Information on the Internet
http://thomas.loc.gov

AIDS

Center for Disease Control (CDC): Division of HIV/AIDS Prevention
http://www.cdc.gov/nchstp/hiv_aids/index.html

Journal of American Medicine (JAMA) HIV/AIDS Resource Center
http://www.ama-assn.org/special/hiv/

Center for HIV Education and Research
http://www.fmhi.usf.edu/hiv

AIDS Resource
http://www.hopkins-aids.edu

CHILDREN, YOUTH AND FAMILIES

National Data Archive on Child Abuse and Neglect (NDACAN)
http://www.ndacan.cornell.edu/

Health Initiatives for Youth
http://www.hify.com/

Stand for Children
http://www.stand.org/

Parents Helping Parents
http://www.php.com

Handsnet Main Home Page
http://www.handsnet.org/

Child Trends
http://www.childtrends.org/

Department of Health and Human Services: Childhood and Youth Policy
http://www.os.dhhs.gov/

Adoption Network
http://www.adoption.org/

Child Abuse Prevention Network
http://child.cornell.edu/

National Children's Alliance
http://www.nncac.org

Research and Training Center on Family Support and Children's Mental Health
http://www.rtc.pdx.edu

DISABILITIES

Commission on Physical and Mental Disability Law
http://www.abanet.org/disability/home.html

DOMESTIC VIOLENCE

Family Violence Prevention Fund (FUND)
http://www.endabuse.org/

Today In Perspective: Family Violence Awareness Page
http://www.famvi.com

GOVERNMENT

The White House
http://www.whitehouse.gov/

Administration for Child and Families
http://www.acf.dhhs.gov/

Center for Disease Control
http://www.cdc.gov/

The Department of Health and Human Services (DHHS)
http://www.os.dhhs.gov/

States
http://www.stateline.org

Social Security Administration
http://www.ssa.gov/

Legislative Information on Congress
http://thomas.loc.gov

National Archives and Records Administration
http://www.access.gpo.gov/

U.S. Department of Education
http://www.ed.gov/

U.S. Department of Health & Human Services
http://www.hhs.gov/agencies/

U.S. Census Bureau
http://www.census.gov/

HEALTH/MENTAL HEALTH

Center for the Study of Issues in Public Mental Health
http://www.rfmh.org/csipmh/

Mental Health Net CMHC Systems Home Page - a technology and
management Information system for human service organizations
http://www.cmhcsys.com/

National Institute of Mental Health
http://www.nimh.nih.gov/home.htm

Mental Health Research Institute -This site requires the use of a
macromedia flash plug in
http://www.mhri.edu.au/

Mental Health Resources - Science and Engineering Library of the
University of California
http://scilib.ucsd.edu

American Network of Home Health Care Social Workers
http://www.homehealthsocialwork.org

Disaster Mental Health
http://ourworld.compuserve.com/homepages/johndweaver

Families USA - The Voice for HealthCare Consumers
http://www.familiesusa.org/

Healthfinder
http://www.healthfinder.gov

Healthy People 2010
http://web.health.gov/healthypeople

Join Together
http://www.jointogether.org

Center for Mental Health Services - Knowledge Exchange Network
http://www.mentalhealth.org/

CMHC Systems—Information systems for behavioral, mental & public
health
http://www.cmhc.com/

National Mental Health Association
http://www.nmha.org/index.cfm

NON-PROFIT ORGANIZATIONS

The Online Non-Profit Information Center (TONIC)
http://www.socialworker.com/nonprofit/nphome.htm

The Foundation Center - National Directory of Corporate Giving
http://www.fdncenter.org/

Independent Sector
http://www.indepsec.org

Global Fund for Women
http://www.Igc.apc.org/gfw

National Network of Grantmakers
http://www.nng.org/

Internet Nonprofit Center
http://www.nonprofits.org/

AmeriCorps: National Service Resources Center
http://www.americorps.gov/

American Red Cross
http://www.crossnet.org/

Gay, Lesbian, Bisexual and Transgender Caucus   Sponsored by the
Boston University School of Social Work
http://www.geocities.com/WestHollywood/Heights/4168

POVERTY AND HOMELESSNESS

Federal Poverty Guidelines
http://www.aoa.dhhs.gov/network/im98povguide.html

Frequently Asked Questions about Homelessness
http://www.wisc.edu/homeless/faq.htm

National Coalition for the Homeless (NCH)
http://www.nationalhomeless.org/

Bread for the World
http://www.bread.org/

RESEARCH

Project STAR (Support and Training for Assessing Results)
http://www.projectstar.org/star/splashpg/Index_blocks.htm

SENIORS

Administration on aging
http://www.aoa.dhhs.gov/network

Environmental Alliance for Senior Involvement
http://www.easi.org/

Senior Net
http://www.seniornet.org

Senior Citizens Website
http://www.intecon.com/senior/about.html

SOCIAL WORK

National Association of Social Workers (NASW)
http://www.socialworker.org

Council on Social Work Education (CSWE)
http://www.cswe.org/

International Federation of Social Workers
http://www.ifsw.org/

National Network for Social Work Managers
http://www.socialworkmanager.org

Social Work Access Network
http://sc.edu/swan/

Social Work and Social Services Websites (GWB School of Social Work)
http://gwbweb.wustl.edu/

Computer User in the Social Services Network (CUSSN)
http://www.uta.edu/cussn/cussn.html

New Social Worker
http://www.socialworker.com

World Wide Web Resources for Social Workers
http://www.nyu.edu/socialwork/wwwrsw/

Social Work Resources from Yahoo
http://www.yahoo.com/Social_Science/Social_Work

SUBSTANCE ABUSE

AL-ANON and ALATEEN (Help for families and friends of alcoholics)
http://www.Al-Anon-Alateen.org

Alcoholics Anonymous
http://www.alcoholics-anonymous.org/

The Center for Education and Drug Abuse Research (CEDAR)
http://www.pitt.edu/~cedar/

The Center for Substance Abuse Prevention (CSAP)
http://www.covesoft.com/csap.html

The Center for Substance Abuse Research (CESAR)
http://www.bsos.umd.edu/

Join Together—Take action against substance abuse and gun violence
http://www.jointogether.org/jto/

The National Clearinghouse for Alcohol and Drug Information (NCADI)
http://www.health.org/index.htm

National Institute on Alcohol Abuse and Alcoholism (NIAAA)
http://www.niaaa.nih.gov/

The Substance Abuse and Mental Health Services Administration
http://www.samhsa.gov/

The Web of Addictions
http://www.well.com/user/woa/

VOLUNTEERISM

AmeriCorps Network Northwest
http://www.nwrel.org/ecc/americorps/index.html.

Corporation for National and Community Service
http://www.cns.gov

Habitat for Humanity International
http://www.habitat.org

National Service Resource Center (for the corporation for National Service)
http://www.etr-associates.org/NSRC/index.html

Peace Corps
http://www.peacecorps.gov

VISTA (Volunteers in Service to America) Website
http://www.friendsofvista.org/

Neighborhoods Online
http://www.libertynet.org/nol/natl.html

SERVE net—website for service and volunteering
http: www.servenet.org

Appendix B

Problem Solving Cases
in Community Organizations

Organizing

Cases 1 — 6

Achieving Goals

Cases 7 — 15

Leveraging Power

Cases 16 — 20

(1) THE COMMITTEE TO ABOLISH ORGANIZATIONS

People in the community were fed up with all the committee meetings. In fact, one night Joe said to Bill, "I'm exhausted from these meetings. I go out every night, and I don't get a chance to see my family."

Bill agreed. "What we need is a committee to get rid of some of these deadwood organizations. We ought to take a look at all the meetings in our community and see which ones we don't need any longer."

So after a number of phone calls, Joe and Bill convinced forty members from different organizations to talk about their idea. People liked it and they decided to set up an organization. Of course, Bill felt they needed different committees, so they created nineteen of them: By-laws, Nominating, Finance, Sunshine, Investment, Evaluation, etc. The committees were to meet once every two weeks.

Joe's not talking to Bill anymore.

1) Is it always necessary to set up a formal structure in order to get things done?

2) To accomplish goals, is it always necessary for organizations to be set up on a permanent basis?

3) Can certain tasks be accomplished by one or two people instead of a committee?

(2) THE DO-NOTHING SOCIAL ACTION COMMITTEE

"What we need is a powerhouse committee that can really get to work on the problems of the city." This is how the president of the local Chamber of Commerce summed up his views before his executive committee that was meeting to decide what to do about the central civic problems. With the approval of his executive board, the president appointed as chairman of Community Action Social Action Committee a man who was senior partner in one of the top law firms in the city and who was a highly-respected person who seemed to have shown concern about the city's problems.

One hour before the first meeting, this is what some of the people were thinking. The chairman: "If I could be highly visible from this position, it might insure my chances to run for State Representative. I will make urban problem solving the major plank in my program. Then if I am lucky enough to get elected, maybe I will run for Senator or for governor and then...."

The president of one of the large industrial firms: "This may be just a waste of my time, but I have got to put in an appearance to show that the business community is concerned. Maybe I will go to one or two meetings and then let my executive assistant attend." Mrs. H., the wife of a prominent physician: " Am I glad to be getting out of the house and away from the kids for a while." The black minister from a large inner city church, somewhat skeptical of the whole operation: "If they think I'm going to be a 'Tom' who will be their front man, they'll have to think again."

1) Why do you think it is likely that this committee will not accomplish very much?

2) Can you describe organizations that were ineffective because of the members' hidden agendas?"

3) Can you recall instances in which members' hidden agendas were compatible with the goals of an organization?

(3) NOTHING SEEMS TO WORK

My name is Jack Green and I own a home in what used to be a fairly decent section of town. But now things are getting pretty rundown. Businesses are leaving the area, some of the kids are breaking windows and stealing and mugging people, and the school seems to be going downhill.

I have tried to do my part to improve the community. For ten years I participated in my street club and I was even president for two years. I have also been active in the church credit union and the area council. But all this hasn't made much difference. It seems that we can't stop the blight from spreading in our community.

Two years ago we had some hope that things would improve. A neighborhood center offered services to the community and a lot of staff came around telling us that if we would stick together we could make things change. So with this new enthusiasm, I became active again. But now, we are even worse off than before. Lots of meetings and lots of rapping, but so little change.

Take for example the smelly sewer down the street. We have been after our Council for three years to get this fixed. We have gone to City Hall, we've called the Mayor—nothing seems to work.

About the only things left for me to do if I want my kids to be raised in a decent environment is to move where people do care.

1) What rewards did he seem to get in his earlier organizational experiences?

2) If you were an organizer whose purpose is to organize a new neighborhood organization, what convincing argument could you use with Mr. Green?

(4) THE SOUTHMOUNT TENANT ASSOCIATION

When a new Human Resources Administration (HRA) regulation was sent out from Washington, many organizations all over the country found themselves in trouble. The regulation stated that all HRA funded groups must provide for equal representation of the 16-20 year age group on the executive committee. The penalty for non-compliance was suspension of funds, followed by withdrawal of support. Organizations had six months to make the change.

One of the groups unconcerned by the news was the Southmount Tenant Service Association. This group had gradually developed a service that provided information and instruction in every aspect of home mainte- nance. The program was unique and so effective in helping tenants achieve household self-sufficiency that its funds were increased.

The executive committee of the Southmount Association was composed entirely of founders of the program, middle-aged women who were confident that they would be exempt from the new ruling. As the president put it, "They don't mean us. We're just the old ladies sewing circle. I can't remember when we had a client under twenty-one, or if we had one at all."

But, in fact, there were quite a number of clients under twenty-one, and they learned about the new regulation from several members who felt the younger people were not getting the full advantage of tenant services.

And so a quiet war began. The young people took every possible orthodox step to gain membership in the group, behaving at all times with restraint and respect. But the executive group, led by the chairperson, became more and more relentless and devious in its efforts to keep the young people out.

1   This episode illustrates factions developing over the interpretation of roles. What other issues might cause factions to develop in organiza- tions?

2) Are you aware of any organizations where there is tension between members of the board about policy making and administration of a program? How did the issue get resolved?

(5) MR. PRESIDENT

George Sweeney was one of the most popular, active and friendly leaders the town had ever known. In fact, unofficially he was often nicknamed "Mr. President," for he had served as president of almost every civic organization, including the United Way, The Society for the Blind, and the Area Councils Association.

Why was he so popular? Well, besides being a wealthy businessman and philanthropist, Sweeny was widely known and admired for his keen wit, his ability to tell interesting anecdotes, and his diplomacy. Sweeney rarely made enemies.

But for some reason every organization he presided over found itself, sooner or later, becoming a "do-nothing." Sharp, fast-reacting groups became sluggish and unresponsive to changing conditions. They lost the clarity of their rational approach and turned muddleheaded in decision-making. In fact, when he finished his term of office, the organization usually had to struggle to survive. Were it not for the affection they felt for him personally, members might have openly used the nickname, "Kiss of Death."

Yes, George Sweeney was a popular president, but he had two flaws; he rarely could make a decision, and he never could stick to one.

1   Why would organizations falter with his kind of leadership?

2) Why would groups choose him to be president?

3) Have you seen this kind of leadership in organizations you know? What happened to them?

4) Which of the leadership problems discussed in the text and the cases are community organizations most likely to encounter?

(6) TO SWIM OR NOT TO SWIM?

The Bellfountain Civic Club was an old and respected organization going back to the foundation of the town when it was instrumental in raising the funds for the first town hall. Since that time, it had proudly furnished Bellfountain with two baseball diamonds, a new fire station and, its latest triumph, a "yes" from the voters for a spectacular new city hall.

Meanwhile, Bellfountain had nearly doubled in size as a result of annexing a large adjacent unincorporated area that had voted to join the town in order to get the benefit of municipal services. Many vigorous residents of this former town ship made joining the Civic Association their first act on the day after the election. They came full of zeal to see a new fire station, recreation areas, and a city road service department substation developed in their part of town.

But the old line members of the organization had not reckoned with any such moves. They had a municipal swimming pool as their next priority item. As a result, the November 22nd meeting of the Bellfountain Civic Club was a loud and fruitless session.

1) What is likely to happen if the township members overwhelm the old liners and get their way?

2) Is there some goal that can unite the members and provide satisfaction for all?

3) Can you think of another organizational situation where members wanted to pursue their agenda in opposition to others who had a different agenda?

(7) BERRYCANT PTA

Mrs. S. looked forward to joining her suburban P.T.A. Her child had just begun kindergarten, and Mrs. S. thought that her participation in the P.T.A. would be a good way to learn about the school district's educational goals and share in improving her child's education. She was particularly interested in seeing about the reduction of class sizes, the development of a human relations course in the curriculum, the improvement of parent-teacher communication, and the search for new and creative teaching methods.

She assumed that she would be involved in these activities because, among the objectives of the P.T.A., were the following:

1) To bring into closer relation the home and the school so that parents and teachers may cooperate.

2) To secure for every child the highest advantages in physical, mental, and social education.

But Mrs. S. learned to her consternation that instead of being involved in activities that would further these goals, Berrycant P.T.A. was planning the following activities for the coming year: 1) Bike Rodeo, 2) Peach Festival, 3) New Mother's Tea, 4) Distribution of Halloween candy to various hospitals. It appeared to Mrs. S. that the local P.T.A. was nothing but a tea party and not at all what she wanted.

1) What are the unofficial goals of this organization?

2) What kinds of programs would more appropriately reflect the stated goals?

3) Can you think of other organizations whose activities do not reflect their goals? Why the discrepancy?

(8) M.A.S.H.

M.A.S.H. (Movement Against Substandard Housing) was formed three years ago by a small group of Protestant, Jewish, Catholic, and Muslim religious institutions. They were concerned about substandard housing in their community and had learned that community funds would no longer be available. The ecumenical group formed a small board of trustees, 50 percent of whom were from the community; the others were selected because of their interest or expertise. Their goal was to rehabilitate housing in their community. They thought they could develop a constituency of concerned community people and then perhaps other housing efforts would be initiated.

Although they were able to rehabilitate sixteen dwelling units in a three-year period, the organization was plagued with problems. The group was never able to develop broad community participation. The lack of sufficient funds and the consequent lack of staff put tremendous pressure of program administration on the volunteers. The organization was ill-equipped to deal with the high costs of keeping the buildings from deteriorating and the problem of tenants not paying their rent on time. As one member of the organization put it, "How can we be a "good" guy and at the same time demand the rent?"

Finally, the organization almost went bankrupt because certain board members were concerned with philosophical issues rather than with current and pressing business problems. They insisted on spending much board meeting time, for example, discussing human behavior, rather than focusing on what needed to be done to repair the plumbing or electrical systems.

1) Give your diagnosis of why M.A.S.H is having trouble achieving its goals.

2) If you were a member of the M.A.S.H. board, how would you deal with its problems?

(9) THE LIBERAL ACTION FORUM

The Liberal Action Forum was formed three years ago by a group of white liberals who were concerned with speeding up open housing in their all-white community. This small group saw that inner city was faced with a crisis and hoped that their efforts to open up housing in their suburb would move the total community in the right direction. They believed strongly that all families, regardless of color or creed, should have the right to live where they chose. The Board of Directors was composed of sensitive and so-phisticated people who involved themselves actively in various functioning committees of the organization.

The organization grew in its impact on the community. It had major influ-ence in modifying school board policy to effect an integrated curriculum, and its support of a school board member sympathetic to integration insured his election. It set up neighborhood discussion groups to discuss race relations, and it created a spin-off organization that solicited support from churches and synagogues on integration. By the end of three years, the organization's membership had grown to about one thousand with a treasury of $10,000. But, while the stated goal of the organization was open housing, most members seemed to want to control the percentage of African America families in the community to preserve integration and a balanced community. Consequently, as more African American families began moving into the suburb, the organization began shifting its emphasis from recruiting African American residents to working on other issues. It broadened its organization's goals to include campaigning for more responsive city councilmen, and getting the city government to tear down dilapidated housing. Increasingly, discussions focused on how to encourage white families to remain in the community and how to attract new white families. The Liberal Action Forum continues to have open housing as its major goal, but its activities are now concentrated elsewhere. So several of the original members, still concerned with open housing, have left the organization.

1) What was the original goal of the organization? What are its goals now?

2) Describe other organizations that become concerned when their goals are about to be achieved.

(10) THE AFRICAN-AMERICAN BUSINESS UNION

The African American Business Union of Johnson City was founded on the idea that if existing black businesses could provide both business expertise and find the seed capital, then they could promote new black businesses.

And so it had worked out. The original businessmen had raised the initial capital by recruiting some three hundred members for the organization and used their dues and contributions as a base. Then they obtained foundation grants for staffing and loan guarantee monies from interested white industrialists. The result of this was that, in three years, they had nourished into being twenty-seven new black businesses in Johnson City. Because members were fiercely proud of the organization's fine record, they continued to pay membership dues, even though this was the extent of their participation. Meanwhile, the Union found that its biggest stumbling block was not funds, but the fact that there was no business orientation among young African Americans. So the Union developed a program for youth designed to foster an entrepreneurial training program at the college level.

Building on its local success, the African American Union decided to move its headquarters to New York, leaving a branch office in Johnson City. Now the AAU has 15,000 members over the country, branch offices in five principal cities, and a record of 271 more new businesses. The youth program is thriving in all branch cities. The only sour note in all this success is that the membership in Johnson City, where it all began, has dropped dramatically from its peak of 300 to 35 currently.

1) If you were a member of this group, how would you have felt about the decision to move?

2) Does the AAU need a large membership? Why?

3) Is there any way a membership of this size could participate besides paying dues?

4) Suppose the original organization in Johnson City had been less effective in expanding its activities but had continued to grow in membership. Would you have considered it a success?

(11) THE HEARTHTOWN PROTECTORS

The Hearthtown Protectors were born out of disaster and nearly died in one. The initial occasion was a tail of a tornado that swept through Hearthtown, ripping a wide swath of total destruction across its center. Since the town had never been hit before, and since the resources of the Red Cross were totally employed in dealing with a much greater disaster in the adjoining city, Hearthtown was left to its own devices, and a group of citizens responded magnificently in overcoming the effects of the tornado.

In the aftermath of the storm, they organized formally, determined that they would never again be caught flat-footed by any disaster. However, there was the problem of keeping the organization going during times of calm so that it would be a functioning unit when storms came. After long debate, the members decided that disturbances in general were consistent with their overall goal. And so they adopted a string of interim goals, including beefing up police and fire protection in town, developing programs for teenagers to keep them out of trouble in the evenings, and fostering interracial understanding in their rapidly integrating municipality.

Ironically, just a year after the first strike, the tornado tail came once again. But the Hearthtown Protectors made a poor showing and distinguished themselves mainly by the amount of quarreling they did among themselves. There was question as to whether the organization would even survive the disaster.

1) What happened to this group that worked so effectively in the first storm? What was the consequence of its goal diversification?

2) How could the Hearthtown Protectors have developed an on-going goal without exhausting their resources in the process?

(12) AT THE CROSSROADS

For two months a group of concerned citizens had been meeting to discuss the lack of programs and facilities in their community. This community of fifty thousand had neither a swimming pool nor a recreation center, and there were only one or two places where children could play ball. Just one neighborhood center existed in the community, and it had limited resources, operating as it did out of a small storefront.

The group was aware that in other parts of the city, recreation centers had been built largely because the residents had put pressure on city officials. However, in preliminary talks with officials they learned that there was no more money available locally for recreation. They also discovered that there was only limited money from such other sources as federal government and foundations.

At a meeting two months after its inception, the group was faced with a major decision: Should it take a chance on planning for a large recreation facility with a swimming pool and gymnasium that would cost an estimated $900,000, or should it attempt a less ambitious but safer program of trying to raise $5,000 to clean up one of the areas for a miniature park?

The group was evenly divided between the alternatives.

1) Which objective would you choose? Why?

2) If you were undecided about which goal you would choose, what other problem-solving steps would you want to go through before making your decision?

(13) RAT CONTROL—AN
IMPOSSIBLE DREAM?

Harmon Jones was a mild man who never looked for trouble and never went out of his way to make it. That is, he was a mild man until the time his baby daughter was bitten by a rat. She now has only a scar on her arm, but Mr. Jones has a wound on his soul that will never heal. Driven by his tremendous commitment to get rid of the problem, he rallied his neighbors for a successful cleanup-extermination day. Everyone rejoiced, not only at the vermin-freedom they had achieved but at the unexpected attractive new look on the block now that all the yards were clean. The block club dissolved, and everyone went home to enjoy their improved neighborhood.

Three weeks later, a rat was seen skittering down the block's only alley and another sneaking out of the basement in back of a store. In another ten days, the rats were nearly as populous on the block as before the cleanup, even though all the yards were still being nicely kept up. Mr. Jones and his nearby neighbors then realized that the trouble lay in surrounding blocks that had not been cleaned up. So the neighbors organized a nine-block area. None the less, the rats came. Obviously, occasional clean-up campaigns were not the answer.

They then met with experts from the City Health Department who advised them that one uncovered garbage can could feed an army of rats and start the problem again. Determined that this would be the year to get rid of rats, they secured funds from the Chamber of Commerce to provide garbage cans to people who could not afford them. Further, they conducted a massive education campaign about the importance of keeping garbage off the streets. All this was coordinated with the city's rodent poison-bait program. It has been a year since the "Get Rid of the Rats" campaign was inaugurated, and Harmon Jones is worried for he has begun to see uncovered garbage cans. The scar on Harmon's baby's arm is a constant reminder that he dare not let the community go back to where it was.

1) Could this effort have any chance of succeeding if it were limited to a few blocks?

2) Can you think of other examples where an ineffective, piecemeal approach was (or should have been) replaced by a more adequate comprehensive one?

(14) A VITAL CONCERN FOR THE CCU

A group of neighborhood people, encouraged by a citizen's action agency, decided to get together to do something about feeling powerless. Too many things were happening in their neighborhood over which they felt they had little control. Within two weeks after they were organized, they were able to get the Department of Public Properties to create playground areas for the neighborhood.   The city also cooperated in a neighborhood cleanup campaign.   The group, calling themselves Concerned Citizens United (CCU), next put on a harvest festival which raised nearly a thousand dollars. It also brought the CCU to the attention of all the area residents, and this produced not just an increased membership but a favorable climate for the organization's forthcoming activities.   Notable among these was a buying club which was coordinated by five university students on assignment in the area.   The club had 100 regular buyers among CCU members, and the enormous amount of paper work was deftly handled by the staff.

Encouraged by these developments, CCU began planning for a center for teenagers and elderly residents, a thrift shop to be stocked largely by a suburban church group, a sewing club doing work on consignment from a local factory, a damaged freight warehouse, and the purchase and rehabilitation of two frame houses. In all of these ventures, they planned to lean heavily on the technical expertise of the staff, and for the first three of them they planned to use the agency area office.

But then the action agency's budget was cut, and it has had to withdraw the staff and abandon the headquarters in the area. This left only the suburban church group as a support for the CCU and no central office for their ac-tivities.

1) How will the reduction in agency resources affect CCU's priorities?

2) If you were a member of this organization, would you continue to try to reach the same short term objectives or be less ambitious? Which would you choose and why?

3) How would you approach a significant reduction in funding in an organization with which you are affiliated?

(15) THE SOCIAL REFORMERS

The people of the neighborhood were angry and discontent because social services in their community were lacking, and agency staff were generally unresponsive to their legitimate requests. They were annoyed at having to wait two weeks for welfare applications to be processed. They were irritated over having to sit and wait an entire day to be seen by a doctor, and they resented the token activity offered by the recreation agencies for their youngsters.

One of the neighbors stirred the others with his claim, "We have got to organize to let these agencies know that we exist." So they started a group called the Social Reformers, developed a campaign to attract several hundred members from the community, and raised several thousand dollars worth of operating funds from within and from foundations. To get the social services they needed, they would have to push for fundamental changes.

While their intent was to reform agencies, they were soon bombarded with so many requests for services that they felt they had to respond directly to those compelling needs. Soon they formed a volunteer bureau to assist people in getting social services, and they began offering extracurricular classes for the neighborhood youngsters. In several months the Social Reformers had become the "Social Servers." Despite their many valuable activities, the community was still lacking basic services.

1) What was the initial ideology of the organization?

2) Did the goals shift because of change in the initial belief or for other reasons?

3) If the group remained true to its original ideology, would it have changed?

4) What other examples can you think of where an organization shifts its goals?

(16) THE ELDERLY CITIZENS TRANSPORTATION COMMITTEE

Two years ago the bus service to the hospital in the Westover area was eliminated. While it affected many people in the area, it was particularly hard on older persons who now had to ride two hours each way and change three buses to reach the hospital.

Annoyed at having to take such a long trip, several of the older people got together to form the Elderly Citizens Transportation Committee (ECTC). Their goal: To get bus service reinstated so that they could ride directly to the hospital. Lacking any overall strategy, in a period of two months they tried to influence the Public Transportation Board (PTB). They decided to collect signatures and within two weeks they had gotten 150 names on a petition which they mailed to the PTB. Although they received a nice "thank you" reply, they were informed that it was financially unfeasible.

Then they decided to attend a PTB meeting. After some discussion they were finally permitted to have 15 of their 30 people enter the hearing room and present their case. A week later the Board proposed that buses used to transport graduates of employment programs to and from factories could be used for hospital transportation in the intervening hours. But this was unsatisfactory because the schedule did not cover early and late appointments at the hospital.

Finally they met with their councilman, who agreed to champion their cause in this election year. As a result, the Board somehow found the money to provide the needed bus service. One of the committee members remarked, "You know, we should have considered taking this to the councilman in the first place, because, after all, the PTB is appointed by the mayor and our councilman is on good terms with the mayor. In an election year like this, that's the smart move.

---

1) Based on the comment at the end of the story, what strategy might the group have adopted from the beginning?

2) What other situations are you aware of that require people of influence to produce change?

(17) THE MILITANT ORGANIZATION OF MOTHERS (MOM)

For years welfare mothers had requested increases in children's clothing allowances, but the most they could get from the County Human Services Department was a total budget of $5,000, which was hardly enough to buy shoes for hundreds of children.

A group of mothers decided to get together to form the Militant Organization of Mothers (MOM). One of them put the reason for the group this way, "By pulling together, we might be able to accomplish what we can't achieve individually." But even when they were organized, the mothers were not able to move the County Human Services Department for higher grants. Always the reply came back, "We just don't have the money to increase local allowances."

Their first tactic was to march as a group to the county commissioners to complain about the lack of adequate clothing allowances. They hoped that this would cause public pressure to mount and get the commissioners to find money somewhere in the county budget. But this proved to be unsuccessful, so they decided on a second tactic: a sit-in at the County Human Services office. Apparently, just the threat of this paid off, for on the eve of the scheduled sit-in, the Human Services Department came through with a small additional clothing allowance for each child.

Some members in MOM were pleased with this victory, but others were angry that the increase was only a token amount and insisted that the group proceed with the sit-in the next day. "We have to show them that we have power on our side and that they must give us a decent income." Others argued that by moving ahead with the sit-in they would lose the sympathy of the general public and their cause. This side lost the debate and the next day, forty-three mothers were jailed for sitting-in at the County Human Services office. The incident did not result in further increases in clothing allowances.

1) Why do you think the threatened sit-in worked and the actual sit-in didn't?

2) What other tactics might the MOM use to bring pressure on the County Human Services Department and the county officials? How might these tactics fit in with the overall strategy of winning public sympathy and support?

(18) THE PAPER TIGER

An experimental social action agency in the community had run a highly successful training program for police officers preparing for a promotional examination. Over 2,200 men and women attended 70 hours of lectures on human relations.

Flushed by high praise from the police department, a staff person from the social action agency decided that the time was ripe to push for improved police-community relations.   So he formed a city-wide grass-roots organization that would be able to apply pressure so the police would become more responsive to the community. Among their goals were enlarging the community relations staff of the police department, relocating police staff in neighborhood centers to improve contact with local people, hiring residents to serve as neighborhood representatives in each of the districts, and developing a permanent police-community relations institute.

After the recommendations were crystallized, a delegation was chosen to present them to the police chief. Two months later, none of the projects had been initiated by the police department. The organization had developed no strategy beyond presentation of its "demands." Meeting attendance was down to little more than the original members who became pessimistic about their ability to make an impact. One of those who stopped attending meetings declared, "I thought this organization would influence the police to make meaningful changes, but it was never more than a paper tiger."

1)   What was the original goal of the social action agency?

2)   What new goal emerged from the staff person's activities? Were these two goals compatible?

3)   What would you recommend to a group that wants to have more leverage and power?

(19) SOCIAL ACTION IN RIVERDALE CHURCH

The meeting of the Board of Trustees of the Riverdale Community Church was tense. People were shouting at each other over whether or not Rev. Smith should have his contract renewed for the coming year. After two hours of debate, the trustees announced that they would go into secret caucus. Here is what brought about the situation: About a year ago, Dr. Jones, a chemist and a new member of the church, convinced ten other parishioners that the church was not taking an active enough role in promoting social causes. He summed up the combined thinking of the small group with, "There's too much emphasis on heaven and not enough on earth."

The initial group of ten formed a social action committee and within two months had fifty active participants. First, the committee influenced the church to participate in a city-wide program using only contractors who had an equal opportunity hiring policy. Then the committee convinced Rev. Smith, for example, to alter his sermons to focus more on people who tend to be targets of prejudice, such as gays and lesbians. But the difference i n style between Social Action Committee members and more conservative church members has caused considerable antagonism.

Initially, the reaction of the members of the church was limited to mumbling of a few members about the Social Action Committee. Slowly at first and then more noticeably, church attendance began to dwindle. Pledge collections fell off by 25 percent. And when several large donors refused to give to the church building fund, claiming they did not like the slant of the minister's sermons and activities, the Board of Trustees felt it was time to reassess Rev. Smith's tenure. The Board of Trustees has just announced it will not renew Rev. Smith's contract.

1) Indicate why you think there is such a strong resistance to change in the Riverdale Community Church.

2) Could the Social Action Committee have anticipated the consequence of its action?

3) In social change situations how likely do you think casualties occur?

(20) THE STUDENT ACTIVISTS VS WATKINS

Ralph Watkins, the right-wing reactionary third party candidate, was due in town in ten days to promote his bid for president. He was to appear at a local nationality hall. In anticipation, the Student Activists had been caucusing for three nights trying to determine the best way to undermine Watkins' campaign. Keenly aware that Watkins would appeal to a broad section of the community, the Student Activists knew they had to find a way to limit his impact. But despite several hours of discussion they were no closer to a decision.

"I say we demonstrate by holding a sit-in at the campaign hall," insisted one student. Another student countered that they demonstrate through picketing. A third speaker advocated a snake dance through the hall.

Cautioned a fourth member, Jerry Henderson, "What good will sit-ins, picketing, or a snake dance accomplish besides getting us arrested and drawing attention to Watkins? Let's fool them this time with something they won't really be expecting from us. Let's steal Watkins's thunder and his audience by holding a neighborhood carnival. People are bound to prefer a fun afternoon to political speeches, and this will cut his crowds in half." After considerable debate about the merits of disruptive tactics vs distraction tactics, Jerry's views prevailed.

Ten days later, the Student Activists had a spectacular street carnival going when the Watkins' cavalcade pulled up to the steps of the hall around the corner. The rostrum had even moved outside in the expectation of a larger crowd than the building could hold, but now people were going in droves with their children to the carnival, lured by prizes and the idea of something given for them instead of wanted from them.

1) If Jerry had not interceded, what would have been the general strategy of the group? What tactics would they have used to carry out this strategy?

2) What was the new strategy? What tactic was used to carry it out?

ADDITIONAL SUGGESTED READINGS

Alinsky, S. (1971). *Rules for Radicals*. New York: Random House.

Auteri, Monica (2003) "The Entrepreneurial Establishment of a Nonprofit Organization" *Public Organization Review* Volume: 3, Issue: 2, June 2003. pp. 171-189.

Babacan, H. (2004). "Community Work Partnership in a Global Context," *Community Development Journal*. Vol. 36, Issue 1. January 2004 pp. 3-17.

Banerjee, M.M. (2001). "Micro-Enterprise Training Program: An Innovative Response to Welfare Reform" *Journal of Community Practice*. Vol. 9, No. 4, 87-108.

Barak, Michàl (2000). "The Inclusive Workplace: An Ecosystems Approach to Diversity Management" *Social Work*: Volume 45, Number 4.

Barker, R.L. (2003). *The Social Work Dictionary*. (5th edition). Washington, D.C.: NASW Press.

Beebe, L., Winchester, N.A., Edwards, R.L., et al. (Eds.). (1997). *Encyclopedia of Social Work*, 2 (19th ed.). Washington D.C.: NASW Press.

Brocklesby, Mary Ann; Fisher, Eleanor (2003) "Community Development in Sustainable Livelihoods Approaches – an Introduction," *Community Development Journal* Volume: 38, Issue: 3, July 2003. pp. 185-198.

Brody, R. and Nair, M. (2000). *Community Service: The Art of Volunteerism and Service Learning*. (2nd edition). Wheaton, IL: Gregory Publishing Company.

Bromley, Ray (2003) "Social Planning: Past, Present, and Future," *Journal of International Development* Volume: 15, Issue: 7, October 2003. pp. 819-830.

Brooks, Arthur C. (2003) "Challenges and Opportunities Facing Nonprofit Organizations," *Public Administration Review* Volume: 63, Issue: 4, July 2003. pp. 503-506.

Carter, C. (January 1999). "Church Burning in African American Communities: Implications for Empowerment Practice," *Social Work,* Vol. 44, No. 1 pp.62-68.

Compton, B., and Galaway, B. (1999). *Social Work Processes* (6ᵗʰ ed.), Pacific Grove, CA: Brooks Cole.

Cox, E.M., Erlich, J.L., Rothman, J. & Tropman, J.E. (Eds.), (2003). *Strategies of Community Organization*, Itasca, IL: Peacock.

Council on Social Work Education (1999). *Curriculum Policy Statement for Baccalaureate Degree Programs in Social Work Education*. Washington, D.C.: Author.

Delgado, M. (2000). *Community Social Work Practice in an Urban Context: The Potential of a Capacity Enhancement Perspective.* NY: Oxford University Press.

Delgado, M and Barton, K (July 1998). "Murals in Latino Communities: Indicators of Community Strengths" *Social Work*, Vol. 43, No 4, pp-346-356.

Dionne, E. J. Jr. (ed). (2003). *Community Works: The Revival of Civil Society in America*. Washington D.C.: Brookings Institution.

Ewalt, P. , Freeman, E. M., and Poole, D. (1997). *Community Building: Renewal, Well-being, and Shared Responsibility*. Washington, D.C.: NASW Press.

Ewalt, P. , Freeman, E., Fortune, A., Poole, D., and Witkin, S. (editors) (1999). *Multicultural Issues in Social Work*. Silver Spring, MD: The National Association of Social Workers.

Fellin, P. (2001). (3ʳᵈ edition). *The Community and the Social Workers*. Itasca, IL: F.E. Peacock.

George, V. and Wilding, P. (2002). *Globalization and Human Welfare*. New York: Palgrave.

Golden, Susan L. and Shrader, Alan (2004) *Secrets of Successful Grantsmanship: A Guerrilla Guide to Raising Money.* San Francisco, CA: Jossey-Bass.

Gray, Mel. (2004). "Social Enterprise: Is it the business of social work?" *Journal of Australian Social Work*. Vol. 56, Issue. 2. January 2004. pp. 141-154.

Hokenstad, M.C. and Midley, J. (1997). *Issues in International Social Work: Global Challenges for a New Century*. Washington,.D.C.: NASW Press.

Hyde, Cheryl A.(2004). " Multicultural Development in Human Services Agencies: Challenges and Solutions," *Journal of Social Work*. Vol. 49, No. 1. January 2004 pp. 7-16

Iglehart, A. and Becerra, R. (2004). Social Services and the Ethnic Community. Boston: Allyn and Bacon.

Kelly, Gail J.; Steed, Lyndall G. (2004). "Communities Coping with Change: A conceptual model," *Journal of Community Psychology* Volume: 32, Issue: 2, March 2004. pp. 201-216.

Kirst-Ashman, K.K., and Hull, G.H. Jr. (1997). *Generalist Practice with Organizations and Communities.* Chicago: Nelson-Hall.

Lackey, A.S., Burkee, R., & Peterson, M. (2003). *Healthy Communities: The Goal of Community Development.* New York: Haworth Press.

Lev-Wiesel, Rachel. (2004). "Indicators constituting the construct of perceived community cohesion" *Community Development Journal.* Vol. 38, Issue 2. April 2004. pp. 332-343.

MacGregor, J., ed.(2003).*Doing Learning Community Assessment: Five Campus Stories.* National Learning Communities Project Monograph Series. Olympia, WA: The Evergreen State College, Washington Center for Improving the Quality of Undergraduate Education, in cooperation with the American Association for Higher Education

MacGregor, J., B L. Smith, R. Matthews, and K. Gabelnick. (2003). *Learning Communities: Creating Connections Among Students, Faculty and Disciplines.* San Francisco: Jossey-Bass.

Mailick, J. D., & Ashley, A. A. (1989). "Politics of Interprofessional Collaboration: Challenge to Advocacy." In B. R. Compton & B. Galaway (Eds.), *Social Work Processes* (pp.622-628), Belmont, CA: Wadsworth.

Martinez-Brawley, E. (1997). Community. In Social Work Encyclopedia (19th ed., pp. 569-576). Washington, D.C.: NASW Press.

McCall, Tony (2003). "Institutional design for community economic development models: Issues of opportunity and capacity." *Community Development Journal* Volume: 38, Issue: 2, April 2003. pp. 96-108.

Murray, Michael (2004). "Exploring equity, diversity and interdependence through dialogue and understanding" *Community Development Journal* Vol. 38, No. 2. Feb. 2004 pp. 287-297

Murphy, P. W., & Cunningham, J. V. (2003). *Organizing for community controlled development: Renewing civil society.* Thousand Oaks, CA: Sage.

Nair, M. (ed) (1998). *Genius in Public Housing: An Anthology.* Wheaton, IL: Gregory Publishing Company.

Netting, F.E., Kettner, P.M., & McMurtry, S.L. (1998). *Social Work Macro Practice* (2nd Ed.). New York: Longman.

Parnell, John A.; Lester, Donald L. (2003). "Towards a philosophy of strategy: reassessing five critical dilemmas in strategy formulation and change," *Strategic Change* Volume: 12, Issue: 6, September/October 2003. pp. 291-303.

Richan, W.C. (1996). *Lobbying for Social Change*. New York: Haworth Press.

Rothman, J. (ed). (1999). *Reflections on Community Organization: Enduring Themes & Critical Issues*. Itasca: IL: F. E. Peacock.

Rothman, J., Erlich, J. L., & Tropman, J. E. (Eds.). (2003). *Strategies of Community Intervention* (6th ed.). Itasca, IL: F. E. Peacock.

Rubin, H. J., & Rubin, I. S. (2003). *Community Organizing and Development* (3rd ed.). Boston: Allyn and Bacon.

Schill, M. and Nathan, R. (1999). *Revitalizing America's Cities*, NY: State University of NewYork Press.

Schneider, R. L. and Lester, Lori. (2001). *Social Work Advocacy*. Belmont, CA: Wadsworth/Thompson Learning.

Smock, Kristina. (2003). "Democracy in Action: Community Organizing and Urban Change." New York: Columbia University Press

Schorr, L.B. (2003). *Common Purpose: Strengthening Families and Neighborhoods to Rebuild America*. New York: Doubleday.

Specht, H. and Courtney, M. (1994). *Unfaithful Angels: How Social Work has Abandoned its Mission*. New York: Free Press.

Temali, Mihailo (2003). *The Community Economic Development Handbook: Strategies and Tools to Revitalize Your Neighborhood:* Amherst H. Wilder Foundation.

Van Vlaenderen, Hilde. (2004). "Community development research: Merging communities of practice." *Community Development Journal*. Vol. 39, Issue 2. April 2004. pp. 135-143

Von Hoffman, Alexander (2003). *House by House, Block by Block: London*, Oxford University Press

Watkins, Patricia and James V. Cunningham. (2003). *Organizing for Community Controlled Development: Renewing Civil Society*: New York. Sage Publications.

Weaver, H. (May 1998). "Indigenous People in a Multicultural Society: Unique Issues for Human Services." *Social Work* Vol.43, No 3. Pp. 203-212.

Weil, M. (1997). "Community Building: Building Community Practice." In P.L. Ewalt, E., M. Freeman, S.A. Kirk, & D.L. Poole (eds), *Social Policy: Reform, Research, and Practice* (1997). Washington, D.C: NASW Press.

Weil, M., and D.N. Gamble. (1995). "Community Practice Models." In the *Encyclopedia of Social Work* (19th ed., 1:577-93). Washington, DC: National Association of Social Workers.

Winkelman, M. (1999). *Ethnic Sensitivity in Social Work*. Dubuque, IA: Eddie Bowers Publishing, Inc.

INDEX